Grammar and Semantics in Medieval Arabic

For all those working in the field of medieval Arabic linguistics

Grammar and Semantics in Medieval Arabic

A study of Ibn-Hisham's 'Mughni l-Labib'

Adrian Gully

Routledge
Taylor & Francis Group
LONDON AND NEW YORK

First published 1995 by
Curzon Press Ltd.

Published 2013 by Routledge
2 Park Square, Milton Park, Abingdon, Oxfordshire OX14 4RN
711 Third Avenue, New York, NY, 10017

First issued in paperback 2014

Routledge is an imprint of the Taylor & Francis Group, an informa business

British Library Cataloguing-in-Publication Data
A CIP record for this title is available on request from the British Library

ISBN 978-0-700-70302-9 (hbk)
ISBN 978-1-138-86983-7 (pbk)

CONTENTS

Acknowledgements vii

Preface ix

1 ML and its place in the medieval Arabic grammatical literature 1

2 Historical and epistemological considerations, and principles of community agreement in ML 27

3 Ibn Hishām and his position as a grammarian in ML 73

4 Polemical categories in Chapter Five of ML 96

5 Particles: the grammarian's stock-in-trade 116

(i) The status of the particle in the Western and Arabic linguistic traditions 116

(ii) The particles in ML 138

(iii) The particles and synonymy according to Ibn Hishām in ML 193

6 Further semantic and structural aspects in Part Two of ML 207

Conclusion 273

Bibliography 279

Index 292

CONTENTS

ACKNOWLEDGEMENTS

One of the pleasures of compiling a piece of work such as this is to be able to thank all those people who made it possible. To the following I owe an enormous debt:

The late Professor M.A. Shaban who advised me so judiciously at an early stage to embark on a study of medieval Arabic in some form. Although it has often been a struggle, I am indebted to him for this direction. I am extremely grateful to Dr Michael Carter of New York University who provided the initial inspiration for the Doctoral Thesis, and whose writings and words of wisdom have continued to stimulate and influence me. Dr Kees Versteegh of the University of Nijmegen has not only been a considerable source of encouragement to me through his writings, but kindly went through the completed version of my PhD thesis in his own meticulous way, and gave me such invaluable assistance with his remarks. In fact, his suggestions added a new dimension to the revision of the thesis; needless to say, however, that remaining imperfections in this work are entirely of my own making. Paul Auchterlonie, the Arabic subject librarian at Exeter University has been unfailing in his assistance with book queries and in chasing references. He is also responsible for the indexing of this work which he has compiled in his own inimitable and flawless style. Thanks are also due to Heather Eva of Exeter University Inter-Library Loans who has been unstinting in her efforts to fulfil all book loan requests. Dr Ian Netton, the Head of the Department of Arabic and Islamic Studies at Exeter has granted all my wishes with a sympathetic understanding. I would also like to extend thanks to Toby Morris and Professor Yasir Suleiman at the University of Edinburgh for their combined assistance in overcoming several typographical problems during the latter stages of preparation of this work, and to Linda Morris for her substantial contribution to the production of the final drafts. My family and friends also deserve a special mention for the many concessions they have made during the period of my writing this book.

Finally, love and thanks are due to my wife Nancy who has not only given us a beautiful daughter, Anya, during the busiest time of my life, but has remained a constant support and encouragement throughout the long days of toil which were necessary to complete this work.

PREFACE

Given the increasing constraints imposed on the development of Arabic grammar after the first few centuries of Islam, it is to the credit of the Arab grammarians that they have provided modern scholarship with sufficient material to inspire the intellectual pursuits that have often proved as fruitful and as stimulating as the polemical debate that spanned the age of medieval Arabic grammar itself. Yet in spite of some of the different approaches adopted to the study of grammar during that period, particularly by those grammarians of the fourth century A.H. who brought principles of logic and philosophy to bear on linguistic analyses, it is fair to say that the later development in particular of the science of Arabic grammar was more lateral than anything else. This is hardly surprising when we consider that the mainstay of grammatical studies was the corpus of material taken from the sacred text. The nature of this material meant, of course, that it could be regarded as nothing less than immutable.

However, this situation has in no way dispirited modern scholarship. In fact, a great deal of time and energy has been spent in attempting to understand and elucidate the types of issues that interested the medieval grammarians. Even if one takes the view that Arabic grammar became an increasingly intellectual and theoretical discipline with decreasing practical value, one can not overlook the complexity of the subject which has stimulated such vast interest. It is perhaps surprising, therefore, that in a discipline where old theories were frequently re-worked, and new ways of saying the same thing were often presented in an innovative fashion, some of the later grammarians also happen to be those who have made a significant and lasting impact on more recent grammatical studies. Indeed, Bohas et al. (1990:15) have noted that it was during this later period in particular that grammatical science reached a 'hitherto unknown degree of formal perfection'. If this is the case, there is every justification for selecting a later grammarian for a more comprehensive analysis. To this end we have chosen to focus on one of the most famous of the later grammarians, Jamāl al-Dīn ʿAbd Allāh ibn Yūsuf Ibn Hishām, who died in 761/1359.

This present work is a revised version of the author's Doctoral Thesis which was examined in July 1991. It focuses on a treatise of grammar and semantics by Ibn Hishām called *Mughnī l-Labīb ʿan Kutub al-Aʿārīb*. The *Mughnī* has always been held in high esteem by scholars of the medieval period who had access to this work. It is clear from the extent to which some of these later scholars incorporated many of I-H's ideas that they regarded it as a major contribution to Arabic grammar. This view has been shared by more recent scholarship too. Yet ML is not merely a work of grammar. I-H himself wrote many tracts along the more traditional lines of other grammatical works which belong to an extremely rich and invaluable linguistic legacy left to us by the medieval grammarians. However, there are many factors which set ML apart from these other contributions to the science. One of the main reasons for selecting ML as the focus of this study is that I-H adopted a technique of analysing Arabic grammar that demonstrates a more acute awareness than many of his predecessors of semantic trends.

Like his predecessors, I-H also lived and studied in a climate of considerable intellectual output. To suggest, however, that ML reflects a general approach to grammatical studies at that time would be to undermine his achievements. On the other hand, evidence is beginning to emerge that he was perhaps not the only scholar of that period who was concerned with issues that pertain more to meaning than form. Larcher (1990/1992) has already described some of the pragmatic elements which are evident in the *Sharḥ al-Kāfiya* of al-Astarābādhī (d.684 or 686/1285-88), for instance, although it should be noted here that the techniques employed by both I-H and al-Astarābādhī were very different. No doubt there is a lot more to be said on this subject and on the latter's work in particular. At all events the question of meaning is never far from consideration in ML, even though I-H may not always treat it as a separate consideration to the form of a given linguistic issue. Of particular interest to us here is whether I-H develops what could constitute a separate semantic theory in ML, since it will soon become clear that his main concern with the language is as much semantic as formal.

We must accept that there are several fundamental problems to be borne in mind at all times when dealing with such a late work, which was written nearly six centuries after that monumental grammar by Sībawayhi, *al-Kitāb*. It is well-known that the later Islamic literature was essentially polygraphic in nature. Material was recorded and handed down for the sake of preservation, which we hardly need add is a prerequisite for a society that adheres to a sacred text as its foundation. It was not necessary for scholars to acknowledge the provenance of their ideas on a given subject. Conversely, to attempt to detect any innovation in methodology or analysis can often prove to be an elusive pursuit, especially as the parameters of the language had, in a sense, been laid down at the outset. That does not mean, however, that scholars could not create new methodologies to examine old problems, or that they could not analyse them in a slightly different way in order to produce a set of different results. Although the question of original contribution is not a straightforward one when examining a work like ML, we are often assisted by I-H's almost immodest acknowledgement that his view on a particular matter is *badīʿ* 'original'.

There is also the question of verification of the authenticity of material which was transmitted as part of the prodigious Arabic grammatical tradition (excepting the Qur'ān, of course, although here too there were disagreements about the accuracy of some 'readings'). This would seem to assume particular significance on a major issue like that of the grammatical arguments of the putative Basran and Kufan 'schools'. In spite of the intermittent efforts of modern scholarship to define the dividing line between what was supposedly Basran and what was Kufan, the matter has still not been satisfactorily resolved. In fact, the resolution of this argument has been made more elusive by the medieval Arab grammarians themselves, including I-H. In ML, he acknowledges the provenance of a given grammatical point as though it is not in doubt. Yet it is unlikely that he would not have been doubtful at times as to whether a transmission had been accurate. It was not beyond the intentions of some of the earlier grammarians to present arguments for the purposes of furthering the reputation of their own so-called school of grammar. This situation creates difficulties for the contemporary scholar who wishes to assess the validity of certain grammatical issues in such a comparatively late work as ML. We shall see later, however, that I-H often attempted to alleviate this problem by employing his own criteria to establish the material on which he felt he could rely.

Throughout this work cross references have been made to several of the main treatises representing other Islamic disciplines which appeared in profusion throughout the medieval period. These disciplines include theology and legal theory, of course, as well as grammar. The references to other works are by no means exhaustive, but are hopefully sufficient to present cogent evidence for an inextricable link between what lies at the foundation of ML and the position of language vis-a-vis Islam. The references made in Chapter Five in particular to many of the works that specialise in a study of the particles are barely adequate: such is the magnitude of this subject that it would benefit a great deal from further attention.

Of particular interest to modern scholars of the Arabic linguistic tradition is the notion that I-H established a reputation for himself as the 'second Sībawayhi' (d.177/798), the pioneer of Arabic grammatical studies. There is no denying that ML in particular made a substantial impact on subsequent medieval writers such as the polymath al-Suyūṭī. Many of I-H's presentations are quoted almost verbatim in some of the later works. Indeed, it is not insignificant that its effect has been even more enduring perhaps than the *Khaṣā'iṣ* of Ibn Jinnī (d.392/1002) which was in many ways a unique work for its time. Although this study does not constitute a forum to compare the relative merits of both Sibawayhi and I-H, a certain amount of attention will be given early on to the significance of this reputation which I-H enjoys.

The present work focuses on the Qur'ān as its main corpus of data, to the exclusion of the considerable wealth of citations from Arabic poetry. Although this decision could be seen as controversial, the reasons for excluding the latter, except for a few references, were twofold. We would argue that the importance of poetry as a form of textual evidence for understanding the Arabic language and its workings was fully acknowledged by I-H. Evidence of this may be found in the one thousand or more citations of parts of poems taken from a wide range of periods which are to be found in ML. However, if our understanding of I-H's intentions in writing ML are correct, he is more concerned with the language of the sacred text than the secular, but with the following important proviso: that even the language of secular texts can not be overlooked because it could, and often did, function as a model of data by which sacred language could be interpreted. In ML, poetry is frequently used by I-H as a linguistic yardstick for this purpose although the converse situation normally obtains. Second, the value of poetry as a form of textual witness, not just in ML, is a stimulating but vast subject which could be taken up in a future study. Baalbaki (1991) gives poetry its deserved status by acknowledging the potential merit of such an inquiry, particularly to deepen our understanding of issues relating to the science of *balāgha* 'rhetoric'. One point which could not be overlooked in this connection, however, is the questionable authenticity of some of the early poetry.

This study does not lay claim to being an exhaustive study of ML. In addition to the parameters set forth above, however, it attempts not only to assess many of the more semantic elements to be found in ML, as opposed to the formal ones, but also to set it in a cultural and epistemological context, and to relate it to some of the other main works of the period which reflect the direction of studies in the Arabic linguistic tradition at that time.

NOTES

1. Throughout this work *Mughnī l-Labīb ʿan Kutub al-Aʿārīb* will be referred to as ML, and Ibn Hishām as I-H.

2. All translations of verses from the Qur'ān are taken from Arberry (1964). The translation of all other texts has been carried out by the author unless otherwise stated.

3. Relevant dates are given in pairs and separated by an oblique: the first date is according to the Muslim era (AH) and the second according to the Christian era (AD).

Chapter One

ML AND ITS PLACE IN THE MEDIEVAL ARABIC GRAMMATICAL LITERATURE.

'...and it (ML) became as famous as Sībawayhi's *Kitāb*'.[1]

A cursory perusal of a selection of biographical and secondary sources substantiates the view that ML has always been held in high esteem by scholars and students of grammar alike.[2] We are not so much concerned here with the generally accepted observation that ML continues to enjoy popularity as a text book of grammar in educational institutions, since that applies to a reasonably large, if select, number of medieval works of Arabic grammar. Rather more benefit could be gained from an examination of the importance of ML within the context of the scholarly community of the time, and an inquiry into why it has so frequently been referred to as a unique work, although this claim, to the knowledge of the present writer, has never been thoroughly substantiated.

Ibn Hishām was one of the last in a line of distinguished medieval Arabic grammarians. He was born and lived in Cairo from 708/1308 until 761/1359, and studied under, amongst others, the famous Spanish grammarian, Abū Ḥayyān al-Gharnāṭī. He became a professor of Qur'ānic exegesis and wrote many works on Arabic grammar for which he achieved considerable acclaim.[3] We can say, therefore, that ML was one of the last great works of Arabic grammar. It has been noted that at least twenty commentaries were devoted to this work during the later medieval period, although only a handful of these are extant.[4] What seems to have captured the imagination of scholars writing about I-H, and ML in particular, is the tribute allegedly paid to him by the eminent historian Ibn Khaldūn. It is rare to find an account of I-H's achievements in the biographical literature and secondary sources without a direct reference to the apparently immortal words of Ibn Khaldūn that describe I-H as 'a better (?) grammarian' (*anḥā*) than Sībawayhi! There is in fact evidence to suggest that Ibn Khaldūn's assessment of I-H's ability to this degree was not based on personal judgement; rather he was merely recounting what he had heard. Nonetheless, it is clear from remarks made by Ibn Khaldūn elsewhere that I-H enjoyed an excellent reputation as a grammarian. It is also worth noting that he was acknowledged as a scholar in the mould of Ibn Jinnī even at that time, which is in itself a significant comparison.[5]

Given the nature of ML, however, it is tempting to pursue this reference to I-H on the understanding that the word *naḥw* is the most accurate generic term employed specifically for syntax. This term should, of course, be seen in juxtaposition with morphology, which is known as *ṣarf*. The use of *naḥw* as an umbrella term for anything to do with grammar has prevailed for some considerable time, and it is certainly a convenient way of describing the discipline to which the *naḥwiyyūn* 'grammarians' subscribed. However, a thorough analysis of ML soon reveals how Ibn Khaldūn's alleged tribute could be interpreted *prima facie* as a comment on I-H's meticulous attention to detail and the finer points of syntax in the Arabic language, particularly in the latter's capacity as the pure expression of the Holy Book. So far as we know there is no obvious reason why I-H should have been so highly acclaimed by Ibn Khaldūn, although these two scholars were contemporaries. Neither is there evidence to lead us to believe that they were friends, nor that there was any form of patronage between them. At any rate, assuming that Ibn Khaldūn was the source of these laudatory words it might be useful to offer two possible interpretations of their significance.

It is barely conceivable that modern scholarship could attempt to determine whether one medieval grammarian was more proficient in his trade than another, particularly when the two grammarians involved are generally held to be among the finest of their profession. As we shall see later, some of the medieval grammarians themselves were not averse to passing judgement on the competence of some of their contemporaries or predecessors. It is unrealistic, however, to subscribe to a belief that I-H was ever considered by Ibn Khaldūn to be a better grammarian than Sībawayhi. Admittedly there is evidence to suggest that the timing of I-H's arrival on the grammatical scene was particularly apposite for Ibn Khaldūn, who had been advocating a resurgence of intellectual advancement in all the Islamic sciences, not least in grammar. So far as he was concerned, the intellectual austerity of that time was destined to restrict any further development of Islamic civilization:

> 'Grammar has come to the point of being allowed to disappear, along with the decrease in the other sciences and crafts which we have noted and which is the result of a decrease in civilization'.[6]

It is in this very context that Ibn Khaldūn alludes to the virtues of I-H. He adds that what sets ML apart from most previous grammars is I-H's avoidance of repetition; this is a point which I-H makes emphatically in his introduction to ML. If I-H has been considered in some circles to be a better grammarian than Sībawayhi, one can only speculate that it was due in part to the former's unequivocal interest in certain grammatical issues which may be subsumed within the domain of semantics. As a starting point to this hypothesis, however, a note of caution should be offered. Any discussion about semantics in relation to medieval Arabic grammar should not lose sight of the formal constraints within which the grammarians worked. It is safer, at this preliminary stage at least, to discuss the issue of meaning within the context of the close relationship between semantics and syntax. In many cases the inquiries of the earlier grammarians were based on the same linguistic material as the later ones; and it was not unusual for them to elucidate their discoveries through the employment of the same grammatical devices, such as *ḥadhf* 'elision' or *taqdīm wa ta'khīr* 'pre/post-posing (of a syntactic element)'. The significant difference, however, is that scholars with an interest in semantic issues would utilize these devices to a different end. According to Versteegh (*to appear*) grammarians like Sībawayhi set out to explain the form of sentences, and although they were interested in meaning it is fair to say that they took it for granted to a certain degree.

The interesting feature about all this is that the application of semantic principles to the linguistic data applied more to the earlier commentators on the Qur'ān than to the main body of grammarians: I-H was perhaps exceptional in his approach. In Versteegh's view (*to appear*) 'from the time of Sībawayhi onwards, the mainstream of the Arabic linguistic tradition was characterized by an emphasis on the formal-syntactic aspect of language'. This may be contrasted with an earlier exegete like al-Farrā' who 'very often includes semantic constraints in his linguistic reasoning' (Versteegh, ibid.). This observation enhances further the value of ML because it suggests that I-H was possibly reviving a long-standing tradition of hermeneutics, but through the eyes of a grammarian. This point forms the main focus of our study here.

The relationship between *naḥw* and *balāgha* (the generic term for the science of 'eloquence') is a complex and, to date, a somewhat indeterminate one. Baalbaki (1983) certainly takes a step in the right direction in his examination of the treatment of certain grammatical features by Sībawayhi and al-Jurjānī.[7] Baalbaki compares the approach taken by both of these medievalists on, amongst other things, one or two of the particles. It is no surprise that the results confirm the restricted nature of Sībawayhi's analysis in a rhetorical context, whilst illustrating the advanced techniques employed by al-Jurjānī. However, the evidence is fascinating, and helps to set our objectives here in a wider and more important context. The complexity of this subject will become more apparent later on as we reflect on the difficulty of identifying the division between purely grammatical issues and those of a more rhetorical nature.

If we return to Baalbaki's argument, it is clear that in spite of some similarities in approach between the two medievalists, the most noteworthy distinction to be made is that al-Jurjānī apparently never draws a line between meaning and form. On the other hand, Sībawayhi 'sometimes focuses on formal issues that have little or nothing to do with meaning' (Baalbaki 1983:12). The relevance of all this to the present study is that in ML, I-H is concerned a great deal with issues that would fit happily into the categories of *ma'ānī* and *bayān*, two of the three main prongs of the science of eloquence. Although this is not the forum for a detailed analysis of these rhetorical devices, (*'ilm al-) bayān* may be defined as '(the science of) clear speech'. On the other hand, (*'ilm al-) ma'ānī* is '(the science of) meanings', which constitutes a skill acquired by the eloquent speaker enabling him to convey the desired meaning in the most accurate fashion using his judgement to manipulate the syntax to that effect. The context of communication often played an important role in this respect. These two concepts overlap inasmuch as they both involve syntax and style, although there is an unequivocal distinction to be made between them: in fact, the lines of demarcation were set by the rhetoricians themselves who understood that such major linguistic phenomena as *majāz* 'figurative usage' belong to *bayān*, whilst elements like *ḥadhf* and *iḍmār* 'suppression' are part of *ma'ānī*. At any rate there is substantial evidence in ML that I-H was well aware of the different ways in which the grammarians tackled these issues. This will be examined later.

To return to the somewhat speculative comparison between Sībawayhi and I-H, any suggestion that the latter's approach to the language was akin to that of al-Jurjānī's cannot be put forward without considerable reservation. In the first instance we may safely assume that I-H's extensive analysis and rigid categorisation of such phenomena as elision and pre/post-posing, or parenthetical sentences (*jumal mu'tariḍa*), for example, indicate a more intricate concern with syntactic and, at times, semantic, elements which constitute a significant part of the category of *ma'ānī*, and, of course, the inimitability (*i'jāz*) of the Qur'ān. Moreover, little consideration is given to morphology in ML - at least not in isolation without consideration of its relationship to meaning- and almost none to phonology; this is not the case in Sībawayhi's *Kitāb*. It is worth adding here that I-H went beyond even the works of later grammarians such as Ibn 'Aqīl and al-Zamakhsharī in terms of the attention he gave to syntax over morphology and phonology.[8] On the other hand, we must be careful not to suggest that I-H's objectives or even the level of sophistication he reaches are necessarily equal to those of al-Jurjānī.[9] Bohas et al. (1990:125), admittedly referring only to I-H's treatment of nominal and verbal sentences, believe that his mature analysis was still bound by formal considerations.

One of the many features of ML which immediately prompts a further investigation is its innovative layout and the methodology employed by I-H. Both of these factors signalled a break from traditional methods of grammatical analysis in which individual grammatical categories were treated in isolation according to 'class'. There is little doubt that scholars of the time were also drawn to the work;[10] some of these factors will be dealt with in more detail later on. On the one hand I-H continued with his painstaking discussions of all grammatical issues in a manner redolent of all his major works; supporting his arguments with innumerable *shawāhid* 'textual evidence' from the Qur'ān, Prophetic Tradition and poetry while refuting the claims and arguments of many preceding grammarians. If we are seeking to determine any overt advantage that I-H might have had over Sībawayhi, then the simple answer may be found in the chronology. I-H was fortunate to be writing nearly six centuries later than Sībawayhi. In many ways, therefore, ML represents an eclecticism and a culmination of those six centuries of grammatical debate, and *prima facie* reflects the view that the later grammarians had few original ideas to offer but found ingenious ways of restructuring arguments based on the same data.[11] The Zahirite Ibn Maḍā' was one who remarked explicitly in the sixth century A.H. that the aims of the grammarians to protect the Arabic language from speech errors and change had been fulfilled and exhausted beyond the call of duty.[12] In mitigation, however, we hope to demonstrate in later chapters how I-H did contribute some innovative ideas to the problem of interpreting syntactic and semantic issues.

ML illustrates unequivocally the ideas of a scholar who derived much benefit from many previous language-related discussions on philosophical, legal and theological matters of an advanced nature that would not have been possible during the Sībawayhi era. He frequently demonstrates the breadth of his accumulated knowledge by referring to such eminent rhetoricians as al-Sakkākī or little-known scholars like al-Mahdawī, where I-H even distinguishes between his particular reference to the latter and another scholar of the same name who was an exegete and not a grammarian (ML 2:420). These points of detail serve to underline the highly eclectic nature of ML.

The classification of chapters in ML is wholly original even by I-H's own standards. It comprises eight chapters in which I-H presents a comprehensive analysis of the syntax of the Arabic language with due consideration being given to a number of semantic issues, as we have already noted. The pivot of the work is *iʿrāb*, a term which incorporates the concepts of inflection, syntactic parsing, and, in a more specific sense, syntax.[13] More than half the work is devoted to the *mufradāt* (a category of single lexical items embodying mainly grammatical particles), while the remainder investigates all aspects and types of the sentence. I-H reveals more overtly perhaps the extent of his aims in ML in Chapter Seven which is entitled 'On the Nature of *I'rāb*', where he notes that 'when the item under scrutiny is a particle, he (the one giving the exposition) demonstrates its type, meaning and operating power (if it is an operator)...then after talking about the *mufradāt* he will go on to talk about sentences' (ML 2:667-68).

Let us return now to the rather unqualified comparison which has been made between I-H and Sībawayhi. There is perhaps a second possible interpretation of the reasons behind Ibn Khaldūn's alleged tribute to I-H which may well be more plausible than the first. When analysing grammatical works, particularly from the medieval and ancient periods, it is paramount to keep in view that the majority of these grammars were compiled with the principal aim of preserving the sacred texts against the corrupting influence of the colloquial language. With regard to Arabic, of course, this would ensure the stability of the Classical language manifested in its purest form in the Qur'ān. Naturally this had vast religious connotations which will be looked at in more depth in Chapter Two. This situation accords nicely with Versteegh's argument (1977:5-6) in which he cites many similar examples; for instance, the Vedas in India and the Confucian texts in China, or the preservation of ancient or sacred literature such as the Homeric epic in Greece or the Sagas in Icelandic literature. In his introduction to ML, I-H states that an understanding of God's Book and the meaning of the Traditions of His Prophet is the way to eternal happiness and the means to attain religious and worldly benefits. From a historical viewpoint it might be useful to add that ML was written during the period of Mamluk rule in Egypt with the ominous Mongol presence in the East and the existence of ruling Spanish armies in the West. In addition there remained the perennial fear of a distortion of the sacred Islamic texts for the reasons outlined above. It also appears that there was an exodus of scholars to Egypt after the fall of Baghdad and, with the encouragement of the Mamluks who built new centres of learning, a new renaissance of scholarship began.[14] All this would have generated the ideal environment to reassert the primacy of Classical Arabic and, therefore, Islam. The argument being put forward here, therefore, is that I-H's preoccupation with syntax and complex problems of exegesis not only elevated him to the ranks of the master of Arabic grammar, Sībawayhi, but also fulfilled a key service to the Islamic community. If our hypothesis is correct the appropriateness of this reaction is not, it seems, without precedent. Wansbrough (1977:103) has observed that 'a conscious resuscitation of past glory by recourse to language...(was) often conceived as a panacea in conditions of social fragmentation'.

All things considered, it must remain our contention here that I-H was not a better grammarian than Sībawayhi since this hypothesis cannot seriously be proved either way, not least because their approaches to grammar were, in the main, very different. Besides, if we are to believe the words attributed to Abū Ḥayyān which claimed that there is no greater grammarian than Ibn ʿAqīl, it appears that the bestowing of such laudatory remarks upon fellow scholars was not unusual in the medieval period.[15] It is far easier to accept another view put forward more recently that describes I-H as the 'second' Sībawayhi![16] Moreover, much of the subject matter of ML had already been dealt with by Sībawayhi in his *Kitāb*, even though he and I-H almost certainly set out to prove different things and often approached issues in a different way. It is worthwhile pausing at this point.

When we talk about a difference of approach in this context it must not be forgotten that the two grammarians under discussion here - and the majority of those who came between for that matter - based their arguments on essentially the same corpus of material. I-H's dependence on the sacred text *qua* text is not unique. Versteegh (*to appear*) observes that for Sībawayhi 'the text of the Qur'ān as it had been codified in the ʿUthmānic codex, constituted the principal and authoritative source of language, even the ultimate source of linguistic correctness'. However, the crucial difference between the two in their interpretation of this data is perhaps best summed up by Carter (1991:131) who remarks that Sībawayhi's theories presume 'a living language', whereas those of I-H are 'based on a text...(in a) universe of discourse which was not only literary in nature but circumscribed in content, being nothing more or less than the Arabic, and only that Arabic, which functioned as the vehicle of expression for the Sunna'.[17] The other point worth making here is that much of the terminology employed by the grammarians over the centuries to interpret their science remained constant. However, not only did some of these terms assume different meanings later on, but their usage also covered a wider sphere as approaches to the study of language diversified. For the present, the relevance of this discussion may be found in the complex issue of the science of eloquence (*balāgha).* In Sībawayhi's *Kitāb* one can readily find such terms as *ḥadhf* 'elision' which are used by all grammarians through to I-H and beyond, and which also constitute an integral part of the rhetorician's repertoire; but the significant factor is the purpose for which these terms were pressed into service in accordance with the aims of the individual. Thus we find that I-H's analysis of elision (ML 2:603-50) is arguably more comprehensive than that of the great master, and would also have been formulated on slightly different criteria, as the foregoing discussion has been attempting to show. If the hypothesis that I-H was keenly aware of matters pertaining to the rhetorical sciences is correct, evidence of this should also emerge through an analysis of the terminology.

As a final point to this discussion on the reputation which I-H supposedly held in the medieval period we may conclude that what Ibn Khaldūn could have meant was that I-H's meticulous attempts to reassert the real meaning of the sacred Islamic literature offered a greater contribution to Islam. After all, I-H asserts more than once that a superficial analysis of the (Holy) text in preference to a deeper examination of the meaning will result in an impaired interpretation (ML 2:529). It is worth noting at this juncture that the science of grammar (*naḥw*) was never a discipline that could be treated in isolation. Knowledge of grammar was regarded as a collective duty, specifically because it assisted in revealing the signs (*dalā'il*) of the Qur'ān and Sunna.[18]

In some ways ML is representative of many of the works which appeared during the period of Islamic Scholasticism that prevailed during the later medieval period. According to Makdisi (1990:pref, p.xx) Scholasticism was a religious movement led by scholars as a reaction to the philosophical approach to theology which developed as a result of the contact with Greek culture. He adds (ibid.:xx) that this movement aimed for 'a juridical theology more in conformity with the nomocracy of Islam...(and it was) the sacred scripture (which) supplied the substance of Scholasticism, and served as a model for human eloquence'. It is in this particular context that ML should be seen. I-H's approach in ML would seem to resemble the problem or question method of early Scholasticism in Western Europe in which the scholar would raise a point, examine all the possible arguments and then (hopefully) reach a conclusion. An example of this may be seen where I-H considers three sides of an argument before discounting two of them by applying an axiom of *taḍmīn* 'implication (of meaning)' which is relevant to the point under discussion (ML 1:226). We shall see later how the ability to argue one's case was not only significant for advancing one's own reputation, but was also an essential ingredient in any attempt to reach a consensus on a given theological issue. Indeed it was only through an elimination of all disagreement that a consensus could be achieved.[19]

To extend the relationship between language and theology in an Islamic context a little further it may be useful to draw an analogy between Latin and Christianity in the Middle Ages. It has been argued that Scholasticism had a positive effect on Christianity in the Middle Ages when a reconciliation took place between Aristotelian philosophy and Catholic theology which resulted in an acceptable harmonization of revelation and reason. As Robins (1979:74) puts it, 'Scholasticism was a system of thought reinforced by and reinforcing the Christian faith of the day'. What is really at issue here, of course, are the efforts of the Scholastic movement to reinforce a religion, viz., Islam, through a sacred text whose language represents the very essence of that society's beliefs. I-H's role in all this should become clear as this present study unfolds. The relationship between Latin and Christianity in the medieval period would appear to share striking parallels with the situation of (Classical) Arabic vis-a-vis Islam. The relationship between the former has been cogently described by Harris (1980:125-26) who observes that 'clinging to Latin, in whatever form, became the only effective resistance available in Western Europe against the barbarian invasions. But clinging to Latin per se might not have been enough, had it not also meant clinging to a religion. It is difficult to say whether the Vulgate saved Europe for Latin, or whether Latin saved Europe for Christianity'.

In this connection it would seem reasonable to suggest that in ML, I-H is attempting to protect not merely a language but a religion. This prerequisite appears to have been overlooked by Fleisch (1961 1:16-17) who, in spite of acknowledging the rigorous demands made by the application of *qiyās* 'sanctioning of linguistic data according to the rules governing the language' within the context of the development of the Arabic language, appears to be seeking in it a '*(une) notion de changement historique*'. Fortunately he does make the point that the (Classical) Arabic language was a static phenomenon at that time. The significant factor here is that any development of a language whose meaning is so tied up in the immutable sacred texts as was the Arabic language at that time will, of necessity, take place within a limited framework. For evidence of this relationship one can look beyond grammatical works to the plethora of linguistic exegeses and commentaries compiled to attempt to interpret the import of these sacred texts. It is hoped that a picture will shortly emerge that a work such as ML, which is first and foremost a grammar, also represents a body of treatises of this nature which constitute exegeses in their own right.

More recently, certain principles of modern linguistics have, for the most part, been successfully applied to medieval Arabic grammatical theory in an attempt to further our understanding of the techniques used by the grammarians.[20] In some cases these attempts have also served as an illustration of the advanced mentality of many of the luminaries of that period, for it is in the light of modern linguistic theory that various suppositions of those scholars may be fully appreciated. For the purposes of this study we are not only proposing to adopt a similar stance at this point, but are also prepared to rekindle an old argument about whether the terms 'descriptive' or 'prescriptive' may be applied to medieval Arabic grammars. Baalbaki (1979:7) gives a brief conspectus of the issue which he actually refers to as a 'controversy'. According to Carter (1980:24) Sībawayhi's *Kitāb* is 'exhaustively descriptive, (although) it does use systematic value criteria to make prescriptive statements about language'. Carter is in little doubt, however, that later grammars were essentially normative in their approach (1983(a):71; 1983(b):116).[21]

Given that we are dealing here principally with the language of the sacred text, particularly in the case of ML, it is fair to say that studies of the state of the (Classical) Arabic language in the medieval period followed a synchronic approach. In the context of historical linguistics, therefore, it would be appropriate to label ML as a descriptive work (cf. Owens 1988:15), not least because it is incumbent on the linguist to describe, and not prescribe, how people speak and write (Lyons 1968:43). On the other hand there is little doubt that not only is I-H's intent in ML prescriptive, but so is his choice of terminology to illustrate some of the errors perpetrated by some of his grammarian predecessors, legal theorists, or even lexicographers. I-H is frequently to be found employing a variety of terms to expose the mistakes of these groups to his students, ranging from *sahw* 'carelessness' to *khaṭa'* 'error'. This will be taken up in more detail in the next chapter. It would be injudicious to argue that ML is given over to a catechetical approach, but there are many traces of didacticism to be found throughout the work. Moreover, one may maintain that it contains a pedagogical intent in the mould of a few of the later grammatical works, of which an obvious example is Ibn Mālik's *Alfiyya,* but that its fundamental objective was that of religious instruction. This manifests itself in particular when I-H is concerned with the meaning of God's word, such as in the section on *ta'alluq* '(syntactico)-semantic connection' (ML 2:530ff). It is clear that any tendency to prescriptivism by scholars in Islamic society must have been motivated by religious exigency and, equally, the requirements of jurisprudence. Ibn Jinnī, for example, was one who recognised that a weakness in language would more than likely result in a straying from the exemplary path of the *sharī'a* (*Khaṣ,* 3:245). To a lesser extent it must not be forgotten that there was also a need for a perfect command of Arabic in bureaucratic circles where Arabic remained the official language. In fact, any excuse for a dogmatic treatment of grammar also provided the ideal disguise for the grammarian to assert his own important position and identity in Islamic society.

This argument has already been discussed elsewhere (Carter 1983(a)) and will be taken up in more detail with specific reference to I-H and ML in Chapter Three.

If we adopt the guarded hypothesis that elements of prescriptivism may be found in ML, I-H's objectives must inevitably fall within the realm of the preservation of linguistic standards. However, modern linguistics offers an appropriate antidote to this rather unrealistic phenomenon by suggesting that these standards amount to nothing more than 'imagined' ones (Crystal 1980:282), or 'some standard selected in advance' (Lyons 1968:42). These standards must be laid down at some point as a result of an agreement amongst certain members of any community of language speakers. Yet this begs the question of who is best placed to judge these criteria of correctness? It is perhaps for this reason that such works can only be wholly appreciated by an educated elite. Certainly in the medieval Islamic community the only members who ever pronounced judgements of this kind on issues relating to language (or law for that matter) were the *'ulamā'* 'scholars'. Mey (1977:243), admittedly discussing Western languages, notes that within the context of normative grammars one can determine that 'the rules of class language dominate, and are dominated by, the language of the ruling class'.

Further evidence of this may be adduced from a cursory look at the role of the traditional grammar of English in the medieval period where there is little doubt that 'the correct way to speak and write was synonymous with the linguistic habits of the upper ruling classes' (Cawthra 1985:4) until towards the end of the nineteenth century. According to Cawthra only those with wealth and influence had access to proper teaching: if they were able to derive benefit from this it was to the exclusion of the majority. It would be unwise to labour the point further except to underline that what emerges above all from this discussion is that language can be, and often is, employed as a powerful tool in society. This would certainly appear to be the case in ML where a number of examples serve to illustrate I-H's aspirations to belong to what is arguably the Islamic equivalent of the 'ruling class'. Specific examples of this may be found in I-H's amusing presentations to his students, whom he frequently includes in his grammatical scenarios, of heinous speech errors or mistakes of *i'rāb* committed by the masses and the educated alike (e.g., ML 2:669,673). On this basis, then, it is not difficult to follow the notion proposed by Wansbrough (1978:99) that sacred languages, of which Classical Arabic is a prime example, belong 'to a view of language as criterion of culture' in which 'edification takes precedence over communication'.

Perhaps this last observation accentuates a need for some refinement of the argument set forth above. So far as Western languages are concerned there is no doubt that the preceding remarks should, on the whole, be interpreted within the context of a 'living' language. The Classical Arabic which is being dealt with in ML, however, presents a paradox. On the one hand we cannot overlook the fact that Arabic has always been a living language. But it should not be forgotten that I-H lived seven and a half centuries after the advent of Islam, and if the notion being put forward throughout this present study is correct, the language of the texts which form the basis of his linguistic corpus is to be seen as the perfect reaffirmation of the stability of the Islamic message within a context of literary discourse.[22]

Further evidence of the prescriptive tendencies of I-H's may be found in the full title of ML; *Mughnī l-Labīb 'an Kutub al-A'ārīb* 'The Book that allows the Wise Man to dispense with all other Books on *I'rāb*', or the title of another of his works; *Mūqid al-Adhhān wa Mūqiẓ al-Wasnān* 'What stimulates Minds and awakens the Sleeper'. We may conclude from all this that I-H's intellectual energies were directed more towards the scholarly community, and that the dissemination of knowledge to all was never seriously contemplated. As was the case in many of the grammatical works, I-H makes frequent implicit assumptions about the extent of his reader's knowledge of the relevant verses from the Qur'ān and poetry which are adduced as textual evidence to support a grammatical point. That the vast majority of the Muslim community would have learned the sacred texts by rote, and to a certain degree some of the more famous lines of poetry, was taken for granted. After all, this was also considered a collective duty of the Muslim community.[23] Nonetheless, the student of ML may find himself faced with an analysis of a grammatical point based on one line of a particular verse, even though reference may be made to omitted parts of the text which are fundamental to the overall meaning.

Perhaps the most obvious indication of the prescriptive nature of ML is to be found in some of the chapter titles themselves. There are two important underlying aims running throughout the work: to correct the errors of interpretation (according to I-H) propounded by scholars of *iʿrāb* (*muʿribūn*), and to guide, or, more appropriately, to instruct students of Arabic on how to reach the most acceptable interpretation of the language based on the application of sound grammatical and semantic principles. In Chapter Five, for example, I-H not only presents objections to the opinions of various grammarians on matters of meaning, but also offers what he considers to be a correct interpretation. At this stage it is clear that the concept of interpretation carries considerable prominence within the context of ML which, as has already been mentioned, is concerned as much as anything with problems of exegesis. It is true that interpretation in itself is hardly a prescriptive term. However, one of the major features which should emerge during the course of this work is that I-H adopted a singularly dogmatic attitude and solution to many of the grammatical issues raised in ML. By way of another example, Chapter Six is an exercise in warning students against making similar errors to the *muʿribūn*. Chapter Four aims to instruct the *muʿrib* on the many types of very common grammatical categories and their differences, and alludes to the inadequacies of those who do not know them. It might be useful here to quote I-H from his introduction to ML after he has informed the reader that he had to rewrite the work after losing the original version on his way back to Egypt after performing the pilgrimage:

> '...so I studied in it (ML) locked issues of *iʿrāb* and opened them up. I also explained and reviewed difficult (subjects) which are obscure to the student, and corrected and alerted them to errors committed by a number of *muʿribūn* and others' (ML 1:9).

Due to the complex and prolix nature of much of the text, it is not surprising that ML is only used as a teaching grammar today at the more advanced levels of study. In spite of this the pedagogical undertones frequently come to the fore, such as in the section on the particle *mā* which has been devised solely for 'practice' purposes (ML 1:315-18). On numerous occasions I-H reminds us that his grammatical exposition in ML is written primarily for the beginner of *iʻrāb* (e.g., ML 1:12; 2:664,668 or 672), although it is difiicult to imagine, with the exception of Chapters Six and Seven perhaps, that he could have meant the totally uninitiated! At the beginning of the section on the *mufradāt* 'single entities' (specifically the particles) he acknowledges that the reason for adopting the alphabetical arrangement is to enable the student to learn and remember them more easily (ML 1:13). In a similar fashion students are encouraged to learn the most economical 'parsing' terms for grammatical and semantic items so that they roll easily off the tongue and can be repeated (ML 2:651). In this connection there are occasions when I-H intrudes into the narrative of the text to apologise for curtailing his discussion of a particular grammatical point because of his striving for brevity. This occurs particularly when he is pointing out the errors and deficiencies of other grammarians (e.g., ML 2:548). Here we are reminded of the aim of the exercise which should be to memorise as much as possible.[24]

It is now time to turn to the question of *iʻrāb* and its significance for I-H in ML. As we have already witnessed from the full title of ML, *iʻrāb* is the key term for I-H. The preceding discussion has already underlined the importance of a sound, if not perfect, understanding of the language, and hence the meaning of the sacred texts in medieval Islamic society. To this end there is no phenomenon more crucial than that of *iʻrāb*.[25] In traditional studies of Arabic grammar, to draw a distinction between what is *muʻrab* 'inflected' and what is *mabnī* 'uninflected' has always been one of the priority tasks of the Arab grammarians. For I-H, a knowledge of *iʻrāb* is no less important; in fact it is the only means to a perfect understanding of God's Book and the Traditions of his Prophet. What might partially explain the reason for the absence of the *muʻrab* /*mabnī* discussion in ML, however, is that I-H is more concerned with the syntactic and semantic value of words, sentences, and parts of sentences than with the purely formal aspects of inflection. The inseparable relationship between *iʻrāb* and *naḥw* had already been alluded to by al-Zajjājī in the fourth century A.H. when he expressed in a similar pious fashion the religious value of a knowledge of *naḥw*, which was not possible without a concomitant grasp of *i'rāb*.[26] We would even go so far as to suggest a certain conformity with Silvestre De Sacy's rendering of *i'rāb* as 'terminational syntax' (Fleisch 1954-:1249), since the two terms are at times synonymous in ML. This was undoubtedly the view of at least two of the principal commentators on ML who wrote in the ninth century A.H. and who might have been offering a definition that had become standard by that time.[27] There is sufficient evidence in ML to conclude that the term *i'rāb* is employed by I-H in many contexts to mean syntax, and this will be taken up later.

On a formal level there appears to have been a consensus amongst the later Arab grammarians in particular that *i'rāb* as inflection is most appropriately defined as the change at the end of a word, viz., in the final vowel, as a result of the *'āmil* 'operator' affecting it.[28] This has obvious ramifications on the syntax of a sentence in which the inflected words will assume a certain syntactic status. In turn this will help to determine the overall meaning of what is being said. We ought to add here that the use of the word *ma'nā* 'meaning' here refers to grammatical as opposed to lexical meanings, since lexical meanings remain unchanged, of course, even after a word has been inflected. A number of the Arab grammarians defined *i'rāb* as the 'means of making clear and distinguishing between meanings'.[29] Ibn Fāris notes that without the existence of *i'rāb* it would not be possible to differentiate between the subject and object of a sentence, nor admiration and interrogative, for example.[30] These examples help to illustrate the syntactic and (hence) semantic value of a full comprehension of *i'rāb*, although it should be noted that for many of the Arab grammarians meaning often seemed to be a convenient consequence of formal considerations.

At this juncture it is worth pointing out that the term *ma'nā*, which we have already translated here as meaning, admits of many different interpretations. Aside from the main usages of the term according to whether it was being employed by the grammarians, logicians or rhetoricians,[31] there were several important contexts which often demanded a different interpretation of the term. In an article which not only offers a comprehensive synopsis of the way in which the term has generally been understood, but also offers fresh ideas, Versteegh (*to appear*) adds three usages to the four main ones put forward by Frank (1981:314 esp.). In spite of the fascinating nature of this subject, however, the interested reader is referred to both of these articles for detailed analyses of the term. For the time being, only those elements of direct relevance to the argument above need concern us here. Bohas (1984:27ff; cf. Versteegh, ibid.) identifies two types of *ma'nā* (*Ma'nā* I and *Ma'nā* II) which illustrate the difference between the lexical meaning on the one hand, and the syntactic / functional meaning on the other. For Bohas the first type of *ma'nā* amounts to the 'semantic content of all the words that are derived from the same radicals, for instance the notion of 'hitting' that is connected with the radicals ḍ - r- b' (Versteegh, ibid.). This lexical aspect of meaning was totally divorced from studies of the science of *naḥw* 'syntax' which were carried out by the Arab grammarians. The second type of meaning identified by Bohas was the one which preoccupied the Arab grammarians. This particular aspect of meaning is explained as 'the meaning or function of the pattern that is applied to these radicals (viz., ḍ - r - b), for instance the function of 'instrument' connected with the pattern *mif'āl* ' (Versteegh, ibid.); in other words the morphological or syntactic aspects. Versteegh goes on to discuss other usages of meaning including *taqdīr* 'reconstruction of elided items' and makes the point that within the context of Bohas' *Ma'nā* II the grammarians paid little heed to the semantic nature of the categories involved because of their principal interest in the *lafẓ* 'the expressed form of a sentence'.[32] It is against this background in fact that I-H's break with tradition in ML, where he makes frequent forays into the realms of meaning, assumes greater significance.

To return to the term *i'rāb* I-H does not define it in the formal manner set forth above, although Chapter Seven of ML entitled 'On the nature of *i'rāb*' constitutes a comprehensive discussion of important aspects of it; rather the relationship between it and meaning is implicit, and, at times, explicit throughout. Nowhere is this more apparent than in the discussion on *ḥattā* where we see how the particle *ḥattā* can take any one of three meanings according to the inflected state of the word following it (ML 1:130), although it should be noted that this particular example is a further illustration of the ineluctable constraints which formal considerations appear to have imposed upon such categories. In other words the significance of *i'rāb* here is as much syntactic as it is semantic.

At the beginning of Chapter Five I-H tells us that the foremost duty of the *mu'rib* is to understand the meaning of what he is parsing or inflecting (ML 2:527). For this reason, parsing of the mysterious letters at the beginning of some of the sūras of the Qur'ān is not permitted, according to those who consider it to be one of the obscurities (*mutashābihāt*) of which only God knows the meaning. In general, however, the only way to comprehend the real meaning of the text is through a perfect command of *i'rāb*. In an analysis of the particle *alā*, for instance, I-H notes how a number of *mu'ribūn* have identified its *i'rāb* 'syntactic / functional ?' status as a particle of introduction (*ḥarf istiftāḥ*) but have neglected the meaning for which it was posited, that of certainty (*taḥqīq*) and drawing attention (*tanbīh*) (ML 1:68). The nature of this remark is in fact much more appropriate to the semantic side of our argument here.

It appears that the inspiration to compile ML arose in part from the positive and encouraging response which I-H received from his students to his short instruction manual called *al-I'rāb 'an Qawā'id al-I'rāb* 'Elucidation of the Rules of Inflection / Parsing / Syntax'. This work is the precursor to ML in terms of its content and is essentially an introduction to the syntax of the sentence, a sort of survival kit that equips the student with a knowledge of the fundamentals of syntax with which to tackle the complexities of *i'rāb*.[33] Both of these grammars were composed in part as a reaction to previous works that purported to treat *i'rāb* as their central theme but often included sections on derivation and internal morphology of the noun. Moreover, what I-H sets out to avoid is repetition of straightforward grammatical issues and a listing of what he calls the *wāḍiḥāt*, grammatical categories such as the subject (of a nominal sentence) and its predicate which had already been dealt with on numerous occasions. We shall see later how I-H's analyses of these issues are based on more complex problems and isolated difficulties rather than a systematic evaluation of simple equational sentences and so on. I-H's prime concern overall, then, is to cover the less obvious linguistic issues which fall within the category of *i'rāb* in as concise a fashion as possible (ML 1:10-12). In practice, of course, an eclectic work like ML could never be concise: at times we are presented with exhaustive analyses of grammatical points in which I-H states all possible variant renderings and interpretations without always drawing a positive conclusion himself as to which is most appropriate.[34] As well as resembling the scholastic technique mentioned earlier this dialectic approach would seem to echo that of the philosophers who, according to Ayoub (1984:5), are known to have been criticised for their prolix and digressive discussions on exegetical subjects.

What is of particular interest in ML, and equally relevant to the concept of *i'rāb*, is I-H's extensive analysis of what we shall loosely call at this stage the particles (*ḥurūf al-ma'ānī*), or, more accurately, the *mufradāt* as I-H refers to them, a category which comprises more than just the particles as we shall see later. More than half the subject matter in ML is given over to discussion of these elements, and they frequently reappear in the analyses of the sentence and its categories. There are a number of important reasons why so much ink has been spent in medieval Arab grammatical discussion on a class of words whose counterparts in the English language, such as 'at' or 'if', do not appear to have ever attracted anything like the same sort of interest. It is not our intention here to initiate an inquiry into what will constitute the basis of much of the later discussion, but it might be useful to point out here that in Arabic the words which fall within the class of *mufradāt* constitute an intrinsic part of the language system, not least because many of them are operators (*'awāmil*) which affect the syntactic (*i'rāb*) status of nouns and verbs around them. In this way, of course, they have a significant bearing on the syntax and, hence, the meaning of the sentence. I-H is not the first grammarian to devote so much space to this class of words, and neither are all his ideas necessarily original. He is, however, the first one to incorporate such an extensive and strictly categorized analysis of the sentence and its concomitant parts into such a detailed study of the particles.

Before moving on to the next chapter a few general points about ML need to be made here. It has been described by Owens (1988:15) as a 'compendious reference work, rich in detail and well-organized' which to some extent makes up for the lack of originality of the later period. By and large this description captures the flavour of the work, and indicates why it was considered of such value at a time when the options for innovation in grammatical studies and in the Islamic sciences generally were limited. It has already been mentioned that one of the more unusual aspects of ML is the influence of the rhetorical sciences on some of I-H's mode of thinking. In this connection it is regrettable that a work mentioned by al-Ashtar (1965:304) called *Qurāḍat al-Dhahab fī 'Ilmay al-Naḥw wa l-Adab* 'Filings of Gold about the two Sciences of Grammar and Literature', an abridged version of ML, did not survive.[35] This work might have shed more light on the way in which I-H viewed the interaction and overlap of the two sciences of grammar and rhetoric. To return briefly to a subject initiated earlier, there is more than adequate evidence in ML of I-H's concern with subjects of a rhetorical nature. Indeed it is no coincidence that al-Irbilī's work entitled *Jawāhir al-Adab* 'The Essences of Literature', which will be referred to in more depth later, is devoted to a comprehensive discussion of the particles.

Finally, much attention has been given by modern scholarship in particular to I-H's position in ML vis-a-vis the so-called Kufan and Basran schools of grammar.[36] It has also been said, for example, that he was a follower of the Ibn Jinnī school of thought,[37] in itself an interesting comparison which could be clarified by further research. What emerges from a closer study of I-H's methodology, however, is that he was not a linguistic arbiter who necessarily supported one view or the other merely because it was propounded by any one of the putative schools of Basra, Kufa or even Baghdad; rather he underlined the acceptability of any grammatical point that concurred with his own views, irrespective of its origins but provided that it conformed to his own understanding and application of *qiyās* in a manner which would further a comprehension of the texts he was endeavouring to interpret.[38]

In the preceding discussion we have attempted to set ML in a context which not only establishes some justification for its acclaim as one of the most famous works of medieval grammar, but also sets the scene for much of the wider significance of that work. To extend the preoccupation with the relationship between the language itself and metalinguistic considerations is the aim of the next chapter.

NOTES

1 Makram (1980:371): wa kāna fī shuhratihi ka mā kāna kitāb Sībawayhi

2 For instance, see any one of al-Suyūṭī, *Bughya*, 293; al-Ashtar (1965:295); al-Afghānī (1968:192); Makram (1980:371).

3 This chronological note is taken from a useful list of medieval linguists provided by Owens (1988:314). Owens use of the term linguists is rather appealing, since it incorporates all the duties required of 'anyone involved in the systematic study of language' (ibid.:266, n.13). However, it might be useful to explain here that the medieval grammarians were not just linguists in the conventional sense of the word but were also required to display varying degrees of 'interpretative' qualities for the purposes of exegesis.

Among I-H's works which are still widely used as teaching grammars today are *Qaṭr al-Nadā wa Ball al-Ṣadā* and *Sharḥ Shudhūr al-Dhahab*. Perhaps the most famous of all, apart from ML, is his commentary on the *Alfiyya* of Ibn Mālik entitled *Awḍaḥ al-Masālik.*

4 These have been noted in al-Ashtar (1965:306-8).

5 See Ibn Khaldūn (1986:324-25).

The quotation '*anḥā min* Sībawayhi' may be found in any number of accounts on I-H and ML, such as al-Afghānī (1968:195), where he quotes Ibn Khaldūn in full. Even if this was not the latter's personal view, there is plenty of evidence that I-H's works made a significant impression on him; for instance, al-Ashtar (1965:305). It is also fair to say that although these commendatory remarks were made not only as a tribute to ML, but also to I-H as a grammarian, nonetheless ML is the most highly regarded of his works.

6 Ibn Khaldūn (1986:324).

7 al-Jurjānī was a grammarian and linguist of the fifth century A.H. Perhaps his most famous work is the *Dalā'il al-I'jāz,* in which al-Jurjāni's theory of *naẓm* 'composition' has been described as 'one of the most sustained, refined, rigourous and durable attempts to construct a theory of the production

of meaning in discourse and of discourse analysis in any language and at any time'. (al-Azmeh 1986:120)

8 Owens (1988:89) gives a brief and contrastive assessment of the relative contributions made by the early and late grammarians to morphology and syntax. It is surprising that no mention is made of I-H's significant contribution in this regard.

9 There are times, in fact, when I-H is made to look like a very ordinary grammarian in the context of rhetorical issues. See, for instance, Baalbaki (1983:15, n.45) where he points out that I-H is sometimes guilty of brevity in his interpretation of semantic problems which could be developed further. For more evidence of this, see below, pp.126

10 See, for instance, al-Shawkānī, *Badr*, 1:401, where he claims it is a unique work. It is only fair to add here that scholarship of such high quality in the medieval period was often readily acknowledged by later writers in this manner. Thus we find al-Suyūṭī, for instance, referring to the *Kāfiya* of al-Astarābādhī as unique (*Bughya*, 248).

11 For a general view on this, see Owens (1988:8).

12 Ibn Maḍā', *Radd*, 64

13 The syntactic significance of the term *i'rāb* will be assessed in Chapter Six.

14 For this, see al-Ashtar (1965:296) and Makram (1980:95-96).

15 al-Shawkānī, Badr, 1:386; '*mā taḥta adīm al-samā' anḥā min Ibn 'Aqīl.*'

This type of comparison had been used in other areas of grammar too. For example it was alleged that Ibn Abī Isḥāq was a greater adherent to *qiyās* than Abū l-'Alā' al-Ma'arrī. See Ibn al-Anbārī, *Nuzha*, 26.

16 See the editor's introduction to al-Irbilī, *Jaw*, *hā'*.

17 At the risk of labouring the point we might also add here the observation that Sībawayhi's system of grammatical analysis involves 'the manipulation of linguistic material to discover the major principles according to which language works' (Baalbaki 1979:22).

18 This has been neatly put by Carter (1983 (a):80), for example. For a more detailed treatment see Ṭāshkubrīzādah, *Miftāḥ*, 1:144, where he states that grammar is one of the *furuḍ*

kifāya 'collective duties' of Islamic law and not a *farḍ ʿayn* 'individual duty'.

19 See Makdisi (1981:112).

20 Of the many examples see, for instance, Owens (1988), Carter (1973; 1980) or Larcher (1990; 1992).

21 It has also been suggested to me informally by Kees Versteegh that Arabic grammar should be characterized as being explanatory in nature as opposed to either prescriptive or descriptive. His reasons for this are that the constraints of the language are not on the production of linguistic material, but on the structure of linguistic arguments. For example, Sībawayhi allows for alternative forms, which means that the speaker often has a choice.
Owens (1988:21-22) observes that 'the main goals of Arabic (grammatical) theory...are to describe the Arabic language and to explain all its aspects'; thus we find an overlap of objectives here. In the first instance what is really at stake is the interpretation of linguistic data, but it is the manner in which some of this material was presented which has given rise in part to the debate on the subject of descriptivism and prescriptivism. No doubt scholars will continue to differ on this subject.

22 cf. Carter's view above.

23 Ṭāshkubrīzādah *Miftāḥ*, 2:401.

24 It is interesting to note that pedagogical considerations had certainly not been overlooked in some grammatical works that preceded ML. It was mentioned earlier that one of the most salient examples of such a work is the *Alfiyya* of Ibn Mālik, a grammar consisting of one thousand verses composed in rhyme. It goes without saying, however, that constraints imposed by the form must have resulted in some reduction of the overall effect of the content.
As further evidence of pedagogical concerns Owens (1990:179-80) lists four works of this nature which had already been written by the early part of the fourth century A.H.

25 According to Ibn Fāris (*Ṣāḥibī*, 76) *iʿrāb* constitutes one of the noble sciences which are unique to the Arabs. Whilst we are not in a position to judge whether he reached this

conclusion by a process of eliminating all other languages without such a system of inflection, we can be sure that this is yet another of Ibn Fāris' attempts to assert the superiority and individuality of the Arabic language.

26 *Īḍāḥ*, 95.

27 al-Damāmīnī, *Sharḥ*, 5; al-Shamunnī, *Munṣif*, 5. The former died in 824/1421 and the latter in 873/1468. The latter in particular is unequivocal about the connection when he says; *ʿilm al-iʿrāb ay ʿilm al-naḥw wa laysa qasīm al-bināʾ* 'the science of inflection, that is to say, the science of syntax, and not the counterpart of non-inflection'.

28 For instance, Ibn Hishām, *Qaṭr*, 16, or al-Zamakhsharī, *Mufaṣṣal*, 16.

29 Try, for instance, Ibn Jinnī, *Khaṣ*, 1:35; Ibn Fāris, *Ṣāḥibī*, 76; al-Zajjājī, *Īḍāḥ*, 72.

30 For example, it is only when you add the endings to the words *aḥsan* and *zayd* in *mā aḥsan zayd* that you know that the meaning is 'How beautiful Zayd is!', and not 'What is the best thing about Zayd ?'.

31 For the latter two groups the concept of meaning was far removed from the one traditionally associated with the grammarians. For the logicians 'meanings' were mental images for which expressions were posited (al-Jurjānī, *Taʿrīfāt*, 235); for the rhetoricians like al-Jurjānī meanings were also far superior to expressions, with the latter being mere 'receptacles' for the former and 'servants' to them (*Dalāʾil*, 46).

32 cf. Carter (1980:25) who notes that 'semantics does not play a great part in Sībawayhi's system...meaning in (his) Book denotes lexical meaning mainly when synonyms are involved'.

33 The version used here forms part of a collection of short grammatical works in al-Maydānī's *Nuzhat al-Ṭaraf.* Of particular interest in I-H's introduction to this version is an apparent typographical error in the title (p.108) which reads; *al-Iʿrāb ʿan Fawāʾid al-Iʿrāb.* I have not found this title elsewhere but should point out the irony resulting from this misprint which offers a title that could be translated thus: 'Elucidation of the Communicative Meanings conveyed by

i'rāb'. In the light of the content of this work and, to a greater extent, ML, this title would seem to be singularly appropriate.

34 Of the numerous examples try ML 1:234 where no conclusion is reached, or ML 2:446-48 where a conclusion is reached.

35 It is proposed that the word *adab* 'literature' be used here in the generic sense incorporating the four sciences of *adab*; *lugha, i'rāb, taṣrīf, balāgha,* as used, say, by al-Yamanī (*Ṭirāz*, 1:20-23). Versteegh (*to appear*) makes the very important observation too that *'ilm al-adab* is the term given to 'the synthesis between the formal-syntactic and the semantic approach...by scholars such as al-Sakkākī and al-Jurjānī' (cf. Versteegh 1989:292). This is particularly relevant to the discussion here.

36 For instance, Makram (1980:386-94) or Nīl (1985:397ff.).

37 This label was apparently given to him by someone as early as Ibn Khaldūn. See the editor's introduction to ML 1:6.

38 For a brief survey of I-H's methodology on *qiyās*, see Nīl (1985:502ff.).

Chapter Two

HISTORICAL AND EPISTEMOLOGICAL CONSIDERATIONS, AND PRINCIPLES OF COMMUNITY AGREEMENT IN *ML*.

> '...and that (meaning) has been agreed upon; so there can be no deviation from it' (ML 1:305).

One of the more fascinating elements of any study of the Arabic language in the medieval period is the rich context from which the many linguistic treatises emerged. That is not to say that relatively context-free studies (e.g., Owens 1990) are ineffective, provided that they help to further our understanding of the mechanics of Arab grammatical theory. However, once we find ourselves within the domain of semantics there is no doubt that epistemological and cultural considerations should come into play. At the very foundation of language studies carried out by the Arab grammarians lies the concept of *waḍʿ* which may be translated for the moment as the 'givenness of speech' (cf. Weiss 1966). It should be added here that for the grammarians the issue of *waḍʿ* was never a problem: linguistic data was put forward as part of a composite whole of a language which had been 'given', and grammarians would freely discuss, say, the meaning of a particle which had been established for a particular sense. In fact discussion of the conventional theory of *waḍʿ al-lugha* was confined to the legal theorists (*uṣūliyyūn*) who devoted much time to determining its principles. Nonetheless, it is worth dwelling for a moment on its significance for ML, not least because of its direct relationship with *ḥaqīqa* and *majāz*, 'literal' and 'figurative' usage of language, and *lafẓ* and *maʿnā*, the '(physical) expression' and 'meaning' of a word or utterance.

The science of *waḍʿ* and its principles have been well-attested[1] and only those principles which are considered to be of direct relevance to ML will be discussed here. One of the major concerns in this present discussion will be to avoid (hopefully) the anachronistic judgement of assuming that I-H, by dint of having lived in the eighth century A.H., had formulated a clear and conscious idea of what was soon to constitute a *sui generis* science of *waḍʿ*. Moreover, any attempt to perceive an overt application of at least some of the principles of *waḍʿ* in ML, or in any grammatical work for that matter, is frustrated to a certain degree by the lack of direct reference to it. Yet the absence of immediate discussion of the theory of *waḍʿ* in ML works to the advantage of our argument throughout the first part of this chapter, which proposes that the influence of *waḍʿ* upon the language was implicitly and even unconsciously accepted by the members of the (scholarly) community or, more precisely, those having anything to do with the direct study of language. This will be illustrated more fully shortly with reference to the concept of logocentrism which appears to underlie medieval Muslim studies of language.

It is appropriate at this point to define briefly the word *waḍʿ* as understood by the scholarly community in the medieval period. al-Azmeh (1986:115-16; cf. Haarman 1974:152-53) notes that 'language is based on *waḍʿ*, the specific positing of a particular phonemic configuration, a word, to designate a particular sense'. Weiss (1987:339) encapsulates the flavour of the function of *waḍʿ* when he refers to it as the 'philosophy of language'. These definitions tie in neatly with the later medieval view that language is made up of expressions posited for meanings, or concepts (*maʿānī*) (e.g. al-Suyūṭī, *Muz,* 1:8) which were perceived as 'mental images' (*ṣuwar dhihniyya*) (al-Suyūṭī, *Muz,* 1:42; al-Jurjānī, *Taʿrīfāt* 242). In fact the axiomatic relationship between *lafẓ* and *maʿnā* is the bastion of *waḍʿ*. According to Weiss (1987:342), 'language comes into being when the two (*alfāẓ* and *maʿānī*) (my brackets) are, so to speak, wedded. Meanings (which before their association with vocables stand as mere ideas) are conceived as discrete, self-contained entities, to which vocables can be correlated in an almost one-to-one fashion'. What lies at the root of this issue, of course, is a movement towards what may be described as a semiotic theory in which names of things (expressions) merely signify ideas.[2] More on this shortly.

What relevance, then, is the theory of *waḍʿ al-lugha* to our understanding of ML ? First it is paramount to note that for many, these expressions (*alfāẓ*) of the relationship outlined above were not necessarily restricted to individual meanings (*ma'ānī*), but were related to the latter in a manner which, if taken to its logical conclusion, encompassed all aspects of the Arabic language. To suggest that I-H's treatment of grammar and syntax in ML is as sophisticated and meticulous as that of the later writers on *waḍ'*, who went to the limits in applying the theory, would be erroneous; moreover it would lead us into the anachronistic trap we are trying to avoid. Indeed, the later treatises on *waḍ'* divided all the main units of sound in the language into formal categories such as words, affixes, or even syntactic structures, and postulated the theory that all these sounds 'had been assigned to a definite meaning'.[3] There is sufficient evidence to be found in al-Suyūṭī (*Muz*, 1:42-45), for example, that later scholars such as Abū Ḥayyān or Ibn al-Ḥājib held the view that the application of *waḍ'* was not restricted to single entities (*mufradāt*) but also worked for combinations of words (*murakkabāt*), viz., the sum total of grammatical parts such as the verb (*fi'l*) and its agent (*fā'il*) The proviso inherent in this argument was that the meaning of these combinations could be based on *waḍ'* provided that they comprised the sum total of the individual expressions and meanings.[4]

This broader appreciation of the relationship between *alfāẓ* and *ma'ānī* based on *waḍ'* is perhaps nowhere more clearly described than in the *Dalā'il* of al-Jurjānī. As a requisite component of his theory of composition (*naẓm*) and inimitability of the Qur'ān (*i'jāz*) he says of this relationship:

> You should know that...single expressions, which are the posited single entities of the language, were not posited so that their meanings (*ma'ānī*) could be known by themselves; rather that they could all be put together so that the (communicative) meanings (*fawā'id*) conveyed by them would become clear' (*Dalā'il* 350).

He then elaborates on this idea:

> 'If you say; Take that! (*khudh dhāka*) this demonstrative (pronoun) is not (used) simply so that the listener knows what is indicated by itself; rather so that he is aware of (exactly) what is intended as opposed to all other (possible) things you

can see and perceive. This is the rule of the expression (*lafẓ*) in association with that for which it was posited' (*Dalā'il* 350).[5]

If the foregoing argument were taken a little further, we might advance the suggestion that what I-H meant (perhaps unconsciously) by his remarks referred to earlier that any analysis of the Arabic language must begin with the single entities and then proceed to the sentences, is that all 'meaningful' components of the (Arabic) language, whether particles or sentences, fall within the framework of *waḍ'* as outlined above, which in itself constitutes what can neatly be described as a logocentric structure.[6] Furthermore, I-H makes the point that the most important requirement of the *mu'rib* is that he understand the meaning (content) of what he is dealing with, whether that be single entities or combinations of (grammatical) structures (ML 2:527) As an example of this responsibility we may cite the case of the *ḥurūf zā'ida* 'the superfluous particles' which could only be discussed with regard to the Qur'ān on the firm assumption that their being elided did not impair the meaning. However, this was not to imply that the speech in question did not have a meaning before the elision occurred.[7] It was pointed out earlier that ML is unique in its comprising such an extensive analysis of syntax together with an exhaustive description of the function and meaning of the particles; in other words all semantically meaningful elements.

It is worth reiterating at this point that the theory of *waḍ' al-lugha* as applied by the post-eighth century A.H. writers was far more scholastic than that put forward by, say, al-Jurjānī. Even if language had always been 'an aggregate of posited entities' (Weiss 1987:344) this view was founded on those authors' strict and extreme application of principles of *waḍ'* outlined above, viz., to every sound of the language, irrespective of its status, such as the past tense markers of verbs. This seems to reflect the notion that by this time scholars were desperately seeking to extrapolate innovative methods with which to study the Arabic language.

It is hoped that the preceding discussion has helped to demonstrate that anyone who supports the view, of which *waḍ'* is the cornerstone, that the 'expressions of the sacred texts have a fixed and constant meaning' (Weiss 1966:1; cf. his succinct argument (1987:343) that these texts display a 'semantic constancy' ensured by the presence of *waḍʿ*), would be correct in thinking that the principles of *waḍʿ* are timeless.[8] In fact, it is likely that they began to play a more important role at least around the time of I-H as scholars searched for ways of reinforcing the primacy of the Word.

Let us turn now to the concept of logocentrism. A brief definition will illustrate immediately how the theory of *waḍʿ al-lugha* fits rather neatly within the parameters of this term. Logocentrism has been defined as 'the belief that sounds are simply a representation of meanings which are present in the consciousness of the speaker. The signifier is but a temporary representation through which one moves to get at the signified which is what the speaker ...has in mind' (Culler 1976:109). It hardly needs to be added here that in the context of the sacred text this definition assumes unquestionable theological dimensions. The corollary to this is that meaning within any culture underpinned by logocentrism has, in a sense, become part of a '*clôture logocentrique*' (Arkoun 1972:9 citing Derrida 1967); thus the process of interpretation becomes purely 'nostalgic' and 'retrospective' (Culler 1976:109). Sharabi (1988: 158) sums this up neatly with regard to the Islamic situation by saying that 'the text is everything and nothing exists beyond it ... the traditional discourse in whatever form it is expressed excludes every other discourse, for it not only contains the only true knowledge but also the solution to all problems'. In an attempt to break away from these confines, sealed by the pioneering work of de Saussure in his *Course in General Linguistics,* efforts have been made to turn meaning into something that is created, not simply recovered, since the latter has indubitable theological connotations and suggests 'the existence of a purified meaning prior to language'.[9]

To extend this argument to the content of ML, it has been suggested more generally that interpretation of a text is merely 'a matter of making present what is absent, of restoring an original presence which is the source and truth of the form in question' (Culler 1975:131). It would seem that this is exactly what is at work in ML, manifested in a literal sense by the detailed analyses and application of the principles of such devices as *taqdīr* or *ḥadhf*, especially as the latter is nearly always dependent on a *dalīl* 'contextual indication' if the absence of one would be detrimental to the meaning or structure (ML 2:603-4). This ties in rather neatly with al-Azmeh's argument (1986:132-37) which looks at the relationship between the 'unit of signification' and knowledge. We should add here that in an Islamic context, that which corresponds to the 'object',[10] i.e., the expression (*lafẓ*) and mental image (*ma'nā*), is inextricably linked to the concept of knowledge as put forward by al-Azmeh. Moreover, the crucial relevance to the discussion here is that this knowledge is essentially 'a prior truth' (ibid.:132) manifested in the form of an understanding of the Qur'ān.

In Western linguistics, logocentrism inevitably falls within the domain of semiotics, the theory of signs in modern linguistics comprising the sign, signifier and signified. There is enough evidence to substantiate the view that the Muslim theory of *waḍ' al-lugha* bears considerable relation to the division of semiotics into these three categories (cf. al-Azmeh 1986:117). Furthermore, it is interesting to note at this point that medieval Muslim discussion on the nature of language also produced conclusions which are singularly commensurate with the modern view. Although some scholars at that time favoured the idea of a natural, or onomatopaiec, theory of language, the consensual opinion was that signification in all languages, not least Arabic, must be arbitrary (cf.Saussure's theory of the arbitrariness of the sign). It was argued then, as it is now, that an absence of the arbitrariness of the sign would lead to everyone speaking the same language. More specific to the Arabic situation was the presence of *aḍdād* 'opposites' in which an expression signifies a meaning and its antithesis. The existence of this phenomenon in particular ruled out the possibility of specific signs being appropriate for particular meanings.[11] At any rate signification (*dalāla*) in the Islamic context does rely largely on the notion of correspondence (*muṭābaqa*) between the expression (*lafẓ*) and its 'concept, representation'(*ma'nā*) (al-Azmeh 1986:115ff; al-Zamlukānī, *Burhān*, 98; al-Āmidī, *Iḥkām* 1:19-20), even if the relationship between sign and meaning is arbitrary. This notion was taken to its limits by one medieval legal theorist who perceived a direct link between the physical quality of a particle with its meaning. This could be exemplified by the particle *wāw* which he argued had been posited for the meaning of *jam'* 'connection' and *'aṭf* 'coordination' because of the position of the lips at the point of pronunciation.[12]

To set the context in a little more detail it is worth noting that the above conclusion on the arbitrary nature of signs essentially followed considerable discussion amongst the medieval legal theorists about the origin of language. Although the theory of *waḍ'* was ultimately based on a principle of the givenness of speech, the medievalists did not neglect to devote some consideration at least to the provenance of that speech. In addition to the onomatopaeic theory of the origin of language, there were those who held that language was a product of divine inspiration; others favoured the view that it was merely a result of human convention.[13] However, it gradually became clear that this type of debate was futile, and that it was not possible to determine exactly who was the original inventor of speech.

If we assess the relevance of all this to I-H's position in ML it is likely that his stance on the issue would have been commensurate with that propounded by Weiss (1987:341-42) vis-a-vis the scholastic scholars of the science of *waḍ'*. Weiss notes that 'although the question of whether language as a whole was the product of one such Positor (God) or many (members of a primordial human society) was never resolved, it was the practice of writers in *'ilm al-waḍ'* to speak of a 'Positor' in the generic sense'. It is true that I-H was not a member of that group of writers, but it is not inconceivable that he would have adhered to this view that had gained currency by that time; that expressions had simply been posited for specific meanings, probably inspired initially by God. Even a glance at religious allegiances does not appear to assist our speculation in this regard. According to al-Suyūṭī (*Bughya* 293), I-H was originally an adherent of the Shāfi'ī school of law and then became a Ḥanbalī. It has been discussed elsewhere that the only two schools of thought to continue to assert the ultimate belief in the divine origin of language were the Zahirites and the Hanbalites. In the case of Ibn Taymiyya, for example, who was a main proponent of the views of the latter school, he believed that the conventionalist view of language had been invented to justify the concept of figurative (extended) usage (*majāz*) (cf. Weiss 1966:34ff.). Yet given I-H's considerable dependence on the consensus of the scholarly community we could scarcely argue that this reflects I-H's mode of thought. If he had not believed in the conventionalist theory to a certain degree at least, then consensual opinion would have been meaningless to him.

Abū Ḥayyān, I-H's teacher, believed in the unquestionable presence of the principles of *waḍʿ* for both the science of Arabic (*ʿilm al-ʿArabiyya*) and the language (*ʿilm al-lugha*): it was not for man to ask why a given construction exists or why a certain word has a particular meaning.[14] This view would seem to equate with the implicit line followed by I-H throughout ML. In other words it was the linguist's responsibility to interpret the corpus of material he had at his disposal, but he was not permitted to distort or even question its value. Once the parameters of the language had been set by the presence of *waḍʿ* the meaning of language was to be found within those boundaries, even for those who accepted the existence of figurative usage. In the case of the latter, who represented a majority, figurative meanings were explained away as having been present in the original act of the givenness of speech.

One need hardly add here that the immutability of the Arabic language continued to have essential legal ramifications. If we take the situation of the particles into account, for example, it soon becomes clear how an assertion of their meanings is one of the ways towards legal guidance. This could be exemplified by the debate on the interpretation of any number of the particles, such as *aw* 'or'; in this case, the issue is the responsibility of the man towards his wife on the question of divorce (ML 1:66). This is one of many examples underlining not only the importance of a sound knowledge of the language for an understanding of the (sacred) legal texts, but also illustrating that the interpretation and comprehension of one of the original meanings for which this particle was posited can have immediate implications within the legal system, as it always has done and always will. Wansbrough (1978:131) notes that 'the law may be disobeyed, it may be forgotten, but it cannot not be altered'. If the inextricable relationship between the language and the law is not to be denied one could almost substitute language for law in this context, with the further substitution of disputed for disobeyed. This would seem to be be particularly relevant in the light of the differences that obtained amongst grammarians and lexicographers on linguistic issues, and the marked competitive spirit which resulted from these disputes. In fact, the nature of this situation is nowhere more clearly documented than in ML (see below, Chapter Three).

Let us return now to the arguments put forward elsewhere that Islam is an essentially logocentric culture. Arkoun's explanation (1972:14) that '*la quête du sens se réduit alors à une simple répétition (taqlīd) des significations déjà constituées, assimilées dans un type de discours*' is without doubt of immense value to our discussion here and, moreover, lies at the very foundation of the main premise of this work.[15] To Arkoun's list of logocentrists we might add grammarians such as I-H, since ML is one of so many works representing the Islamic sciences - of which grammars were as important as any - that 'act as a substitute for the direct linguistic experience of Islam as it was in Muḥammad's lifetime...' (Carter 1983 (a):69). Carter's suggestion that Islam is essentially a 'verbal construct' (ibid.:66) is a neat postcript to the foregoing argument. Furthermore, it is interesting to note how the particles, for example, which are particularly relevant to this work, are described by Carter (1981:293, n.12.92) as 'kinds of linguistic acts'. In support of this view we shall see later that the meaning and function of the particles in an Islamic context are, in effect, one and the same. In ML, then, I-H's strategy to attempt to recover the meaning of the sacred texts and to categorise the particles (with their concomitant meanings and functions) together with an exhaustive rule by rule analysis of syntactic categories (often with their semantic significance) is no more than a reinforcement of the 'logocentric' ideal.

It was mentioned earlier that elements of signification in the Arabic linguistic system may be looked at in the light of a modern semiotic theory. In this connection we are particularly concerned with the particles which have always carried an indeterminate status because of their apparent lack of a qualifiable meaning. However, a penetrating analysis by Eco (1976) could provide a felicitous explanation for the position of the particles as they are represented in the medieval Arabic situation. Within the context of the meaning of a term Eco propounds a case for the replacement of the expression 'referent' by the term 'cultural unit'. If we are to understand his thesis correctly a theory of codes works on the premise that signs are 'social forces', and that words do not necessarily require referents that are readily identifiable phenomena (Eco ibid.:65). To clarify this point one of the examples proposed by Eco is the word /transubstantiation/ in relation to Christian theology, and its significance for Christian believers. According to Eco (ibid.:67) it is simply enough to be able to identify the 'cultural unit', viz., 'anything that is culturally defined and distinguished as an entity', which corresponds to the content of a particular word. To extend this argument a little further - and herein lies its direct relevance to ML - Eco proposes that the erroneous identification of the meaning with the referent (the latter being essentially any readily identifiable part of the word in association with its expression) would inevitably exclude from discussion of meaning 'all sign-vehicles (Saussure's 'signifiers') [my brackets] not corresponding to a real object' (Eco ibid.:66-67). This would include the syncategorematic terms of a language which we can loosely call the particles, such as /to/ /the/ /of/, which are terms devoid of referents. Presumably the consequent emergence of what Eco calls the 'referential fallacy' (ibid.:63) goes some way towards explaining why scholars have traditionally found difficulty in dealing with such terms.

Now the inestimable importance of the language - culture relationship in Islamic society has already been alluded to on more than one occasion so far, and is further underlined in the light of Eco's remarks which are singularly appropriate to the issue under discussion here. The analysis of the syncategorematic terms in ML, viz., the particles, constitutes more than half of its subject matter. Moreover, if one is to conclude that the particles are essentially the pivot around which meaning in Arabic, not least in the Qur'ān, appears to function, it is reasonable to suggest that referents, as defined above, were not considered as such because of the notion of *muṭābaqa* 'correspondence' which obtained in Arabic linguistic theory. This correspondence is founded on a direct relationship between the expression (*lafẓ*) and the concept (*ma'nā*) of that expression. Moreover, according to al-Azmeh (1986:117) it would seem that a word was 'primarily posited with reference to (a) representation (mental image), not to the reality that this representation indicates'. That the phonemic combination *mīm nūn*, for example, which makes up the particle *min* 'from', had been posited for the idea or concept of *ibtidā' al-ghāya* 'beginning [point] of a specific aim', was sufficient for it to be included as an intrinsic part of any semantic study. Unlike a linguistic system that strives to attach identifiable referents to its words, the individual components of this particular category of words which, after all, constitutes the third part of speech in the traditional tripartite system, appear to have possessed as much semantic and semiotic value as any other word in the Arabic language.[16] For further evidence of this we may cite Ibn Fāris (*Ṣāḥibī* 166) who indicates his astonishment at the legal theorists who discussed some of the particles and omitted others from their books on legal theory. One would assume from Ibn Fāris' remarks that the particles as a category were of equal importance in the language, and that any study of them should reflect that status. To sum up, then, the presence of *waḍ'* ensured that the Muslim community had its own set of 'cultural units' corresponding to the content of a particular word.

Let us turn now to the role of *waḍ'* related notions in ML. It is quite clear that when I-H is discussing the function of a particular particle, or the verb, for example, he is fully aware of the concept of the establishment of speech. He employs derivatives of the root *wāw ḍād 'ayn*, namely *wuḍi'a* or *mawḍū'*, to convey the idea of words having been established for a particular function, on at least twenty five occasions. For instance, the particle *hal* has been established for (the idea of) seeking verification from positive questions (*li ṭalab al-taṣdīq al-ījābī*) (ML 2:349). By way of further examples we may cite I-H's pronounced judgement on the reason for the establishing of the verb (ML 1:227) which is to bind the action to the inferred time (*li taqyīd al-ḥadath bi-l zaman al-muḥaṣṣal*).[17] With regard to the particle *ḥattā*, it has been established to convey the connection (of the import) of the verb preceding it, by degrees, to its aim (*li ifādat taqaḍḍī l-fi'l qablahā shay'an fa shay'an ilā l-ghāya*) (ML 1:124). The significant factor in this explanation is that the presence of the notion of the establishment of speech is often vital to distinguish between two particles which *prima facie* share the same meaning. In this case both *ḥattā* and *ilā* have in common the idea of *intihā' al-ghāya* 'end (point) of a specific aim', but I-H is able to draw upon the reason for which each was posited in order to determine the exact difference in meaning. A similar situation obtains for the example of the particle *hal* given above. This particle is, in fact, unique amongst the interrogative particles in that it seeks verification, viz., a 'yes' or 'no' response, from a question, whereas the other interrogative particles (*hamza* excepted) are for ascertaining which of the two or more things being asked about is either being done, or is actually doing the verb (*li ṭalab al-taṣawwur*).

The view that I-H was writing at a particularly interesting time historically and intellectually was deployed earlier in this work, and the major commentaries on ML have undoubtedly contributed to underlining this situation. What is of interest to the present discussion is the way in which one of those commentators displays a tendency to interpret some of I-H's views in the light of the scholastic theory of *waḍʿ al-lugha* which developed in fact around the time of I-H. In his commentary al-Damāmīnī tells us (*Sharḥ* 17) that what I-H meant by his very first words in ML, viz., *fī tafsīr al-mufradāt* 'to explain the single entities...(ML 1:13)', was 'an elucidation of the meanings for which the *mufradāt* were posited in correspondence with those meanings' (*tabyīn al-maʿānī allati wuḍiʿat tilka l-mufradāt bi izāʾihā*).[18] There is nothing unorthodox in this explanation, but the commentator then elaborates on this idea during the ensuing discussion of the *alif* (or, more correctly, the *hamza*) as a 'particle with which someone nearby is called' (*ḥarf yunādā bihi l-qarīb*) (*Sharḥ* 18; cf. ML 1:13). He notes that the *hamza* here is a vocative particle (*ḥarf nidāʾ*) in terms of its denotatum (*bi iʿtibār al-musammā*). However, according to al-Damāmīnī its full title should be 'the name of a particle with which someone is called' (*ism ḥarf yunādā bihi*), just as the *bāʾ*, for instance, is the 'name' of a particle of obliqueness (*ism ḥarf jarr*).[19]

The above example is significant because it reflects a trend which had begun already with al-Ījī (d.756/1355) to concern oneself with the theory of 'name-giving' which was the outstanding trademark of the scholastic theory of *waḍʿ*. Weiss (1966:90ff.) notes that the idea of the positing of expressions for mental images, and not names of objects in the outside world, would seem to bear substantial similarities with the modern linguistic theory of name-relation. Given that al-Ījī died even before I-H, and that the concern with 'name-giving' was well-established within a century of I-H's death, it is not inconceivable that I-H would have been aware of this trend. Indeed, there is some evidence to support the view that I-H was also concerned with the naming of all formal elements of the language, such as the attached pronoun suffixes of verbs. For instance, he tells his students (ML 2:664-65) that when they are parsing a verb like *ḍarabtu* they must describe the subject marker *tā'* as the *fā'il* 'agent' *tā'* and not as a 't'. With regard to the particles I-H notes that a particle comprising a single consonant, such as the *bā'* or the *wāw*, for example, must be parsed and expressed in terms of its particular name; likewise those particles made up of two consonants such as *qad* or *hal* must be expressed as such, and not as the phonemes *qāf* and *dāl* or *hā'* and *lām*. In this connection I-H criticises al-Khalīl and Sībawayhi for representing the definite article *al* as 'the *alif* and the *lam*,' even though his criticism of the latter appears to be based on the opinion that their description was too verbose (ML 2:664-65). What I-H is doing here, of course, is asserting the morphemic nature of the particles and thus giving them a meaning (grammatical in this case), although there would seem to be an apparent concern with their names too. Indeed, it is not a coincidence that the nature of the particles aroused great interest amongst the later writers on *waḍ'*, and that whole short treatises were devoted to that subject (cf.Weiss 1976:24-28). There had been a marked increase in attention given to the particles initially towards the end of the fourth century A.H., which is reflected in some of the works which we shall be looking at later in conjunction with the beginnings of a much more detailed approach which emerged during the seventh century A.H.

As part of the process of laying the peripheral foundations of this study it is now time to turn our attention to the issue of *ḥaqīqa* and *majāz* which has fascinated contemporary scholars for some time now. In essence the former conveys the idea of literal meaning, whilst the latter may be translated as figurative or extended meaning, although only in a later context of, say, the third century A.H. onwards, or even after that date. Before assessing the immediate importance of these terms to ML, a sketch of the history of the terms may be in order here.

It is generally held that the *ḥaqīqa* of an expression is the result of the original positing of expressions for concepts (Ibn

Qayyim al-Jawziyya, *Mukhtaṣar,* 1:6). More specifically we may cite the succinct definition of Ibn Taymiyya (*Īmān* 101; cf. al-Zarkashī, *Burhān,* 1:99) that *ḥaqīqa* is what is literal in language, that which signifies by itself without a *qarīna* 'associative indication'. Bloomfield (1970:149) arouses a certain interest in this connection in his discussion of what he calls 'normal' or 'central' meaning in relation to 'marginal' or 'metaphoric' or 'transferred' meaning. He notes that 'we understand a form (that is, respond to it) in the central meaning unless some feature of the practical situation forces us to look to a transferred meaning'. It is tempting to speculate that the concepts of *waḍʿ* and *ḥaqīqa* fit neatly into Bloomfield's notion of central meaning.

To attempt to comprehend the precise nature of *majāz* requires a little more explanation. There is evidence to suggest that the term *majāz* was employed by Abū ʿUbayda (d.209/824-25) in a manner which sets it aside from the later understanding of the term vis-a-vis *ḥaqīqa.*[20] It has been noted by Heinrichs (1984:112), however, that Abū ʿUbayda's use of the term appears to constitute a 'prefiguration' of its later acceptance as figurative speech. According to Heinrichs (ibid.:127), we can say that *majāz* as it is presented in the work of Abū ʿUbayda denotes an 'explanatory re-writing of a given phrase which consists in establishing its *maʿnā* by various means of 'going beyond' the original wording'. Although the idea of figurative speech does not pervade Abū ʿUbayda's employment of the term, Heinrichs suggests that the distinction between this earlier and the later usage is not so vast. He maintains (ibid.:123) that perhaps the most important difference to be borne in mind is that for Abū ʿUbayda, *majāz* does not refer to the linguistic phenomena as it does later when used in the context of *ḥaqīqa*; rather it appears for the most part to possess a similar identity and to perform a function which is analogous to *taqdīr.* Perhaps the best conclusion one can reach is that Abū ʿUbayda used his *majāz* method to safeguard correct textual comprehension of unusual language and to prove that this unusual language was not incorrect' (ibid.:139).

By the time of I-H, of course, the term *majāz* was being widely used as the counterpart of *ḥaqīqa,* and is best understood in this context as figurative language.[21] In essence, figurative usage is made up of expressions which are employed for meanings other than that for which they were established, and which also depend on an associative indication to indicate the meaning (e.g., al-Baṣrī, *Mu'tamad,* 1:31; al-Zamlukānī, *Burhān,* 1:99; Ibn Taymiyya, *Īmān* 101). The presence of *majāz* is vital for I-H's purposes in ML: in fact, we can safely say that all meanings discussed in such a work are dependent on the presence of either a literal or a figurative meaning, even when this is not explicitly stated, since these two categories constitute the whole of language. The consensual view acknowledged that the purpose of *majāz* was to embellish language (al-Suyūṭī, *Muz,* 1:358; al-Zarkashī, *Burhān,* .2:255); some even went so far as to suggest that the majority of language is figurative (al-Suyūṭī, *Muz,* 1:357). The basis of the argument put forward by those who firmly believed in the existence of figurative usage was that if the Qur'ān, as the perfect example, were devoid of such features as *ḥadhf* or *tawkīd* 'emphasis', it would lose the aesthetic beauty which makes it so unique.

What is the immediate relevance of all this, then, to ML? We are told by al-Suyūṭī (*Muz,* 1:358) that figurative devices in language include elision, pre-posing and post-posing (*taqdīm wa ta'khīr*), and correlating the meaning of a word or a part of syntax with another (*al-ḥaml 'alā l-ma'nā*). All these devices feature prominently in ML which is a study of, above all, the Qur'ān. Morever, if we are to follow the unequivocal line of the Mu'tazilites, God communicated to man in the Qur'ān in figurative speech (al-Baṣrī, *Mu'tamad,* 1:30). Another of the alleged advantages of figurative speech over literal usage is that the former is more flexible due to the expansive nature (*ittisā'*) of Arabic. For instance, it allows you to use the word 'ask' in 'Ask the village' (*is'al al-qarya*) (should be 'Ask the people of the village') in a way that you could not if *ḥaqīqa* were in force (al-Suyūṭī, *Muz,* 1:358).[22]

Aside from some of the figurative devices mentioned above which are dealt with at length by I-H in the second part of ML (to be reviewed here in Chapter Six), there are also other features of equal significance which neded to be taken into account, such as the application of *majāz* to whole groups of words (*murakkabāt*) as well as to single entities (*mufradāt*) (al-Zamlukānī, *Burhān,* 1:100). This view is very much in line with that of al-Jurjānī's on the function of *waḍ'* which we looked at earlier. With regard to the *mufradāt* it is clear that such an exhaustive analysis of the particles, for instance, would not be possible without the admittance of figurative usage. This could be exemplified in ML by the interrogative *hamza* which has eight 'extended' meanings beyond that of interrogation. These meanings comprise such rhetorical devices as the invalidatory denial (*al-inkār al-ibṭālī*) which occurs frequently in the Qur'ān as a means of denoting that what really happened is the converse of the apparent meaning of the verse: thus anyone who claimed the literal meaning would be an infidel. An example of this is the following from Sūra XXXIX vs.36: *a laysa allāhu bi kāfin 'abdahu* ? 'Shall God not suffice His servant ?' (ML 1:17).[23] It is worth noting here that on this and many other occasions, I-H employs the verb *kharaja 'an* 'to go beyond' to render the extended function of a given particle. For instance, he says of the *hamza* that it may go beyond (*qad takhruju 'an*) the (meaning) of *istifhām ḥaqīqī* 'literal interrogation' and occur with eight (other) meanings (ML 1:17).[24]

Another useful example of the presence of figurative usage in ML can be seen in the section on the particle *bā'*. Scholars have agreed that the original meaning for which it was established is *ilṣāq* 'adhesion', but according to I-H a distinction must be drawn between the literal and the figurative meaning. In the former the verb is related in essence to what follows the preposition (*ilā nafs al-majrūr)*, as in *amsaktu bi zaydin* 'I grabbed (hold of) Zayd'. On the other hand, the figurative idea is conveyed by the verb which merely 'approaches' the essence of what follows the preposition, as in *marartu bi zaydin* 'I passed by Zayd' (ML 1:101). What I-H fails to make clear, however, is that although the particle *bā'* admits of several other interpretations, the sense of *ilṣāq* underlies them all (al-Irbilī, *Jaw* 36). Such examples abound in ML, and many of these will be encountered in later chapters of this study.[25]

A picture should gradually be emerging that figurative usage was viewed as an intrinsic part of the *i'jāz* 'inimitability' of the Qur'ān, at least by those scholars who accepted its existence. A further illustration of this may be found in the particle *in* 'if', for instance, of which the underlying meaning is that of *sharṭ* 'condition'. Yet its meaning can assume more significance than that in both current usage and the Qur'ānic text, for 'the verb with it (can) convey a certainty that something has or will actually happen' (ML 1:26). We might add to this that it can also imply that something actually is the case. In Sūra II vs.278, for instance, the words *in kuntum mu'minīn* 'if you are believers' does not cast doubt on the faith of those being addressed; rather these words adopt the meaning of condition with the extended meaning of *tahyīj* 'provocation' and *ilhāb* 'inciting', just as you say to your son: 'If you are my son, do not do that', although he is unquestionably your son (ML 1:26; cf. al-Dasūqī, *Ḥāshiya* 33). This last example raises a particularly important issue as to whether there exists an overlap between Qur'ānic and secular rhetoric, although an investigation of this issue is beyond the purview of this study.

The original (*waḍ'ī*) meaning of words or particles can be replaced by similar categories with the same import by a process called *taḍmīn* 'implication (of meaning)'. Once again this will be examined in more detail in later chapters but merits a mention here because of its relationship to the original *waḍ'*. For instance, I-H notes how in the sentence *Zaydun a'qalu min an yakdhaba* 'Zayd is too intelligent to tell lies', the elative (*ism al-tafḍīl) a'qalu* (lit. 'more intelligent') has assumed, by implication (*ḍummina*), the meaning of *ab'adu* (lit. 'too remote'). The reason for the application of implication here is that a literal (*ẓāhir*) interpretation would suggest that Zayd is much better in terms of intelligence than he is at telling lies (*tafḍīl zayd fī l-'aql 'alā l-kadhb*). With the presence of implication, though, the import of the sentence would be that Zayd is far too remote in terms of merit to tell lies. In this case the implied meaning overrules, figuratively at any rate, the originally posited meaning (*al-ma'nā l-waḍ'ī*) of the elative (ML 2:548).[26] This is one of the many illustrations to be found throughout ML of the relationship between *ḥaqīqa, majāz* and *waḍ'*.

If we accept that the communicative meaning (*fā'ida*) of *taḍmīn* is to allow one word to indicate, or to convey, the import or meaning of two words (ML 2:530,685), it is hardly surprising that the interpretation of certain individual lexical items in the Qur'ān necessitates the application of this device. An example of this may be cited from Sūra II vs.261 where, according to I-H, a correct understanding of the verb *amāta* rests in this particular context on the implication of the verb *albatha* in the first instance, then *labitha*. The reason for this is that the original (or established) meaning of *amāta* is the taking away of life; but the opposite is meant here, and this is reflected in the implication of the latter verb which carries the meaning of abiding (ML 2:530). The availability of this device inevitably gives the language and its users more options and flexibility, but ensures the preeminence of *waḍ'*. It should be noted at this point, however, that there were those who believed that everything should adhere to its original meaning. A very clear indication of this is to be found in al-Irbilī (*Jaw* 263) when he notes that 'they (the Kufans) argued their case by stating that according to the primary form (*aṣl*), every particle should be used for that which it was established, so it does not lead to confusion and an elimination of the intended meaning of the *waḍ'* '.

It is time to review the position so far. The immediately preceding discussion has looked in more depth at the underlying concomitants of *waḍ'*, which in itself is a concept that admits of comparisons with the logocentric idea as we saw above. It is worthwhile pursuing this notion a little further in order to illustrate briefly a few more principles at work in ML that help to ensure the stability of the (Classical) Arabic language vis-a-vis the Qur'ān within that framework.

In his stimulating article on logocentrism, Arkoun notes (1972:11) that *'la notion décisive d'aṣl'* ensures the impermeability of the *'clôture logocentrique'*. The concept of *aṣl* lies at the foundation of all linguistic studies together with *waḍ'*, and it is mentioned explicitly on several occasions in ML. In the first instance it is tempting to compare the function of the *aṣl* in a syntactic context with the notion of deep structure in the transformation theory of modern linguistics, especially as the former often invokes an element of elision (*ḥadhf*) or reconstruction of the original syntax (*taqdīr*) (e.g., ML 1:28,267; 2:615). For example, in accordance with the primary form, there is a syntactic requirement that the predicate (*khabar*) follow the topic of a nominal sentence (*mubtada'*), although an inversion of the two is perfectly legitimate in certain circumstances (ML 2:613). However, Owens (1988:220-26 esp.) has shown that caution must be applied when comparing the two systems, and that we must not assume that the theories of the Arab grammarians are necessarily commensurate with those of the generativists of today.

As a yardstick for testing the validity of existing linguistic data and generating grammatical forms in ML, I-H employs the term *qiyās*. This term is normally translated as 'analogy', although a proposed translation here is 'the sanctioning of linguistic data according to the rules governing the language' (see Chapter One). The issue of *qiyās* is a profound one with a long history. It should be underlined here that although I-H's employment of the term is not original, it played a significant role in his system of grammatical and semantic analysis.[27] Although *qiyās* is one of the main bastions of the Islamic legal system it has always been an important criterion of any grammatical study. Indeed its significance in this respect inspired the immortal quote of Ibn al-Anbārī in the sixth-century A.H. that 'whoever denies (the existence of) *qiyās* denies (the existence of) grammar (*naḥw*)' (*Luma'* 95), even if al-Anbārī's remarks emanated from his skilful attempts to equate the principles of grammar with law.

In ML *qiyās* is used to judge the validity of a wide range of grammatical points or to generate grammatical forms (e.g., ML 1:25,43; 2:418,504,524,525,626,695). Although this function is not original, it is interesting to note its importance in non-grammatical matters such as the orthography of the Qur'ān (e.g., ML 1:254). What is of more interest, however, is the use of such terms as *thabata* or *ithbāt* and their attendant verbs. This root would seem to imply the establishment or assertion of a grammatical point. In some ways it appears to be performing a similar function to *qiyās* in the sense that any grammatical issue under scrutiny must meet the required standard. On the other hand the former would intimate the need for some sort of agreement in asserting that a given point has been attested (e.g., ML 1:38,70,81,171,177,324; 2:403). On one occasion, however, I-H is more explicit in revealing the precedence of *qiyās* over *thabata* when he states that even if the grammatical rule in question has been attested (*thabata*), it does not fall within the realms of *qiyās* nor the established usage of the eloquent speakers of the language (*al-fuṣaḥā'*) (ML 1:91): in other words, being attested is not necessarily sufficient evidence for the sanctioning of linguistic data. One would also expect to find the word *shādhdh* 'anomalous material' used in the context of *qiyās*, but it is often found in ML in direct association with *ithbāt* (ML 1:38,70,324). *Shādhdh* also occurs in association with *samā'*, which has been proposed as 'the pure reporting of linguistic usage as it has been transmitted from the ancient Arabs' (Bohas et al. 1990:26). *Samā'* was also a vital antithesis to *qiyās,* and was accepted to varying degrees by the grammarians. Other terms which appear to assume similar properties to *thabat* and its derivatives are *ta'yīn* and *ta'ayyun* (e.g., ML 2:569,595). In fact, a study of the terminology deployed for these purposes would constitute a very worthwhile pursuit, for it is clear from the foregoing modest assessment that the various terms bear considerable and, in some cases, subtle significance.

There is little doubt that of all the principles underlying I-H's approach in ML the assertion of the primacy and supremacy of the Qur'ānic text is paramount. This merits some elaboration here. Indeed, I-H expressed this view in less defined terms in another of his works where he states that whenever he discusses a grammatical issue he applies to it a relevant verse of the Qur'ān (*Shudhūr* 10). This process works in reverse, too, since the Qur'ān, or the *tanzīl* 'Revelation' as I-H prefers to call it, would not be subjected to interpretation with any parts of speech or citings from poetry that were irregular (*shādhdh*), incorrect Arabic (*laḥn*), or weak (*ḍa'īf*). The following examples should suffice to illustrate I-H's view of the supremacy of the *tanzīl*. He says, for instance (ML 1:270-71), that 'I have found a verse in the *tanzīl* in which the predicate (of the particle *anna* after *law*) occurs as a derived noun (*ism mushtaqq*). It was not pointed out by either al-Zamakhsharī...nor Ibn Mālik, otherwise he (the latter) would not have cited poetry as proof (of its occurring in this form)'. The argument being put forward here, of course, is that had Ibn Mālik discovered it he would have given the Qur'ānic verse precedence as textual evidence. The advantage gained here by I-H is twofold: to underline the primacy of the *tanzīl* and to assert his authority and further his standing as a grammarian in the service of Islam. A few more examples are in order here:

'...and the first (view) is correct, because the predicate after *mā* only occurs in the *tanzīl* without the *bā'* when it is in the accusative (dependent) case (*manṣūb*)' (ML 2:595).

'...and al-Zamakhsharī. claimed that it is irregular and rare, but that is not the case because of its occurring in (several) places in the *tanzīl* ' (ML 2:505).

'...moreover there are several places in the *tanzīl* where it occurs like that, and that is indisputable' (ML 2:621).

'...and this is not permitted in poetry, so how can it be (allowed) in the most perfect of speech (*afṣaḥ al-kalām*)' (ML 2:544; cf. ML 1:13, 35, 87, 156, 189, 231; 2:594).

The reverse procedure involves the interpretation of the Qur'ānic text according to a given form or word from other sources, normally poetry. The two terms used in relation to this process are *al-ḥaml 'alā l-ma'nā* 'the correlating of the meaning of a word or a part of syntax to another' and *al-takhrīj 'alā* 'interpreting a piece of Qur'ānic text according to a grammatical form or word'. The employment of these two terms may be exemplified by the following:

'...because the Qur'ān is never interpreted on the basis of anomalous material' (*li'anna l-tanzīla la yatakharraju 'alā l-shādhdh*) (ML 1:199).

'I said; he acknowledged that it was bad (Arabic) (*ridā'a*); thereafter to interpret the *tanzīl* by it would also be unacceptable' (ML 2:589).

'...to apply the nominative/independent case to the verb with this meaning is very rare, so it would not be good practice to interpret the *tanzīl* by it' (*inna majī'a l-raf' bi hādhā l-ma'nā qalīl jiddan*; *fa lā yaḥsunu ḥaml al-tanzīl 'alayhi*) (ML 2:482; cf. for *ḥaml* and *takhrīj*, 1:84, 114, 184, 231, 233; 2:282, 324, 325, 482, 509, 510, 548).

It is worth pausing at this juncture to consider the value of poetry as textual evidence for an interpretation of the sacred text.

It was indicated earlier that for I-H poetry is just one example of textual material in a universe of discourse expressed in an Arabic language which represents nothing less than the language of the Sunna. Nonetheless, although poetry was doubtless deemed by I-H to be a worthy and reliable source of recourse in linguistic matters involving the sacred text, it is also clear from his remark noted above concerning the perfection of the latter that they were not to be equally exalted in his view. This may be seen in contrast to the observations of Carter (1993:147) on Ibn Fāris (d.395/1004) who apparently viewed the language of human poetry and the Qur'ān as 'equally sublime'.

To conclude this section on significant, recurring terms in ML that help to illustrate the underlying principles present in it which we would argue are prerequisites for any elucidation of the meaning of the Qur'ān, it is worth noting the use of the word *dalīl* 'proof, indication' in ML. This word is used in context with a proliferation of citations of verses taken mainly from the Qur'ān, and to a lesser extent poetry, as proof of the acceptability of the meaning of a particle (ML 1:104), for instance, or a point of grammar (ML 2:536). It also functions as a proof, for example, that two particles are more or less synonymous in the opinion of I-H based on citations of two separate verses of the Qur'ān where the meaning would seem to concur, although different particles have been used (ML 1:148).[28] The term *dalīl* occurs frequently in ML in a wide range of contexts outlined above, and it is worth dwelling a moment here on what we consider to be its real importance. Earlier in this chapter we looked at the Islamic concept of signification and supported the view that it is the very unit of knowledge. Now, a thorough knowledge of the Arabic language, which includes knowing what is literal and figurative, an understanding of the principles of elision and suppression (*iḍmār*), is what can lead to a knowledge of the significations expressed in the Book and the Sunna (al-Āmidī, *Iḥkām*, 1:9). If the unit of proof, or signification (*dalīl*), is what leads to knowledge (al-Rāzī, *Maḥṣūl*, 1:15), then it is not inconceivable that an ability to be able to cite proofs in the form of Qur'ānic verses as I-H does in ML professes a command of that knowledge, and an ability to go some way towards reaching that truth.

The next point of discussion pertains to an issue already alluded to in this study that in spite of the indisputable nature of the sacred Islamic texts there was by no means a perfect harmony of opinion on grammatical issues amongst the grammarians. The more personal aspects of points of agreement and disagreement will be examined in the next chapter. What concerns us here once more is what lies at the foundation of the discussion of meaning and grammar in ML that permits I-H to attempt to draw conclusions based on these proofs as to what was really meant in the texts. After all, I-H draws on opinions from a plethora of sources, balancing one view against another and, in most cases, adhering to a majority conception if he does not offer an innovative solution himself.

The wisdom of associating a particular language with a specific type of linguistics would in many circumstances be open to question. Nonetheless we believe that there is sufficient evidence in ML to suppose that if we had been privileged to meet I-H he might have accepted the view to be argued here that (Classical) Arabic, particularly in its Qur'ānic form, was a member of the 'contractualist' type of languages. The case for upholding this view of language has been put forward at length in a cogent argument by Harris (1980:102ff.) with specific reference to Western languages. Although his discussion is based on the opinions cast by Hermogenes on the Greek language that it is based on 'convention' and 'agreement', there would seem to be a great deal of relevance in Harris' examination to the situation of Arabic as we see it in ML.[29]

Harris (ibid.:102) defines contractualism as 'essentially a form of social contract'[30] in which 'a language is thus envisaged as the manifestation of a tacit collective understanding between members of a community as to how a certain range of social affairs shall be conducted'. With regard to the Arabic situation, of course, the Qur'ān is and always was the axiomatic guide for Muslims in their daily lives, the prescription for social conduct and the application of the law. If we follow the line put forward earlier in this chapter that by the time of I-H the discourse of the text represents nothing less than a constant reenactment of the message of the sacred word, it is not difficult to conclude that a work like ML functions as a reaffirmation of the contract established amongst the Muslim community at the time of the

Prophet, even though it was written nearly seven and a half centuries later. Harris (ibid.:110) notes that a 'linguistic convention' of this kind is normally maintained without question 'so long as it continues to serve its social purpose adequately'.[31]

It is worth noting here that for the purposes of the contract the origin of language was irrelevant. Indeed it did not matter how language had originally evolved because the factors concerning the provenance of the contract may not always be subject to scrutiny (Harris ibid.:111). The most important factor was the presence of a 'contract', in the form of the revered Arabic language outlined above, whose continuation would be overseen by the *ʿulamāʾ*. This large and diverse body of scholars have been described by Hourani (1991:158) as the 'keepers of the moral conscience of the community'. The obligation of these scholars was to Islam, of course, and the grammarians, many of whom were exegetes in their own right, had all the tools at their disposal to help maintain this contract.

Every contract requires a guarantor. In ML, the *ijmāʿ* 'consensus of the community' is the ultimate guarantor of the contract, based perhaps on what Wansbrough (1978:130) calls a 'concept of authority' founded in the notion of 'precedent'. Wansbrough adds that through this process the preservation and transmission of the sacred texts brings the past into the present and even the future (cf. the discussion on the logocentric nature of Islam above). The *ijmāʿ* is nothing less than the optimum form of agreement on linguistic issues, although we shall see later that there is some doubt as to whether a total consensus on such matters was ever really possible. In ML, various terms are pressed into service in a seemingly hierarchical fashion to deal with the different levels of agreement reached by the grammarians on a given linguistic point: at the head of the hierarchy is *ijmāʿ*, followed by *ittifāq*, and to a lesser extent *iṭbāq*, which seem to convey the idea of a general agreement, but certainly not a consensus. *Jumhūr* and *jamāʿa* 'group' are two categories which suggest a majority opinion, but alongside the occurrence of these terms one may well find mention of one or more grammarians who dissented from a particular viewpoint. Except for *ijmāʿ*, it is not immediately clear whether I-H's application of these terms is systematic or arbitrary; further detailed study would be necessary to investigate this. The significance of *ijmāʿ* in its more familiar legal context, however, has been well-documented. Given the inextricable link between the language and the law alluded to above, its prominent role in linguistic matters is hardly surprising. For the legal theorists *ijmāʿ* was the most important of the foundations of religion (*uṣūl al-dīn*) (al-Amidi, *Iḥkām*, 1:316) and exhibited a character of infallibility (Gardet 1981:121-22). We shall return shortly to the manner in which *ijmāʿ* and its concomitant terms are employed in ML.

To understand the intellectual climate in which ML was written, it is worth considering at this point the prevalence of debate and dispute amongst scholars of the Islamic sciences, of which the study of grammar was a vital component. In spite of the indisputable nature of the sacred texts there was by no means a perfect harmony of opinions on grammatical issues any more than on matters relating to other theological or legal problems. In fact the literature is laden with polemical material, and whole books devoted to the disagreements that took place between scholars on linguistic or legal matters have come down to us (e.g., al-Baṭalyawsī's or Ibn al-Anbārī's *Inṣāf*). It is important to realize that even the outcome of discussions on legal issues tended to rest on a grammatical or linguistic consideration. In this connection, according to al-Anbārī (*Lumaʿ* 95) a man could not only consider himself a fully-fledged legal theorist until he had perfected his command of grammar. In ML, the question of who said what on a particular point and its validity within the context of interpretation is pivotal to I-H's style of debate. It is inevitable that many scholars will have differed on a linguistic issue. What I-H does throughout ML is to present the many different views on a given point and then normally reach his own conclusion based either on the evidence itself, hence applying his own unique interpretation, or on the conclusions of the consensus, or on the strength of the agreement reached between scholars. What happens to the contract, however, in cases of disagreement amongst the members of the (scholarly) community ?

In this regard Harris (1980:105-6) poses some highly pertinent questions. For instance, 'does the contract break down?...are certain parties in breach of contract ?...are there a number of equally valid contracts operative?'. More on this shortly; but for the moment, this brings us back to the question of prescriptivism raised earlier in this study. Harris (ibid.:106ff.) argues that it was indeed these considerations that led to the genesis of the prescriptive or normative approach as scholars sought to select (and set) standards by which to judge their language. Such judgement naturally depends on the existence of a 'class of professional language experts', as Harris puts it (ibid.:106), an educated elite who attempt to ensure that the purity of the language is maintained.[32] Harris adds that these experts will base their opinions on 'a body of prestigious texts..., handed down from earlier generations..., (and which) will tend to be regarded as authoritative in respect of linguistic matters'. The relevance of all this to I-H and ML is too great to ignore. As we have already seen I-H does not just use the sacred text of the Qur'ān as the ultimate yardstick for the purity of the Arabic language but he also gives due deference to the validity of secular language, including pre-Islamic poetry.

The body of prestigious texts also admits of a further interpretation in the case of ML. Given that it was written nearly six centuries after Sībawayhi's *Kitāb*, I-H was able to draw on a wide range of grammatical works as the main substance for his arguments. If we take these works, of which ML automatically became one, as the prestigious texts to which the community had recourse on linguistic issues, I-H's own position within this elite group becomes even more prominent. He does not rely on these previous works, but rather leans on them as a gauge for his own standards. It is in this context that his unique, corrective, and at times almost informal chatty style with which he addresses his students, assumes greater significance. The following examples demonstrate this approach.

Throughout the presentation of his arguments I-H avails himself of a full range of descriptives to discount the opinions of other grammarians or linguists. These range from the frequent use of *sahw* 'carelessness' to the prescriptive *ma'īb, ghalaṭ* or *khaṭa'* 'error'. It is the latter type that concerns us here. The acknowledgement of *laḥn* 'solecisms', perpetrated equally by the literati and the masses, is to be found at various points in the text, as in *al-fuqahā' yalḥanūna fī qawlihim...*'the legal theorists speak incorrect Arabic when they say...' (ML 2:669). Verdicts imposed by I-H on certain grammatical issues include *wa hādhā lā yaṣaḥḥu fī l-ʿarabiyya* 'this is not acceptable in the Arabic language' (ML 2:543), or in cases where, for example, grammarians give too much attention to the *ṣināʿa* 'grammatical form' at the expense of the *maʿnā* 'meaning', as in *kathīran mā tazillu l-aqdām bi sabab dhālik* 'lit: 'feet often slip because of that', i.e., 'people often fall into this trap' (ML 2:527). An error (*khaṭa'/ ghalaṭ*) can be committed in a structural or semantic context; for instance, when certain grammarians assume that the inverted *sharṭ* 'condition' can be linked to what precedes it when the conditional verb is in anything other than the simple past tense, which is a *khaṭa'* (ML 2:545), or when they misinterpret the role of the *mutaʿalliq* 'syntactico-semantic connector' in a particular verse of the Qur'ān. Of this I-H says: *fa (hādhā) ghalaṭ awqaʿahum fīhi ʿadam fahm al-mutaʿalliq fī l-āya* ...(ML 2:685). The didactic, instructive elements in ML are perhaps at their most prominent in the short, but detailed, chapter devoted to the nature of *iʿrāb* (*fī kayfiyyat al-iʿrāb)*, which represents, after all, the main thrust of the work. I-H addresses his students in an almost conversational style, as in, for instance, 'I asked some of my students one day how they would parse the following...' (ML 2:673), or 'Students were very fond of asking about His (God's) word in...' (ML 1:260). One can almost perceive a catechitical approach in his prescription to the learner to parse everything about the noun, as in *lā budda li l-mutakallim*...'the speaker must...' (ML 2:666), or the verb, as in *yanbaghī an tuʿayyina li l mubtadi' nawʿ al-fiʿl*...'You should define the type of verb for the beginner...' (ML 2:667). Additionally we may cite the instruction given by I-H to his students at the beginning of Chapter Six in ML as a warning (*taḥdhīr*) on linguistic matters for which the grammarians have become famous. I-H notes that the correct versions are in fact the opposite of what they maintain (*wa l-ṣawāb khilāfuhā*) (ML 2:650).

What I-H achieves through this technique is to ensure as far as possible that the contract is not corrupted by further grammatical error. In practice, of course, the purity of the contract could never be guaranteed. Yet the consequences of breaching it are unequivocal: one falls into religious error. It was Ibn Jinnī (*Khaṣ,* 3:245) who said that a weakness in language leads to a straying from the path of the *sharīʿa*. At any rate there are two important terms in ML that relate to the contractual idea and to those questions raised above by Harris concerning the validity of the contract. These are *kharq* 'breach' and *khilāf* 'disagreement'.

To return to the terms introduced earlier, the presence of *ijmā'*, and, in the event of a lesser agreement, *jumhūr* or *jamā'a,* ensures that the contract does not actually break down. This does not mean, however, that certain parties could not be in breach of the contract. I-H employs the term *kharq* 'breach' at various points in relation to a view held by one grammarian or more. For instance, in the discussion on the meaning of the particle *alif* as a vocative particle with which something close by is addressed, the grammarian Ibn al-Khabbāz claimed that it was used to call something at middle range, and that the particle *yā* was used for calling something or someone close by. I-H calls this a 'breach of their consensus' (*wa hādhā kharq li ijmā'ihim*...ML 1:13). On another occasion, I-H claims that a particular view held by Ibn Mālik was a breach of the consensus of the grammarians (ML 1:46).

Much more prevalent throughout ML, however, is the underlying theme of *khilāf* 'disputation'. Although these disagreements between scholars on a given linguistic issue did not constitute a breakdown of the contract, they ensured the coexistence of a number of equally valid sub-contracts, as suggested by Harris above. I-H's non-acceptance of the material contained within some of these sub-contracts could not justify their removal. In many cases the evidence was simply insufficient for a consensus to be reached. This could be exemplified by the discussion on the preposition *rubba*, where I-H argues that its meaning is not always for a small number of things (*al-taqlīl),* in contrast to (*khilāfan li)* the belief of the majority (*al-aktharīn)*; likewise it is not always for many things (*al-takthīr)*, in contrast to the view of Ibn Durustawayhi and a group (*jamā'a*)' (ML 1:134). I-H offers a compromise on this issue by citing examples of the occurrence of *rubba* in the Qur'ān, ḥadīth and poetry, although he is unable to rule out categorically these widely held interpretations.

It must be said that debate and disputation (*khilāf/ ikhtilāf*) amongst the *'ulamā'* of the Muslim community was a way of life. Makdisi (1981:111) puts this succinctly when he says that 'to become an accomplished master-jurisconsult one had to become proficient in disputation'. He adds (significantly) (ibid.:112) that 'the absence of *khilāf* could lead to consensus (*ijmā'*)'. This serves to corroborate the argument here that the sub-contracts based principally on *khilāf,* notwithstanding the underlying meaning of that word, viz., 'to deviate from a good course' (Makdisi 1981:110), could not be overruled by a consensus, but could continue to exist in that context. A significant contribution to our understanding of the nature of disputation in the medieval period was made by al-Baṭalyawsī (*Inṣāf* 19) when he said that 'controversy and disputation is embedded in our nature, and is an intrinsic part of our being (*markūzan fī fiṭrinā, maṭbū'an fī khalqinā*)'. According to al-Baṭalyawsī the disagreement is never about the truth itself, but about ways of reaching the truth.

In ML it appears that a consensus in the strict sense of the word never really occurs, so long as there were grammarians prepared to offer a different opinion.[33] I-H normally claims an *ijmā'* in cases where just one or two scholars have followed a different line (try ML 1:78; 2:397,551,593), although there are occasions when the consensus appears to be unanimous (ML 1:98; 2,606). In one instance I-H refutes al-Sīrāfī's claim to have acquired a consensus on a given point by listing the names of eight grammarians who disagreed with his view (ML 2:354). The concept of *naql* 'transmission' was also important in ensuring the validity of a consensus, and, *ipso facto*, the stability of the contract. We are told, for example, how the grammarian Ibn 'Uṣfūr transmitted a consensus on a grammatical feature of the particle *immā* (ML 1:60).

We suggested earlier that a hierarchy of agreement on linguistic issues would seem to be in operation in the form of the terms *ijmā'*, *ittifāq, jumhūr,* and *jamā'a.* This point would, admittedly, merit further examination, although there is evidence to conclude that *ittifāq* constitutes a more authoritative form of agreement than either of the latter two forms. For instance, I-H states that a particular meaning in a line of poetry and some verses of the Qur'ān has been agreed upon; hence there can be no deviation from it (ML 1:305). Moreover, on the question of annexing the *asmā' al-zamān* 'nouns of time' to the sentence, for example, we see how the choice was between '*idh' bi ittifāq* 'by agreement', '*idhā*' '*inda l-jumhūr* 'majority group' or '*lamma*' '*inda man qāla bi ismiyyatihā* 'those who asserted that it was a noun' (ML 2:419). On one occasion at least, I-H offers an innovative interpretation (*badī'*) on whether the quasi-sentence can be semantically connected to the particles. His own view on this overrides that of the *jumhūr* (ML 2:432). It is highly unlikely, however, that he would take such liberties on an issue that had been agreed upon (*muttafaq 'alayhi*).

It is hoped that the preceding discussion has outlined the role of the guarantors of the contract. Let us now look more closely at the contents of the contract in the form of the subject matter of ML. Of particular interest to this part of the proceedings is I-H's analysis of the particles (*ḥurūf al-ma'ānī*) which constitutes more than half of that work. The particles, and the nouns and adverbs which imply the meaning of particles, are analysed extensively according to their meanings. Although it was generally agreed that the particles did not signify a meaning in themselves, but rather 'in something else', their significance within the Arabic language system cannot be overestimated. We would even go so far as to suggest that they are pivotal to the whole issue of meaning, a fact which did not escape the notice of I-H. The particles are presented systematically and, for the most part, alphabetically, according to their meanings. Thus the particle *bi,* for example, has fourteen meanings, the first and most important of which is *ilṣāq* 'adhesion'. This can be seen in either a literal context, as in *amsaktu bi zaydin* 'I grabbed Zayd', or in a figurative one, as in *marartu bi zaydin* 'I passed by Zayd' (ML 1:101). For the particles, their meaning is essentially their function. By presenting them in an easily assimilated fashion, and illustrating their function with numerous examples, many of which are taken from the sacred texts, it can be argued that I-H provides a valuable service to Islam through a reinforcement of the logocentric ideal. More on this shortly.

If we return to another substantial part of Harris' thesis there are further parallels to be drawn between the status enjoyed by the monolingual dictionary in Western society and its effects on that civilisation, and the potential effect of the contents and mode of presentation of ML on its users; in particular the manner in which the former imposed itself as a type of 'straitjacket' on further developments of lexicology and vocabulary. Harris

(1980:131) notes that in addition to the monolingual dictionary providing the language with its 'lexical inventory' it also 'set the standard, from which any departure invited a query, if not a charge of idiosyncrasy, or ignorance, or error'. He adds (ibid.:130ff.) that the dictionary became the 'final court of appeal' in cases of dispute concerning correctness. In addition to 'fixing' the meanings of words and, in a sense, discouraging its users 'from seeing a language as consisting in a form of continuous activity', the dictionary system introduced what Harris calls a 'lexical egalitarianism, which sees each word as being as important and as independent as the next'. Harris remarks that these developments recreated a new version of the 'classical fallacy' referred to above.

The significance of all this to the Arabic situation is too great to ignore. In practice it was impossible to prevent the emergence of new meanings for words, but the acceptance of them was subject to clearly defined rules. Muslim scholars, such as the legal theorist al-Āmidī (*Iḥkām*, 1:36-37), acknowledged that a new meaning for a word was only acceptable on the basis that it had become part of common linguistic usage (*al-lafẓ al-musta'mal fī mā wuḍi'a lahu bi 'urf al-isti'māl al-lughawī*), which naturally included figurative usage. As we can see from al-Āmidī, the underlying meaning of a word, viz., the originally posited one (*mā wuḍi'a lahu*) remained, and all additional meanings would be explained away figuratively, for instance. This is evident in many places in ML, such as in the discussion of the particle *bi* (ML 1:101) where the meaning of adhesion is evident in all fourteen meanings of the particle, since that was the meaning for which it was originally established. There was no place for neologisms though. Any innovation of this type had been ruled out explicitly by the grammarian Abū Ḥayyān who said that the innovation of either a new expression or a grammatical construction is not permissible because these things are posited entities (al-Suyūṭī *Muz,* 1:42-43). It was also a grammarian, al-Sīrāfī, who in his defence of the Arabic language against the infiltration of logic, told the logician Mattā that 'one can not invent a language that is already fixed among those who speak it' (Mahdi 1970:79). Weiss (1987:343) puts all this very neatly when he notes that for the Muslim community, Arabic 'represents a fixed deposit of vocables and corresponding meanings which must never be altered or abandoned so long as that community seeks to understand and do God's will'. He adds that 'this semantic constancy presupposes the absolute normativeness of the <original> and therefore essential Arabic language'.

To return to Harris' remarks on the effect of the dictionary on Western civilization, it should be acknowledged that ML is not a dictionary in the true sense of the word. It is not a lexicographical account of meanings of all the words in the Arabic language, since that service was provided by a rich collection of dictionaries dating back to the medieval period. Nonetheless, there are two significant aspects of ML which lend themselves singularly well to the dictionary idea. The first point concerns a fundamental difference between the treatment of the particles in earlier Western dictionaries and in the medieval Arabic material. We have already argued that lexicographers in the former tradition were uneasy about how to define words such as 'of' or 'to', for example, because they lacked an immediate referent. In the earlier dictionaries only scant grammatical information was supplied as lexicographers concentrated on definitions of the so-called hard words (nouns, for instance). It is true that some of the more modern dictionaries offer what might be called rule-based definitions of this class of words, but the inherent grammatical nature of these words allows them to be more at home in a grammar than in a dictionary (cf. Jackson 1980:39-44). Given the nature of the particle in the medieval Arabic situation, however, they were equally at home in either a dictionary or a work like ML, since their definitions and examples of their function would be one and the same. Moreover, in contrast to this above situation we have already seen that the notion of referents was not important for the Arab scholars.

The second point to be made here is that the manner in which I-H presents the particles in ML is, in fact, akin to the dictionary arrangement. This mode of presentation is likely to have been a result of some reflection by I-H, since studies of the particle were not without precedence. Most previous studies had been presented according to the number of constituent consonants of each particle, beginning with those particles with only one consonant, such as *bi,* through to those with four, such as *lākinna.*[34] I-H adopted the alphabetical arrangement in common with only one of the works devoted to a study of the particle, that of al-Mālaqī (*Raṣf*). It is worth reiterating here that the context for this choice must be theological. I-H acknowledges at the outset (ML 1:13) that he has presented the particles in alphabetical order (according to first consonant only) to enable students to assimilate their meanings more easily: learning by rote was, of course, a duty of all Muslims. By this method, therefore, not only was it easier for the Muslim to learn the function of the particle, but the real significance of the particle and its contribution to the issue of meaning became more prominent. It should be noted that descriptions of the particles were nothing new. Even Sībawayhi had recognised the particle as one of the three main parts of speech and had discussed the meanings and function of some of them. In ML, however, I-H penetrates much more acutely than most of his predecessors the whole question of meaning and the particles. Moreover, the piece-meal presentation by scholars like Ibn Yaʿīsh, for instance, who were more concerned with the grammatical qualities of the particle - hence one finds *ḥattā,* for instance, under the section on particles of obliqueness (*ḥurūf jarr*) and also coordinating particles (*ḥurūf ʿaṭf*) (Ibn Yaʿīsh, *Sharḥ,* 8:15-16 and 102-3) - is discarded in favour of the alphabetical approach.

Therefore, it may be argued that in structuring the section on the particles in this way, I-H guarantees the semantic constancy mentioned by Weiss above. Thus the first part of ML became a repository of this class of individual lexical items, a type of seal of the contract, in which we would argue lies the key to the question of meaning in Arabic, and consequently, a path to a deeper understanding of the religious texts. It became an easy reference for future generations and, more important, helped to ensure the stability of those texts, depicting the language of Islam as a type of 'closed system', as Harris puts it (1980:133). That the particle was indeed part of the essential baggage of the grammarian becomes clear from a perusal of a short, but valuable, work of I-H's in which he lists some of the more important particles (*Iʿrāb* 115ff.) which the grammarian must have at his disposal. The famous legal theorist-philosopher al-Ghazāli recognized their importance when he said that '...(an understanding of) legal issues rests on them and the need for them is very great' (*Mustaṣfā,* 1:229). But the carefully structured nature of ML is not restricted to the presentation of the particles; rather it is also to be found in I-H's sentence analysis which constitutes the second part of ML. In many cases the straitjacket metaphor could also be applied to this part of ML, such as in the section comprising ten occasions in which the nominal sentence may begin with an indefinite noun (*musawwighāt al-ibtidā' bi-l nakira*).[35]

It could be said then that I-H was a codifier to a certain degree. ML does assume encyclopaedic proportions but not in the same way as, say, some of the works of the polymath al-Suyūṭi. In different ways they both appear to have subscribed to the transmission of material around which the view of the 'nostalgic nature of Islamic history' (Carter 1983 (a):66) is centred. However, a scholar like al-Suyūṭi was indiscriminate in his recording of linguistic material. He was concerned with anything to do with language, whether it was morphology, phonology, or syntax; on the other hand, I-H was concerned only with syntax and semantics. Therefore, by presenting syntactic rules as described above under neat headings for the various types of sentence in Arabic, many of which are determined by semantic considerations, he consolidates the issue of meaning in a manner which also aids learning. Furthermore, I-H's interest in *ḥadhf* 'elision' (ML 2:603ff.), *taḍmīn* 'implication (of meaning)' (ML 2:525ff., 685-86 esp.), and *ta'alluq* 'syntactico-semantic connection' (ML 2:530ff.), is much greater than that of his grammarian predecessors. These three concepts in particular hold the key to a much more profound understanding of the meaning of the contract; and in the case of examples of the latter two it is the particle that features prominently once more.

It is now time to turn to the second part of the discussion. So far we have been considering a view of a religion as language bound by a contract for all time. At the root of this argument lies the concept of knowledge (*'ilm),* an epistemology of history in which linguistic data (of the past) is subject to continuous analysis but not, of course, on the basis of empirical verification. Yet a religion founded in revelation cannot ignore the past. Weiss (1985:84) describes this situation very accurately when he notes that 'the edifice of Islamic revelation as a whole had to rest upon a foundation of unassailable historical certainty'. I-H's position as a linguist in this environment is not dissimilar to that of the historian. Although his knowledge of the 'contract' described above is for him (like that of the historian's) a reality of what actually happened, i.e., the (language) event of revelation, he is not in a position to recover the actuality of the event. As in any form of historical enquiry a number of ground rules or principles should be applied.

Lass (1980:47ff.) propounds a stimulating notion of language change based on principles of historical reconstruction. At the root of the enquiry are 'witnesses' which are responsible for providing the historical evidence. Lass (ibid.:49) suggests that in the case of the historian these witnesses might take the form of buildings, archaeological sites or documents. If we transpose this argument to the context of ML there would seem to be ample justification to label the texts on which I-H bases his own linguistic enquiry as witnesses to the revelation event (*tanzīl*). Moreover, one may discern a parallel between the use of this term and the body of prestigious texts which forms a substantial part of Harris' thesis, as we saw earlier. According to Lass (ibid.:50) the validity of a historical enquiry rests on the implementation of a strict methodology and the foundation of 'a general theory of history' which admits of an identification of the potential witnesses and an evaluation of their validity. Fundamental to this theory is a 'hierarchy of responsibility' in which the data is assessed from the stage of the admission of the documents into the system through to the present time (whenever that may be). The potential ramifications of an error at some point in the chain of transmission could be disastrous of course, especially at what Lass (ibid.:50-52) calls the 'local theory' level, such as 'the admission of a document that is not properly part of the record'. In other words, the contract is susceptible to failure at any point; hence the need for the hierarchy of responsibility, or in this case, the group of language experts.[36]

Lass' argument appears to be of much relevance to I-H and ML. We have already seen the necessity for an accurate interpretation of linguistic material which is verified by a body of scholars in the form of *ijmāʿ*, *jumhūr* and so on. It is vital that these texts, which we have chosen to call 'witnesses', stand the test of time if they are not to be excluded from the contract. Only through a combination of these principles can I-H select what Lass (ibid.:52) calls 'a criteria of reliability and meaning', based on a 'uniformitarian axiom' of historical postulates. With specific regard to linguistic history this axiom admits of the premise that 'if someone reconstructs a language with, say, the vowel system / e o a / we can reject it on methodological grounds because no living language has been observed with such a system' (ibid.:56). The prerequisite of this argument is that with the application of the correct principles one can establish that what took place in the past may well be applicable to the present. In ML there is widespread evidence to suggest that these criteria of selection are in operation. However, I-H is able to base his arguments on an even more solid foundation than that proposed by Lass. The reason for this, we would maintain, is the existence of *tawātur* in Islam which functions as a direct substitute for empirical knowledge about the past.

Most of the information about *tawātur* has come down to us through the works of the legal theorists. There is no direct reference to the term in ML, so a certain amount of speculation is in force here. In essence *tawātur* is the transmission of the language of the Qur'ān, the Sunna and the (pure) language of the Arabs (*kalām al-ʿarab*) amongst a sufficient number of believers who agree on its authenticity to preclude fabrication at any point in the transmission.[37] It lends unquestionable emphasis, therefore, to the validity of the language of Islam at any given time. In this theological context language, history and knowledge are inseparable entities. Weiss encapsulates this idea when he remarks (1985:86) that 'the knowledge that a statement about a past event is true is taken to be tantamount to a knowledge of the event itself'. Given that the language was, in essence, the event itself, we would argue that only through *tawātur* could I-H possess the conviction that words such as *samā'* 'sky, heavens', or *arḍ* 'earth', for example, were used with the same meaning then as they were at the time of the Prophet. According to al-Suyūṭī (*Muz,* 1:118) the philosopher al-Rāzī held that the major part of language and grammar is made up of necessary knowledge (*ʿilm ḍarūrī*) which had been established (*mawḍūʿ*) in the past. Therefore, not only did individual lexical items mean now what they did then, but so too did grammatical categories; for instance, the agent of the verb (*fāʿil*) is still in the nominative/independent case (*marfū'*). However, one crucial element in all this should not be overlooked; that of the human role in affirming the authenticity of the 'witnesses' through the medium of consensus and the like. Again in al-Suyūṭī (*Muz*, 1:59) we find that Ibn Jinnī put this whole issue into a rational perspective when he acknowledged that language could not be based purely on transmission (*naql maḥḍ*) of the nature described by people like al-Rāzī, but that it could also be known by associative indications (*qarā'in*), such as figurative usage. Without this proviso there would be no place for the human element in the interpretation of texts along the lines of what we see in ML.[38] An example of this may be seen concerning the interpretation of Sūra IV vs.127: *wa targhabūna an tankiḥūhunna* 'and yet desire to marry them' (ML 2:604). I-H's view is that the preposition, viz., either *fī* or *'an* has been elided because of an associative indication. He adds that the *'ulamā'* disagreed (*ikhtalafū*) on which of the two prepositions should be reconstructed (*muqaddar*) because of their disagreement about the reason for the revelation of the verse. However, I-H's conclusion is that in reality the dispute was over the *qarīna*. This appreciation of the different views of the *'ulamā'* leads appropriately into the final part of the discussion which concerns I-H's responsibility to the community of believers.

The concluding element to our paper has once more been inspired by a further epistemological question proposed by Lass (1980:153ff.). He discusses a notion which focuses on an individual's perception of the world, which inevitably includes religious matters. In this case he examines that of the linguist. An axiom of this perception is the way in which one shares one's personal belief with a wider audience. Central to Lass' thesis are three types of 'rationality': private, community and public. He examines how a 'purely private conviction' can become part of a wider community one and eventually a public matter if argued in the correct manner. The position of I-H in ML seems very relevant to this situation.

The preceding summary of the principles of *tawātur* has hopefully demonstrated that members of the Muslim community have always been able to experience the revelation event, viz., the Qur'ān and the words of the Prophet Muḥammad, with a certain degree of 'epistemic conviction' (ibid.:154). With regard to the Christian situation, Lass says that there is a large community of (intellectual) [this word is significant here] believers who are convinced of the proposition that Christ rose on the third day who 'can assume its relegation to unproblematical background knowledge within that community'. Moreover, it can function happily as an 'ordering function' in their life. If we transpose this principle to I-H and his position vis-à-vis ML and the Muslim community, we can say that he is one of those intellectual believers who of course do not doubt that the Qur'ān is the word of God: on that point they are in unanimous agreement. Where their views differ, however, is on how to reach the essence of that knowledge on which intellectual debate is founded.

At the level of private rationality, therefore, we may assume that I-H would share his views about the meaning of the Qur'ān (c.f. Lass' example of Christ) with the community of believers, notwithstanding the differences that obtained amongst the *'ulamā'* on how to get to the essence of the truth. Lass (ibid.:155) poses this particular problem for the linguist in such a situation: how does he convince the public at large that his views are correct and thus persuade them to join him ? Although it would not be strictly appropriate to regard the people to whom I-H is reaching out as a wider public, given that a work of this nature was, in the first instance at least, only accessible to an educated elite, I-H was still faced with the problem of convincing his fellow grammarians and exegetes, including his 'disciples' (students), that his line of argument was the correct one. It is in this context that the absence of direct empirical evidence of the past can be replaced by what Lass calls (ibid.:155) 'well-formed metaphysical arguments' that in the case of I-H underline his standing as a grammarian and a scholar.

The scholastic approach adopted by I-H is singularly appropriate to this end. He achieves this by presenting well-constructed arguments and drawing on an extensive range of opinions of other linguists, discarding those which he considers invalid for one reason or another. Furthermore, by defaming certain grammarians ('I used to think so-and-so was a good grammarian until I heard him say...') and replacing their erroneous or misguided views with cogently argued alternatives, he is inviting those whom he is addressing to share his private rationality. In addition to some of the ways in which I-H supports his arguments set forth above, we may add one or two further examples of how he asserts his own position within the community and makes his case for others to join him. One of the devices employed by I-H is to quote the names of other grammarians ('name-dropping' ?)who have apparently solicited his opinion on a given linguistic issue. An example of this is when Abū Hayyan, who was once I-H's teacher but for whom the latter appears to have lost all affection, asked I-H in front of a large audience about the conjoining of a certain word in a piece of poetry by Zuhayr. I-H tells us that his former teacher was impressed by the reply (*fa istaʿẓama dhālika*...ML 2:528). On other occasions I-H presents a long list of viewpoints on, say, a line of poetry, and then rounds off the argument by saying, for instance, *wa hādhā alladhī dhakartuhu fī l-bayt ajwad mā qīla fīhi* ... (ML 2:439) 'and what I have mentioned concerning this line is the best thing to have been said about it'. He is also inclined to present an argument based on what the grammarians have said but on which he has a more accurate interpretation, as in *wa l-naḥwiyyūna yaqūlūna...wa l-ṣawāb mā bayyantu* (ML 2:467) 'the grammarians say..., but the correct (interpretation) is the one I have demonstrated'.

To conclude this argument it should be pointed out that the linguistic data of medieval Arabic could never be looked at in a vacuum so long as it was based on the material of sacred texts. A society founded on a revealed religion requires the mechanism to guarantee the validity of those texts at all times. This is the role which was performed by the *ʿulamāʾ* on behalf of the Muslim community. However, for this to function successfully the members of that community must be agreed on one thing: that they are all members of the same contract. The preceding discussion has attempted to show that the contract as displayed in ML is the language of the Arabs and Islam. It was only through a comprehensive knowledge and understanding of the small print of the contract that man could even begin to interpret the meaning of God's word. Moreover, it was incumbent on the scholar who embarked on this mission to present his arguments in a manner which could gain the confidence of his fellow community members. Without that element of faith not only was the scholar himself likely to be excluded from membership of the contract, but so too was the linguistic material which he had set out to prove.

In ML, I-H states his case successfully. This may be seen in the acclaim which that work has received amongst modern scholars and, perhaps even more important, in the extent to which medieval scholars like al-Suyūṭī acknowledged his ideas by quoting them in detail in their major works and offering them as the last word on a given linguistic issue.[39]

We shall return to many of the arguments set forth in this chapter in subsequent discussions. Let us look more specifically now at the grammarian's position in society and, in particular, I-H's own situation within that domain.

NOTES

1 See the profound studies by Bernard Weiss (1966; 1976; 1987).

2 Weiss (1966:91) perceives a relationship between the theory of *waḍ'* and the concept of name-relation in modern linguistics.

3 Weiss (1987:342); for instance, the particle *min* 'from' is assigned to {from}, or even {from-ness}.

4 It should be noted that this opinion was not without opponents. Ibn Mālik, for instance, claimed that knowledge of the signification of speech (*dalālat al-kalām*) was a rational (*'aqlī*) one and not a posited (*waḍ'ī*) one. Attempts to assess I-H's views in this matter are further complicated because the debate appears to have settled down by the tenth century A.H. at least. According to Ṭāshkubrīzādah (*Miftāḥ*, 1:144) the subject matter of grammar is both *mufradāt* and *murakkabāt*.

5 In order to appreciate al-Jurjānī's views on *waḍ'* more fully the reader is referred to pp.350-55 of the *Dalā'il*. Of particular further interest are his comparisons between the positor (*wāḍi'*) of speech and the builder, in the sense that the former resembles the latter in the manner in which he assembles parts of something, i.e., speech, to make a whole (*Dalā'il* 73). Similarly the positor of speech is like a jeweller in the way in which he creates one piece (of speech) from many individual pieces (*Dalā'il* 269-70).

6 The notion of logocentrism in Islamic culture is not new: it has been discussed at length by Arkoun (1972) and developed by Wansbrough (1978:141ff), whilst its implications for Arabic grammar have been put very nicely by Carter (1983(a)). In this chapter it is the intention to take the idea a little further with specific reference to ML.

7 See al-Zarkashī, *Burhān*, 1:305. More specifically the issue rests on whether the word *zā'id* 'superfluous' can actually be associated with anything in the Qur'ān because of its negative connotations.

8 To this we may add the view of al-Shāfiʻī that Arabic was 'a deposit of linguistic data preserved in the memories of the community as a whole' (Weiss 1966:45; Kopf 1956:27).

9 Coward and Ellis (1977:124).
The attempts to reverse the role of meaning appear to have been initiated by Derrida in his *De la Grammatologie.* For an acute analysis of Derrida's ideas, see Culler (1975:131-32 esp.; 1981:40 esp.). In essence, what Derrida sets out to do is avoid reducing his texts to an 'ultimate meaning' which amounts to no more than a 'semantic reduction' in his view. (Norris 1982:32).

10 The word 'object' is employed here in the same sense as by Eco (1976:58).

11 For all this see, for example, the discussion by al-Suyūṭī, *Muz,* 1:48, or Ibn Jinnī, *Khaṣ,* 1:40ff. For a good modern assessment of the situation which highlights particularly the role of the legal theorists in the debate, see Ḥammūda (1973:171ff.)

12 Ibn Qayyim al-Jawziyya, *Badāʼiʻ,* 1:82. This ingenious theory could not hold, of course, for many other particles, especially those comprising more than one consonant.

13 See, for instance, al-Suyūṭī, *Muz,* 1:16ff.

14 Abū Ḥayyān, *Manhaj* 230.

15 The logocentric issue is a fascinating one and deserves to be recounted in more depth with particular reference to the works of Arkoun and Wansbrough (1978). Of especial interest is the juxtaposition of the terms '*l'histoire vraie*' and '*l'histoire réelle*' (cf. Arkoun 1972:41 esp.), and the conclusions of Wansbrough (1978:131,141ff.) that Islam is part of a 'salvation' history that is inherently 'nostalgic'.

16 Ibn Qayyim al-Jawziyya points out the value of the conditional particles, for instance, when he notes that they connect two sentences whose meanings can only be understood with their presence. See his *Badāʼiʻ*, 1:43.
Of relevance to the foregoing discussion is the view put forward by Almagor (1979:314-15) that 'the medieval Arab speaker did not apparently feel the need for a clear distinction between the lexical meaning of a word, the abstract idea

which it comes to convey, and the mode of conveying this idea'.

17 It is regrettable that I-H does not say more about the posited nature of the verb. For additional information we need to look to the impressive al-Irbilī (*Jaw* 16)who says that verbs, according to their establishment (*ḥasaba waḍ'ihā*) are of two kinds: transitive (*muta'addin*) and intransitive (*lāzim*).

18 Another of the commentators on ML makes the very important point that this 'positing' may be one of three types; an originally posited one (*waḍ' lughawī*), one in customary usage (*waḍ' 'urfī*), or a figurative usage (*majāz*). See al-Dasūqī, *Ḥāshiya* 26.

19 To underline further the importance of the distinction between meanings often brought about by the original *waḍ'* of language, al-Damāmīnī (*Sharḥ* 18) tells us that the secret in the establishment of the *alif* as a device for calling someone who is nearby, is that in order to call someone far away you must raise your voice.

20 For the purposes of this discussion we shall concentrate principally on the article by Heinrichs (1984). For a wider perspective of the issue the reader is referred to Almagor (1979) and Wansbrough (1978:21ff.).

21 There is a firm suggestion that the deployment of the term *majāz* to mean figurative language was a creation of the Mu'tazilites who used it as a 'theological tool' to explain linguistic elements and theological controversies involving metaphor which were found in the text of the Qur'ān. For all this see Heinrichs (1984:117 and 139 esp.).
The above view was propounded principally by Zahirites such as Ibn Taymiyya who notes (*Īmān* 75) that the division of the terms *majāz* and *ḥaqīqa* did not effectively occur until at least the fourth century A.H.

22 This interpretation may be applied much more readily to the later Arabic situation. Versteegh (1990) has shown that the term *ittisā'* was used by Sībawayhi in a specific syntactic context.

23 I-H's application of a quasi-philosophical equation to the meaning of this verse in which the *hamza* is followed by a negative clause is not wholly insignificant. He notes that the

negation of a negative equals an affirmative; therefore it is indisputable that God should suffice His servant.

24 It is interesting to cite Heinrichs here (1984:126) when he refers to a particular passage in which Abū 'Ubayda uses the term *khurūj al-ma'nā* where one would normally expect *majāz*. Given the clear link between the two established by I-H, it is difficult to accept Heinrichs' translation of the former as 'the emerging of the meaning'.

25 For the present the reader is directed to the folllowing explicit references of *ḥaqīqa / majāz* in ML 1:50, 53, 142, 147, 148, 164, 203, 205, 206, 212, 214, 253, 310, 323.

26 In a future article we shall be looking at the concept of *taḍmīn* in much more depth. For the moment, however, it is significant that I-H acknowledges explicitly that the application of *taḍmīn* entails a change in the meaning of the primary form (*aṣl*) (ML 1:226). It is also worth pointing out that al-Suyūṭī (*Ashbāh,* 1:72) was also concerned with this concept - as indeed he was with anything related to the study of language - and noted that *iḍmār* 'suppression' is a more straightforward category (*ashal*) than *taḍmīn* because the latter changes the original *waḍ'*. In ML (2:226) I-H assesses the difference between *ḥadhf* and *taḍmīn* in the same way as al-Suyūṭī compares his two categories. What is of even more interest in this connection is that *iḍmār* and *ḥadhf* are themselves two terms which admit of close comparison and differentiation (cf. Carter 1991:123).

27 A thorough evaluation of the historical development of *qiyās* is still awaited, although Baalbaki's work (1978) constitutes a valuable study of the earlier period. Such remarks as those by Versteegh (*to appear*) that 'for (Sībawayhi) the *qiyās* was no longer an instrument of speech production, but an explanatory argument' serve as further illustration of the complexity of the subject.

An extremely useful assessment of the status of *qiyās* is to be found in Bohas et al. (1990:22-26 esp.). The conclusion that the process of reasoning involved in *qiyās* can be as much inductive as deductive (ibid.:23) is particularly enlightening; as indeed are the other conclusions reached about the possibility of two different interpretations of the validity of a *qiyās* even if they are based on the same set of data (ibid.:24).

28 The use of the term *dalīl* here should be seen as a category which is totally independent from that which features principally in the section on elision. The import of the latter is distinguished by the requirement of a contextual indication (*dalīl ḥālī, maqālī*) which will be looked at in Chapter Five.

29 The main substance of this argument has appeared in a chapter of Suleiman (ed.), 1994, entitled '*Medieval Arabic as a form of 'social contract', with special reference to* Ibn Hishām*'s Mughnī l-Labīb*'. I am grateful to the respective editor and publisher for the concession of allowing some of the material to be reprinted here.

30 According to Harris the use of the word 'essentially' is crucial to the argument. With regard to the Greek situation it was the agreement itself that determined how a thing should be called: coincidence played no part in this whatsoever.

31 Harris underlines the significance of the use of the word 'convention' by noting (ibid.:110) that it is more appropriate to speak of linguistic conventions than linguistic rules because a particular form of a contract cannot always be explained away rationally. The crucial factor is that people adhere to the contract, whatever it may be.

32 This approach created what Lyons (1968:9) terms the 'classical fallacy' in some cultures, where a certain standard of language was deemed superior to another. In other words a community of scholars would decide on what was correct in their language and exclude from the contract what was deemed incorrect.

33 The editor of al-Irbilī's *Jaw*, 341, n.2. asks whether a consensus in grammar is ever attainable when he questions al-Irbilī's claim to have reached one on the function of the particle *min* as a superfluous particle in a particular context.

34 For works devoted exclusively to a study of the particle see, for instance, al-Harawī (*Uzhiyya*), al-Murādī (*al-Janā*), al-Irbilī (*Jaw*), al-Mālaqī (*Raṣf*), or al-Rummānī (*Ma'ānī*). Special mention could also be made here of Ibn Fāris' contribution to the study of the particles (*Ṣāḥibī* 166ff.), not so much for its detail, but more for the importance he appears

to have accorded to them. He also adopted a quasi-alphabetical arrangement for his presentation.

35 It would be unfair to overlook the work of Ibn ʿAqīl (*Sharḥ* 193-200), a contemporary of I-H, who used a similar technique of presentation for such categories. However, it is fair to say that it is a grammar very much in the traditional mould, and any serious comparison with ML ends here.

36 To the 'hierarchy of responsibility' we could add here a hierarchy of grammatical rank and standing. I-H held unequivocal views on the incompetence of some grammarians on the one hand, but also commended the artistry of others, such as Sībawayhī whom he called the *imām* of 'grammatical form' (*ṣināʿa*) (ML 2:575).

37 People differed on the agreement of the minimum number of people required for *tawātur* to be valid, but it seems that seventy was the most popular figure (Ibn al-Anbārī, *Lumaʿ* 84).

38 An interesting counter-argument to this was propounded by al-Āmidī in a theory which maintains that the (sacred) texts harbour a meaning which is clear from the texts themselves, independent of any external interpretation e.g., by consensus. For all this see Weiss (1984).

39 Of the many examples compare, for instance, the section in al-Suyūṭi's *Itqān,* 1:190ff. on the particles, or his *Ashbāh,* 2:95ff. on the coordinating particles. Alternatively try the section in his *Muʿtarak,* 1:309ff. on elision.

Chapter Three

IBN HISHĀM AND HIS POSITION AS A GRAMMARIAN IN *ML*.

> '...but those were times when, to forget an evil world, grammarians took pleasure in abstruse questions. I was told that in that period, for fifteen days and fifteen nights, the rhetoricians Gabundus and Terentius argued on the vocative of 'ego', and in the end they attacked each other with weapons'. [1]

A picture should gradually be emerging that the grammarian was certainly not a maverick of medieval Islamic society, but that he performed a particularly important role in making accessible an understanding of the complexities of the Arabic language which, as we are already witnessing in the case of ML, would extend into the realms of exegesis and an elucidation of the sacred texts to varying degrees. Before taking a closer look at I-H's own position within that society, and the way in which his linguistic arguments appear to establish him as a unique and sophisticated grammarian in some ways, a summary of the general background of the life of a grammarian at that time would seem to be in order here. There is little doubt that the intellectual climate of the medieval era engendered an atmosphere of competitiveness and even rivalry amongst the grammarians, and this is clearly reflected in many places in ML. Nonetheless, what should also be borne in mind in this connection is that in spite of the importance of grammar for that society, the grammarians were not always given the status they necessarily deserved, nor, we may suggest, the recognition they would have liked.

In a most stimulating article Versteegh (1989) assesses the profession of the grammarian based on information provided mainly by the rich Arab biographical tradition. He notes (ibid.:290) that one may estimate the number of grammarians mentioned in the medieval Arabic literature to be somewhere between 3,500 and 4,000. The foundation of our study so far is wholly commensurate with the view held by many of the grammarians that 'without grammar there could be no Islamic sciences' (ibid.:290). Yet in spite of the potential prominence of the science of grammar it was often treated with flagrant disregard by the *'ulamā'* who were concerned principally with the negative effect it had on other subjects, such as poetry, language and literature (cf. Makdisi 1981:214ff.). According to Makdisi (ibid.:214) 'it was liable to place (these) subjects within the category of the profane'. It is both interesting and amusing to note that evidence of the lowly status accorded to grammar in that period may be seen in the instruction given to librarians to stack the manuscripts on grammar and poetry at the bottom of the pile of works on all the Islamic sciences (Versteegh 1989:290, n. 3). Evidence also suggests that doubt might also have been cast on the levels of piety attained by some grammarians. Makdisi notes (1981:215) that it was said of one grammarian that he was 'trustworthy and religious, and rare it is that a grammarian is religious'. Further proof of the minimized appreciation of the grammarians' contribution to medieval Islamic society may be seen in the fact that being a grammarian did not constitute a profession as such. In order to eke out a living a grammarian was obliged to work in the educational system, for example, as a scribe or a private teacher to sons of the ruling class, or as a copier of books and manuscripts, or even in the manual sector as, say, a weaver or a glass cutter. A number of them also worked as lawyers or Qur'ān readers. It should be added here that even within the education system no provision was made to establish a curriculum for grammar.[2] Nonetheless, there is no doubt that the grammarians' own self-aggrandising enabled them to create an environment which contains all the hallmarks of a prevailing competitive spirit.

The question of whether two distinct 'schools' of grammar existed in Basra and Kufa, with the formation of a subsequent eclectic school in Baghdad, has not yet been fully resolved, although research carried out during the last three decades or more has made considerable progress in establishing a clear foundation for a thorough typological evaluation of this issue.[3] Until this has been fulfilled, however, it is probably more appropriate to speak of differences that obtained between the groups rather than schools.[4] The polarised nature of this debate has undoubtedly become more pronounced as a result of the biographical works of such scholars as al-Zubaydī who categorised the grammarians within those rubrics in his *Ṭabaqāt al-Naḥwiyyīn wa l-Lughawiyyīn*. Of much more relevance to the later period, say, from the late sixth century A. H. onwards, is the issue of personalities and their views rather than the school to which they might have adhered; and this is what is of interest to the argument here. It is true that I-H frequently acknowledges the provenance of a particular view in ML, whether it be Basran or Kufan, and he even makes a very general remark on at least two occasions which suggests that he upheld the existence of a group of grammarians from Baghdad whom he could justifiably argue as consensual adherents to a given grammatical point (ML 1:232; 2:394). Nonetheless, we have already seen that ML constitutes a lively debate in which I-H takes issue with views propounded by grammarians from all periods, not least those who resided in Egypt during the later period.

Given the overwhelming evidence set forth above one must accept that the professional rivalry and competitive spirit which is evident in the works of some of the grammarians was, to a large degree, of the grammarians' own making. It is not inconceivable that they would have felt considerable frustration at their potential, yet unfulfilled and unrecognized, importance within the society of that time, and that this situation may well have contributed to the inexorable attempts of some grammarians to assert their self-perceived superiority over others. At any rate this element of competitiveness which is described by Carter (1983 (a)) would seem to have reached its zenith by at least the time of Abū Ḥayyān (d. 745/1344), of whose grammatical ethos we may derive some idea from the title of a satire he wrote on a work of one of his instructors, Ibn al-Ṭabbā', entitled *An Exposition of the Errors in the Teaching of Ibn al-Ṭabbā'*.[5] The manner in which he refutes many of the ideas of Ibn Mālik in his commentary on the *Alfiyya* is not, therefore, a total surprise; neither is it wholly implausible that Abū Ḥayyān's intellectual battle with Ibn Mālik was borne out of envy at the latter's revered position as an *imām* of grammar, a title which might have been particularly difficult for Abū Ḥayyān to contend with given that both grammarians were of Spanish origin.[6]

In this connection it is worth noting that Ibn Mālik himself once undermined the position of both Ibn al-Ḥājib (d. 646/1248) who wrote the formidable *al-Kāfiya fī l-Naḥw*, and al-Zamakhsharī (d. 538/1143), when he said that the former learned grammar from the latter who was a grammarian of little standing.[7] One could easily offer the explanation that al-Zamakhsharī did not enjoy popularity with Ibn Mālik, amongst others, because of his Mu'tazilite views. The same could be said of the attitude shown at times by I-H towards al-Zamakhsharī in ML, although his remarks are normally confined to the linguistic issue in hand. In fact, the disagreements between the orthodox grammarians and the Mu'tazilites on grammatical points would constitute an extremely interesting study, especially as so many of the grammarians from the fourth century A. H. onwards were from the latter group. In ML, it is clear that the infrequent direct reference to their theological views (e.g., ML 1:103) belies a much greater concern for I-H. One of the many examples of this may be found in I-H's rejection of a view held by Abū 'Alī l-Fārisī (d. 377/987) who was a Mu'tazilite. In Sūra LVII vs. 27 Abū 'Alī claimed that the construction *rahbāniyyatan ibtada'ūhā* '(and) monasticism they invented' is of the same grammatical kind as *zaydan ḍarabtuhu* (viz., *ḍarabtu zaydan ḍarabtuhu*, and therefore, *ibtada'ū rahbāniyyatan ibtada'ūhā*) [my brackets]. Abū'Alī's argument rests on the belief that God cannot be the creator of what they invented; for this interpretation one needs to look back at the verb *ja'alnā* 'we made' in the previous line. I-H's response to this is, not surprisingly, negative, so he sets out the well-known rejoinder that *rahbāniyya* is coordinated (*ma'ṭūf*) with what precedes it, that *ibtada'ūhā* is its adjectival complement (*ṣifa*), and that the first term of an *iḍāfa* is to be reconstructed (*muqaddar*) here, viz., *ḥubba rahbāniyyatin* 'love of monasticism' (ML 2:577). What is surprising here is I-H's lack of reference to al-Zamakhsharī who held the same view as Abū 'Alī on this issue.[8]

Much has been made in the medieval biographical literature in particular of I-H's apparent ambivalent relationship with Abū Ḥayyān whom we have already pointed out was one of I-H's teachers in Egypt. We know, for instance, that I-H severed contact with him at some point during his career (al-Suyūṭī,

Bughya 293; al-Shawkānī, *Badr,* 1:401). Once more it is difficult to ascertain the exact reasons for this, although one could suggest that he broke away for professional motives in order to establish his own position, or even that he resented the eminent standing held by a scholar who originated from a different country and was not a pure Arab. What is more conceivable, however, is that I-H held no personal disaffection for Abū Ḥayyān, but merely disagreed with many of his views. In spite of the claims that their opinions on grammatical issues were frequently at variance[9] I-H takes issue far more frequently in ML with the views held by Ibn Mālik, Ibn al-Ḥājib or al-Zamakhsharī, for example. Moreover, any number of scholars including Sībawayhi or al-Farrā' from the early period, or Abū 'Alī or Ibn Jinnī from the middle period, are mentioned far more frequently in ML than Abū Ḥayyān. It is perhaps the manner in which I-H opposes the latter's opinions that gives rise to an impression of animosity.[10]

Ironically I-H's polemical approach in ML bears considerable resemblance to that of Abū Ḥayyān's in his *Manhaj al-Sālik* in terms of the vocabulary and style employed to discount the opinions of other grammarians: the frequent employment of such terms as *sahw* 'carelessness', *ta'assuf* 'incorrect use of language', *ta'adhdhur* 'non-feasibility' and *tawahhum* 'misconception'[11] is prevalent throughout the two works. In fact, these terms are often used by I-H with direct reference to Abū Ḥayyān, and would seem to reflect an intent by I-H to gain the upper hand on his former master. In contrast to the example cited earlier illustrating how I-H was able to impress Abū Ḥayyān with his response to a question about the meaning of a line of poetry, we find I-H unstinting elsewhere in his criticism of his former teacher's apparent ignorance of one of the rhetorical sciences, that of *bayān* 'clear speech' (ML 2:399). On this and on other occasions we find I-H defending the views of al-Zamakhsharī, and even Ibn Mālik, which represents further testimony perhaps that the question of who said what was less important to I-H than an exposition of rational argument and sound knowledge.

The reference to *bayān* here underlines a need for an understanding of the difference between the grammarians' and the rhetoricians' interpretation of certain linguistic categories. In this particular example the issue under discussion is one of the aspects of *i'tirāḍ* 'parenthesis', a syntactic device belonging to one of the categories of sentence devoid of syntactic status and function within the context of the sentence under discussion (*jumla lā maḥalla lahā min al-i'rāb*). More on this later. However, the main point to be made here is that the function of parenthesis is the separation of two clauses by another clause; in essence the reinforcement and sealing off, or embellishment of speech (*li ifādat al-kalām taqwiyatan wa tasdīdan aw taḥsīnan*)[12] in a manner which actually enhances the meaning. This definition, we would presume, is intended by I-H to apply to the rhetoricians, because we see that in the example above *i'tirāḍ* is identified by those versed in *bayān* in a manner that does not obtain for the grammarians. I-H acknowledges that for the *bayāniyyūn* the sentence 'to Him we surrender' (Sūra II vs. 127) could admit of the interpretation that it is an emphatic parenthetical sentence (*jumla i'tirāḍiyya mu'akkida*) stressing God's Oneness. On the other hand, he notes that the grammarians' understanding of parenthesis does not extend beyond the sphere of two items of request (*shay'ayni mutaṭālibayn*).[13]

Further disparaging remarks made by I-H towards his former teacher may be seen in a short analysis of the particle *wāw* in Sūra XIX vs. 72 which the latter allegedly claims to be the '*wāw* of oath'. Inconvenienced by this misrepresentation I-H points out that this is an error which would not be perpetrated by even the most junior student! (ML 2:404). This mode of refutation seems mild, however, in comparison with the harsh rejoinder of Ibn al-Shajarī (d. 542/1147) towards Abū 'Ubayda (ML 2:546). Not only was the former incensed when he heard that Makkī (d. 437/1045) had relayed the story that Abū 'Ubayda had once interpreted the particle *kāf* in Sūra VIII vs. 5 as a '*kāf* of oath', but he went so far as to add that 'if anyone said *ka allāhi la af'alanna* (By God I shall do (such and such)), he would deserve to have his face spat in'. That this type of outburst was not atypical may be seen in a quote from Ibn Qutayba who said that 'a grammatical mistake in speech is uglier than smallpox in the face' (cf. Carter 1983 (a):71-72).

In ML it is not unusual for I-H to perpetuate further the notion of an existence of hierarchy in grammatical circles by referring to such grammarians as Ibn Khālawayhi (d. 370/980) as 'weak' (ML 2:362). Furthermore, in a lengthy refutation of the view expounded by several scholars on the function of the particle *wāw* as the *wāw al-thamāniyya* '*wāw* of eight', which they claimed occurs before the eighth item of a sequence as a separate item, viz., that the preceding seven items constitute a homogeneous group and the eighth is a 'number of recommencement' (*'adad musta'nif,* e.g., Sūra XVIII vs. 22), I-H siezes the opportunity to exploit what in his view are the misguided contentions of scholars from three major sciences: *adab*, grammar and exegesis (ML 2:362). Once again he displays a judgement and knowledge that would surely have impressed his followers. On another occasion I-H informs us that al-Khaḍrāwī (d. 646/1248) was a grammarian on whom he only relied for one grammatical point (ML 1:127). In addition to the so-called weak grammarians I-H applies a similar criticism to al-Tha'labī (ML 1:358) whom he describes as a weak exegete.

The quest for knowledge, of course, is an issue that can not be over-emphasized in the medieval context. *'ilm* 'knowledge' and its antithesis *jahl* 'ignorance' are often in direct relation in ML, although the latter may be couched in slightly less subjective terms.[14] The trend to denounce the intellectual acumen of another scholar appears to have been well-established by at least the time of I-H, and it did not stop there. For instance, the manner in which I-H discounts an interpretation of the verb *amina* in a line of poetry by al-Mutanabbī (ML 1:86) is mirrored by one of the principal commentators on ML well into the ninth century A. H. when al-Damāmīnī refers to what is ostensibly vague wording by I-H on the function of the particle *hal* by declaring that 'this is a simple matter, even if some of those in this country who claim to have knowledge (*'ilm*) make it difficult' (*Sharḥ* 59). It is important to note here that the commentary on ML by al-Shamunnī was written in part as a work of arbitration to counter some of al-Damāmīnī's harsh indictments on I-H. In addition to all this I-H's criticism of those who claim to have *adab* (ML 1:86) is particularly interesting if we take *adab* to be synonymous with knowledge as we saw in Chapter One of this study.[15] This denunciation could include that of the incompetence of those scholars who blindly follow the erroneous views of others (e.g., ML 2:385), or even the inaccuracies of transmission of linguistic data or interpretations by some grammarians (e.g., ML 2:526). I-H's interest in the errors or misconceptions of others may extend to the acknowledgement of works of other grammarians by name who exploit the carelessness of their rivals, such as Abū ʿAlī's work called *al-Aghfāl*, in which he discusses the faults of al-Zajjāj's arguments in his work on the meanings (*maʿānī*) of the Qur'ān.

Although we would generally agree that the grammarian did not, in his capacity as a language expert, necessarily hold any position of power within society at large, there is little doubt that a relationship existed between knowledge and power within what we might call the grammarians' own micro-society, as the first part of this chapter has been attempting to show. Indeed, this nexus of knowledge and power has been adequately described by Carter (1983 (a)) who adds to the scenario the very important concept of leadership (*ri'āsa*), which evidence would suggest was also a major consideration and aspiration of the grammarians within their own conception of the hierarchy of language experts. To extend this view a little further we might propose an appropriate syllogism which encapsulates the relationship between language, knowledge and power: if signification (and hence language) is the unit of knowledge (as we saw earlier), and knowledge is the way to power, one may conclude that language is ultimately power. Such a conclusion merely echoes a view that has been propounded throughout history.

If an assertion of one's knowledge was seen as a prerequisite of survival in the medieval intellectual climate this may provide one solution as to why scholars often chose to record ideas expounded by their predecessors without acknowledging their provenance. In ML the evidence that many of I-H's views on the meaning of the particles, for example, have been taken directly from some of the works by earlier writers on the subject is nothing short of conclusive. Of the principal writers on the subject I-H acknowledges the opinions of al-Mālaqī on five occasions, and al-Harawī on three occasions. Significantly no mention at all is made of either al-Murādī or al-Irbilī who both made a considerable contribution to studies of the *ḥurūf al-maʿānī*. Yet in some places in ML there is substantial evidence to suggest that verbatim borrowings have occurred from at least one of these works in the first instance. It is true that the process of recording and preserving large parts of the literature at that time was so crucial to Islam, as we saw earlier. Moreover, not only did this religious exigency function as the perfect disguise for the detailed transmission of earlier views and data, but it also meant that plagiarism, for example, was a very difficult accusation to support. In mitigation, however, medieval Islamic society owes much to the efforts of such scholars as al-Suyūṭī who, in his works like *al-Ashbāh*, frequently acknowledges the source of his information: at times both the scholar and the relevant work; at other times just the scholar. In an implicit fashion al-Suyūṭī appears to accept that he is preserving information 'just for the record'.

At this point it would seem appropriate to draw an analogy between the characteristically systematic nature of ML which represents, amongst other things, the eclecticism that was so invaluable at that time, and the type of scholarship which prevailed in the Middle Ages in the West. Lewis (1964: 5) notes that medieval culture displayed an 'overwhelmingly bookish or clerkly character' in which 'every writer, if he possibly can, bases himself on an earlier writer'. To add to this one might say that 'medieval man...was an organiser, a codifier, a builder of systems... (and) of all our modern inventions (it is likely) that they would most have admired the card index' (Lewis 1964:10). The foregoing views would all seem to be reflected in the type of works of which ML was one. Indeed, even the title of ML which, as we saw earlier, suggests an attempt to dispense with all previous books written on the subject of *iʿrāb*, reflects perhaps a conscious decision by I-H to codify and build an exhaustive system which would serve as the 'Model' in the same way as Aquinas' *Summa* or Dante's *Divine Comedy*.[16] In broad terms ML has certainly remained unsurpassed as the last comprehensive work of its kind on the Arabic language.

If we move even further back in time it is tempting to make further analogies between the position of scholars, including philosophers and medical doctors, in Greek times, and that of medieval Muslim scholars like I-H. The Greek situation has been argued very commendably by Lloyd (1987) who approaches the issue from several angles including that of the egotistic scholar who, in the competitive intellectual environment of the time, seemed to face no alternative but to present himself as a strong personality. In the same way as I-H frequently enters into the narrative of ML, particularly in his more prescriptive chapters, Lloyd notes (ibid.:65) how this was a technique employed by many of the Greek doctors in their medical treatises. No doubt this method was part of the effort to reinforce or develop one's reputation, especially if it was combined with a system of discrediting the ideas of those who had previously written on the subject, as is the case in ML. As Lloyd indicates one of the dangers inherent in this method is that it illustrates the extent to which 'the question of whether or how far to follow tradition was openly contested'.

Wisdom, then, was a key word in that society, and it appears that little had changed by the time of I-H. In Greek society the scholar would 'naturally try to justify his own position and undermine those of his opponents, and one way he might attempt to claim superiority for his own ideas was by stressing their novelty' (Lloyd ibid.:90). Although the scope for innovation in the Islamic context was much more restricted, there are numerous occasions in ML when I-H reverts to this technique; in cases where little innovation could be offered on a given problem the next best thing perhaps was not to acknowledge the provenance of a given viewpoint.

As a final point of analogy in this connection it is worth noting another important observation recorded by Lloyd (ibid.:108):

> 'A certain self-consciousness in the investigations and an awareness of alternatives, at least of rivals, were tolerably durable legacies bequeathed by early Greek to Hellenistic science, part what then became, for some, revered tradition. .. (for this to occur, however), what was needed was not just written texts ... but, among other things, texts that through a strong authorial presence implied a personal accountability for the claims they contained'.

The parallels that may be drawn between this situation and that of I-H in ML are too relevant to ignore. First, ML did not automatically become part of the revered tradition mentioned above; rather it had to earn its place within that tradition. Second, it is certainly the case that I-H showed himself to be aware of the alternatives offered by his rivals, as we have already seen in this and the preceding chapter. Moreover, the question of personal accountability is exactly what was under discussion too in the latter stages of the previous chapter. The legacy left by ML to later writers is ample testimony to the enduring effect of I-H's erudite and cogent arguments which were clearly regarded as definitive in many ways.

At any rate there was undoubtedly much at stake for all in the medieval Islamic scholarly community. The necessity to lend sufficient credence to one's argument may well have contributed to the misquoting or occasional misrepresenting of the ideas of other scholars; even I-H is apparently not inculpable in this respect.[17] It is worth reminding ourselves that I-H lived during a period of considerable intellectual revival. In fact, I-H was one of at least four of the most eminent grammarians of all time who lived and died within one hundred and sixty years of each other; the others being Ibn Mālik, Ibn al-Ḥājib and Abū Ḥayyān. Given that I-H died some sixteen years after Abū Ḥayyān it is fair to say that he was writing from a position of strength and hindsight. On the other hand this fact should in no way undermine the value of ML which was not only probably the last great work on Arabic grammar, but also arguably the most unique. If the anecdotes dispersed throughout the grammatical literature are to be believed, a sound knowledge of grammar often turned out to be a priceless commodity for which a grammarian could receive prizes or large sums of money. I-H recounts several of these tales in ML in a manner which captures the absurdity of the occasion, even if this was not his intention (e.g., ML 1:53,88; 2:539).

Due to the nature of many of the texts with which the grammarian concerned himself, his repertoire often extended beyond that of mere linguistic analysis. He was at once responsible for much of the hermeneutical practices of *tafsīr* and *ta'wīl*.[18] I-H was a teacher of *tafsīr* (Makram 1980:357), and he states in ML (2:650) that he wrote that work for both students of Classical Arabic (*al-'Arabiyya*) and exegesis (*tafsīr*). Carter (1983 (a):79) refers to the grammarians as the 'front line troops of exegesis' which is certainly a felicitous description of the role of some of them. However, it is clear that not all the grammarians made as profound a contribution to exegesis as I-H, for instance. Second, exegesis was often carried out by its own band of scholars, *mufassirūn*, who would not necessarily be classed as grammarians. It is beyond the scope of this study to examine the differences between the two groups, but the existence of a certain degree of professional tension between them could not be ruled out. Paradoxically we gain an insight into the extent of the convergence of the respective roles of the exegete and the grammarian (*mu'rib*) from a comparison of a remark made by I-H in his *I'rāb* (115) and the same reference noted by three later writers. The case in point concerns I-H's description of the particles of which knowledge is required by the *mu'rib* (*fī tafsīr kalimāt yaḥtāju ilayhā l-mu'rib*). The other three writers essentially repeat I-H's words, but substitute *mufassir* for *mu'rib* (al-Suyūṭī, *Itqān*, 1:190; Ṭāshkubrīzādah, *Miftāḥ*, 2:417; al-Zarkashī, *Burhān*, 4:175).

To add to this overlap of roles we might also consider the axiomatic contribution of the rhetoricians of whom 'Abd al-Qāhir al-Jurjānī is a prime example. He was well-known to his contemporaries for his contribution to grammar, but he is perhaps best known today as a rhetorician through his two principal works on rhetoric, the *Dalā'il* and *Asrār al-Balāgha*. That a thorough knowledge of exegesis was incumbent upon a scholar attempting to elucidate the 'inimitability' of the Qur'ān is indisputable, yet a picture is gradually emerging that the division between the grammarians and rhetoricians could have been almost as clearly defined in the medieval Arabic situation as it was, say, in the Classical Greek period where the grammarians had to tolerate a status inferior to that of the latter (cf. Harris 1980:118-19). Moreover, there is sufficient evidence to be found in ML that the rivalry amongst the *'ulamā'* was not necessarily confined to scholars within one particular discipline such as grammar; rather it filtered through to some of the other equally important Islamic sciences. If the hypothesis put forward throughout much of this present study so far is correct, one may argue for further parallels between the Greek and Arabic situations inasmuch as the contractualism (discussed in Chapter Two) functioned as the 'professional creed' (Harris 1980:119) of the grammarian, and the classical fallacy was very much his 'professional charter' (Harris 1980:119). In both cases the grammarian was apparently the unpromulgated bastion of intellectual society. In the Greek context he was always to be found striving to achieve parity of status with the rhetorician, and even the logician. With regard to the Arabic situation there are indications in ML that by the time of I-H a knowledge of grammar alone was insufficient for a linguist to project himself as a serious exegete. One often had to penetrate beyond this.

In his *Ṭirāz* al-Yamanī presents an enlightening and detailed account of the different functions expected of and performed by the lexicographer (*lughawī*), grammarian (*naḥwī*), and rhetorician (*ṣāḥib 'ilm al-bayān wa l-ma'ānī*). From this description it is possible to conjecture what lay at the root of I-H's intentions when writing ML. After all, there are many occasions when I-H demonstrates a sound knowledge of all four disciplines. Moreover, he would appear to support al-Yamanī's criticism of certain exegetes who fall short of expectation by restricting themselves to an exposition of the grammatical meanings (*ma'ānī i'rābiyya*) and the significations of the posited expressions (*madlūlāt al-alfāẓ al-waḍ'iyya*) without demonstrating any knowledge of *balāgha* nor, more important, *i'jāz*. Implicit in al-Yamanī's argument is that only through a thorough grasp of the above disciplines is it possible to conduct a proper exegesis.[19] I-H himself was not averse to overruling the decisions of such eminent exegetes as al-Rāzī and al-Ṭabarī (e.g., ML 1:119; 2:584).

How does all this relate to I-H's position ? If he did possess the extensive knowledge of linguistic disciplines outlined by al-Yamanī his position as a better grammarian than Sībawayhi admits of an even more worthy interpretation. In ML I-H displays a sufficient understanding of the language (*lugha*) to enable him to oppose interpretations on lexical and grammatical issues by eminent purists like al-Ḥarīrī (d. 516 /1122) (ML 1:149,156,288-89; 2:439,524) who was deemed to hold exemplary standards in these matters. In fact al-Ḥarīrī appears to have established his own classical fallacy through his works on *laḥn* 'solecisms'.[20] What is equally significant is that I-H did not refrain on occasions from discounting lexical interpretations by the lexicographers such as al-Jawharī (e.g., ML 1:154,320; 2:512). Perhaps the reason for this becomes clear if we acknowledge the received wisdom at that time on the relationship between the lexicographer and the grammarian.

According to al-Suyūṭī (*Muz.*, 1:59) it was generally held that their relationship was similar to that of the Ḥadīth specialist (*muḥaddith*) and the legal theorist (*faqīh*). In other words the grammarian must take up what has been passed on to him by the lexicographer and form grammatical rules according to it; and the lexicographer must be as accurate in his transmission as the *muḥaddith.* This would suggest that I-H was at times doubtful about the interpretation of his predecessors, and even the transmission of certain lexical items, and thus set out to offer a more accurate assessment.

I-H's interest in rhetorical issues has already been alluded to several times so far. Although he never departs from his principal position as a grammarian it is in his analyses of such devices as parenthesis, which may be interpreted on a grammatical or a rhetorical level, that the aims set forth in his introduction to go beyond a superficial discussion of grammar are revealed. Once again it would be useful to compare a few arbitrary examples furnished by al-Yamanī in his *Ṭirāz*, a work which purports to transcend the basic issues of *iʿrāb* and to reach the secrets of rhetoric and eloquence, with some of those in ML. In the section on parenthesis, for example, I-H notes in the first instance all the occasions in which it can occur, such as between a conditional sentence and its result clause, or a noun and its qualifying adjective. There are three particular instances noted by I-H that also occur in al-Yamanī's *Ṭirāz* which merit a mention here.

It was acknowledged by al-Yamanī (*Ṭirāz,* 2:168) that part of *iʿtirāḍ* 'parenthesis' pertains to *iʿrāb*; this would seem to be the aspect referred to by I-H in the examples above. However, al-Yamanī accepts that these types of examples bear no significance to the basis of his work which is principally a study of the 'science of meanings' (*ʿilm al-maʿānī*). He discusses a number of occurrences of parenthesis in the Qur'ān which exemplify the art of rhetoric, and set it above the level of mere *iʿrāb*. I-H has recorded three of the most 'perfect' examples discussed by al-Yamanī,[21] although naturally I-H does not acknowledge that they have been discussed elsewhere. It is worth dwelling for a moment on the essence of the different approaches adopted by the grammarians and the rhetoricians to such categories. The distinction drawn by al-Yamanī between the grammatical aspects of parenthesis, and the rhetorical ones whose existence he defines as necessary for the communicative meaning (*min ajl al-fā'ida*), underlines the importance of the assessment made by Bohas et al. (1990:125) concerning the profound difference of approach between the grammarian and the rhetorician. Citing the case of relative sentences Bohas notes that for the grammarian they do not fill 'a functional position', whereas 'they would be considered as 'secondary sentences' in rhetoric, since they necessarily play a qualifying role of some sort in the utterance'. In this connection it is important to retain sight of the extent to which I-H moves away from the traditional mould of the grammarian into the realms of rhetoric. Our conclusion at this stage would be that his position seems to fall somewhere between the two. The following examples will help to illustrate this.

That I-H has recorded the three so-called perfect examples mentioned above is evidence of his awareness of the rhetorical aspects of parenthesis. Yet he does not elaborate on these examples by pointing out their sublime significance in the same way as al-Yamanī. Moreover, I-H retains the grammarian's shackles by recording examples of parenthesis which do nothing to further an understanding of the secrets of rhetoric, as in the occurrence of an oath between two terms of an annexed construction (*iḍāfa*) in *hādhā ghulāmu wallāhi zaydin* 'This is the slave boy, By God, of Zayd', but which actually offend the sensibilities of scholars like al-Yamanī (ML 2:392; cf. *Ṭirāz*, 2:168). On the other hand one may draw certain parallels, even on the basis of some cursory cross-referencing, between the apparent intent of I-H's analyses and those of the eminent al-Jurjānī in his *Dalā'il*, as we saw in Chapter One above. On many occasions in ML I-H draws on issues which constitute a main focus of al-Jurjānī's work to demonstrate the rhetorical and more profound significance of a verse in the Qur'ān. This could be exemplified by the pragmatic considerations inherent in Sūra XXI vs. 63: *a anta fa'alta hādhā* 'So, art thou the man who did this (unto our gods, Abraham)?' *bal fa'alahu kabīruhum hādhā* 'No; it was this great one that did it'. In this verse I-H notes (as did al-Jurjānī) that the *hamza* (viz., *a*...) here is not employed to ask about the act itself nor to establish that it actually occurred; rather what is at issue is who actually did it (*al-fā'il*).[22] On another occasion I-H discusses an area of syntax in which some grammarians erroneously assume an element of elision merely because an element of syntax is missing. In order to remedy this superficial analysis I-H examines the deeper meaning contained within by illustrating how in certain contexts it is not necessary to mention or even intend the object (*maf'ūl*) of the verb if the meaning itself (within the verb) and the agent (*fā'il*) is all that needs to be demonstrated (cf. ML 2:612 and *Dalā'il* 111).

I-H's position as a grammarian with more than just a passing interest in rhetorical issues is strengthened in the light of a pertinent assessment by Bohas et al. (1990:128) of the contrasting views of al-Jurjānī and the grammarians on what Bohas calls 'displacement'. He argues that although the grammarians acknowledged that certain elements of a sentence could occur elsewhere in other than their customary position, 'they never worried about identifying what effect these displacements could have on the semantic content of the sentence'. Moreover, according to Bohas they often argued that a change in word order had no effect on the meaning of a sentence. This was viewed by al-Jurjānī as tantamount to 'disfiguring' the language. Baalbaki (1991:92) firmly underlines al-Jurjānī's disparagement of the grammarians when he notes that 'he accuses them of failing to discover nuances of meaning in a single subject, and asserts that their reader can do without what they have to offer but badly needs that which they ignored'. In the case of ML a genuine concern with the semantic effects of displacement and other syntactic phenomena such as elision is apparent in many cases throughout. What is also clear in ML is that I-H champions the precedence of *ma'nā* 'meaning' over *lafẓ* 'form' in a manner resembling that of the rhetoricians like al-Jurjānī and al-Yamanī; this will be dealt with in more detail later. Indeed, evidence of this point can be found throughout ML, but for the present, however, we may refer to a discussion of the *ḍamīr al-faṣl* 'pronoun of separation' (ML 2:496) in which I-H notes that the majority of grammarians restricted their understanding of its communicative meaning (*fā'ida*) to the formal aspects, whereas the *bayāniyyūn* were more concerned with the semantic elements. The latter is a view which I-H appears to favour.[23]

The diversity of views held by the grammarians, rhetoricians and even legal theorists represents a frequent undercurrent of conflict which runs throughout ML. We have already mentioned that to attempt to establish a consistent line in I-H's arguments is not always a straightforward task. In contrast to the previous example in which he supports the case of the rhetoricians, we find him on more than one occasion upholding a consensus of the grammarians against the other two groups concerning a particular interpretation of the particle *mā* (e.g., ML 1:309). Moreover, if we return to the comparison begun above between I-H and al-Jurjānī there is sufficient evidence to support the argument for these inconsistencies, such as the respective analyses of Sūra XXXV vs. 26: *innamā yakhshā allāha min ʿibādihi l-ʿulamāʾu* 'Even so only those of His servants fear God who have knowledge'. For al-Jurjānī the importance of this verse lies in the word order and the position of the word *ʿulamāʾu*, whereas I-H cites this verse to demonstrate the possibility of the *mā* being the *mā l-kāffa* 'nullifying *mā*', or conveying the meaning of the relative pronoun *alladhī* (cf. ML 1:308 and *Dalāʾil* 231).

Before moving on to examine in more detail the type of subject matter that constitutes much of the linguistic debate in ML it is worth pausing for a brief examination of two further issues which help to set I-H's own position in some sort of perspective. The first of these considerations is I-H's use of Prophetic Tradition (Ḥadīth) as textual evidence. It is generally held that grammarians were reluctant to use Ḥadīth as textual evidence until the time of Ibn Mālik (d. 672/1273). In the early period, of course, before the time of the canonized collections of Ḥadīth literature of al-Bukhārī and Muslim, there would have been no standard versions of Prophetic Tradition from which grammarians could draw. Reference to Ḥadīth in early grammars is extremely rare, therefore, although I-H may be added to the list of grammarians to quote the famous debate taken from Prophetic Tradition involving the grammatical case of the character Abū l-Dardāʾ, which began as early as Sībawayhi. Even in the post al-Bukhārī era it is held that scholars persisted in their reluctance to use Ḥadīth as textual evidence on the grounds that the transmission of material might have incurred some inaccuracies during the two centuries or so after the death of the Prophet Muḥammad. If the accuracy of modern scholarship is to be accepted all this appears to have changed with Ibn Mālik who allegedly demonstrated a special interest in the use of Prophetic Tradition for textual evidence. To corroborate this view sources reveal that he was even prepared to accept a particularly vulgar expression similar to the famous *akalūnī l-barāghīthu* because it had been accepted by al-Bukhārī and Muslim (Fück 1955:188-89; Makram 1980:431). After this it appears that the employment of Ḥadīth as textual evidence became more acceptable, and was certainly adopted by al-Astarābādhī (d. 688/1289) in his *Sharḥ al-Kāfiya*. With regard to ML there are a number of interesting observations to be made in this connection.

First, it is worth noting that the actual incidence of citations of Ḥadīth in ML amounts to a total of sixty one (Nīl 1985:496). Although I-H has been acknowledged as the grammarian most dependent on Prophetic Tradition after Ibn Mālik (e.g., Makram 1980:431; Nīl 1985:496) this figure still represents a low proportion of the total number of individual citations of textual evidence taken from the Qur'ān and poetry. Furthermore, it is significant that I-H does not automatically accept the accuracy of a particular transmission without putting it to the test, unlike the impression we are given of Ibn Mālik's liberal selection procedure. In fact, there are occasions in ML when I-H disputes the validity of material recorded by al-Bukhārī (and Muslim), and proceeds to cite other textual evidence as a counter-argument to support his point (e.g., ML 1:114,183). It is also significant that I-H opposes Ibn Mālik's interpretation of Ḥadīth on a number of occasions by producing cogent alternative conclusions, and in one case citing another Ḥadīth to support his own contention in addition to the original one under discussion (ML 1:94-95). On balance, however, there is little doubt about I-H's views on the potential validity of Ḥadīth as a form of textual evidence. On at least one occcasion he acknowledges that a citation of Ḥadīth to support a grammatical point constitutes one of the strongest proofs (*min aqwā l-adilla*), on which basis it may be argued that for I-H it represented another form of sacred text that could not be overlooked within the context of the logocentric domain, even if it was to be subjected to the same minute grammatical scrutiny as the rest of the evidence. The same could be said perhaps of the variant readings of the Qur'ān (*al-qirā'āt*) which constitutes the final issue of this chapter.

It has been noted elsewhere that I-H did not restrict himself to an acceptance of just the seven traditional variant readings of the Qur'ān; rather he would try to accommodate as many as possible without classifying them as *shādhdh* 'anomalous'. The reason for this would seem to lie in the words of al-Suyūṭī who claimed that 'reading of the Qur'ān is a custom to be followed, accepted and adhered to' (Makram 1980:420-22). In this regard I-H's citings from, and acceptance of, more readings from the non-ʿUthmanic codice of Ibn Masʿūd than from any of the seven official readers is particularly noteworthy. In keeping with the argument maintained throughout this study it is likely that for I-H these readings could be regarded with equal justification as a representation of the undisputable sacred text ; that is not to say, however, that he did not disagree with and, indeed, oppose certain readings.

It is hoped that the context of the linguistic and social background to this work is now firmly set. Let us now turn to the detailed material of the text on which this study is based.

NOTES

1 Eco (1984:312).
2 For all this see Versteegh (1989:293ff.).
3 Of the many assessments of this subject see, for example, Owens 1988:8ff.; 1990:203ff.), Carter (1990), Fleisch (1961) or Bohas et al. (1990:6-8esp.).
4 The use of 'school' (*madrasa)* as a handy nomenclature persists in fact to the present day. See, for instance, the work of Makram (1980), although it should be added that the content of that work would suggest that the author has employed the word 'school' more as a reflection of the geographical situation than as a representation of a unified body of grammatical opinion.
5 See Glazer's introduction to the *Manhaj al-Sālik* by Abū Ḥayyān, xx.
6 This is not to deny, of course, that a detailed study of the *Manhaj* would almost certainly reveal genuine differences of opinion on grammatical issues.
7 al-Suyūṭī, *Bughya* 55: '*wa ṣāḥib al-Mufaṣṣal naḥwī ṣaghīr*'.
8 See the *Kashshāf* of al-Zamakhsharī, 4:67. The commentator on this work criticises both Abū ʻAlī and al-Zamakhsharī for their views which are unacceptable to orthodox Islam.
9 al-Suyūṭī, *Bughya* 293; al-Shawkānī, *Badr,* 1:401.
The latter notes how it was commonplace for scholars to challenge the position held by their predecessors, as did Abū Ḥayyān, for instance, with al-Zamakhsharī. The biographical work by al-Shawkānī is particularly important because it is one of the few such works containing information about the scholars of the eighth century A.H. Given that he died in the middle of the thirteenth century A.H. he could never be considered a part of the intellectual scene at that time; therefore he was able, in a sense, to take an objective and retrospective glance at the situation.
10 For an overview of I-H's assessment of the views of different grammarians in ML, see Nīl (1985:417ff.).
11 For an exceptional meaning of *tawahhum* see Baalbaki (1982). As Baalbaki points out, I-H was one of the few grammarians who demonstrated an awareness of the

ambiguity of the term *tawahhum* which was sometimes used in a positive sense. With reference to I-H this will be looked at in Chapter Six.

12 ML 2:386.
According to Isbir / Junaydī (1981:135) the term *i'tirāḍ* belongs to *'ilm al-badī'* which is the third of the rhetorical sciences, and the one generally associated with 'tropes'. Nonetheless, there appears to have been a considerable overlap between many of the terms pertaining to the rhetorical sciences in the later period, so we should not be deterred or confused by the fact that I-H relates it to *bayān* in ML 2:399.

13 I-H does not elaborate here but it is likely that he is referring to the concept of *ṭalab* which is the generic term for the imperative, prohibitive and requestive moods of the verb (Isbir / Junaydī 1981:577).

14 See, for instance, ML 1:22: *fa yaẓannu man lā ma'rifa lahu...* 'he who has no knowledge may think...'.
We are aware that in general Islamic terms there is an important distinction to be made between *'ilm* and *ma'rifa* , although I-H would seem to be referring specifically here to knowledge of the subject of grammar. The difference between the two is not always apparent, however, in ML. Yet I-H does appear to be cognizant of the connotation of knowledge contained within the term *adab,* as we shall see presently. For interpretations of *'ilm* and *ma'rifa* see Rosenthal (1970:282ff.) or al-'Askarī's *Furūq.*

15 The more general meaning of *adab*, noted by Rosenthal (1970:286) is 'education'. This would also be an appropriate translation here.

16 For the idea of the 'Model' see Lewis (1964:11-12).

17 cf. ML 2:593 and al-Zamakhsharī, *Kashshāf,* 2:37. Try also ML 1:64 and *Kashshāf,* 1:345, where al-Zamakhsharī merely explores the possibility of the particle *wāw* assuming the meaning of *ibāḥa* 'unlimited choice' (Sūra II vs.196), and then draws the conclusion that this is unlikely to be one of the meanings of that particle. Not only does I-H omit his conclusion in the discussion, but he adds that this particular interpretation has only been advanced by the *bayāniyyūn*

such as al-Zamakhsharī and al-Qazwīnī, and that the grammarians would not interpret it in this way. Yet we are told by al-Damāmīnī (*Sharḥ* 138) that I-H actually argued the case of *wāw* for *ibāḥa* in his *Ḥāshiyat al-Tashīl*. On other occasions al-Damāmīnī criticises I-H for an incomplete representation of the argument of another grammarian (cf. ML 1:25 and al-Damāmīnī, *Sharḥ* 55). It should be noted here that it is often difficult to perceive a consistent line in I-H's argument when he seems to oscillate between a support for the grammarians against the *bayāniyyūn*, and vice-versa.

18 The issue of *tafsīr* and *ta'wīl* is a vitally important one but can not detain us here. In brief, the latter is the undertaking of a more esoteric investigation as opposed to the more interpretative nature of *tafsīr* which was concerned more with the literal meaning of a text. For a concise definition of each of these terms see al-Jurjānī, *Ta'rīfāt* 42,65.

The etymological significance of *ta'wīl* is worth noting, however. It comes from *tarjī'* 'returning something to its original place', which seems to parallel perfectly the view of Todorov (1983:110) that 'the end result is known in advance; what the exegete is looking for is the best way to get there'.

19 For all this see al-Yamanī, *Ṭirāz*, 1:17-19. It is particularly interesting to note that al-Yamanī died only twelve years after I-H, which at least gives some indication that this might have represented an established view at that time. For the advantages of *balāgha* over mere *i'rāb* see *Ṭirāz*, 2:168-69.

We have already seen how titles of inaccessible or non-extant sources can stimulate speculation on the value of the contents; this context is no exception. In a book written in the tenth century A.H. called *Asrār al-Naḥw* by Ibn Kamāl Bāshā, there is a reference (p.14) to a treatise by the author in which he assesses the similar role and function required of the lexicographer and the scholar of *ma'ānī*. To the knowledge of the present writer this treatise is only available in manuscript form in the Staatsbibliothek in Berlin.

20 I-H does not always oppose the views of al-Ḥarīrī, but considers himself sufficiently well-informed to ratify the contention of a tripartitite agreement on a matter of *lugha* involving al-Ḥarīrī, al-'Askarī (two experts on the language,

and the latter also in *balāgha*), and Ibn al-Shajarī, a grammarian. See ML 1:57.

21 cf. ML 2:389 and *Ṭirāz*, 2:171-72 on Sūra XVI vs.102; ML 2:390 and *Ṭirāz*, 2:169; ML 2:393 and *Ṭirāz*, 2:171.

22 cf. ML 1:18 and *Dalā'il* 87. See also al-Damāmīnī, *Sharḥ* 36. This particular verse is recorded by al-Zamakhsharī as one of the beauties of Arabic and *'ilm al-ma'ānī*. Abraham is being sarcastic in his reply, of course, by saying that it was the eldest one of them who destroyed the idols. This may be compared to the situation where, say, you are a famous calligrapher, and you are asked by an infirm and illiterate person: 'Did you write this ?", to which you reply: "No, you wrote it!'; thereby affirming that you wrote it, but mocking the questioner at the same time.

23 As far as the distinction between the *bayāniyyūn* and the *uṣūliyyūn* is concerned Heinrichs notes (1984:140) that from the late fifth century A.H. onwards the two groups held different, although interdependent, views on the *ḥaqīqa / majāz* theory. These differences appear to have been centred around the role of the *qarīna* 'associative indication' and its relationship to *majāz* (Heinrichs 1984:114-15, n.8).

Chapter Four

POLEMICAL CATEGORIES IN CHAPTER FIVE OF *ML*

> '...and this (particular) grammarian asked the right question but gave the wrong answer' (ML 2:528).

The reader should have been able to formulate an impression by now of the polemical nature of ML which runs throughout that work. This chapter represents an attempt to extend the content of the argument set forth above by assessing the subject matter of a chapter in ML which would seem to encapsulate the whole ethos of I-H's approach to grammar; that there is no simple solution to a grammatical problem but that one can normally be reached by a thorough and logical analysis, often by the employment of a system of elimination in which a panoply of opinions may be discarded along the way. To this end it is our intention to look more closely at the content of the main part of Chapter Five in ML, with a view to delaying a more detailed study of I-H's vitally important evaluation of elision, which also appears in that section, until the final chapter of this study.

In this chapter of ML I-H examines grammatical categories (*jihāt*) which have been treated by the grammarians in a manner to which I-H objects. At the same time one is expected to learn from these misinterpretations in order to avoid falling into the same traps. The first two categories are concerned with the juxtaposition of meaning (*ma'nā*) and (grammatical) form / structure (*ṣinā'a / lafẓ*).[1] The occurrence of the word *lafẓ* as the antithesis of *ma'nā* is not new. Of particular interest here, however, is I-H's use of the word *ṣinā'a*, as opposed to *lafẓ*, as the converse of *ma'nā*. Owens (1988:92-93) notes that the term *ṣinā'a* was used as early as Ibn Jinnī, although with some degree of inconsistency. To the knowledge of the present writer, however, it is only in ML that we are presented with a more comprehensive picture of the significance of the term. As we have pointed out before it was incumbent upon the grammarian (*mu'rib*) that he understood, first and foremost, the meaning of what he was parsing. I-H's concern in the first category of this discussion is that the grammarian may devote too much attention to the overt grammatical form at the expense of meaning (*yurāʿī mā yaqtaḍīhi ẓāhir al-ṣināʿa wa lā yurāʿī l-maʿnā*) (ML 2:527), or similarly those examples where the meaning is adulterated for this reason (*amthilatan matā buniya fīhā ʿalā ẓāhir al-lafẓ wa lam yunẓar fī mūjab al-maʿnā ḥaṣala l-fasād*) (ML 2:529). The employment of the terms *ṣināʿa* and *lafẓ* in these two examples, which appear to be conveying the same idea, suggests that they are used synonymously in this context. In the second category under discussion in this section the precedence of meaning over form is reversed. In this connection I-H criticizes those who pay attention to the correct meaning but omit to consider how it fits into the grammatical form (*yurāʿī l-muʿrib maʿnan ṣaḥīḥan wa lā yanẓuru fī ṣiḥḥatihi fī l-ṣināʿa*) (ML 2:539). We shall return to this in more detail shortly.

There is little doubt, therefore, that *ṣināʿa* (like *lafẓ*), in the sense of grammatical form or structure, is intended as the exact opposite of *maʿnā*. The use of the two terms is contrasted on several occasions in ML. In addition to the above examples, witness the analysis of the particle *kull* in a line of poetry of Abū al-Najm (ML 2:498), in which to interpret it as an object of the verb would be pernicious to the meaning (*kāna fāsidan maʿnan*) because its occurring where it does in relation to the negated verb demands that the whole thing be negated (*in waqaʿa l-nafy fī ḥayyizihā iqtaḍā l-salb ʿan kull fard*) (ML 1:201). On the other hand it is also weak in terms of the grammatical form (*ḍaʿīfan ṣināʿatan*) because *kull* with an attached pronoun can only be used for emphasis with a definite noun, or as the topic (or subject) of a nominal sentence, neither of which is applicable nor possible here. On another occasion I-H disputes al-Baṭalyawsī's interpretation of Sūra III vs.92 : *wa li allāhi ʿalā l-nāsi ḥajju l-bayti man istaṭaʿa ilayhi sabīlan* 'It is the duty of all men towards God to come to the House a pilgrim, if he is able to make his way there' (ML 2:536). I-H's objection is based on two grounds: first, al-Baṭalyawsī's thesis that *man* as the agent (*fāʿil*) with the verbal noun (*maṣdar*) [here, *ḥajj*] results in an impaired meaning (*fasada al-maʿnā*) because it consequently implies that all people will be guilty of sin if even one able person refrains from performing the pilgrimage. Second it is also weak in terms of the grammatical form (*fīhi ḍuʿf min jihat al-ṣināʿa*), since the occurrence of the agent after the annexing of the verbal noun to the object is anomalous (*li'anna l-ityāna bi l-fāʿil baʿda iḍāfat al-maṣdar ilā l-mafʿūl shādhdh*). Already a picture is emerging of the frequent juxtaposition of the verb *fasada* and its derivatives with an incorrect meaning (*maʿnā*), whereas the verb *ḍaʿufa* and its derivatives are normally associated with an imperfect grammatical form (*ṣināʿa / lafẓ*).

This assessment of the relationship between *ṣināʿa* and *maʿnā* merits one final illustration here because it underlines the essence of this study that I-H was as much interested in semantic issues as he was grammatical ones. In his long and detailed section on elision I-H commences with a look at contextual considerations and the conditions under which elision takes place (ML 2:603ff.). One of his early arguments focuses on establishing the correctness of two situational examples which bear similar properties, but with one significant difference. I-H notes that the *jumhūr* did not allow the sentence *lā tadnu min al-asadi ya'kulka* 'do not go near the lion, it will eat you', with the verb *ya'kul* in the jussive (*jazm*) mood, because if the reconstructed condition (*al-sharṭ al-muqaddar*) were restored as an affirmative, viz., *fa in tadnu...* 'if you go near...', it would not be commensurate with the verb of prohibition (*fiʿl al-nahy*) which is an indication of it. Moreover, if the reconstructed condition were negative, viz., *fa lā tadnu...* 'if you do not go near...', the meaning would be impaired, i.e., how can the lion eat you if you do not go near it ? However, if one changed the type of verb in the result clause to, say, *taslam* 'you will be saved', then even if the reconstructed condition is a negative, the sentence would be correct from the point of view of both *maʿnā* and *ṣināʿa*, i.e., 'if you do not go near the lion you will be saved' (ML 2:604-605).[2]

Let us now return to the first of these categories in which I-H assesses some examples of meanings which have been misinterpreted by some grammarians because they have accorded excessive attention to the grammatical form. I-H lists twenty-two such examples but our analysis here must of necessity rest on a selection of these. What is of particular interest in this section is that many of these examples involve the relationship between the particle present in the piece under discussion (normally taken from the Qur'ān) and the other components, normally the verb. At the foundation of this relationship is the concept called *ta'alluq* '(syntactico)-semantic connection' which has already been mentioned in this work.[3] I-H's definition of this term as *al-irtibāṭ al-ma'nawī* (ML 1:440) concurs exactly with the idea of semantic connection which we have been trying to convey so far. Further useful information on this concept is to be found in the *Amālī* of Ibn al-Ḥājib. He notes (2: 685) that *ta'alluq* always occurs in the context of the particle connecting the meaning of the verb to the noun (*īṣāl al-ḥarf ma'nā l-fi'l ilā l-ism*), as in, for example, *marartu bi zayd* 'I passed by Zayd'. He then adds that the meaning which is connected (from the verb to the noun) is also the one to which the particle is semantically connected, as in *sirtu min al-baṣra* 'I went from Basra'. In this example the particle *min* connects the meaning of 'going' (*al-sayr*) to Basra according to the meaning of commencement (*ibtidā'*), which is also semantically connected to the particle. The other important point to be made here is that *ta'alluq* normally occurs within the context of *taḍmīn* 'implication of meaning' which has already been mentioned on several occasions in this study and will appear again later. The reason for this is that I-H's interpretation of a particular verse is often based on one particle assuming the meaning of another, or a particular verb implying the meaning of another. In many such cases a consideration of the semantic connection between components is vital,[4] and this should become clearer in the following discussion. The technique adopted by I-H in this section is to say that 'one would initially think (*fa innahu yatabādaru ilā l-dhihn...*) that such-and-such a particle were (semantically) connected to a certain part of the sentence...', and then to discount that view by offering an alternative based on the 'intended' meaning of the piece. The following examples help to illustrate the purpose of this category.

In Sūra II vs.250 we find the following: *fa man shariba minhu fa laysa minnī, wa man lam yaṭ'amhu fa innahu minnī illā man ightarafa ghurfatan* (ML 2:533) 'God will try you with a river); whosoever drinks of it is not of me, and whoso tastes it not, he is of me, saving him who scoops up with his hand'. I-H argues that one would initially connect (semantically) the particle of 'exception', *illā*, with the second sentence, viz., *wa man lam*...etc., but this is incorrect because it would necessitate that he who scooped up a handful were not of him. However, that is not the case because the scooping up of a handful is permissible. Therefore the 'exception' must be from the first sentence. I-H criticizes Abū l-Baqā' for this misconception, and goes on to say that it is as though there were no separation (*faṣl*) here of the two sentences because mentioning that he who drinks is not of him necessitates (implicitly) that he who does not taste it is of him.

Another illustration of this argument may be seen in the prescription to the Muslims for preparing for prayer in Sūra V vs.8: *fa ighsilū wujūhakum wa aydiyakum ilā l-marāfiq* (ML 2:533) '...wash your faces, and your hands up to the elbows...'. Although we have already been told in the section on particles that one of the meanings of *ilā* is to convey the 'end of the aim' (*intihā' al-ghāya*) (ML 1:74) the question still remains as to the extent of that aim, i.e., does the verb extend to the noun following *ilā* in a full sense. According to I-H one would instinctively connect the particle *ilā* in the example above to the verb *ighsilū*. However, this had already been discounted by some on the basis that what precedes the aim, viz., the meaning of the verb, must be repeated before that aim is reached; this is why you may say *ḍarabtuhu ilā an māta* 'I beat him until he died', but you may not say *qataltuhu ilā an māta* 'I killed him until he died'. However, in the case of the verse above the hands are not washed repeatedly before reaching the elbow because the (word) hand includes the fingertips to the elbows and everything in between. The correct interpretation, therefore, is that *ilā* is semantically connected to the elided verb *asqiṭ* 'bring down!', which would then include the washing of the elbows in the ritual. I-H explains that the consensus on the meaning of the verb *asqaṭa* is that it applies from the shoulders down and ends at the elbows, and does not work from the fingertips upwards. On the question of the majority view that what follows *ilā* is not normally included in the act, I-H appears to eschew this problem by saying that even if the elbows are not included in the process of *isqāṭ* one can assume that they are part of the command, and should be washed. The implication of the elided verb in this verse represents I-H's attempt to move away from an interpretation bound by the grammatical form of the text, and to provide a solution which is more faithful to the meaning.

Another example of this category is to be found in Sūra XI vs.88-89: *a ṣalawātuka ta'muruka an natruka mā ya'budu ābā'una aw an naf'ala fī amwālina mā nashā'* (ML 2:536) '...does thy prayer command thee that we should leave that our fathers served, or to do as we will with our goods ?'. I-H claims that one would immediately think that *an naf'ala* is coordinated with *an natruka,* but that is 'nonsense' since He (God) did not order them to do what they wished concerning their goods. According to I-H *an naf'ala* is coordinated with the *mā* which is the thing operated on by the 'leaving'. In this case the meaning should be that they abandon doing what they wish concerning their goods (*natruka an naf'ala*). The reason for this misconception is that the *mu'rib* is influenced by the presence of the particle *an* and the verb on two occasions and the presence of a coordinating particle, viz., *aw.* Once more it is their adherence to the grammatical form which I-H takes issue with here.[5]

Moving away for the time being from the question of *ta'alluq* we find I-H taking the grammarians to task over the interpretation of Sūra VI vs.124: *allāhu a'lamu ḥaythu yaj'alu risālatahu* (ML 2:531) 'God knows very well where to place His Message'. I-H argues here that one may well assume initially that the particle *ḥaythu* is an adverb of place (*ẓarf makān*) since that is how it is used in speech. However, this view can be rejected on the grounds that God knows the place that deserves his Message, not that his knowledge is actually in that place. In this case *ḥaythu* is the direct object (*maf'ūl bihi*), not the adverbial object (*maf'ūl fīhi*).

Yet another example of I-H's objections to erroneous parsing by certain grammarians which has distorted the meaning is from Sūra XVIII vs.1-2: *wa lam yaj'al lahu 'iwājan qayyiman* (ML 2:534) '(who has sent down upon His servant the Book) and has not assigned to it any crookedness; right,(to warn of great violence)'. I-H refutes emphatically the suggestion that the word *qayyiman* in this verse is an adjective (*ṣifa*) of *'iwājan,* since something crooked cannot be right at the same time. We gain a sense of I-H's irritation at this type of error when he adds that 'I would show mercy on the readers (of the Qur'ān) who paused on the word *'iwājan'* (*taraḥḥamtu 'alā man waqafa min al-qurrā'...*).

A very interesting debate centres on the following from Sūra XLVI vs.27: *fa law lā naṣarahum alladhīna ittakhadhū min dūni allāhi qurbānan ālihatan* (ML 2:537) 'Then why did those not help them that they had taken to themselves as mediators, gods apart from God ?'. According to some the original structure (*aṣl)* is *ittakhadhūhum qurbānan* in which the pronoun (*hum*) and *qurbānan* are both objects (*maf'ūlāni*) of the verb, and *ālihatan* is a substitution (*badal*) of the latter. The erroneous meaning of this interpretation had already been noted by al-Zamakhsharī but he did not give reasons for his objection. However, we find a very clear elaboration on this issue in the commentary, or more specifically, the refutation of Mu 'tazilite views in the *Kashshāf* which is summarised in ML by I-H, although once again he does not acknowledge the provenance of his explanation. The only possible parsing of *ālihatan* here is that it is a second object; as for *qurbānan* it can only be an 'accusative of condition'(*ḥāl*). What follows is I-H's explanation of why the original interpretation is incorrect:

> ...and if they are being blamed for taking as mediators other than God then the import is that they are being urged to take God as a mediator just as when you say 'Do you have a teacher other than me ?' you are telling him to take you as a teacher and noone else' (ML 2:537).

Unfortunately I-H is a little vague as to why this is not the intention in the verse. However we learn from the commentator on the *Kashshāf* (*al-Intiṣāf,* 3:526-27) that what is really at issue is their relating 'Godship' *(ilāhiyya)* to other than God. They both agree on the fundamental premise that God may stand as a mediator, but that He cannot be used as a mediator through which to reach other Gods (*wa allāhi ta'ālā yutaqarrabu ilayhi bi ghayrihi wa lā yutaqarrabu bihi ilā ghayrihi*). It is examples of this nature which help to underline the importance of meaning to I-H in ML.

Conversely we find him adopting a slightly different approach in the second of the categories of Chapter Five. In this section I-H's concern is not so much with the meaning (although he suggests that misrepresentations have occurred in certain selected examples) but rather with the breach of the rules of grammatical form (*ṣinā'a*). Once more we must confine ourselves to a small number of illustrations of this.

The issue of (syntactico)-semantic connection (*ta'alluq*) features frequently again here, but principally from the point of view of grammatical correctness. The element of *ṣadāra* 'initial position' carries considerable importance in this section as certain grammatical considerations may be accepted or ruled out on the basis of the application of some principles of grammatical form. This could be exemplified by Sūra LIII vs 50: *wa annahu ahlaka 'Ād al-ūlā wa Thamūdan fa mā abqā* (ML 2:539) '(and that he destroyed Ad, the ancient, and Thamood, and he did not spare them'. I-H claims that some people said that *Thamūdan* here is a pre-posed 'object' (*maf'ūl muqaddam*). He discounts this view, however, on the grounds that the negative particle *mā* should be (grammatically) at the head (of its clause) (*li mā l-nāfiya al-ṣadr*), and that what follows it cannot operate upon what precedes it. In that case *Thamūdan* will either be coordinated with *'Ād* or will be preceded by a reconstructed verb, viz., *ahlaka* (although this is not strictly necessary because it already appears in the verse).

We find other examples in this section of particles requiring *ṣadr,* such as those of interrogation (*istifhām*) or condition (*sharṭ*) (e.g., ML 2:542-43,545). In the latter's case I-H states that in addition to the normal conditional particles requiring this status[6] the same obtains for the particle *idhā* 'of surprise' (*idhā al-fujā'iyya*) since '(this particle) has the grammatical status (*manzila*) of the conditional *fā'* '. The verse in question is from Sūra XXX vs.24: *thumma idhā da'ākum da'watan min al-arḍi idhā antum takhrujūna* (ML 2:543) 'then, when He calls you once and suddenly, out of the earth, lo you shall come forth'. According to I-H this interpretation by the exegetes would require that the meaning be: 'Lo, you shall come forth from the earth', since they would be connecting (semantically) what precedes *idhā* with what follows it, but this is unacceptable in the Arabic language. In other words they would come forth, but not out of the earth. It is only the call which would come from there. Therefore I-H is indicating that a misinterpretation of the grammatical form here will consequently necessitate an impaired meaning.

The third category in Chapter Five is very brief. I-H takes issue here with opinions and explanations of grammatical data based on what has not been attested (*mā lam yuthbat*) in the Arabic language. Significantly he attributes these errors either to ignorance or carelessness by the *mu'ribūn*. It is true that I-H attempts in certain cases to offer some mitigation for the errors by exploring possible sources of explanation. For instance, he applies a method of 'interpretation of an interpretation' (*ta'wīl 'alā ta'wīl*) as used for Sūra X vs.28, to the situational example *Zaydun a'qalu min an yakdhaba* (ML 2:547-48; al-Shamunnī, *Munṣif*, 2:211) (already cited above in Chapter Two) in order to attempt to accomodate the notion offered by Ibn Mas'ūd al-Zakī that the particle *an* may occur with the meaning of the relative pronoun *alladhī*. In this instance I-H's argument runs as follows. In Sūra X vs.28 the interpretation of *mā kāna hādhā l-Qur'ānu an yuftarā* 'This Qur'ān could not have been forged' requires that *yuftarā* undergo a transformation to become the verbal noun *iftirā'*, and then a further one to become a participle *muftaran*, viz., *mā kāna muftaran*. I-H accepts, however, that the attempt to apply the same process to the situational example fails because it results in a meaning which implies a 'preference over something lacking; and there is nothing preferable in that' (*al-tafḍīl 'alā l-nāqiṣ lā faḍla fīhi*). What is meant here is that after the interpretation by which the *an* and its verb become a verbal noun, which in turn becomes a descriptive element (*waṣf*), the resulting meaning would be *zaydun a'qalu min al-kādhibi* 'Zayd is more intelligent than the liar (he who lies)'. Consequently I-H presents his own favoured interpretation which was noted above in Chapter Two, p. 43). Thus we witness the ingenuity of I-H at work. Other examples in this section include I-H's categorical assertion that the particle *kāf* cannot occur for *qasam* 'oath' (ML 2:546), that the elision of the particle *wāw* of 'accompaniment' (*wāw al-maf'ūl ma'ahu*) has not been attested in Arabic (ML 2:547), and that neither has a superfluous *tā'* at the beginning of the 'past tense' of what is generally known today in Western circles at least as Form V of the verb (ML 2:547).

The fourth category of Chapter Five in ML reinforces once more the importance of interpreting the Qur'ān according to sound principles. I-H is concerned here with the interpretation by some of the *mu'ribūn* of linguistic issues according to unlikely and weak arguments as opposed to the more likely and more plausible ones, which is further evidence of the symmetrical and antithetical nature of the terminology deployed to gauge the standard of these arguments; *ba'īd* is used as the opposite of *qarīb*, and *ḍa'īf* as the converse of *qawī*. In this connection I-H adds that the the *mu'rib* is guilty of a sin if the most likely interpretations did not even occur to him! What he appears to be doing here is creating a further sub-hierarchy of linguistic standards of which evidence has already been adduced during this work. The category under discussion here assumes prescriptive dimensions in the sense that the grammarian is excused, or even commended, if a presentation of both extremes of an argument is adopted merely to illustrate the possiblities or to train the student. However, this is not an acceptable approach when interpreting the material of the Qur'ān because that must be interpreted according to the most predominant and likely view of what was intended. If there is no prevailing opinion then a demonstration of the possible interpretations is acceptable; but if the intention of the *mu'rib* is merely to show people the most unlikely interpretation and to highlight the numerous possibilities then that is extremely difficult to accept. The student is subsequently presented with several examples of this by I-H to avoid committing the same errors (ML 2:548-49).

The first example of this category is perhaps the most significant for a number of reasons. It comprises a selection of examples taken only from the Qur'ān, with refutations by I-H of various scholars' interpretation of them. The main point of contention for I-H concerns the coordination (*'aṭf*) of one verse to another. Once more I-H creates an order of 'unlikelihood': '...and even more remote than this is the idea that...' (*wa ab'ad minhu...*) or (*wa dūna hādhā fī l-bu'd*). His objections are based on both purely syntactic grounds, such as the unacceptability of the pre-posing of the result clause of a conditional sentence, or semantic, such as the occurrence of the particle *thumma* 'then' in Sūra VI vs.155. for the 'sequence of informing' (*tartīb al-akhbār*) and not 'sequence of time' (*tartīb al-zamān*) (ML 2:549). I-H's overriding objection to most of these interpretations is that the distance between the verses is too great for coordination to occur between them. This could be exemplified by al-Zamakhsharī's suggestion that Sūra XXXVII vs.149: *fa istaftihim a hum ashaddu khalqan* 'So ask them for a pronouncement - Are they stronger in constitution ?', is coordinated to vs.11: *fa istaftihim a li rabbika l-banātu* ' So ask them for a pronouncement - Has thy Lord daughters ?'. I-H's conclusion here is that these two verses are so far apart in the text that coordination is extremely unlikely (ML 2:549).

In this section I-H makes particular use of the terms *ḍa'īf* and *ḥasan* (and their derivatives). We saw earlier that the employment of these terms is not original. Nonetheless, it is interesting to note that *ḍa'īf* is used, with rare exception, as a judgement on poor grammatical form (*ṣinā'a*). Conversely, *ḥasan* is almost always employed to pass judgement on good meaning (*ma'nā*). An appropriate example of this may be drawn from the second point made by I-H within this category which concerns the interpretation of the concept of *ighrā'* 'inducement' in two separate verses of the Qur'ān (ML 2:550). In Sūra II vs.153: *fa lā janāḥa 'alayhi an yaṭūfa bihimā* 'it is no fault in him to circumambulate them', I-H refutes the interpretation of *'alayhi* as 'inducement' on the grounds that *ighrā'* of the 'third person' (*al-ghā'ib*) is *ḍa'īf*. On the other hand, in Sūra VI vs.151: *qul ta'ālaw atlu mā ḥarrama rabbukum 'alaykum an lā tushrikū bihi shay'an...*'Say: Come, I will recite what your Lord has forbidden you: that you associate not anything with Him...', I-H considers an interpretation of *'alaykum* as *ighrā'* to be good (*ḥasan*). We may assume two reasons for this; the use of *ighrā'* with the second person and, more than this, the interpretation of a pause (*waqf*) after the words *rabbukum*. I-H adds that the presence of the meaning of 'inducement' here is not responsible for the idea of necessity (*ījāb*) in the particle *'alā* since it always conveys that sense.[7]

The fifth category in this section constitutes an analysis of some categories of which certain possible overt interpretations have been overlooked by the grammarians; in this regard I-H adheres to one of his aims set out in the introduction to ML to avoid repeating well-covered ground. The technique he employs here is to select isolated issues, *masā'il*, on such essential subjects as the topic (*mubtada'*) of the nominal sentence (ML 2:556) and the verb *kāna* in conjunction with what can follow the same grammatical rules (ML 2:559). Once more he acknowledges that this form of presentation by means of individual *masā'il* enables the student to learn them more easily. He also adopts an approach much favoured throughout ML in which he takes two or three similar grammatical concepts and argues for the coexistence of both or all of them in a given context. It is this latter approach we are concerned with here.

In the section on *manṣūbāt mutashābiha* 'obscure accusatives (dependent entities)' I-H makes a few important observations from examples in which the accusative could be either a *ḥāl* 'accusative [though not always] of condition' and a *tamyīz* 'accusative of specification' (ML 2:563-64). The first example is the following: *karuma zaydun ḍayfan* which may be translated as either 'Zayd's guest was noble' or 'Zayd was noble as a guest'. According to I-H the accusative here, viz., *ḍayfan,* is a *tamyīz* if the guest is other than Zayd, on the basis that it is averted from being the grammatical agent (*muḥawwal 'an al-fā'il*), i.e., Zayd here (Ibn 'Aqīl, *Sharḥ,* 1:587), and cannot take the particle *min*, i.e., *min ḍayfin* because the *tamyīz* can only be in the oblique (*jarr*) case following *min* if it is not an agent in terms of meaning. In this instance, of course, it is a semantic agent just like, say, the word *nafs* in *ṭāba zaydun nafsan* 'Zayd is a pleasant soul', for which you cannot say *ṭāba zaydun min nafsin*.[8] However, if you 'restored' the words *nafsahu* to our original example here then the accusative *ḍayfan* could be either a *ḥāl* or *tamyīz* [upon which Zayd would then be the guest].[9]

That notwithstanding, according to I-H the most suitable way of identifying the *tamyīz* is in fact to insert a particle *min,* which constitutes the most felicitous analysis of *hādhā khātamun ḥadīdan* 'this is an iron ring' (ML 2:564). He argues that this example is more likely to be a *tamyīz* than a *ḥāl* to 'avoid forming a *ḥāl* with an underived noun' (*li l-salāma bihi min jumūd al-ḥāl*), although I-H has demonstrated previously that this is possible (ML 2:463). Moreover it is more likely to be a *tamyīz* because the *ḥāl* in the example is not transitory (*ghayr muntaqil*); in other words, the adjective *ḥadīd* is a permanent type of adjective, but *ḥāl* adjectives are normally transitory.[10] Finally, the subject of the *ḥāl* here is an indefinite noun whereas the *ḥāl* normally functions with definite nouns (c.f. *Ibn 'Aqīl*, *Sharḥ*, 1:556).

To conclude this brief look at the fifth category in this section the following represents another unequivocal example of the polemical and, at times, almost patronising, nature of I-H's response to the opinions of certain predecessors. He notes how the *ḥāl* can either be of the agent or the object, as in *ḍarabtu zaydan ḍāḥikan* 'I hit Zayd laughing'. In other words we do not know if I was laughing as I hit Zayd or if he was. The same applies to the following in Sūra IX vs.36: *wa qātilū l-mushrikīna kāffatan* 'And fight the unbelievers totally'. However, I-H objects to al-Zamakhsharī's similar interpretation of the following in Sūra II vs.204: *udkhulū fī l-silmi kāffatan* 'Enter the peace, all of you'. I-H refers to this interpretation by al-Zamakhsharī as a misconception because *kāffa* is specifically for rational things (*man ya'qalu*); therefore the only possible interpretation is that it is a *ḥāl* of the agent, to wit, in the verb *udkhulū,* because the 'peace' cannot be entered totally. Even worse than this is his making *kāffa* an adjective (*na't*) of an elided verbal noun in Sūra XXXIV vs.27, thereby denuding it of its *ḥāl* function. Finally we witness the extremity of I-H's attack on al-Zamakhsharī when he cites an example from the narrative of the latter's own introduction to his *Mufaṣṣal* where he uses *kāffa* as the first term of an *iḍāfa* and thereby deprives it of its accusative function (ML 2: 564). A heinous sin indeed!

The sixth category comprises numerous examples of what we have already referred to as misconception (*wahm*) in which scholars demonstrate considerable inconsistency by not observing the correct categories for certain grammatical rules because they confuse the conditions (*shurūṭ*) laid down by their own grammatical system. However, in this section I-H's arguments are based far more on formal considerations than semantic ones; therefore we shall move swiftly on to the seventh category which would seem to constitute an attempt by I-H to reinforce the consistency of the Arabic language, principally that of the Qur'ān, in the light of inconsistent analyses by certain *mu'ribūn*. In particular the application of (linguistic) proof (*dalīl*) is important here as I-H illustrates the way in which the grammarians may accord a given proposition to something, in spite of the existence of another similar usage as textual evidence (and proof) which contradicts their view (*...an yaḥmila kalām 'alā shay' wa yushhadu isti'māl ākhar fī naẓīr dhālika l-mawḍi' bi khilāfihi*) (ML 2:593). Two examples will suffice here.

In Sūra VI vs.95: *inna allāha fāliqu l-ḥabbi wa l-nawā yukhriju l-ḥayya min al-mayyiti wa mukhriju l-mayyiti min al-ḥayy* 'It is God who splits the grain and the date-stone, brings forth the living from the dead; He brings forth the dead too from the living', al-Zamakhsharī (*Kashshāf,* 2:37) argues that the sentence beginning ...*mukhriju* is coordinated with ...*fāliqu l-ḥabbi*...etc., since it is more appropriate to coordinate the noun with the noun, which in this case is the active participle (*ism al-fā'il*). However, both I-H (ML 2:593) and the commentator on the *Kashshāf* (2:37) note that the occurrence of the verb in the second part of Sūra X vs.33 where the same words are repeated with this one difference, i.e., *yukhriju l-ḥayya min al-mayyiti wa yukhriju l-mayyita min al-ḥayyi...*, is sufficient proof to contradict al-Zamakhsharī's argument. In another example I-H cites a verse as textual proof to show that the verb *za'ama* 'to assert' normally occurs with the particle *anna* and its connecting clause (*ṣila*) and not with two direct objects. We are told that in the Qur'ān it never occurs with the latter (ML 2:594). To support his case I-H argues that in Sūra XXVIII vs.62: *ayna shurakā'ī alladhīnā kuntum taz'amūna* 'Where now are my associates whom you were asserting', the reconstructed version of this should be *taz'amūna annahum shurakā'* (since the antecedent of the relative pronoun requires a relating element here) and not *taz'amūnahum shurakā'* as suggested by some. To prove his case I-H cites from Sūra VI vs.94: *wa mā narā ma'akum shufa'ā'akum alladhīna za'amtum annahum fīkum shurakā'u* 'We do not see with you your intercessors, those you asserted to be associates in you'. Therefore, not for the first time do we see I-H using Qur'ānic text as the ultimate support for his linguistic arguments.

As further evidence of the presence of grammatical hierarchy and aspiration to excellence I-H follows all this with the eighth category, in which error and misinterpretation is even more likely to occur than in the previous category. The apparent reason for this likelihood is the subtle nature of the issues under discussion. This applies particularly to certain verses of the Qur'ān as I-H brings together a number of semantic issues whose interpretation is in many cases influenced by the immutability of the *rasm*, the orthographical representation of Qur'ānic Arabic which determines the grammatical status of a given word. It is interesting to note that I-H avails himself of this term in this section on at least six occasions (ML 2:595-98), yet it is rarely to be found elsewhere in ML. The term *rasm* would, in fact, seem to evoke rather sublime connotations. It is certainly to be found in the *Kashshāf* (e.g., 2:194) of al-Zamakhsharī where he underlines the importance of *rasm* in the Qur'ān, and its superior standing over the ordinary Arabic script. He notes, for example, that the *fatḥa* was written as an *alif* (cf. Sūra IX vs.47 or XVII vs.20) in the Qur'ānic text (*muṣḥaf*) before the Arabic script came into being; the latter was 'invented' (*ukhturiʿa*) shortly after the sending down (*nuzūl*) of the Qur'ān.[11]

To return to I-H's use of *rasm* in ML we see, for example, how a correct interpretation of the *rasm* can establish that there is no difference between him who repents in the face of death and him who dies an unbeliever. In Sūra IV vs.22: *wa lā alladhīna yamūtūna wa hum kuffārun* 'neither to those who die disbelieving', I-H maintains that the *wa lā* must be coordinated to a previous sentence *li alladhīna yaʿmalūna l-sayyi'āti* 'towards those who do evil deeds' on the basis that the two categories of people are of the same kind, viz., that God has prepared a painful chastisement for them both. I-H's interpretation runs contrary to that of the grammarian al-Akhfash who appears to put only those who die disbelieving into the category of those who will face God's wrath, on the understanding that the line about repentance in the face of death which comes between these two lines earns those people a reprieve. The relevance of the *rasm* to this argument is that al-Akhfash argued that the *lā* of *wa lā* denotes the 'inchoation of a nominal sentence' (*ibtidā'*) and that the *alif* is superfluous. Through his interpretation I-H establishes an important Islamic precept concerning faith and lack of it.[12]

A further important interpretation supported by I-H may be seen in Sūra XI vs.82: *fa asri bi ahlika bi qiṭʿin min al-layli wa lā yaltafit minkum aḥadun illā imra'atu/a/ka*. (ML 2:597) 'so set forth, thou with thy family, in a watch of the night, and let not any one of you turn round, excepting thy wife'. According to al-Zamakhsharī, whoever put *imra'a* into the accusative/dependent case implied that the exception (*istithnā'*) was from the sentence beginning *fa asri*... On the other hand, whoever put it in the nominative/independent case implied that it was from *wa lā yaltafit...*,etc. However, I-H rejects this view because of the contradiction [in meaning] of the two readings. In other words the wife (of Lot) would be taken on the travels according to the nominative reading but left behind according to the accusative reading. In I-H's view this is open to discussion since excluding her from the prohibitive (*nahy*) sentence does not [automatically] mean that she was taken with them on their travels at night; rather it shows merely that she was with them. Indeed, it was related that she followed them and that when she turned round and saw the punishment and screamed, she was hit by stones which killed her. I-H's verdict on this one is that the reading of the majority, which opted for the accusative case, is not neccessarily the more likely; rather I-H asserts that the 'exception' in the verse is from the imperative sentence in both readings. The proof of this is that in the reading of Ibn Masʿūd's the whole sentence *wa lā yaltafit minkum aḥadun* was omitted. Moreover, the exception is disjunctive (*munqaṭiʿ*), as proven by the omission of the same sentence in Sūra XV vs.66: *fa asri bi ahlika...wa lā yaltafit minkum aḥadun* 'So set forth, thou with thy family, in a watch of the night, (and follow after the backs of them), and let not any one of you turn round'. As a final proof I-H explains that what is meant by the 'family' here is the 'believers' even if they were not from the people of his house, not the people of his house even if they were not believers (ML 2:598).

It has been our contention throughout this study that what I-H achieved above all through his meticulous approach was the compilation of a major compendious work of grammar and exegesis that provided an invaluable service to Islam. It has already been acknowledged that parts of his contribution were by no means wholly original. Nonetheless, there is further evidence of the above achievements in the ninth category of this particular chapter of ML in which he criticizes certain grammarians for not paying sufficient attention to the existence of potential obscurities (*mushtabihāt*) for which a delicate mode of interpretation is required. The first example concerns the interpretation of the meaning and function of the verb *aḥṣā* 'to calculate, count, store in the mind'. In the situational example *zaydun aḥṣā dhihnan* (ML 2:598; c.f. al-Zamakhsharī, *Kashshāf,* 2:474; *Ibn ʿAqīl*, *Sharḥ*, 1:584-85) 'Zayd has a better/the best mind for calculating' *aḥṣā* is an elative noun and the accusative/dependent noun is a specification (*tamyīz*). In the example *ʿamrun aḥṣā mālan* "Amr counted [his] money' *aḥṣā* is a past tense verb and the accusative noun is an object (*mafʿūl*). I-H cites a verse from the Qur'ān as a corroboration of this. He then goes on to disagree with the misconception that Sūra XVIII vs.11: *aḥṣā limā labithū amadan* ('we might know which of the parties) would better calculate the while they had tarried', is of the first type, viz., *zaydun aḥṣā dhihnan*. He notes that the *amad* 'period of time' cannot be the calculator but can only be calculated; for it is one of the conditions of the specification after an elative that it be an agent (*fāʿil*) in terms of the meaning. This is exemplified by the situational example *zaydun aktharu mālan* 'Zayd has more / the most money' in which *māl* is the agent in terms of meaning, viz., you could say *kathura mālu zaydin.*

Other interesting examples in this section include the interpretation of *shāʿir* 'poet' in the example *zaydun kātibun shaʿirun* 'Zayd is a writer and a poet', as either a predicate (*khabar*) or an adjective of the (first) predicate. However, in the example *zaydun rajulun ṣāliḥun* 'Zayd is a righteous man', which is structurally identical to the previous example, the word *ṣāliḥ* 'righteous' can only be an adjective because the word *rajul* cannot be a predicate by itself since it does not carry any communicative meaning (*fā'ida*) in relation to Zayd whom we know from his name is a man.[13] Examples of a slightly different, but nonetheless equally interesting, nature illustrate I-H's concern with the semantics of a sentence which in turn determine the grammatical status of certain words. For instance, in *ra'aytu zaydan faqīhan* 'I considered Zayd (to be) a legal theorist' *faqīh* is a second object because the verb *ra'ā* here 'pertains to knowledge' (*ʿilmiyya*), as opposed to the more common meaning of 'to see'. However, in the example *ra'aytu l-hilāla ṭāliʿan* 'I saw the crescent moon rising' the verb *ra'ā* 'pertains to vision' (*baṣariyya*); therefore, the word *ṭāliʿ* can only be an 'accusative of condition' (*ḥāl*) (ML 2:598-99).

The tenth aspect deals with interpretations by certain *muʿribūn* which run contrary to the original structure (*aṣl*), or even the outward form (*ẓāhir*), for no apparent reason. This section deals mainly with unnecessary interpretations of elision and leads into I-H's important discussion of that issue.

It is hoped that this chapter in conjunction with the previous one has gone some way towards highlighting the type of contentious issues that prompted I-H to devote a whole chapter of ML in which he raises objections to many of the views held by other grammarians. It should be added here that it is not always immediately clear what distinguishes certain categories from others. Moreover one can find similar objections raised elsewhere in ML. What should have emerged, however, is an unequivocal indication that I-H was concerned as much as anything with the question of meaning, and that faulty interpretations, of which there were plenty according to I-H, had to be refuted for the benefit of the sacred texts and, of course, for the purposes of Islam. We shall now move on to an analysis of the particle which is arguably the most significant part of speech in the Arabic language from the point of view of meaning.

NOTES

1 Owens (1990:91-92) distinguishes between the terms *ṣināʿa* and *lafẓ* by translating the latter as 'form'. The reason for this is that its function throughout the period of medieval Arabic grammar would seem to have oscillated between that of 'a phonetic form, a phonetic form that correlates with a meaning, and a grammatical as opposed to a semantic entity'.

2 Of the many other examples try ML 2:617, 622. On at least one occasion we see how a lack of contextual indication can lead either to a corrupted meaning (*ḍarar maʿnawī*) or a corrupted grammatical form (*ḍarar ṣināʿī*) (ML 2:604).

3 An historical study of the employment of this term would probably produce some interesting results. Although it appears to be a term used more predominantly by the later writers, say, from the fifth century A.H. onwards, we would not rule out the possibility of its having been used before that time. In his commentary on the *Adab al-Kuttāb* of Ibn Qutayba, al-Baṭalyawsī uses the term *taʿalluq* to explain some of Ibn Qutayba's more superficial explanations of the potential substitution of one preposition for another.

4 A short analysis of the question of the substitution of one particle for another can be found at the end of Chapter Five. For a more comprehensive analysis the reader is referred to Gully (1994 (a)). In a future article I shall be looking at the significance of *taḍmīn* in a wider context.

5 It is important to bear in mind that not all I-H's views here are necessarily wholly original. The example of Sūra IX vs.88-89, for example, is to be found in the commentary on al-Zamakhsharī's *Kashshāf* where the explanation is described as one of the 'niceties' (*laṭā'if*) of Arabic. It is safe to assume that I-H was aware of this commentary for two reasons: first, the commentator, al-Munayyir, died some time before I-H in 683 / 1284. Second, according to Brockelmann (1943 2:31) I-H wrote what appears to have been an abridgement of that work entitled *Mukhtaṣar al-Intiṣāf*. As we have suggested before it is often not the originality, or lack of it, of a particular point, but the context and manner in which it is presented which makes ML such a valuable and appealing work.

6 I-H rejects the Kufan view that the result clause can pre-pose the conditional clause (ML 2:545).

7 For further examples of the application of *ḍaʿīf* in the context of poor grammatical form, try, for instance, ML 2:551,552,555. For further instances of the deployment of *ḥasan* for good meaning, try, for example, ML 2:552,554.

8 For this see Ibn ʿAqīl, *Sharḥ*, 1:587, and 1:585 for the testing device for this argument which shows that the original structure (*aṣl*) for this example would be *ṭābat nafsu zaydin*. Therefore, if one applied this device to I-H's example it would produce *karuma ḍayfu zaydin*.

9 A more comprehensive discussion of the differences between the *ḥāl* and the *tamyīz* can be found in ML 2:460-64.

10 For a discussion of *ḥāl* and the *ṣifa mutanaqqila / thābita* see Isbir / al-Junaydi (1981:421). See also, for example, Ibn ʿAqīl, *Sharḥ*, 1:556, and al-Astarābādhī, *Sharḥ*, 1:199 for *intiqāl*.

11 One cannot fail to make mention of Ibn Fāris in this regard who appears to have used the term *rasm* in his *Ṣāḥibī* in a special way. Carter (1993:141) compares the term to Derrida's 'trace', and notes that Ibn Fāris uses it in the context of 'the *rasm* of the past, its written record'. What is even more significant in Carter's analysis is that what was once direct knowledge for the community is now nothing more than 'subtle discourse about the basic and derived principles of the faith, about law and inheritance, about grammar, prosody and so on' (ibid.:141 quoting Ibn Fāris, *Ṣāḥibī*, 72). This idea ties in very neatly with the argument set forth in the latter part of Chapter Two of this present study.

12 cf. Yusuf Ali (1934:184) who notes that when someone sins without compunction, it is too late to repent in the face of death. This would appear to be commensurate with I-H's view if we understand his linguistic reasoning correctly.

13 cf. Ibn al-Sarrāj in his *Kitāb al-Uṣūl*, 1:73 (as quoted by Frank 1981:265; Versteegh *to appear*) who said that the sentence 'fire is hot' does not have any communicative value (*lam tufid maʿnan*).

Chapter Five

PARTICLES: THE GRAMMARIAN'S STOCK-IN-TRADE

'One of the grammarians said: 'The particles do not actually need to be defined because they (amount to) a restricted number of words' ... but it is not as he said, because (the particle) is an essential and indispensable (part of speech)'.[1]

The status of the particle in the Western and Arabic linguistic traditions

The importance of the particle as one of the three main parts of speech has already been alluded to on a number of occasions so far. Before moving on to a closer analysis of the significance of the particle in ML, a glance at the historical development of the term *ḥarf* would seem to be order here. Modern scholarship has devoted considerable attention to the various possible interpretations of the term, on the basis that it was used to convey a diversity of meanings in addition to its most readily understood sense nowadays of particle. What has stimulated the debate above all is the definition given by Sībawayhi (*Kitāb*, 1:12) that speech is made up of a verb, noun, and *ḥarf jā'a li ma'nan laysa bi ism wa lā fi'l*. Given the apparent complexity of the term we prefer Carter's translation (1981:15, n.1.25) of *ḥarf* as a 'bit', hence 'a bit which comes for a meaning'. Carter lists a number of different meanings for the term which include grapheme, phoneme, consonant, radical, and morpheme; and in any event these meanings reflect the fact that the *ḥarf* is, in a sense, 'a bit (more technically a particle) which is not, morphologically, a noun or a verb' (ibid.:15).

More recently, Fischer (1989) has suggested that the term has passed through various stages of development according to the context in which it was being employed. In ancient poetry, for instance, it was only used in the sense of 'edge' or 'border', whilst within the domain of early Qur'ānic exegesis it assumed the sense of 'to write letters or consonants' in the text, which led to a new interpretation of the term amongst the readers of the Qur'ān as 'letters, characters, or consonants' (*Buchstabe*). In the field of early grammar it was used in the sense of 'word', and it was not until the time of Sībawayhi that it began to be used in a far more limited capacity as the term for particle, although it continued to be deployed in the sense of 'consonant'. According to Fischer (ibid.:145) these older meanings of the term soon became obselescent.[2]

What really concerns us at this juncture, however, is to examine the way in which the term *ḥarf* was interpreted as particle in the later period of the Arabic linguistic tradition, and to draw a few brief parallels with the perception of the term 'particle' in the Western linguistic literature. Fortunately, whatever Sībawayhi really meant by his leading remark on the *ḥarf* in no way interferes with, nor obscures, our understanding of the later definition of the particle, which is to be found at least as early as al-Zajjājī (*Īḍāḥ*, 54), that the particle is essentially 'something that signifies a meaning in something else' (*mā dalla ʿalā maʿnan fī ghayrihi*). We shall return to this shortly. In the meantime, the brief foregoing discussion has already illustrated that the term *ḥarf* carried heavy baggage. In broad terms it was employed to cater for any words which did not fit within the rubrics of noun or verb. It remains to determine the range of words which are covered by the term particle, therefore, on the premise that it is little more than a handy nomenclature from which both the medieval Arabic situation and Western linguistics have benefited.

In both Western linguistic literature and amongst Muslim scholars of the medieval period, the definitions of what lies outside the categories of noun and verb have varied. To be more precise, the conclusions as to which words can safely be subsumed within the rubric of particle, or *ḥarf* in the Arabic context, have differed. In the Western literature scholars have frequently avoided the use of the term in favour of a more vague description, as we shall see presently. In the Muslim literature the term *ḥarf* (pl. *ḥurūf*) to denote particle(s) was soon extended to *ḥurūf al-maʿānī* 'particles of meaning', presumably to distinguish this part of speech from the consonants, for which the term *ḥarf* (pl. *ḥurūf*) was also extended to *ḥurūf al-mabānī*, which neither have a meaning in themselves (unlike the verbs or nouns), nor in relation to what surrounds them in the sentence (unlike the particles). It is interesting to note, however, that I-H and many of his successors, particularly those like Ṭāshkubrīzādah who was clearly influenced by I-H, did not use the term *ḥurūf al-ma'ānī*. The reason for this choice, we would suggest, is that I-H broadened the scope of the particle by subsuming certain types of noun and adverb, and even verbs, within the rubric of his particles, or what he preferred to call *mufradāt* 'single entities'. We shall be looking at this in more detail shortly.

The following definition of the term particle would seem to encapsulate the view being put forward here that this category of words appears to defy the application of a generic term like particle which is relevant to all words of its kind:

> '(particle is) a term used in grammatical description to refer to an invariable term with grammatical function, especially one which does not readily fit into a standard classification of parts of speech' (Crystal 1980:258).

It should be noted here that the particle in the Arabic literature under discussion also performed a syntactico-semantic role too, in addition to its grammatical function either as an operator (*'āmil*) or non-operator (*hāmil*) on the nouns and verbs which followed it. Indeed, it was the former type of analysis carried out by such scholars as I-H which represented a significant change in emphasis from the more traditional formal studies of the particle. At any rate, I-H used the term *mufradāt* as the generic term for the particles in preference to the more common *ḥurūf al-ma'ānī* which is conspicuous by its absence in ML. For I-H the term *mufradāt* not only incorporates the conventionally accepted particles (*ḥurūf*), but also the nouns and adverbs (*asmā' wa ẓurūf*) which contain the same (grammatical) meaning (*wa mā taḍammana ma'nāhā*) as the particles (ML 1:13). [3]

Although I-H does not elaborate on this usage an important indication of what he probably meant is located elsewhere (*Majma'* 1934-35:183). Apparently the term *taḍmīn* (which is related to the *taḍammana* used by I-H) was employed originally by the ancient grammarians (*qudamā' al-naḥwiyyīn*) for the noun in its conventional sense to signify a meaning which should have been signified by the particle, such as the *asmā' l-sharṭ wa al-istifhām* 'conditional and interrogative nouns' (cf. ML 2:530); this is, in fact, one of the bases of non-inflection (*'ilal al-binā'*). What is meant here is that words such as *ḥaythu* are technically adverbs (*ẓurūf*), but are uninflected and assume a conditional sense because of their containing (*taḍammunuhā*) the meaning of the conditional particle *in*. In other words they now assume a partial meaning (*ma'nan juz'ī*) which should be conveyed by a particle, in this case the condition conveyed by the expression *in*. It is also worth noting that later writers on this subject such as al-Suyūṭī (*Itqān,* 1:190) and Ṭāshkubrīzādah (*Miftāḥ,* 2:417) preferred the term *adawāt* which they qualified in much the same manner as I-H by noting that this meant the particles and the adverbs, nouns, and verbs that resemble them. Other scholars such as al-Zarkashī (*Burhān,* 4:175) used both terms. Of particular interest in this connection is that the term *adawāt* is normally associated with adherents of the Kufan 'school', which was not only used much earlier on in the Arabic linguistic tradition, but which we are tempted to conjecture would not at that time have covered these extra categories. Indeed, Owens has established (1990: 161) that al-Farrā', the famous Kufan grammarian, employs the term *adaat* but only rarely, and that he certainly does not distinguish between this term and *ḥarf.* However, according to Owens (ibid.: 197) Abū Bakr al-Anbārī (d.328/939) uses the term *adaat* in his *Kitāb al-Mudhakkar wa l-Mu'annath* as a means of differentiation, i.e., he uses it for those words that 'occur initially, do not occur with a preposition, and must be followed by the topic', such as *law*, *layta*, *hal* and *inna*.[4]

Let us cast a glance now at the various assessments of the role of the particles offered by the modern Western linguistic tradition. The deployment of rubrics such as 'empty forms' (Lyons 1981:47-48) to categorise words like 'the', 'of', 'and', or 'to', as opposed to 'full' forms for what could be described as proper nouns, verbs or adjectives; for instance (/man/, /came/, /green/), certainly suggest a subordinate status for the particle within the language system. What is meant, in fact, is that this class of words generally carries less meaning than the full word forms. Lyons adds that alternative expressions to empty forms include 'structural', 'form' or 'function' words, of which the latter would seem to be particularly appropriate to the medieval Arabic situation. There is little doubt that the prevalent view in both Western and medieval Muslim literature that the immediate importance of particles lies in their affecting the meaning of what surrounds them in the sentence, viz., that their distribution relies to a large extent on the syntactic rules of a given language, fits this description. However, we would suggest that the analogy ends here for the time being for two reasons. First, although it is fair to say that some of these so-called empty word forms in English (and other languages) are devoid of even a grammatical meaning, which may be proven in their frequent omission from headlines and telegrams (Lyons 1981:46), for instance, it is also clear from I-H's section on elision in Chapter Five of ML that the same phenomenon can occur in the Arabic language with some of the particles (ML 2:635-45 esp.), although the reconstruction of those elided items by *taqdīr*, or their suppression by *iḍmār*, ensures that the underlying meaning is never far away.[5] Second, we have already seen on several occasions so far how important each individual particle was within the Muslim conception of meaning. In this connection Weiss (1976:27) affirms that so far as the Muslim philologists were concerned all particles were bearers of meaning to a degree, even if that meaning was essentially in something else. He notes that 'the notion that some particles function as pure markers, having no semantic value at all, was apparently never seriously considered'.

Although the Arabic situation may well be concurrent with that of many Western languages inasmuch as this particular category of words did not have a proper independent meaning, it would be unwise to conclude that they had no independent meaning, be it lexical or grammatical, merely because they do not relate directly to what we might refer to as worldly objects or tangible concepts (direct referents). The former view is certainly compounded by evidence which has been passed down concerning the Stoic doctrine, for example, of the classification of the parts of speech in which anything other than nouns or verb, which were considered to be elements of *logos*, viz., 'significant utterances or sounds', were categorised as elements of *lexis*, i.e., 'an utterance (or sound) composed of letters...presumably on the grounds that these have no meaning in themselves but depend for it on the nouns and verbs' (Long 1971:61).[6]

In Chapter Two of this study it was suggested that the treatment of the particles by the medieval Muslim scholars demonstrated without doubt a sophisticated approach to the study of language. It was also pointed out that whilst early Western dictionaries did not contain detailed information on these so-called empty forms (hard words), the Arabic situation was very different. However, there is evidence now that Western dictionaries have, in some cases, made good this deficiency and this enables us to make a brief, but interesting, comparison between the definition of a particle taken at random from a Concise English Dictionary, and one of the meanings given by I-H in ML (which as was stated earlier is not a dictionary as such) for the corresponding particle. A fundamental premise for this comparison is an agreement with the view propounded by Robins (1980:20) that the meaning of particles and their concomitants, which we may say rarely occur in isolation, can only be adequately described by 'saying how they are typically used as part of longer sentences and how those sentences are used'. If we compare the following modern definition of the word 'the':

> 'applied to a person or thing or persons or things already mentioned, implied, or definitely understood' (Concise English Dictionary, 1167)

with one of the meanings of the definite article *al* given by I-H in ML:

> '(the definite article) of indicating previous knowledge ... its accompanying part is known because it has already been mentioned (*fa l-'ahdiyya ... an yakūna maṣḥūbuhā ma'hūdan dhikriyyan*) (ML 1:50),

we find an extraordinary resemblance between the two descriptions. That such definitions can be found in the Muslim literature even earlier than ML, however, gives some indication of how advanced was the thinking on linguistic matters at that time.

A particularly appealing and felicitous description of the problem of defining the status of pronouns, articles, prepositions and other 'minor parts of speech' has been afforded by Ullmann (1962:35). He argues that these parts of speech are 'words in some respects and mere grammatical tools in others'. Now, nowhere does the function of this class of words appear more as grammatical tools than in some of the works of I-H, not least in ML, and even more emphatically perhaps in his short work *al-I'rāb...*, a much shorter and more concise work, in which he summarises twenty of the most important types of particles (although he calls them words) required by the *mu'rib* (*kalimāt yaḥtāju ilayhā l-mu'rib*) (*I'rāb*, 115) in a manner redolent of, say, a description of the essential requirements of a tool kit! Indeed, it is not difficult to perceive the striking resemblance between Ullmann's use of the word tool here and the Arabic word *adawāt* which also means 'tools' in some contexts.

The importance of the particle in a syntactic and semantic context was underlined earlier during the discussion of *ta'alluq*, where a correct understanding of the meaning of the particle was a prerequisite for a proper interpretation of the sentence in which it appeared. This gives an illustration too of why such a class of words is normally referred to as syncategorematic as opposed to categorematic, or synsemantic as opposed to autosemantic. This applies very much to Western languages too.[7] Needless to say that in each case the former is (fully) meaningful only when it occurs in a sentence, in other words it is context-bound, whereas the latter type is meaningful by itself. A description of the perceived function of the particle according to the earlier Arab grammarians can be found in Frank (1981:291) who notes that 'the meaning of a given particle is that which it contributes to the basic phrase or sentence, as it functions syncategorematically within the sentence by virtue of its syntactic relation to one or another of the grammatical units or to the sentence as a whole'. This description serves to uphold the argument being made here that the role of these syncategorematic words should not be underestimated. We saw earlier how they are in fact nothing less than 'fundamental elements in the process of signification' (Eco 1976:67).

The preceding discussion has attempted to acknowledge in a general fashion the importance of the particle in both Western languages and, in this context, Arabic. In addition we have seen how the particles constitute part of a class of words that was, and remains, somewhat difficult to define. It is now time to extend the references made to the particles throughout this work so far, and to look more specifically at the importance of this class of words in the Islamic literature, culminating in a detailed study of the particles as viewed by I-H in ML, with some reference to other similar works of the medieval period.

The discussion of the particle amongst scholars in the medieval Islamic literature spanned several centuries and was accorded varying importance by those who tackled the issue. It was, of course, a subject of immense importance to anyone involved in a study of any part of the Arabic language which involved syntax; for this reason one can find information on the particle in all the grammar books from *al-Kitāb* through to ML and beyond. It is generally held that the particles 'make their contribution to the grammar of sentences rather than to their referential meaning' (Jackson 1980:143). This would explain in part why they are of great interest to the grammarian, and why they featured so frequently in the Arabic grammatical literature. What is at issue here, however, is the distinctions that may be drawn between one scholar's analysis of them and another. It is no coincidence that the particles were a part of speech which appealed to the linguistic sensibilities of the rhetoricians like al-Jurjānī who demonstrated their semantic and even pragmatic values to fascinating effect in parts of his *Dalā'il.* I-H also devoted considerable interest to this aspect of the particles in ML, although perhaps in not so much detail. Nonetheless, even if he sometimes fell well short of the profound conclusions of al-Jurjānī [8] there is more than enough evidence to show that the particles held a unique place for him.

As we saw earlier, the position of the particles in medieval Arabic was that such rule-based definitions as they were accorded were equally at home in a dictionary as in a grammar. In a way the recording nature of Islamic literature created a situation in which the grammar books and dictionaries complemented each other by fulfilling the role of preserving language and, therefore, the quintessence of the Islamic religion. This last point brings us briefly to the works of the legal theorists which represent another significant category of Islamic literature in which the particles underwent considerable study. It hardly needs to be stated that the unquestionable theological dimensions of much of the linguistic debate of the medieval period was paralleled by its legal significance, given that the Qur'ān also represents a sacred law. The legal importance of a firm understanding of the language has been neatly put by Weiss (1984:15) who notes that 'if someone is going to determine what the law requires, he must be versed in the language of those instruments or sources in which the law is embodied'. Eminent legal theorists such as al-Āmidī (*Iḥkām,* 1:85ff esp.; 2:46ff.), al-Baṣrī (*Mu'tamad,* 1:38ff. esp.), Ibn Qayyim al-Jawziyya (*Badā'i',* 1:passim), or al-Ghazālī (*Mustaṣfā,* 1:228ff. esp.), all demonstrated an acute interest in the function of the particle. These individuals are not unique amongst legal theorists, however. In fact, the setting out of linguistic premises appears to have been one of the priority tasks of the jurisprudent in any work on the law, although as we saw earlier from the dissatisfaction expressed by Ibn Fāris, the descriptions of the particles carried out by some lawyers were not necessarily exempt from the charge of inadequacy. At any rate, it is often in this type of work that we are furnished with some of the most pertinent explanations of, or allusions to, the importance of the particle. For instance, Ibn Qayyim (*Badā'i',* 1:51) tells us that 'speech is based in its entirety on certain parts being connected to others, such as the tying (*irtibāṭ*) of the adjectival appositives (*tawābi'*) to the nouns they follow ... (and the category of) exception (*istithnā'*), (for example) cannot stand alone but is only acceptable when it is tied to what precedes it'. Admittedly in the second part of this quotation Ibn Qayyim is referring to the grammatical category of exception as opposed to the particle of exception, but the underlying argument is effectively one and the same; that so long as the full meaning of particles is reflected in what surrounds them in a given sentence, their pivotal role in the language is unequivocal. The importance of the particle as set out by al-Ghazālī (*Mustaṣfā,* 1:229) becomes even more marked when he notes that '...(an understanding of) legal issues rests on them (particles), and the need for them is very great'.

Before proceeding to a general survey of the grammarians' view of the particle it is perhaps worth noting briefly a couple of slightly different approaches to the subject afforded by two of the illustrious rhetoricians mentioned previously, al-Jurjānī and al-Yamanī. In his discussion the latter notes that the secret of the particles lies, in the main, in what is related to the science of *i'rāb*; that is to say, it falls within the domain of the grammarian. However, he selects a number of particles (*Ṭirāz*, 2:200ff.) which he considers to be an intrinsic part of *balāgha* 'rhetoric' and *faṣāḥa* 'eloquence': these include *innamā*, the particle of 'restriction', *inna*, the particle of 'affirmation', and *mā*, *lā*, *lam* and *lan*, particles of 'negation'. It can be assumed that these particles have been singled out because they offer clear evidence of the influential role of the particle in conveying the full meaning of a sentence. In his own inimitable fashion al-Jurjānī (*Dalā'il*, 6-7) reaches the heart of the issue concerning the axiomatic function of the particle, with his penetrating description which may be summarised as follows. There are three ways in which the particle is (semantically) connected to the noun and the verb:

i) where it mediates between the two, namely as a preposition which makes verbs transitive that would not be so without it; for instance, the *bā'* in *marartu bi zaydin* 'I passed by Zayd'.

ii) where it makes a (semantic) connection of coordination (*'aṭf*) in which the second noun functions grammatically like the first; for instance, *jā'a zaydun wa 'amrun* 'Zayd and 'Amr came', and *ra'aytu zaydan wa 'amran* 'I saw Zayd and 'Amr'.

iii) where it makes a (semantic) connection of the whole sentence, such as the negative particle, or interrogative, or conditional sentences; for instance, in the sentence *mā kharaja zaydun* 'Zayd did not go out' the *mā* does not negate 'going out' altogether, but only Zayd's 'going out'.

These interesting observations notwithstanding, however, there is much more to be said on the rhetoricians' views on the particle which are unfortunately beyond the scope of this study.

Before moving on to the main theme of this chapter which will concentrate on the grammarians' view of the particle, and in particular that of I-H in ML, it is worth noting one final, pertinent description of the significance of the particle made by the lexicographer Ibn Sīda (d.458/1065) (*Mukhaṣṣaṣ*, 14:45). He affirms the following:

'The particles of meaning are, of necessity, the smallest part of speech, yet the most widely used one because they are required by the verb and the noun, or the sentence. However, these other categories (i.e., the noun and the verb) are different because they can stand by themselves. These particles are like the machine (*āla*), and the other two parts (i.e., the verb and noun) have become the deed (*al-ʿamal*) for which the machine and its actions have been prepared'.

Of especial interest in these remarks is not only the 'work' metaphor which underlines the onerous duty performed by the particle at all times, but also the reference to the machine, whose Arabic word *āla* may also be translated as 'tool'. This term echoes the use of *adawāt* 'tools' which we saw earlier.

So far as the grammarians were concerned the final consensus on the function of the particle was in fact that it signified a meaning in something else (cf. al-Zajjājī, *Īḍāḥ*, 54; al-Zamakhsharī, *Mufaṣṣal*, 283). This definition does necessitate further qualification, however, because of the feeling amongst some that the particles were not totally devoid of meaning when they stood alone. Indeed, an objection to this definition noted by al-Suyūṭī (*Ashbāh*, 2:4) was raised by the grammarian Ibn al-Naḥḥās and supported by one of no less standing than Abū Ḥayyān. They claimed that the particle did indicate a meaning in itself. If this opinion is not taken as a direct contradiction to the standard view, but as an indication of the uncertainty over the exact status of the particle, it lends further conviction to the overall value of the particle within the Arabic language system which we have been attempting to stress throughout this study.

One further point should be made here concerning the perceived relationship between the particle and the noun. Some scholars claimed that there was very little difference between the noun and the particle in terms of their respective relationship with other components of the sentence. al-Zajjājī (*Īḍāḥ*, 49)notes the following:

'It has been said that the noun signifies its nominatum (*musammāhu*) but does not convey a communicative meaning (in isolation) until it is connected to a noun like it, or a verb or sentence...likewise the particle: if you mention it, it signifies the meaning for which it was established. But it does not convey a communicative meaning by your mentioning it until you connect it with something to complete its meaning. In this regard there is no difference between the noun and the particle.'

The issue becomes at once clearer and more complex if we examine the views of two eminent grammarians, Ibn Yaʿīsh and al-Astarābādhī. The latter reiterates the former's view that certain nouns convey a meaning in something else, such as the interrogative nouns (*asmā' al-istifhām*) or conditional nouns (*asmā' al-sharṭ*). It was already pointed out by Ibn Yaʿīsh that these nouns also convey a meaning in themselves in terms of their 'noun-ness' (*bi ḥukm al-ismiyya*); for example, *ayna* signifies 'place', *kayfa* signifies 'condition', *man* signifies 'someone rational', and *mā* signifies 'something non-rational'. In other words, they bear the status of a noun inasmuch as they signify the nominatum, viz., the meaning for which they were established, and the status of a particle because they convey a meaning 'in something else'. One can only identify them as signifying interrogation or condition, for instance, by interpreting them as particles (*ʿalā taqdīr ḥarfayhimā*). To put this more clearly, *man*, for instance, implies the meaning of *in*, the particle of condition, and links the conditional and result clause in, for example, *man yaqum aqum maʿahu* 'Whoever stands up I shall stand up with him'. Ibn Yaʿīsh adds that the particle *bā'*, for example, does not properly signify *ilṣāq* 'adhesion' until it is added to the following noun; thus the meaning of *ilṣāq* cannot be attained when the *bā'* stands alone.[9] Perhaps a poignant remark made by Ibn Yaʿīsh (*Sharḥ,* 8:150) on the subject of *istifhām* 'interrogation' puts this whole issue into a neat perspective. He notes that 'since interrogation is one of the meanings (in language), tools (*adawāt*) to convey that meaning became essential, and the particles were posited to convey meanings'.

It was possibly in the light of the ambiguity surrounding the exact status of the particle that al-Astarābādhī (*Sharḥ,* 1:36) chose to modify the earlier definition of the particle, viz., *mā dalla ʿalā maʿnan fī ghayrihi* 'what indicates a meaning in something else' to *lā yadullu illā 'alā ma'nan fī ghayrihi* 'only indicates a meaning in something else'. It is tempting to conjecture that the rationale behind this lies in the evidence set forth in the discussion by Ibn Ya'īsh. In other words, if the interrogative and conditional nouns, for instance, indicate a meaning both in themselves and in something else, then the particle must, in essence, be something that can only indicate a meaning in something else. In order not to labour the point, the final word in this connection must rest with al-Suyūṭī (*Ashbāh,* 3:2-3) who says the following:

> 'We can understand from both the noun and the verb when they stand alone, the essence of what is understood by them when they are put into a construction. This is different from the particle because the meaning understood from it in a construction is more complete (*atammu*) than when it stands alone'.

The value and relevance of the foregoing discussion may be seen in two conclusions which can be drawn from all this. First, it is now easier to comprehend why I-H did not restrict his analysis in ML to the particles, but also included nouns, adverbs, and even verbs which resemble them, notwithstanding the fact that an explicit debate as to what constitutes a particle and its concomitants is sadly lacking in ML. Second, although the balance of the argument about the status of the particle seems to suggest that its main significance lay in its relationship to everything around it in a sentence, al-Suyūṭī's suggestion above that the meaning of a particle is 'more complete' in context with other items indicates that it was not wholly meaningless when standing as an isolated entity.

A few other general points about the ingredients of the particle will be made here. As we have just seen it is generally held to be a part of speech requiring a verb or a noun within its context in order to fulfil its real value, except in specific cases where the verb has been elided and the particle alone is used, such as *balā* or *na'am* (e.g., al-Zamakhsharī, *Mufaṣṣal,* 283) in response to a statement or question. The particle can be neither a predicate, nor can it be predicated; likewise speech can only be completed with a noun or a verb (Ibn al-Sarrāj, *Mūjaz* 27). In addition to these considerations what were the criteria which the grammarians had at their disposal to differentiate between a particle and a noun? In other words, how could I-H in ML, for instance, decide that certain *mufradāt* are in fact nouns? He is able to apply some universals of grammar in this regard which assist him in identifying that *mahmā* 'whatever', for example, is a noun (in certain contexts at least) because of the presence of a pronoun later on in the sentence to refer back to it; particles do not require a relating pronoun (ML 1:330). Similarly, *maʿa* 'with' must be a noun (in certain contexts) because it can take nunation (*tanwīn*) (ML 1:333). Throughout I-H's analysis of the particles one reaches the conclusion that their ultimate grammatical status was often indeterminate, with different grammarians admitting of various interpretations. Perhaps this lack of a precise definition enabled I-H to incorporate a wider range of this type of words than some of his predecessors who wrote extensively on the particles, such as al-Murādī (*al-Janā*) who does not include many words like *bayda* 'other than, on account of', *thumma* 'then', *ghayr* 'non-, other than' and *kayfa* 'how', which are indisputably not particles. More will be said on this later. At this juncture it is hoped that the preceding pages have illustrated why the application of the term particle with regard to the medieval Arabic situation is not a wholly satisfactory one, even if it suffices as a quasi-generic term in the absence of a more suitable one.

Given the unequivocal importance of the particle and its concomitants, therefore, it is perhaps a little surprising that relatively few works devoted exclusively to the subject have come down to us. Although a detailed study of some of these extant works is regrettably beyond the realm of duty here, considerable benefit can be gained from setting ML in context with some of those works by making scant reference to them here. Three of the earliest extant works on the particle reflect a trend which began in the fourth century A.H. and continued for almost a century. The first of these works is the *Ḥurūf al-Maʿānī* of al-Zajjājī, a useful but rather short and brief work which at least gives us an insight into how the importance of these words as a separate issue had been recognised, even if al-Zajjājī failed to categorise them into a neat and cohesive form. The layout of the particles in this small work is arbitrary, and the amount of information provided on each particle is scant. The second of the three works is the *Kitāb Ma'ānī al-Ḥurūf* by al-Rummānī (d.384/994). a much more detailed and useful work which seems to have inspired the treatise by al-Harawī (d.415/1024) called *Kitāb al-Uzhiyya fī 'Ilm al-Ḥurūf.* In this work al-Harawī appears to have developed the more logical and systematic approach begun by al-Rummānī. It was not until some three to four centuries later that the next group of tracts on this subject appeared, although in terms of the level of sophistication reached in these works one could say that it had been worth the wait. The three principal extant works of that period, in addition to I-H's ML, are the *Raṣf al-Mabānī* of al-Mālaqī (d.702/1302), the *Jawāhir al-Adab* by al-Irbilī (d.741/1340), and *al-Janā l-Dānī* by al-Murādī (d.749/1348).

Of particular interest here is that all three writers lived within the lifetime of I-H. This has inevitably led to speculation about which writers influenced the others, since there is often conclusive evidence to show that a degree of borrowing of ideas took place. What is fairly certain is that by the time this collection of treatises had been compiled there was little more to be said on the role of the particle in the Islamic scheme of things. Within these works, though, are to be found some very interesting differences of opinion and variations of terminology; some of these will be examined shortly. In the meantime it is worth noting the different layout adopted by each writer which may in itself lead to some worthwhile conclusions, or at least initiate a degree of speculation.

With the exception of al-Zajjājī and al-Harawī, the scholars mentioned above who devoted complete works to the study of the particle followed a specific methodology which was aided, to a large extent, by the manner in which they presented their material. Moreover, there is at least one very significant difference between the way in which material on the particle is presented in traditional grammars which cover every aspect of the grammatical system, and these more specialised works. In conventional grammar books the particles are presented in a piecemeal fashion, and in some cases under many different rubrics. They are examined in terms of their grammatical and syntactic function, but are located in various sections under such headings as *ḥurūf al-iḍāfa* 'particles of annexation', *ḥurūf al-'aṭf* 'coordinating particles', or *ḥurūf al-nafy* 'particles of negation', for instance. Given that many of the particles possessed several meanings, it was not unusual for them to be discussed under several different headings. Ibn Ya'īsh (*Sharḥ*, 8:15-16; 102-103), for example, discusses the particle *ḥattā* within the sections on 'particles of annexation' and' coordinating particles'. Not only does this particular layout create difficulties for the user who wishes to consult the meanings and function of a given particle, but the arbitrary categorisation often adopted within these sub-sections further complicates matters.

On the other hand, a much more logical user-friendly format was set out by al-Rummānī who was apparently influenced by the Aristotelian approach to studies of the particle (*Ma'ānī*, 24). He classified the particles according to the number of their constituent consonants, and this pattern was subsequently followed by al-Murādī and al-Irbilī. In contrast I-H appears to have been influenced by al-Mālaqī who opted for the alphabetical arrangement which might well have been received at that time as a revolutionary aid for memorising the particles and their meanings. This was undoubtedly the principal aim behind that system as we have already seen, presenting them like 'troops on the parade ground', or in what is tantamount to a 'linguistic straitjacket' (Harris 1980:134). Let us look in a little more detail at some of the principles on which these works appear to have been founded.

In the introduction to al-Rummāni's work, the editor notes (p.24) that the author was concerned mainly with what operates upon a sentence (*'āmil*), and what does not (*hāmil*). He adds that al-Rummānī analysed not only the *ḥurūf al-ma'ānī* but also the *adawāt*. In effect, then, he undertook to examine, for instance, what was either a particle or a noun, such as *'an*; this raises a number of points of interest. First, it suggests that a firm idea was already developing of the complexity involved in defining the exact status of words of this nature. Second, it is interesting that the editor uses the term *adawāt* in exactly the same way as it was employed by some of the medievalists, even though al-Rummānī did not use the word himself. Moreover, it appears that the complex nature of the particles and their concomitants created a problem which has not been fully resolved until now. Thus we find the translation of *adawāt* as 'particle' in a modern Arabic dictionary,[10] even though in the medieval period at least there is little doubt that the term was employed to incorporate more than just the particles. The evidence adduced by Ibn Ya'īsh earlier which gave us an illustration of the real function of the *adawāt* as 'tools' should suffice to determine this fact. We may recall that their function is specifically to convey the meaning of a concept, such as *istifhām,* which may be conveyed equally by a noun or anything resembling a particle. Third, there are several inconsistencies to be found in al-Rummānī's work (as indeed there are in all of these major works): why, for example, does he include verbs resembling particles, like *khalā* and *ḥāshā*, but omit important nouns such as *kull*? Notwithstanding this last point, al-Rummānī's work is of considerable value, not least because he already appears to be tackling some of the more rhetorical aspects of the particles in addition to the purely grammatical features. He acknowledges, for example, that the meanings of the *hamza* include *inkār* 'denial', *tawbīkh* 'reprimand' and *istirshād* 'seeking guidance' (*Ma'ānī*, 24).

The pioneering work of the three later major tracts on the particle mentioned above is that of al-Mālaqī. There seems little doubt that this work influenced the later writers to varying degrees, and that the alphabetical format which he adopted might have been the inspiration for I-H to chose this method in ML. Indeed, to facilitate the learning of these particles (by rote, presumably) and to make their assimilation an easier process had already been acknowledged as a main objective by al-Mālaqī (*Raṣf*, 2). It is in this work that we are presented for the first time with a detailed view of the diverse opinions of some of the *'ulamā'* on certain particles. In a climate where it was apparently not always deemed necessary to disclose the source of one's ideas if they were not original, it is not wholly surprising that I-H mentions al-Mālaqī by name on only a handful of occasions; and even then most of these references are made in connection with a contradictory viewpoint offered by I-H (e.g., ML 1:20,55,229,276,336). Moreover, with the exception of a rare reference to al-Harawī I-H eschews any mention of the scholars who wrote on this subject. In contrast, al-Murādī mentions al-Mālaqī on at least forty occasions in his *al-Janā*. It is tempting to suggest that if I-H did intend to produce the definitive work on the syntax of Arabic, which of course included a major contribution to the study of the particle, he would not have wished to give the impression that other works had been a source of motivation or even assistance to him in this objective.

Unfortunately it is not possible within the scope of this present study to examine the extent to which some of these scholars influenced others by their writings. Such a subject would, nonetheless, undoubtedly merit further examination, not least because amongst the similarities one can find many differences, particularly in the area of terminology. Of exceptional interest is the work by al-Irbilī who, at first glance, appears to have adopted a more philosophical approach to the subject, borne out by some penetrating notes on *waḍʿ*. The editor of that work advances the firm conviction (*Jaw*, 5) that both al-Murādī and I-H were influenced by some of his ideas, and it is significant that al-Murādī opted for the same style of presentation by arranging the particles according to the number of constituent consonants, as we saw earlier.

Chronologically, then, I-H was the last in this line of writers who dealt with the particle in such depth. According to his own introduction to ML we see that he began writing it just a few years after the death of al-Murādī. If we assume, therefore, that he did have access to this work - and it will be demonstrated later that there is little doubt of this - he was certainly writing from a position of strength. Perhaps it was the tangible and self-contained nature of the particle which above all inspired the production of these works. In addition to this, in comparison to the number of nouns and verbs in the Arabic language their number was relatively few. This point was made even during the medieval period by the legal theorist al-Zarkashī (*Burhān*, 4:291) who suggested that this fact accounted for the significant amount of attention accorded to the particles by the grammarians. At that time, however, it appears that the need to compile separate books on the subject was not taken seriously; al-Zarkashī adds that it was only for nouns and verbs that separate works were required in the form of dictionaries. At all events, let us turn now to some of the factors which interested I-H in his analysis of the particles in ML, with initial cross-referencing to some of the important treatises mentioned above.

In addition to the emergence of the alphabetical form of presentation, one of the most salient differences between some of those major works on the particle, particularly the later ones, and the treatment of the particles by the grammarians as just one of the parts of speech, is that certain words are simply not included by the latter group. On balance ML is the most useful of the former category in this regard because of the extent to which I-H went in incorporating all the *mufradāt*, which included those nouns and adverbs and even verbs which resembled particles, but which required a special explanation. A clear pattern emerges, in fact, from a brief comparison between the treatises specialising in the particle concerning words whose status is undeniably not a particle, but either a verb, noun or adverb. The word *kayfa*, for example, can only ever be a noun; for this reason I-H is the only writer to record it. Likewise I-H is unique amongst his contemporaries in discussing the word *kull*, although it may be found in al-Zajjājī's short contribution. Words which can only be either a noun or an adverb, such as *maʿa* or *ʿinda* are also to be found only in ML. In general al-Murādī adheres to the rubric of *ḥurūf*, although we find a discussion of *ʿasā* which is only accorded the status of a verb, and *mahmā* which can only generally be a noun. On the other hand, all the major works include any word which admits of two (or more) interpretations, provided that at least one of those possibilities is a *ḥarf*, such as *ʿalā* which can be either a particle or a noun. There was even a place for *laysa* with some scholars because it was claimed that it could be particle and not a verb.[11] To give one illustration of I-H's methodological criteria for determining that a word is a noun, for example, and not a particle or verb, we may cite the case of *kayfa* (ML 1:204ff.). He advances two reasons why *kayfa* can only be a noun, using the situational example *kayfa kunta* 'How were you?': first, it cannot be a particle because it can be used as a predicate (*li l-ikhbār bihi*), and second, it cannot be a verb because it can be followed immediately by another verb which would be unacceptable in the Arabic language.

It is worth remaining with *kayfa* for the time being to underline the importance of its inclusion in a work like ML. After all, *kayfa* occurs frequently in the Qur'ān and in this respect is no less significant than any of the other words of its kind. I-H notes that *kayfa* can assume a conditional (*sharṭ*) or an interrogative (*istifhām*) sense. In the former case the essential requirement is that the two verbs concur in both *maʿnan* 'meaning' and *lafẓ* '(grammatical) form', but that neither should be in the jussive mood, unlike most other conditional situations. Therefore you can say *kayfa taṣnaʿu aṣnaʿu* 'Whatever you do I shall do', but you cannot say *kayfa tajlisu adhhabu* 'Wherever you sit I will go', since that does not make sense. With regard to the interrogative *kayfa* there are two kinds; one which conveys the literal meaning, such as *kayfa zaydun* 'How is Zayd ?', and the other which carries the figurative meaning, as in Sūra II vs.26: *kayfa takfurūna bi allāh* ? 'How do you disbelieve in God?'. In this example the use of the word *kayfa* brings out the meaning of *taʿajjub* 'astonishment' on the understanding that a disbelief in God is simply not possible.

We should recall at this stage the axiomatic conclusion drawn by the majority of medievalists that the meaning of a particle was, in essence, to be found in 'something else'. The example of *kayfa* here raises an interesting issue: does one assume that the same applies to concomitants of the particle like nouns and adverbs ? If the preceding example is used as a gauge the answer to this question must be yes. The inevitable relationship between grammatical status and meaning is further revealed in I-H's discussion of *kayfa* as a *ḥāl* 'circumstantial' noun (ML 1:205-6), in, for instance, *kayfa jā'a zaydun* 'How did Zayd come ?'. The significance of this does not become clear until I-H affirms that *kayfa* may also occur as a *mafʿūl muṭlaq* 'absolute object' when it appears to be a *ḥāl.* To support his point I-H cites one recurring verse from the Qur'ān, Sūra LXXXIX vs.5: *kayfa faʿala rabbuka* 'how thy Lord did'. There is a theological issue at stake in the interpretation of *kayfa* here, since it can not be a circumstantial of the agent who is God because one is forbidden to describe God with the concept of *kayfiyya* 'how-ness'. I-H proposes that the only meaning can be 'What deed did your Lord do ?' (*ayya fiʿl faʿala rabbuka?*), with the pre-posing of the absolute object.

Although this study has sought from the outset to prove that I-H showed considerable interest in semantic issues, it has never been the intention to overlook the formal considerations which were inevitable in the circumstances. We have to remember that much of his work represents a response to exegetical problems which are unlikely to have warranted or even permitted any scholar to develop what we might call a theory of semantics.

Nonetheless, as we have seen, and shall continue to witness, the two notions of form and meaning appear to run concurrently throughout ML, with a characteristic leaning more towards one than the other at various junctures. Whilst the discussion of some particles appears to be founded more on semantic interests, there are other occasions when formal considerations appear to take precedence. One such case is the verb *ʿasā* about which we learn that its basic meaning is *al-tarajjī fī l-maḥbūb* 'looking forward to something desired, or *al-ishfāq fī l-makrūh* 'shunning something detested' (ML 1:151-54; cf. Wright 1933 2:15,107). I-H cites an example of where both meanings occur in Sūra II vs.212: *wa ʿasā an takrahū shay'an wa huwa khayrun lakum wa ʿasā an tuḥibbū shay'an wa huwa sharrun lakum* 'It may happen that you will hate a thing which is better for you; and it may happen that you will love a thing which is worse for you'. Yet beyond this there is little in the section on *ʿasā* of semantic interest, especially as the remainder of the discussion rests mainly on its grammatical status within various contexts.

Before moving on to a more detailed study of individual particles in ML a useful illustration of I-H's technique of presentation will be given. Although not all particles are discussed within such neatly defined rubrics as the word *idhan* we are in no doubt as to the potential categories which apply to each particle and the like. I-H divides the section on *idhan* into four parts (ML1:20-22), and in each one he assesses a different property of the word. In other words, it is to be regarded in terms of:

(i) its *nawʿ* 'type', i.e., is it a particle or a noun.

(ii) its *maʿnan* 'meaning', i.e., is it for the result of a conditional clause, as Sībawayhi said, in every case or in just some instances.

(iii) its *lafẓ* 'physical form', i.e., does it have a final *alif* or *nūn*.

(iv) its *ʿamal* 'operating value', i.e., does it put the verb into the subjunctive /dependent mood only when it has precedence (*taṣdīr*) in the sentence.

As a continuation of this we have already seen that one of I-H's principal aims in ML was to be as brief and as pertinent to the point in hand as possible in matters of *i'rāb*. Thus he avoids any discussion of the phonetic properties of particles such as the *hamza* which is treated at length by al-Irbilī, for example, in this regard. One of the many aspects about which he informs us is that it is a pharyngeal particle (*ḥarf ḥalqī*). He also provides supplementary phonetic information about particles whose consonants are also letters of the alphabet, such as *bā', sīn* and *wāw* (*Jaw*, 12,34,52,68). Similarly I-H eschews the type of exhaustive preamble on the back ground to the *alif* and its relationship to the meaning of the *hamza* as presented by al-Mālaqī (*Raṣf*, 8-34). The same writer (*Raṣf*, 394) even considers the particle *sīn*, a future marker, in its capacity as an infix of what is known in the West as derived form X of the verb. I-H rarely embarks on a discussion of the morphemic nature of the particles because his overriding concern is with the *mufradāt*, although he was criticised by his commentators for professing to follow this policy even though he discussed some particles which they claimed were *murakkaba* 'composite', as opposed to *basīṭa* 'made up of one part'. One such example of this is *mahmā* which I-H discounts as being made up of two components, *mah* and the conditional *mā* (ML 1:331).

In the same way as the noun contains binding syntactic regulations, so too does the particle. Although I-H does not discuss these under one neat heading one can formulate a profile of its functional limits from information disseminated throughout ML. Its restrictions include the following:

(i) that it cannot operate on a direct object (of a verb) (ML 1:59).

(ii) two particles cannot be coordinated to each other (ML1:60).

(iii) particles are more likely to be superfluous (*ziyāda*) than nouns, although we have already seen that superfluous normally meant emphatic (ML 1:180).

(iv) that they themselves do not have any syntactic status (ML 2:496).[12]

It is now time to turn to a more detailed study of the particles. Given that the main interest of this work is I-H's semantic contribution to grammatical analysis the following discussion will be selective. We are concerned mainly with what I-H had to say on meaning, principally, although not exclusively, in the Qur'ān, with more than a passing interest in what could be considered as an original contribution from I-H. In some cases an interesting piece of information has been documented even if it is likely that I-H borrowed the idea from one of his predecessors. One final decision to be taken was that there would be little merit in merely listing all the individual meanings of a given particle, especially as in some cases they have been listed elsewhere (e.g., Wright 1933 2:147-157 on *al-lām al-mufrada*). It was clearly the meaning of a particle which interested the writers on this subject, even if in some instances those meanings were bound by formal constraints. In fact, so enthusiastic were some of them for their students and future generations to learn those meanings that they even wrote poetic verses to facilitate the rote learning process (e.g., al-Murādī, *al-Janā*, 116,151,325).

The particles in ML

al-alif al-mufrada

It is well-known that the 'literal' meaning of the 'single *alif*' (or *hamza*) is *istifhām* 'interrogation'. Among its most significant devices in this regard is its capacity to be used in the sense of *taṣawwur* 'in request of establishing the individual (concerned with the verb)', as in *a zaydun qā'imun am 'amrun* 'Is Zayd standing or is it 'Amr?'. According to I-H the secret of this rhetorical device is that you know one of them is standing but do not know which. Conversely, the other main function of this particle is *taṣdīq* 'in request of verification', as in, for example, *a zaydun qā'imun* 'Is Zayd standing ?', when you require knowledge of whether he is standing as opposed to, say, sitting (ML 1:15).[13]

The main interest in this section, however, are the 'figurative' usages of the single *alif*. I-H does not claim (ML 1:17) to be the first to acknowledge that one of its figurative uses is *hamzat al-*

taswiya 'the *hamza* of equalization', but he adds supplementary information to that provided by his predecessors when he notes that it is not only employed after the word *sawā'un* 'whether', but also after expressions such as *mā ubālī* 'it makes no difference to me', or *mā adrī* 'I do not know'. He adds that what should be made clear above all is that it is the *hamza* 'which precedes a sentence that can be replaced by a verbal noun' (*al-hamza al-dākhila 'alā jumla yaṣaḥḥu ḥulūl al-maṣdar maḥallahā*). By way of example we may cite Sūra LXIII vs.6: *siwā'un 'alayhim a istaghfarta lahum am lam tastaghfir lahum* 'Equal it is for them whether thou askest forgiveness for them or thou askest not forgiveness for them', which according to I-H becomes *siwā'un 'alayhim al-istighfār aw 'adamuhu*. With regard to the second category above I-H indicates that a similar transformation may take place, such as in the example *mā ubālī a qumta am qa'adta* 'It makes no difference to me whether you stand up or sit down', which becomes *mā ubālī bi qiyāmika aw 'adamihi.* What is happening here, of course, is that the verbal noun is replacing not only the sentence, but the *hamza* itself, without affecting the meaning (al-Damāmīnī, *Sharḥ* 32). The additional information provided here by I-H is useful because it is not to be found in any of the other major works on the particle. It also serves as an illustration that any change in the structure must be accompanied by careful scrutiny of the meaning, a point which I-H makes emphatically in his criticisms of the grammarians (see Chapter Four above).

Another of the figurative aspects of the *hamza* is that of *inkār ibṭālī* 'invalidatory denial' (ML 1:17) in which either what follows it is not real or has never actually taken place, or that he who claims its validity is in fact a liar. This could be exemplified by Sūra XVII vs.42: *a fa aṣfākum rabbukum bi l-banīna wa ittakhadha min al-malā'ikati ināthan* 'What, has your Lord favoured you with sons and taken to Himself from the angels females?' in which the meaning of the verse after the *hamza* is a negative one because the very suggestion being put forward in the verse is preposterous. Conversely, Sūra XXXIX vs.36, for example: *a laysa allāhu bi kāfin 'abdahu* 'Shall God not suffice his servant?', is an illustration of the opposite function in which the negation of the sentence after the *hamza* creates an affirmative meaning. In other words, if the starting point is that what follows the *hamza* is negative in meaning, and that coincides with a negative verb, the whole meaning is affirmative (*nafy al-nafy ithbāt*).[14] The opposite category of the above is *al-inkār al-tawbīkhī* (ML 1:17-18) 'reproachful denial' in which what follows the *hamza* has actually occurred, or where the doer of the act is being reprimanded, as in, for example, Sūra XXXVII vs.94: *a taʿbudūna mā tanḥatuna* 'Do you serve what you hew ?', in which they are being reprimanded for doing just that.

The fourth category of figurative usage discussed by I-H is that of *taqrīr* 'confirmation'. It is employed for soliciting confirmation or an acknowledgement from the person being addressed that a matter did or did not occur. However, perhaps the most important factor to be taken into account in this regard is that the *hamza* must be followed directly by the act or action being asked about, otherwise other considerations come into play which suggest a preoccupation with more pragmatic issues. This could be exemplified by the following situational examples cited by I-H (ML 1:18) in which the person requesting the information must be asking about a different aspect of the question in each case. In the sentence *a ḍarabta zaydan* 'Did you hit Zayd ?' it is clear that the confirmation being sought is the act of hitting. Compare this, however, with *a anta ḍarabta zaydan*, which translates in exactly the same way, but with an emphasis now on the *fāʿil* 'doer/agent' of the act, or *a zaydan ḍarabta* which now requires an interpretation in which the emphasis is on the *mafʿūl* 'object' of the act, viz., the recipient of the hitting. I-H illustrates this category with a customary citation from the Qur'ān which in this case could admit of two interpretations. In Sūra XXI vs.63: *a anta faʿalta hādhā* 'Art thou the man who did this ?', it is possible that the meaning here could be a 'literal interrogative' (*istifhām ḥaqīqī*), on the understanding that they genuinely did not know that the person being addressed was the agent. On the other hand, it could also be of the *taqrīr* type on the assumption that not only did they know who was the agent of the verb, but also that they could not have been enquiring about the act itself, nor seeking a confirmation of it, because the *hamza* does not (directly) precede it. Moreover, the response from Abraham was *bal faʿalahu kabīruhum hādhā* 'No; it was this great one', i.e., the emphasis of his reply was on the agent.[15] What these examples show is that I-H was at times concerned with issues of emphasis and displacement in a sentence which affected the meaning. Indeed, these considerations were not traditionally a part of the grammarians' business, but they help to illustrate that I-H was often interested in matters normally dealt with by the rhetoricians.

an

The first point relevant to our discussion here is the function of *an* as a *mawṣūl ḥarfī* 'relative particle' (ML 1:28-30). In this section I-H revives the important question of whether this particle can be followed directly by a command (*amr*). He appears to agree with Sībawayhi's view that the sentence *katabtu ilayhi an qum* 'I wrote to him to stand up' is permissible, i.e., that the particle can be followed directly by an imperative verb. According to Abū Ḥayyān, however, this is unacceptable because the meaning of command disappears as soon as the verbal construction *an qum* is replaced by the underlying implied verbal noun, viz., *katabtu ilayhi bi l-qiyām.*[16] In this case, according to Abū Ḥayyān the *an* particle in this syntactic position must assume the meaning of *tafsīriyya* 'explanatory'. However, I-H notes that connecting the command verb to the particle and the preceding verb which results in the loss of the imperative element (*al-amriyya*) produces a result which is no different to connecting a past tense or imperfect indicative verb to *an* and the preceding verb, i.e., that once the verbal noun replaces the verb, the 'tense' element is partially lost, as in Sūra XVII vs.76: *law lā an thabbatnāka* 'and had We not confirmed thee', which would become *law lā tathbītunā*, and so on. In the original example above the command element does in fact disappear, but what is really meant is *katabtu ilayhi bi l-amr bi l-qiyām* 'I wrote to him giving him the command to stand up' (al-Damāmīnī, *Sharḥ* 61). Moreover, I-H discounts Abū Ḥayyān's view that the *bā'* in the original example is superfluous (*zā'ida*) by saying that all prepositional particles, irrespective of whether they are superfluous or not, can only precede the noun or what is interpreted as one. In other words, the presence of the *bā'* as a preposition here necessitates an interpretation of the *an qum* clause above as being replaceable by the verbal noun type construction, and not as an explanatory type, especially as prepositions cannot precede explanatory particles.

To continue this important debate on *an* as an explanatory particle, I-H demonstrates some sympathy with the Kufan view that it never assumes this meaning because the explanatory sentence should always convey the essence of (*nafs*) of what precedes it (ML 1:31). For example, when you say *hādhā ʿasjadun ay dhahabun* 'this is gold, that is to say, gold', *dhahab* conveys the essence of *ʿasjad*, viz., they amount to the same thing. By contrast, in the sentence *katabtu ilayhi an qum* the verb 'to stand' does not convey the essence of 'to write'; therefore, how can the particle be explanatory here ? A counter argument to I-H's example is put forward by al-Damāmīnī (*Sharḥ* 67, citing al-Astarābādhī) when he notes that the function of the particle could be explanatory in this example on the basis of the presence of an object (*mafʿūl*) with an underlying expression (*lafẓ*) indicating the meaning of what is being said. In other words, if we take the example *nādaynāhu an yā Ibrāhīm* 'We called him *O Ibrāhīm*', the words *yā Ibrāhīm* constitute an underlying object of *nādaynāhu*, viz., *nādaynāhu bi lafẓ huwa qawlunā yā Ibrāhīm*. By the same token the underlying structure of *katabtu ilayhi an qum* is *katabtu ilayhi shay'an huwa qum* 'I wrote something to him, it is 'stand up'.

On balance, however, I-H does acknowledge that the particle *an* may sometimes occur with the meaning of explanation, and he lists several occasions when this may occur. Yet we are told that there are restrictions to these cases, such as when the sentence preceding the particle *an* must contain the meaning of 'something said' (*qawl*), but must not actually contain the consonants *qāf wāw lām* nor anything related to the root 'to say'. Thus the sentence *qultu lahu an ifʿal* 'I told him, that is to say, do...' is unacceptable because of the absence of the one being addressed when the incident is being recounted. However, I-H agrees with al-Zamakhsharī (ML 1:32) that the *an* particle in Sūra V vs.117: *mā qultu lahum illā mā amartanī bihi an uʿbudū allāha* 'I only said to them what thou didst command me; Serve God...', could be explanatory because of the possible interpretation of the verb 'to say' as 'to command'.

One final point of interest worthy of note in this section is the discussion of an issue concerning the superfluous *an* particle

(ML 1:34-35). In defence of al-Zamakhsharī, I-H dismisses a claim by Abū Ḥayyān that he ascribed the meaning of *ta'qīb* 'immediate consequence' (al-Dasūqī, *Ḥāshiya*, 46) in addition to the common meaning of *tawkīd* 'emphasis' to the particle *an* with regard to a couple of similar verses in the Qur'ān. The two verses in question are Sūra XXIX vs.33: *wa lammā an jā'at rusulunā Lūṭan sī'a bihim* 'When that Our messengers came to Lot he was troubled on their account', and Sūra XI vs 72: *wa lammā jā'at rusulunā Ibrāhīma bi l-bushrā qālū salāman* 'Our messengers came to Abraham with the good tidings; they said, 'Peace!''. According to I-H Abū Ḥayyān misinterpreted what al-Zamakhsharī (*Kashshāf*, 3:205) actually said about these two verses, because the latter neither affirmed nor denied the function of *lammā* in the above verses; rather he notes that the particle *an* assumes the function of emphasis in the former, and confirms that the two actions conveyed by the verbs, viz., the 'coming' of the messengers and the 'being troubled' occurred more or less at one time, i.e., Lot's being troubled followed on immediately from their arrival. I-H adds that the particle *lammā* conveys the meaning of the second verb following on from the first one in any case, whilst the particle *an* is merely an emphasis of that. Furthermore, Abū Ḥayyān appears to have confused the two verses by implying that they are to be found in the same Sūra, possibly because the same words as those in the former verse are to be found in Sūra XI vs.79, but without the particle *an*. A further consideration noted by I-H is that Sūra XI vs.72 does not actually contain the particle *lammā*, in spite of what Abū Ḥayyān said; we can only assume, however, that this is according to some readings (e.g., 'Abd al-Bāqī, *al-Mu'jam al-Mufahras*, 356) where the particle *laqad* occurs, viz., *wa laqad jā'at rusulunā..* I-H's other point of disagreement with Abū Ḥayyān's analysis is that by asserting the extra meaning which al-Zamakhsharī allegedly put forward, he is implying that in Sūra XI vs.72 the greetings must have been delayed after their arrival, due to the absence of the particle *an*. One final consideration which enters the scenario here is that three verses before the occurrence of the particle *an* we find the following in Sūra XXIX vs.30: *wa lammā jā'at rusulunā Ibrāhīma bi l-bushrā qālū innā muhlikū ahli l-madīna* 'And when Our messengers came to Abraham with the good tidings, they said,

We shall destroy the people of this city', in which the *an* does not occur. What I-H suggests with regard to this verse is that the decision to destroy the people of the city did not follow immediately after the arrival of the people, which supports the occurrence of *an* three verses later to emphasize the immediacy of Lot's being troubled.

anna

Of particular interest in this section is I-H's analysis of *anna* plus *mā* to convey the meaning of *ḥaṣr* 'restriction' in the same manner as *innamā*.(ML 1:39-40). Once again he takes Abū Ḥayyān to task for his interpretation of Sūra XXI vs.108: *qul innamā yūḥā ilayya annamā ilāhukum ilāhun wāḥidun* 'Say: It is revealed unto me only that your God is One God'. In the first instance, Abū Ḥayyān claims that only *innamā* can occur with this meaning. Second, he claims that it cannot mean restriction here because this would suggest that the oneness (*tawḥīd*) of God would be the only thing revealed to him. I-H discounts the first claim by citing the verse above, and overrules the second point by indicating that this is an example of limited restriction (*ḥaṣr muqayyad*) because the only ones being addressed are the polytheists. In other words the meaning is that the only thing revealed to him in the verse concerning His Lord-ship is the oneness of God.[17] I-H adds that this interpretation is also known as *qaṣr qalb* 'restriction of reversal' whereby the belief of the person being addressed is reversed.

In relation to the argument set forth above I-H also provides us with an interesting and corrective interpretation of Sūra III vs.138: *wa mā muḥammadun illā rasūlun* 'and Muḥammad is naught but a messenger'. According to Abū Ḥayyān the *mā* must be for negation and the *illā* for restriction, if his original analysis of the particle *annamā* above is correct. However, this would suggest that the description of the Prophet were restricted to his being merely a messenger, which is not the case; rather it is the fact that there was only one Muḥammad, and that when people glorified his death they established for him eternal life. According to I-H this verse represents the category of *qaṣr ifrād* 'restriction of oneness', and again represents an example of *qaṣr qalb* (al-Damāmīni, *Sharḥ*, 85).

am

The most relevant section for our purposes in the discussion of this particle is that which tackles the meanings of the *am munqaṭi'a* 'disjunctive *am*'. This particle has the following three meanings (ML 1:44-45) which are all based on an underlying meaning of *iḍrāb* 'retraction':

(i) 'interrogation' and 'retraction' with the sense of the particle *bal* 'nay, rather' (al-Damāmīnī, *Sharḥ*, 92), and 'retraction' without 'interrogation' with the sense of *bal.*

(ii) 'retraction' with 'invalidatory interrogation' (*istifhām inkārī*).

(iii) 'retraction' with 'requestive interrogation' (*istifhām ṭalabī*).

The first meaning could be exemplified by Sūra XIII vs.16: *hal yastawī l-a'mā wa l-baṣīru am hal tastawī l-ẓulumātu wa l-nūru am ja'alū li allāhi shurakā'a* 'Are the blind and the seeing man equal, or are the shadows and the light equal ? Or have they ascribed to God associates'. According to I-H the first *am* in the verse must be a combination of interrogative and retractive because on a structural level an interrogative cannot immediately precede another interrogative. The meaning of the second *am*, however, is determined by semantic factors, and can only be for retraction here because it affirms their conviction of ascribing partners to God which is, of course, unacceptable.

An example of the second meaning may be found in Sūra LII vs.39: *am lahu l-banātu wa lakum al-banūna* 'Or has He daughters and you sons ?'. I-H points out that the reconstruction of the syntax (*taqdīr*) of this verse gives *bal a lahu al-banātu wa lakum al-banūna* 'rather, does He have daughters and you sons?', which demonstrates a combination of retraction and invalidatory interrogation, since to interpret it without an element of the latter would suggest that God does have daughters, which is absurd.

The third type of meaning is also of some interest, not least because of a significant difference of opinion between I-H (ML 1:45) and al-Harawī (*Uzhiyya*, 136) based on the following line of poetry: *innahā la iblun am shā'un* 'they are either camels or sheep', in which the *taqdīr* according to I-H is *bal a hiya shā'un.* I-H claims that this represents an example of retraction and requestive interrogation; on the other hand, al-Harawī considers this to be an indubitable case of retraction because of the poet's certainty that they are sheep after doubting that they were camels.

al

The definite article *al* received much attention from the medieval scholars who specialized in studies of the particle. Yet in spite of its importance it is perhaps surprising that like so many of the particles only a relatively small amount of information about its meanings and function has been documented in more recent times. One of the most significant elements of the *al* particle is its relationship with previous knowledge (*al-ʿahdiyya*) which has been noted by Wright (1933 2:243), although this sense is developed to a more profound level by I-H. According to I-H (ML 1:50) there are three different types of previous knowledge in this connection:

(i) that which is *maʿhūdan dhikriyyan* 'known because it has already been mentioned' in speech or in the previous sentence and so on. An interesting point here is that one may include within this category a sentence where a pronoun replaces the definite article and its noun, as in, for example, *ishtaraytu farasan thumma biʿtu l-farasa* 'I bought a horse then sold the horse', which becomes *ishtaraytu farasan thumma biʿtuhu* 'I bought a horse then sold it'.

(ii) that which is *maʿhūdan dhihniyyan* 'known by the speaker alone', although there is a case here for claiming that it can be known by the speaker and the listener; the important thing is that it has not been mentioned hitherto (al-Damāmīnī, *Sharḥ*, 106), as in, for instance, Sūra XLVIII vs.18: *idh yubāyiʿūnaka taḥta l-shajara* 'when they were swearing fealty to thee under the tree'. The reference to 'the tree' here is a reminder of what took place at an earlier point in history when God sent down his Shechina[18] upon the believers.

(iii) that which is *maʿhūdan ḥuḍūriyyan* 'known by its presence'. I-H challenges the views of Ibn ʿUṣfūr on the application of this catgory. The latter claims that the aspect of presence only occurs after demonstrative pronouns, as in, for example, *jā'anī hādhā l-rajulu* 'this man came to me', or with the vocative, as in *yā ayyuhā l-rajulu* 'O man!', or with the particle *idhā* of surprise, as in *kharajtu fa idhā l-asadu* 'I went out and there was the lion', or with the noun of the present time, such as *al-āna* 'now'. However, I-H notes that are other occasions involving the idea of presence when the definite article is employed, such as when you are talking to a man who is insulting another at that time, so you say to him *lā tashtum al-rajula* 'Do not insult the man'. In addition, I-H maintains that the use of *al* after the particle of surprise in the example of the lion is not for the identification of something present at the moment of speech, because the lion would not be there when the story is being told.

Having examined the three types of definite article associated with previous knowledge I-H identifies three types of *al* which function as *jinsiyya* 'generic'. These are as follows:

(i) *li istighrāq al-afrād* '(to encapsulate) the totality of the individuals', for which the word *kull* 'all' could be substituted in its literal meaning, as in, for example, Sūra CIII vs.2: *inna l-insāna la fī khusrin illā alladhīna āmanū* 'surely Man is in the way of loss, save those who believe'. In the section on *kull* I-H notes (ML 1:193) that its original posited meaning was *li istighrāq afrād al-munakkar* '(to encapsulate) the totality of undefined individuals'. It is this function that would seem to be in operation in the verse here, viz., each human being is in the way of loss except the believers.

(ii) *li istighrāq khaṣā'iṣ al-afrād* '(to encapsulate) the totality of certain characteristics of individuals', for which *kull* could replace it figuratively, as in *zaydun al-rajulu ʿilman* 'Zayd is the man of knowledge', where Zayd is complete, and every man in terms of his knowledge; similarly the phrase *dhālika l-kitābu* 'that Book' taken from the Qur'ān means that it is every book in terms of its guidance because it constitutes the perfect Book.[19]

(iii) *li ta'rīf al-māhiyya* 'to identify the essence', as in, for instance, Sūra XXI vs.32: *wa ja'alnā min al-mā'i kulla shay'in ḥayyin* 'and of water fashioned every living thing'. For this type the definite article cannot be replaced by the word kull at all because the meaning here is not that every living thing was created from every water.

ammā

This particle has three meanings which are all worth noting here. I-H's initial suggestion that *ammā* is a conditional particle (*ḥarf sharṭ)* (ML 1:56) is somewhat inaccurate, because it soon becomes clear that it merely implies the meaning of the conditional, not that it was posited for that purpose (cf. al-Damāmīnī, *Sharḥ* 120; al-Irbilī, *Jaw*, 515; al-Murādī, *al-Janā*, 482). At any rate, that it assumes a conditional function is indicated because it cannot occur without the particle *fā'* at the beginning of the result clause. I-H cites Sūra II vs.24 as evidence of this: *ammā allādhīna āmanū fa ya'lamūna annahu l-ḥaqqu min rabbihim* 'As for the believers, they know it is the truth from their Lord'. He notes that if the *fā'* were for coordination (*'aṭf*) and not condition here, it would not precede the predicate of the second clause, viz., *ya'lamūna*...because the predicate cannot be coordinated with its topic (*mubtada'*). Moreover, if it were superfluous (*zā'ida*) it could be omitted, but that is not possible here. I-H acknowledges that the proof of this syntactic function of *ammā* had already been advanced by Sībawayhi who, in order to explain the occurrence of *ammā* in the sense of condition (ML 1:57) in this type of sentence, said that the paraphrase of *ammā zaydun fa dhāhibun* 'As for Zayd he is going' is *mahmā yakun min shay'in fa zaydun dhāhibun* 'Whatever the case Zayd is going'.

The second meaning of *ammā* noted by I-H is that of *tafṣīl* 'elaboration', as suggested by Ibn Mālik (al-Murādī, *al-Janā*, 482) and others. According to I-H this applies to the majority of instances when the *ammā* occurs in conjunction with the *fā'*, as in, for example, Sūra II vs.24: *fa ammā alladhīna āmanū fa ya'lamūna annahu l-ḥaqqu min rabbihim wa ammā alladhīna kafarū fa yaqūlūna...* 'As for the believers, they know it is the truth from their Lord; but as for the unbelievers, they say...'. However, there are two sub-categories of this which are essential to note if the parts of the text in the Qur'ān containing this particle are to be fully understood. The first of these possibilities is when the *ammā...fa* should be repeated to contrast the sense of a verse, but it is omitted because the sense of the verse should be sufficient to imply what follows. An example of this is Sūra IV vs.174: *yā ayyuhā l-nāsu qad jā'akum burhānun min rabbikum wa anzalnā ilaykum nūran mubīnan fa ammā alladhīna āmanū bi allāhi i'taṣamū bihi fa sa yudkhilūnahum fī raḥmatin minhu wa faḍlin* 'O men, a proof has now come to you from your Lord; We have sent down to you a manifest light. As for those who believe in God, and hold fast to Him, He will surely admit them to mercy from Him, and bounty...'. I-H affirms that a further *ammā...fa* clause is implied here, viz., as for the unbelievers, they will have..., and so on. The second of these sub-categories involves an omission once more, but on these occasions what follows the original *ammā...fa* construction compensates for the omission, and explains exactly what the meaning would have been in the additional construction, as in, for instance, Sūra III vs.5, where the idea is that an implication follows the verse about those who follow 'ambiguous' verses from the Holy Book in an attempt to divert from the truth, that others actually believe in everything it contains, viz., 'as for others...'.

The third possible meaning of *ammā* is *tawkīd* 'emphasis', which was only mentioned by a small number of scholars, in particular al-Zamakhsharī. He suggested (ML 1:57; cf.*Kashshāf*, 1:261)that the communicative meaning of this particle is to give speech the benefit of emphasis. Therefore, the sentence *zaydun dhāhibun* 'Zayd is going' becomes *ammā zaydun fa dhāhibun* if you want to emphasize his going, or the inevitability of his going, or that he is on the point of going, or even his determination to go. In essence this is little more than a clarification and extension of what Sībawayhi meant, according to I-H.[20]

immā / aw

Although the particle *aw* has thirteen meanings as opposed to the five of *immā*, it shares those five meanings with the latter; this is the focus of our brief analysis here. On the syntactic level I-H was one of a minority of grammarians who held that *immā* was not a coordinating particle, unlike *aw*. A feasible explanation for this is that *immā* always occurs in a pair, and must be repeated; therefore the coordinating function is performed by the *wāw* 'and' particle which always precedes the second *immā* (Carter 1981:284-85). However, it was clearly the meanings of the two particles which interested I-H more. These shared meanings are as follows (ML 1:59-68):

(i) *shakk* 'doubt', as in, for example, *jā'anī immā zaydun wa immā 'amrun* 'Either Zayd or 'Amr came to me', or Sūra XVIII vs.19: *labithnā yawman aw ba'ḍa yawmin* 'We have tarried a day, or part of a day'.

(ii) *ibhām* 'obscurity', where some doubt is left in the mind of the recipient of the information, as in, for example, Sūra IX vs.107: *wa ākharūna murjawna li amri allāhi immā yu'adhdhibuhum wa imma yatūbu 'alayhim* 'And others are deferred to God's commandment, whether He chastises them, or turns towards them', or Sūra XXXIV vs.24: *wa innā aw iyyākum la 'alā hudan aw fī ḍalālin mubīnin* 'Surely, either we or you are upon right guidance, or in manifest error'.

(iii) *takhyīr* 'limited choice', viz., one of two things, but not both, as in, for instance, Sūra XVIII vs.85: *immā an tu'adhdhiba wa immā an tattakhida fīhim ḥusnan* 'either thou shalt chastise them, or thou shalt take towards them a way of kindness'. I-H raises a significant point when he discounts the opinion of Ibn al-Shajarī who claimed that the verse above from Sūra IX was also of this type. Although I-H fails to substantiate the reason for his dismissal of this view it is likely that in the example from Sūra IX, God reserves the right to make that decision, and it is not for Man to speculate. On the other hand, in the example from Sūra XVIII the person responsible for making the decision is no more than a mortal human being.

The particle *aw* occurs in this sense after request (*ṭalab*), as in, for example, *tazawwaj hindan aw uhktaha* 'Marry Hind or her sister', where you may only marry one of them. With regard to this meaning we find I-H once again attempting to deliver a settlement of an issue which has repercussions for the Muslim and his duty towards others. It was argued by some scholars that the idea of connection (*jam'*) was possible within the context of limited choice in Sūra V vs.91: *fa kafāratuhu iṭ'āmu 'asharati masākīna min awsaṭi mā tuṭ'imūna ahlīkum aw kuswatihim aw taḥrīri raqabatin* 'whereof the expiation is to feed ten poor persons with the average of the food you serve to your families, or to clothe them, or to set free a slave', and Sūra II vs.192: *fa fidyatun min ṣiyāmin aw ṣadaqatun aw nusukin* 'then redemption by fast, or freewill offering, or ritual sacrifice'. However, I-H maintains that one's expiation and redemption are not dependent on the carrying out of all three requirements, but only one of each category. Therefore, the idea of connection is not permissible here.

(iv) *ibāḥa* 'unlimited choice', where either option is possible, or both, or even more, as in, for instance, *ta'allam fiqhan wa immā naḥwan* 'learn either legal theory or grammar'. An example of *aw* in this sense is *jālis al-'ulamā'a aw al-zuhhāda* 'sit with scholars or ascetics', where the particle also occurs after request, but with the possibility of connection here. Therefore, in the latter example one may sit with either group of people or both.

(v) *tafṣīl* 'division', as in, for example, Sūra LXXVI vs.3: *immā shākiran wa immā kafūran* 'whether he be thankful or unthankful', where the opposite ideas are expressed. As for the particle *aw*, it appears that the term *taqsīm* was employed by some to convey the sense of division (ML 1:65), as in, for example, *al-kalima ism aw fi'l aw ḥarf* 'a word is either a noun, verb or particle', but *tafṣīl* by others (e.g., al-Mālaqī, *Raṣf*, 132; al-Irbilī, *Jaw*, 257). However, this category was named *tafrīq mujarrad* 'pure differentiation' by Ibn Mālik as in, for instance, Sūra IV vs. 134: *in yakun ghanīyyan aw faqīran* 'whether the man be rich or poor', on the grounds that one of the functions of the particle *wāw* is more suited to the idea of *taqsīm*.

A significant contribution to the question of associative indications (*qarā'in*) and extra-linguistic context (*umūr khārijiyya*) is made by one of the commentators on ML (al-Damāmīnī, *Sharḥ* 143). He observes that the original posited meaning for both *immā* and *aw* was for a choice between one of two or more things (cf. ML 1:67). If it were not for the external considerations mentioned here, and for those noted by I-H (ML 1:67) that the other meanings of *aw* are only understood from external matters (*mustafāda min ghayrihā*), then the category of *ibāḥa* (ex. iv. above) would not be acceptable for either of these particles. I-H acknowledges this point himself at one stage (ML 1:60). Not for the first time on the subject of extra-linguistic considerations, for example, do we witness the unequivocal difference between the approach of the earlier linguists and those of I-H's era (although dependence on these factors developed some time before I-H). I-H adds that it was the earlier grammarians (*mutaqaddimūna)* who held that *aw* had been posited for one of two things or more, thereby implying that the interpretation of the rest of the meanings based on external factors came later.

To conclude the discussion of these two particles, *aw* is arguably a more functional particle than *immā* because it has many more meanings. In fact, it is in the concluding section on *aw* that I-H's concern with meaning comes to the fore once more (ML 1:67). For example, as part of his assessment of the supposed tenth meaning of the particle *aw* being for *taqrīb* 'nearness', I-H affirms that the *aw* in *mā adrī a sallama aw wadda'a* 'I do not know whether he said hello or goodbye' can only be for doubt, or that the sense of *taqrīb* can only be merited if one asserts the resemblance between (the gestures of) greeting and departing. He adds that a case cannot be made for *taqrīb* as such because of the obvious time lapse between the two acts.

At any rate the most important meanings of both particles are shared, and in this sense they are very similar; but there is one essential difference between the two concerning the unique repetition of the latter in speech which is duly noted by I-H. He says (ML 1:61) that 'with *immā* (a piece) of speech is based from its outset on the doubt that (this particle) brings on account of that speech. Therefore it must normally be repeated (in speech). However, with *aw*, when speech begins it is based on certainty (*jazm*), and then (the question of) doubt is raised. Thus it is not repeated'.[21]

illā

It would be fair to say that the function most immediately associated with the particle *illā* is that of *istithnā'* 'exception', as in, for example, Sūra II vs.251: *fa sharibū minhu illā qalīlan* 'But they drank of it, except a few of them', or Sūra IV vs.69: *mā fa'alūhu illā qalilun minhum* 'they would not have done it, save a few of them'. However, the most interesting element in I-H's discussion of this particle, which is most relevant for our purposes here, is that of *illā* in its capacity to function with the meaning of *ghayr* 'other than' (ML 1:70-72).

I-H cites two examples of *illā*, one from the Qur'ān and the other from a situational context, which not only support the immediate argument, but which demonstrate how a situational example can often serve to untangle any theological complexities which may be associated with the meaning of a particular verse of the sacred text. It hardly needs to be reiterated here that this is a common and effective technique of I-H's deployed on many occasions in ML. The example in hand taken from the Qur'ān is Sūra XXI vs.22: *law kāna fīhimā ālihatun illā allāhu la fasadatā* 'Were there gods in earth and heaven other than God, they would surely go to ruin'. The situational example is illustrated by *law kāna ma'anā rajulun illā zaydun la ghulibnā* 'If there had been with us a man other than Zayd we would have been defeated'.

In both of these cited examples there is an issue of meaning (*ma'nan*) and grammatical form (*lafẓ*) to be taken into account. I-H advances two reasons why *illā* in the examples cannot be for exception. In the first example, if this interpretation were proposed on the level of meaning it would imply in the first instance that if they had gods but God was not among them they would have gone to ruin. This would then necessitate that if they had gods, and God was among them, they would not have gone to ruin, but this is not what is meant; rather the intended meaning is that their 'going to ruin' (*fasād*) is caused by their adhering to many gods instead of one God. As for the issue of grammatical form the word *ālihatun* 'gods' is an indefinite plural, and therefore has no generality (*'umūm*). In this case it can not be excepted from, just as you cannot say *qāma rijālun illā zaydan* 'Men got up except Zayd'.

In the second example the word *rajulun* 'man' is indefinite and therefore has no generality, as in the previous instance. On a semantic level it is again incorrect to interpret *illā* for exception. On this occasion such an interpretation would suggest initially that if there were a group with us of which Zayd was not one, we would have been defeated. This would imply that if there were a group with us of which Zayd was one, we would not have been defeated. Now, this latter meaning is perfectly acceptable of course, as I-H notes (ML 2:538), but what is really intended here is that Zayd's presence alone is sufficient for us not to be defeated, and that the presence of anyone other than him would not have sufficed to save us from defeat. I-H's explanation for the above interpretations apparently rests on a self-acknowledged uniqueness, and in support of his claims to originality it must be said that the following explanation is not to be found in any of the other major works on the particle at least.

The most important consideration for the interpretation of *illā* with the sense of *ghayr* is the distinction between two types of *waṣf* 'descriptive element': *mukhaṣṣiṣ* 'specifying' and *mu'akkid* 'emphatic'. According to I-H this descriptive element is made up of the word *illā* itself and what follows it (*fa yūṣafu bihā wa bi tālīhā*). I-H maintains that in the Qur'ānic verse above (Sūra XXI vs.22) this descriptive element must be an emphatic one because it is based on an understanding of 'many (i.e., gods) described by being other than one' (*muta'addid mawṣūf bi annahu ghayr al-wāḥid*). The *ḥukm* 'logical predicament' (Carter 1981:476) for this is that if what follows *illā* contradicts the thing being described by it in terms of its singularity (*ifrād*) (in this case God) and so on, it must be an emphatic descriptive element. On the other hand, the *waṣf* in the situational example must be a specifying one, just as you would say *jā'a rajulun mawṣūfun bi annahu ghayru zaydin* 'a man came described as being other than Zayd'. The logical predicament for the specifying descriptive element is that if what follows *illā* corresponds to what is being described by it, the *waṣf* actually specifies it.

What seems to emerge from all this is that if the descriptive element differs from what precedes it in terms of number or species, for instance, it is to be interpreted as an emphatic one, provided *illā* occurs with the sense of *ghayr*. I-H qualifies this further by recalling an issue discussed by the grammarians concerning the difference between the following two sentences (ML 1:71): *lahu 'indī 'asharatun illā dirhaman* and *lahu 'indī 'asharatun illā dirhamun.* The grammarians agreed that in the first example the speaker is owed nine dirhams, but in the second example he is owed ten. However, according to I-H the secret (*sirr*) of this is that he is owed ten of something, but not dirhams. In other words, every ten of something would be described in this way, so the attribute here, viz., *dirhamun*, is *mu'akkida* 'emphatic' and could be elided (*ṣāliḥa li l-isqāṭ*). What may be inferred from this is that in the first case the *illā* is for exception, whereas in the second one it occurs with the sense of *ghayr*. Moreover, in the second example the descriptive element is emphatic because the dirham is of a different type to the ten things owed.

ilā

Of all the particles *ilā* is amongst those which have received extensive attention from the grammarians, as well as those medieval scholars who specialized in studies of the particles. One plausible explanation for this is that in addition to its one fundamental meaning of *intihā' al-ghāya*, its seven other senses would seem to focus mainly on its capacity to occur with the meaning of other particles, and to replace them by a process of *niyāba* 'substitution'. It is perhaps significant that Sībawayhi and al-Mubarrad only recorded this one main meaning since many of the Basrans apparently did not accept the phenomenon of 'substitution' (ML 1:111; cf. al-Irbilī, *Jaw*, 422, n.1), which entailed the exchange of one particle for another in certain contexts.[22] A further related explanation is even more likely: that the later attention afforded to the question of associative indications (*qarā'in*) offered so many more options for semantic interpretation. In this connection it was al-Mālaqī (*Raṣf*, 80) who once again underlined the fact that it was only the later scholars who recognised the importance of these external considerations in this context.

There are two types of *ilā* which occur with the sense of *intihā' al-ghāya* (ML 1:74). One of these is *zamāniyya* 'temporal', as in, for instance, Sūra II vs.183: *thumma atimmū l-ṣiyāma ilā l-layli* 'then complete the Fast unto the night'; the other type is *makāniyya* 'spatial', as in, for example, Sūra XVII vs.1: *min al-masjidi l-ḥarāmī ilā l-masjidi l-aqṣā* 'from the Holy Mosque to the Further Mosque'. What is of more interest to our discussion here, however, and perhaps even more representative of the type of issues with which I-H was preoccupied, is the question of whether *ilā* operates upon what follows it, according to whether the particle and what precedes it are considered part of the particle in a semantic sense or not, due to the presence of an asociative indication. An example of where what follows the particle is not deemed on a semantic level to be part of it nor what precedes it is Sūra XVII vs.1 just cited. On the other hand, it is likely that an associative indication exists to signify a connection between those elements in the example *qara'tu l-*Qur'ān*a min awwilihi ilā ākhirihi* 'I read the Qur'ān from the beginning to end', where the intended meaning is that the whole Book was read.[23] According to I-H some said that there was only a connection if what follows the particle is of the same (semantic) species (*jins*), whilst others maintained that it was connected at all times. Of these two types the former could be exemplified by *sir bi l-nahāri ilā waqt al-'aṣri* 'travel during the day until the mid-afternoon period', and the latter by *sir bi l-nahāri ilā l-layli* 'travel during the day until night-time' (al-Damāmīnī, *Sharḥ*, 161). Others said that a connection never existed, which is the argument favoured by I-H because he notes (ML 1:77) that it represents an opinion held by the majority (*al-akthar*), and this must be adhered to in times of indecision (*fa yajibu l-ḥaml 'alayhi 'inda l-taraddud*).

idhā

In much the same way as the meaning of the previous particle is clearly reflected in the other components of the sentence in which it features, the function of *idhā* may be assessed in the same manner. I-H's discussion of this particle begins with the *idhā li l-mufāja'a* 'of surprise' (ML 1:87), which we learn only occurs as part of nominal sentences (*jumal ismiyya*), does not require a result clause (unlike the conditional *idhā*), and cannot occur in an initial position (of speech) (*fī l-ibtidā'*). This last point requires clarification.

The fundamental premise underlying the position of *idhā* in speech is that the intention behind it is to signify that what follows it occurs after what precedes it in a manner of surprise. Therefore, if it occurred at the beginning of speech it would not fulfil this function. This may be exemplified by the sentence *kharajtu fa idhā l-asadu bi l-bābi* 'I went out and there was the lion at the door'. Once again we are presented with a firm indication of how the particle is the pivot around which meaning is apparently conveyed.

The grammatical status of *idhā* of 'surprise' is also given considerable attention by I-H because it was clearly an issue for the earlier grammarians. For al-Akhfash it was a *ḥarf* 'particle', for al-Mubarrad it was a *ẓarf makān* 'adverb of place', and for al-Zajjāj it was a *ẓarf zamān* 'adverb of time'. To establish this status becomes particularly important when one is faced with a topic of an equational sentence without a predicate as in, for instance, *kharajtu fa idhā l-asadu.* I-H notes that *idhā* of 'surprise' never occurs in the Qur'ān without an expressed predicate. This necessitates that all such occurrences of *idhā* have a predicate, since the Qur'ān is the yardstick by which grammatical points will be judged. In the sentence just cited, therefore, *idhā* must be a predicate for al-Mubarrad on the assumption that it means 'in attendance' (*bi l-ḥaḍra*). But this interpretation would not be commensurate with the view of al-Zajjāj because the (adverb of) time cannot be predicated by a concrete noun (*juththa*); neither would it concur with al-Akhfash's opinion because a particle cannot predicate nor be predicated. However, if you changed the word *asad* 'lion' to *qitāl* 'battle' it would become acceptable as a predicate to al-Zajjāj, and, of course, al-Mubarrad because the topic, viz., 'battle', would then be an abstract noun (*ism maʻnan*) (ML 1:87; al-Damāmīnī, *Sharḥ*, 188).

The second category of this particle discussed by I-H is its function as an adverb of future (time) implying the meaning of condition (*ẓarf li l-mustaqbal muḍammina maʻnā l-sharṭ*) (ML 1:92). Contrary to the *idhā* of 'surprise' it occurs only in verbal sentences. To illustrate this difference I-H employs a customary technique of his which is to cite a verse of the Qur'ān in which the particle occurs twice within close proximity, but with a different meaning in each case (ML 1:93). On this occasion he cites Sūra XXX vs.24: *thumma idhā daʻākum daʻwatan min al-arḍī idhā antum takhrujūna* 'then, when He calls you once and suddenly, out of the earth, lo you shall come forth', in which the first *idhā* implies condition, and the second one is for surprise. Even when the rule about *idhā* of 'condition' not occurring next to nouns is contravened, it can often be explained away as an example of elision, as in, for example, Sūra CXXXIV vs.1: *idhā l-samā'u inshaqqat* 'When heaven is rent asunder'. In this instance the noun *al-samā'* is an agent of an elided verb which performed the condition of explanation (*sharīṭat al-tafsīr*), i.e., *idhā inshaqqat al-samā'u inshaqqat.*

I-H then tests each of the three main properties of *idhā*; adverbial, future tense and conditional, to determine if it ever occurs with an additional meaning. In the first instance he concludes that according to the majority (*jumhūr*) it is always adverbial, in spite of several opinions of various grammarians to the contrary. His attempts to prove whether it occurs beyond the senses of future or conditional require some elaboration here.

In spite of its normal future function I-H appears to accept the view that *idhā* can occur with the past (*al-māḍī*), as exemplified by Sūra IX vs.93: *wa lā alladhīna idhā mā atawka li taḥmilahum qulta* 'neither against those who, when they came to thee, for thee to mount them, thou saidst to them'. As for the view that it occurs for the *ḥāl* 'present' after an oath (*qasam*), I-H has much to say on this. In Sūra XCII vs.1: *wa l-layli idhā yaghshā* 'By the night enshrouding', I-H refutes the view that the particle signifies the present here, because 'semantic connection' (*ta'līq*) (of the particle) with the non-affirmative oath (*al-qasam al-inshā'ī*)[24] is incorrect on the grounds that something as eternal (as God's oath) has no time factor (*lā zamān lahu*); rather it precedes all time. Moreover, some argued that *idhā* is an adverb for an elided 'being' (*kawn maḥdhūf*) which would be a *ḥāl* 'circumstantial' of *wa l-laylī.* However, they maintained that if the particle signified the future here then this argument would not hold because of the contradiction between the present and the future. I-H discounts this view by affirming that there is nothing to prevent the suspension of the word *kā'inan* as a circumstantial of *wa l-layli* which some argued would preclude the occurrence of *idhā* in its future capacity. As proof of this I-H cites a situational example containing a reconstructed circumstantial element, even though the meaning still conveys the future. He notes that in *marartu bi rajulin ma'ahu ṣaqrun ṣā'idan bihi ghadan* 'I passed by a man who had a falcon with him with which he was going to hunt tomorrow', the reconstructed meaning is that he will hunt with it tomorrow. Even more elucidatory than this is to say that he was intending (*murīdan*) to hunt with it tomorrow, just as the word *qumtum* in Sūra V vs.8: *idhā qumtum ilā l-ṣalātī* 'when you stand up to pray', is to be interpreted as *aradtum,* viz., 'if you want / intend to stand up to pray'. In other words, the *ḥāl* in the example about hunting carries the meaning of intention and future time (ML 1:95-96; al-Damāmīnī, *Sharḥ*, 203).

With regard to *idhā* occurring outside of its conditional function, I-H maintains that this may happen in some cases; one such example is Sūra XCII vs.1 (above), or Sūra LIII vs.1: *wa l-najmi idhā hawā* 'By the star when it plunges'. I-H notes that if *idhā* were a conditional marker here, then what precedes it would be the result in terms of meaning, just as when you say *ātīka idhā ataytanī* 'I would come to you if you came to me' the result precedes the condition. In other words, the reconstructed version of the verse above would then become *idhā yaghshā l-laylu wa idhā hawā l-najmu aqsamtu* 'If the night enshrouds, and if the Star plunges, I will swear an oath to it'. However, I-H advances a firm rejection of the argument that the particle here may indicate the meaning of condition (ML 1:100). He repeats the earlier premise that the non-affirmative oath is not semantically connected, and adds here that this is because non-affirmative (speech) is to 'make something happen' (*īqā'*), whereas something semantically connected may or may not happen (*wa l-mu'allaq yaḥtamilu l-wuqū' wa 'adamahu*). In contrast to the situational example *in jā'anī fa wa allāhi la ukrimannahu* 'If he comes to me, By God I shall certainly honour him', in which the result (in terms of meaning) is the verb of honouring (*fi'l al-ikrām*) because it is caused by the condition (*li'annahu l-musabbab 'an al-sharṭ*), and in which the oath has only occurred between the two clauses for emphasis, the situation in the Qur'ānic verses is very different. According to I-H the result element of the 'By the night' verse, viz., *inna sa'yakum la shattā* 'Surely your striving is to diverse ends', is permanent (*thābit*), whilst the result of the 'By the Star' verse, i.e., *mā ḍalla ṣāḥibukum wa mā ghawā* 'Your comrade is not astray, neither errs', is in the past (*māḍin*) and is continuously being discounted (*mustamirr al-intifā'*); therefore, neither of these result clauses could be caused by a future matter (*amr mustaqbal*) in the form of the conditional clause, with the particle as the conditional marker (cf. al-Murādī, *al-Janā*, 362).

It is noteworthy that I-H's discussion of the particle *idhā* occupies thirteen pages of ML. The aspects considered above represent only a modest proportion of his study, although it is hoped that the salient points of contention have been brought to the fore. To underline further our objectives here, it was decided to omit the long and famous discussion involving Sībawayhi and al-Kisā'ī about the extent of the sting of the scorpion and the hornet (*al-mas'ala al-zunburiyya*), in which a fervent debate ensued about the grammatical status of the pronouns following *idhā* (ML 1:88-92). On the other hand, the later examples in this section here have illustrated once more the finer points of meaning which interested I-H.

bā'

The particle *bā'* (in context *bi*) is a preposition which has fourteen meanings (ML 1:101). Many of these meanings have been well documented too in Western grammars of Arabic (e.g., Wright 1933:395). There are two particular points of interest which will be assessed in this first section on the *bā'* which is clearly a very important and highly functional particle.

First, for I-H and most of the grammarians and scholars who specialized in studies of the particles, the principal meaning of this particle in its prepositional capacity was *ilṣāq* 'adhesion', as we saw earlier (above, Chapter Two). In essence, this meaning underlies all the other meanings, as I-H notes (ML 1:101) when he says that this meaning is always a part of what the *bā'* conveys (*ma'nan lā yufāriquhā*).[25] It is not surprising then that in the early period Sībawayhi restricted his cursory discussion of this particle to this meaning, and that of *ikhtilāṭ* 'association'. Whilst the several additional meanings listed by I-H and others clearly serve to illustrate how the study of the more rhetorical aspects of the particles, particularly their figurative usages, began to develop, it is interesting to observe that Sībawayhi, for instance, was not wholly unaware that this particle carried out other functions. A useful illustration of the significance of these figurative usages is revealed in I-H's discussion of whether it is more correct to say *marartu bi zaydin* or *marartu ʿalā zaydin* for 'I passed by Zayd'. The issue here rests on the fact that neither the *bā'* in its capacity as a particle of adhesion, nor the *ʿalā* as a particle denoting elevation (*istiʿlā'*) are being employed in their literal (*ḥaqīqī*) sense. I-H's conclusion as to which of the two is more correct is founded on the premise that when two implications of figurative usage are equal, the interpretation should be based on whichever of the two is more frequently used (in speech) (*fa idhā istawā l-taqdīrānī fī l-majāziyya fa l-akthar istiʿmālan awlā bi l-takhrīj*) (ML 1:102).

The second main point of interest concerns several differences of terminology to be found in ML and some of the other major works on the particles. Most agree that one of the meanings of the *bā'* is *istiʿāna* 'to indicate the instrument used for assistance', as in, for example, *katabtu bi l-qalami* 'I wrote with the pen'. However, al-Irbilī (*Jaw*, 38), for example, does not identify a category by this name; rather he subsumes it under a category called *sababiyya* 'expressing the reason or cause', which he defines as 'the function in which the noun put in the oblique case (by the preposition) can actually be the agent of the verb' (*wa hiya l-mawḍiʿ alladhī yajūzu an yujʿala l-majrūr fīhi fāʿil li l-fiʿl*). Therefore, you can say *kataba l-qalamu* 'The pen did the writing'. Similar reservations about using the term *istiʿāna* were expressed by al-Murādī (*al-Janā*, 103-4) based on what Ibn Mālik said in his *Tashīl* that this term cannot be used about God. This appears to have been behind al-Irbilī's reasoning too, although it does not appear to have been an issue for I-H who notes that the *bā'* has the function of *istiʿāna* in the *basmala* 'to say In the name of God...etc.', since the act of saying it is only complete with the particle. One's imagination is also stirred by Ibn Fāris' use of the term *iʿtimāl* for examples like 'I wrote with the pen' and 'I struck with the sword' (*al-Ṣāḥibī*, 133).

If we stay with I-H's category of *sababiyya* for the moment we find some rather more fundamental differences between his examples and those of some of the other writers on this subject. For instance, al-Murādī, who preferred to use *sababiyya* for what I-H calls *istiʿāna*, employs the term *taʿlīl* (also expressing reason or cause) (*al-Janā*, 104) for the Qur'ānic examples cited by I-H under the category of *istiʿāna*. He points out that *taʿlīl* must be the category in question when the *bā'* could be replaced by a *lām* (also used for cause or purpose). In some cases the issue appears to amount to no more than a battle of terminologies, although there is sufficient evidence to suggest that semantic, or even theological, reasons were behind some of the terms adopted. In the first instance it is difficult to perceive any distinction between the function of the *bā'* for *sababiyya* in Sūra II vs.52: *innakum ẓalamtum anfusakum bi ittikhādhikum al-'ijla* 'You have done wrong against yourselves by taking the Calf', and the *lām* for *ta'līl* which could be readily substituted for it. On the other hand, an interesting difference in terminology and interpretation of a particular category emerges from a comparison between I-H's section on *sababiyya* and those of al-Mālaqī and al-Irbilī with regard to the situational example *laqītu bi zaydin al-asada* 'I found in Zayd the lion'. According to I-H the interpretation of this is 'on account of my finding him' (*bi sabab liqā'ī iyyāhu*) (ML 1:103). However, al-Mālaqī (*Raṣf*, 147) classifies this as an example of *tashbīh* 'simile', whilst al-Irbilī (*Jaw*, 41) subsumes it in a section called *tajrīd* 'absolution', so called because it strips the noun being qualified of all description except the one in hand, whether that be praise or blame.[26]

Further semantic considerations emerge in I-H's section on the transitivizing (*ta'diya*) *bā'* (ML 1:102). This is the *bā'* which takes the place of the *hamza* (known in the West as the marker of the derived form IV of the verb) in making the *fā'il* 'agent' a *maf'ūl* 'object'. It normally occurs with an intransitive (*qāṣir*) verb, as in, for instance, *dhahaba zaydun* 'Zayd went', which would become either *dhahabtu bi zaydin* or *adhhabtuhu* 'I did away with Zayd'. Two of the earlier grammarians, however, al-Mubarrad and al-Suhaylī, claimed that the two methods of making the verb transitive displayed here are not the same; in other words, they argued that if you say *dhahabtu bi zaydin* the meaning can only be that you actually went with him. I-H discounts this argument in customary fashion by citing a verse from the Qur'ān in which the *bā'* occurs in the above capacity, and comparing this with the original sentence which features the *hamza*. In Sūra II vs.16: *dhahaba allāhu bi nūrihim* 'God took away their light', I-H points out that it is not possible to describe God as 'going' somewhere, or with something. The test for the validity of his view is that the intended meaning can be derived from the original *adhhaba allāhu nūrahum* 'God took away their light'.

I-H then explains (ML 1:102) why the *hamza* (form IV marker) and the *bā'*, which are both used to make a verb transitive, cannot occur together. But how does he explain away the occurrence of both in a verse in the Qur'ān like Sūra XXIII vs.20: *tunbitu bi l-duhni* '(...and a tree issuing from the Mount of Sinai) that bears oil...' (where the verb *anbata* is used in its present indicative mood)? He advances several possible explanations for this, such as the *bā'* being superfluous, or for accompaniment (*muṣāḥaba*).

Another of the many meanings of the *bā'* noted by I-H is *muqābala* 'recompense' (also known as *bā' al-'iwaḍ*). The particle here precedes a recompense or a price, although these do not necessarily have to be financial ones. Examples of this function are *ishtaraytu bi alfin* 'I bought it for a thousand', or *kāfa'tu iḥsānahu bi ḍi'fin* 'I rewarded his good turn with double its value'. We have already seen how theological issues may, not surprisingly, play a part in determining the views on linguistic issues of individual grammarians. Not least in this regard is I-H's refutations of Mu'tazilite arguments on particular points. A further example of this may be seen in his rejection (ML 1:104) of such an argument concerning the particle *bā'* in Sūra XVI vs.34: *udkhulū al-jannata bi mā kuntum ta'lamūna* 'Enter Paradise for that you were doing'. According to the Mu 'tazilites the *bā'* here is for cause or purpose; but I-H affirms that it is for recompense because the giver, i.e., God, not only gives recompenses, but may also give something for nothing (*qad yu'ṭī majānan*). Therefore, as there is no cause (*sabab*) there is nothing caused (*lā yūjad musabbab*). In other words, what they are actually doing is not necessarily the reason for their eventual entrance to Paradise. This view, of course, runs contrary to the Mu 'tazilite belief in the causal ralationship between man's deeds and the eternal reward.

I-H's interest in semantic related matters may be seen elsewhere in the section on the *bā'*. In his analysis of this particle as a superfluous one attached to the agent of a verb (ML 1:106), he notes how the majority considered its superfluity essential in the example *aḥsin bi zaydin* 'How wonderful Zayd is'. They said that the original version of this was *aḥsana zaydun* with the meaning *aḥsana dhā ḥusnin* 'He (Zayd) has become wonderful'. Then the affirmative mode (*ṣīghat al-khabar*) became a requestive (*ṭalab*), viz., imperative (*amr*), and the particle became superfluous 'to serve as an embellishment of the grammatical form, or expression' (*iṣlāḥan li l-lafẓ*). I-H then poses a rhetorical question: what happens if someone said that it has now become an imperative in terms of both its grammatical form and meaning, and that the pronoun of the second person is concealed within it ? I-H's reply to this is an inspired one, for he notes that if this were the case, the particle would be a transitivizing one (*mu'addiya*), as it is in the example *umrur bi zaydin* 'Pass by Zayd!'.

A further illustration of the diverse functions of the *bā'* may be found in the section on its function as superfluous when attached to an object of the verb (ML 1:109). In an illuminating example I-H invokes the concept of *taḍmīn* 'implication of meaning' again to demonstrate how the *bā'* may accompany the verb *qara'a* 'to read' to assume the implied meaning of *tabarruk* 'being blessed' in a certain context. Therefore, you can say *qara'tu bi l-Sūrati* 'I read the Sūra' because it has the sense of blessing, i.e., you are doing something for God, but you can not say *qara'tu bi kitābika* 'I read your book', because the idea of blessing no longer applies.

The final category of *bā'* as a superfluous particle concerns its function as an emphatic with the words *nafs* and *'ayn* 'self' (ML 1:111). Once more I-H alludes to the necessity for a correct interpretation of the meaning with reference to Sūra II vs.227 and vs.234: *yatarabbaṣna bi anfusihinna* 'They (the women) shall wait by themselves'. Some scholars interpreted the *bā'* in these particular verses in conjunction with the word *anfus* to be purely for emphasis (*tawkīd*). However, I-H argues that on the level of form, the attached nominative/independent pronoun emphasized by the words *nafs* or *'ayn* should be emphasized in the first instance by the independent pronoun as in, for example, *qumtum antum anfusukum* 'you yourselves got up'. On the level of meaning, I-H suggests that the emphatic element in the Qur'ānic verses is lost because there is no doubt about who is being ordered to wait, unlike when you say *zāranī l-khalīfatu nafsuhu* 'the Caliph himself visited me', in which you wish to stress that it was actually the Caliph in person who came.

According to I-H the word *anfus* in Sūra II above was mentioned to increase the inducement to wait, and to make him (the man) really feel the woman's contempt of him, and her desire to wait. The context of all this, of course, is divorce or death of the husband, and the woman's rights in that connection, not least in the time in which she should wait after a divorce or death of her spouse.

bal

I-H's discussion of the particle *bal* is comparatively brief, but once again it is fair to conclude that he makes a significant contribution towards clarifying its meanings and functions, particularly with regard to his correction of the interpretations offered by some of his predecessors.

The function of *bal* as a particle of *iḍrāb* 'retraction' is reasonably well-documented in Western grammars of Arabic (e.g., Wright 1933 2:335). It can be followed by either a sentence (*jumla*), or a single entity (*mufrad*). In the case of the former, there are two types of retraction noted by I-H. The first is that of *ibṭāl* 'invalidation', where the statement of the previous sentence is invalidated and replaced by something to the contrary, as in, for example, Sūra XXIII vs.72: *am yaqūlūna bihi jinnatun, bal jā'ahum bi l-ḥaqqi* 'Or do they say, 'He is bedevilled'? Nay, he has brought them the truth'. The other type of 'retraction' is that of *al-intiqāl min gharaḍ ilā ākhar* 'transferring (the meaning) from one intention to the other'. The essence of this meaning is that it does not invalidate what precedes the particle, but transfers what follows it into a new meaning. It is here that I-H's comments are particularly valuable because he notes that Ibn Mālik, for instance, failed to identify the meaning of invalidation in one of his works. According to Ibn Mālik this particle only occurred in the Qur'ān in this latter sense, which could be exemplified by Sūra LXXXVII vs.14: *qad aflaḥa man tazakkā wa dhakara isma rabbihi fa ṣallā, bal tu'thirūna l-ḥayāta l-dunyā* 'Prosperous is he who has cleansed himself, and mentions the Name of his Lord, and prays. Nay, but you prefer the present life'.

If *bal* is followed immediately by a single entity it assumes the function of a coordinating particle. Of particular interest in this connection is I-H's refutation of a claim by al-Mubarrad and one 'Abd al-Wārith (ML 1:112) that the meaning of the negative (*nafy*) and prohibitive command (*nahy*) preceding the particle *bal* is transferred to what follows it. Therefore, they made no distinction between *mā zaydun qā'iman bal qā'idan* 'Zayd is not standing, but sitting' or ... *bal qā'idun*. However, I-H remarks that there is an unequivocal difference between the two because in the first example Zayd is neither standing nor sitting, whereas in the second instance he is standing as opposed to sitting (al-Damāmīnī, *Sharḥ* 234).[27]

ḥattā

Of all the particles which have been well-documented in the Western grammars of Arabic, *ḥattā* ranks among those that have received most attention (e.g., Wright 1933 2:146-47). The function of this particle has often been assessed in particular in relation to the particle *ilā* and the similarities and differences that obtain between them. I-H devotes a fair proportion of his section on *ḥattā* to this subject, as we shall see below. What has pushed *ḥattā* to the fore as a key particle more than anything perhaps, is the frequently quoted situational example *akaltu l-samakata ḥattā ra'su/a/i/hā* 'I ate the fish, even its head' (cf. Carter 1981:290-91) about which grammarians debated for centuries concerning the merits of the respective case-endings, and the implications of each for the meaning (ML 1:123).[28] Remarks in this section will be restricted to those elements which seem to be important from a semantic viewpoint.

It was generally held that the principal meaning of *ḥattā*, like *ilā*, is *intihā' al-ghāya* 'end of a specific aim / limit'. In spite of this common ground, however, there are some interesting differences between the two. One of the main distinctions is the unacceptability of exchanging one of the particles for another in, for instance, *katabta ilā zaydin wa anā ilā 'amrin* 'You wrote to Zayd and I (wrote) to 'Amr'. In this regard what you mean is 'he is my specific aim' (*ghāyatī*). Yet it is not possible to substitute *ilā* for *ḥattā* here because as we saw earlier, the latter was established to 'convey the connection (of the import) of the verb preceding it, by degrees, to its aim" (*li ifādat taqaḍḍī l-fi'l qablahā shay'an fa shay'an ilā l-ghāya*). In other words, in this context at least it does not go so far as *ilā* in reaching that aim. We may conjecture that this was the reason for Ibn Ya'īsh's redefining of the meaning of *ḥattā* (*Sharḥ*, 8:15) as the 'end of the beginning of the (specific) aim' (*muntahā ibtidā' al-ghāya*). A further important example illustrating the non-interchangeability of these two particles is *sirtu min al-baṣra ilā l-kūfa* 'I walked from Basra to Kufa'. In a similar way it is not possible to substitute *ḥattā* for *ilā* because of this 'weakness'. According to I-H (ML 1:124) the overwhelming proof of this is that it cannot be employed as a direct contrast to the preposition *min* whose meaning is 'the beginning of the (specific) aim' (*ibtidā' al-ghāya*) in the same way as *ilā*. As an illustration of this you cannot say *kharajtu min al-baṣra ḥattā l-kūfa* 'I went out from Basra to Kufa' by replacing *ilā* with *ḥattā* (al-Damāmīnī, *Sharḥ*, 255).

I-H's neat and concise section on the incidence of the particle *ḥattā* followed by the verb in the nominative/independent mood (*raf'*) (ML 1:126) offers further evidence of the inextricable link between *i'rāb* and meaning. There are three conditions in which the verb may occur in this form after the particle. The first of these is when the verb is actually happening at the time the speech is being said (*ḥikāyat al-ḥāl*), as in, for example, *sirtu ḥattā adkhuluhā* 'I walked until I am entering it (now)'. The same situation obtains if it is in reported speech (*mu'awwal bi l-ḥāl / maḥkiyya*). The second of these occurrences is when what follows the particle is caused by what precedes it (*an yakūna musabbaban 'ammā qablahā*). Therefore, you cannot say *sirtu ḥattā taṭla'u l-shamsu* 'I walked until the sun came up', because the sun's rising is not dependent on your walking. Likewise you cannot say *mā sirtu ḥattā adkhuluhā* 'I did not walk until I entered it', because entering would not be the result of not walking. In addition, you cannot say *hal sirta ḥattā tadkhuluhā* 'Did you walk until you entered it', because the reason has not yet been realized, i.e., walking has not been confirmed. What you can say, however, is *ayyuhum sāra ḥattā yadkhuluhā* 'Which one of them walked until he entered it', because the walking has been confirmed, and the doubt rests merely with who did it. By the same token you may say *matā sirta ḥattā tadkhuluhā* 'When did you walk until you entered it', because the only thing in doubt is the time of walking, not the walking itself. The third occasion in which the verb may occur in the *raf'* mood is when the verb is a redundant proposition (*faḍla*). Therefore, you cannot say *sayrī ḥattā adkhuluhā* 'My walking until I entered it', because the particle *ḥattā* would then become one of inception (*ibtidā'*), and the sentence following it would then be a sentence of recommencement (*musta'nifa*), but without a predicate, which is unacceptable.

al-sīn al-mufrada

I-H's main contribution to the particle *sīn* as a future marker appears to be that he prefers to use the term *tawsī'* 'extension' to denote its function, in preference to the more common *tanfīs* 'amplification'. That there should be a significant difference between the two is not clear from ML, since I-H does not explain why his term should be more appropriate than the other. What he does offer, however, is an explanation for the choice of the term *tawsī'* which he opts for 'because it transfers the imperfect mood (*muḍāri'*) from its narrow time (scale) (*al-zaman al-ḍayyiq*), which is the present (*al-ḥāl*), to a wide(r) time (scale) (*al-zaman al-wāsi'*), which is the future' (ML 1:138).

An interesting discussion follows on from this in which I-H discounts the view of one scholar that the function of this particle was to denote continuity (*istimrār*), not future (*istiqbāl*). The verse cited as putative evidence of this was Sūra II vs.137: *sa yaqūlu l-sufahā'u min al-nāsi mā wallāhum 'an qiblatihim* 'The fools among the people will say, What has turned them from the direction they were facing'. He claimed that the words 'the fools among the people will say' were revealed after their saying 'what has turned them away', on the basis that the particle *sīn* informs of the continuity, not the future, i.e., with the idea that they have turned away and continue to do so. It was al-Zamakhsharī, however, who offered a rebuttal of this argument by saying that the force (*fā'ida*) of informing about what they will say even before it has happened is that 'the element of surprise involved with something reprehensible is much stronger, and that knowing about it before it occurs eases the anxiety when it does occur' (*al-mufāja'a li l-makrūh ashadd wa l-'ilm bihi qabla wuqū'ihi ab'ad 'an al-iḍṭirāb idhā waqa'a*). In other words, people are being prepared for their turning away by what the fools will say.

On the issue of continuity, I-H affirms that if one is to accept that it does have a place here it can only be derived from the imperfect indicative mood, not from the particle itself. Hence, if you say *fulānun yaqrī l-ḍayfa wa yaṣna'u l-jamīla* 'so-and-so is hospitable to the guest and does nice things', what you really mean is that he does this continuously (*dhālika da'buhu*). On the other hand, I-H adds that although the *sīn* is the future marker, the idea of continuity is obviously connected to the future. In this connection he appears to support an argument put forward by al-Zamakhsharī (ML 1:138-39) that if the particle precedes a verb of endearment (*maḥbūb*) or reprehension (*makrūh*) then it communicates the meaning that the action is already taking place (*wāqi'*). I-H suggests that this interpretation was not particularly clear to other scholars, so he qualifies it by saying that the particle communicates the promise (*al-wa'd*) that the act of the verb will actually occur. Furthermore, he notes that its preceding a promise or a threat (*wa'īd*) is essential to emphasize it and consolidate what is meant by it. He cites the verse which al-Zamakhsharī used to illustrate his point, i.e., Sūra II vs.132: *fa sa yakfīkahum allāhu* 'God will suffice you for them', in which the particle *sīn* conveys the meaning that God's sufficiency is already in existence, even if it will be delayed until the right time. Another example is Sūra IX vs.73: *ūlā'ika sa yarḥamuhum allāhu* 'upon them God will have mercy', in which the particle conveys the meaning of the inevitable existence of (God's) mercy, thereby emphasizing the promise in the same way as it emphasizes the threat in, for instance, *sa antaqimu minka* 'I shall get revenge on you!'. What we may derive from all this, then, is that verbs of this type are already part of a plan, whether that plan belongs to God, as in the Qur'ānic examples, or even on a secular level in which the future event will not just occur, but is part of a pre-meditation by the one who either promises or threatens with something. It is in this regard that the important properties of the particle *sīn* as a future marker may be found. What this section demonstrates is I-H's consistent concern with semantic issues. Although the basis of the second part of our discussion above is not derived from I-H's own views as such, it shows that he is always prepared to consider and enlarge on the opinions of others if they are commensurate with his objectives.

'inda

Of all the major works on the particles a discussion of *'inda* is to be found only in ML. The reason for its omission from these other works is conceivably due to its being a noun. On the other hand, it is not surprising that I-H includes a section on it in ML, given its large number of occurrences in the Qur'ān. I-H tells us (ML 1:155) that it is a noun which denotes presence (*ḥuḍūr*), either of a perceptible (*ḥissī*) kind, as in, for example, Sūra XXVII vs.41: *wa lammā ra'āhu mustaqirran 'indahu* 'Then, when he saw it settled before him', or an abstract (*ma'nawī*) type, as in, for instance, Sūra XXVII vs.40: *qāla alladhī 'indahu 'ilmun min al-kitāb* 'Said he who possessed knowledge of the Book', or for proximity (*qurb*), as in, for example, Sūra LIII vs.14: *'inda sidrati l-muntahā 'indahā jannatu l-ma'wā* 'by the Lote-Tree of the Boundary nigh which is the Garden of the Refuge'. The function of this noun is either adverbial, or the noun which follows and is operated on by the preposition *min*.

On a note of terminology, I-H defines this noun (ML 1:156) as one denoting the place of presence (*li makān al-ḥuḍūr*) in preference to Ibn Mālik's definition of its simply denoting presence (*li l-ḥuḍūr*). The reason for this is that it is an adverb, not a verbal noun. In addition it also functions as a noun denoting the time of presence, as in, for instance, *ji'tuka 'inda ṭulū'i l-shamsi* 'I came to you at sunrise'.[29]

qad

Although I-H discusses the initial meaning of *qad,* which is expectation (*tawaqqu'*), at some length, he advances a revised view on this meaning with particular reference to its occurring with the simple past tense of the verb. In fact, only al-Murādī (*al-Janā,* 269-75) from the major writers on the particles offers such a detailed account of *qad* and its senses.

I-H notes how you say, for example, *qad rakiba l-amīru* 'The prince has mounted (probably his horse)', when he has finally mounted, to someone who was expecting him to mount. It was probably this aspect which led some to argue that expectation (signifies) waiting for (the event) to happen, whereas the past has already happened. Therefore, how can expectation, in the form of the particle here, signify the past? I-H concludes that the opinion of those who affirmed its existence for this purpose was based on the past tense being expected until it was informed about (*qabla l-ikhbār bihi*), not that it is expected now. However, I-H has further views on this, because he states that *qad* did not originally communicate the meaning of expectation; this may be seen in its dispensability with the imperfect indicative verb, as in, for example, *yaqdamu l-ghā'ibu* 'the absent one may arrive' where the idea of expectation lies within the sentence. With regard to the use of the past tense with *qad*, I-H makes the following pertinent observation (ML 1:172):

'If it is correct to affirm the (meaning) of expectation for *qad* in the sense that it precedes what is expected, then it is correct to say about *lā rajula* 'there is no man' that it occurs for interrogation (*istifhām*), because it only occurs as a reply to whoever says *hal min rajulin* 'Is there a man ?' (In other words) what comes after *lā* is being asked about by another person, just as the past is expected by another person after *qad*.

I-H thus supports what Ibn Mālik concluded about *qad* and its relationship with the past; that it precedes an expected past, not that it communicates the meaning of expectation (by itself).

More interesting points emerge in I-H's detailed analysis of this particle. He explains, for instance (ML 1:174), how the *la* of *laqad* came to assume its status as a past tense marker. Originally it was the *lām al-ibtidā'* 'the *lām* of inception' which preceded the noun in, for instance, *inna zaydan la qā'imun* 'Indeed Zayd is standing'. Then it came to precede the imperfect indicative because of its resemblance to the noun, as in, for example, Sūra XVII vs.125: *wa inna rabbakum la yaḥkumu baynakum* 'surely thy Lord will decide between them', where the word *ḥākim* could replace the verb; finally, it came to precede the past when the time factor was approaching the present, as in *inna zaydan laqad qāma* 'Indeed Zayd has stood up (i.e., is standing)'.

He also includes a linguistic issue (*mas'ala*) (ML 1:175) which is not to be found in any of the other principal works on the particles. This issue concerns the possibility of *zayd* occurring in the accusative/dependent (*naṣb*) case due to *ishtighāl* '(syntactic) occupation/preoccupation'[30] in the example *kharajtu fa idhā zaydun yaḍribuhu ʿamrun* 'I went out and there was ʿAmr beating Zayd'. Some scholars maintained that it was always possible; others said it was totally unacceptable. I-H adheres to the latter view because the *idhā* of surprise can only be followed by nominal sentences, as we saw earlier. If preoccupation were taking place here it would turn the sentence into a verbal (conditional) one, i.e., *idhā yaḍribu zaydan*..., and Zayd would then be operated upon by the preceding verb. Some scholars maintained that *ishtighāl* was possible with the insertion of the word *qad* in, for instance, *fa idhā zaydun qad ḍarabahu ʿamrun* 'and there was Zayd having been beaten by ʿAmr'; *fa idhā ḍaraba zaydan* ... but not possible without it. I-H concludes that this view is erroneous because the main reason for the occurrence of *idhā* of 'surprise' with the noun is to distinguish it from the conditional one which always occurs with verbal sentences. Moreover, if *qad* is inserted then the difference becomes clear in any case, because the sentence consequently becomes a nominal one since the conditional type of sentence is never connected with *qad.*

Thus we witness a little more of I-H's ingenuity in this argument.

qaṭṭu

This is an adverb of time which is always connected, in its first and principal function, with the negative verb to convey the totality of what has passed (*li istighrāq mā maḍā*), as in, for instance, *mā faʿaltuhu qaṭṭu* 'I have never done it'. According to I-H (ML 1:175) it is uninflected because of its implying (*li taḍammunihā*) the meaning of *mudh* and *ilā*. The meaning of the above sentence, therefore, is 'I have not done it' *mudh an khuliqtu ilā l-ān* 'since I was born until now'.

What is interesting about this word is not just that it was not included by any of the other writers on the particles, but that I-H decided to include it, even though it does not occur in the Qur'ān.

kallā

It is perhaps surprising that with the exception of al-Murādī (*al-Janā*, 525-26), I-H is the only one of those writers specialising in studies of the particles who included a discussion of this particle which occurs on thirty three occasions in the Qur'ān (ML 1:189; al-Murādī, *al-Janā*, 526). In fact, it constitutes a particle of some importance, not just for the frequency of occurrence, but also because its meanings provoked different and diverse interpretations amongst the earlier grammarians in particular.

The majority of Basrans of the earlier period, including Sībawayhi, held that its sole meaning was *radʿ* 'averting' and *zajr* 'rebuking'. This is the only meaning to have been recorded by at least one comprehensive Western grammar of Arabic too (Wright 1933 1:287). Many grammarians also argued that it was only to be found in the later Meccan sūras of the Qur'ān because it conveyed the meaning of threat (*tahdīd* and *waʿīd*) (ML 1:188), since the Meccans were those most resistant to the Islamic message. However, I-H is somewhat cautious in his interpretation of this particle, not least because of several instances in the Qur'ān where he considers the argument for such a meaning to be unjustified. Three such examples are Sūra LXXXII vs.7, LXXXIII vs.6, and LXXV vs.19. Although the verses leading up to the particle *kallā* are too long to quote in full here, I-H's refutation of the foregoing interpretation is that some grammarians held that in each case the recipients of God's word were being ordered to cease doing a particular thing. However, I-H maintains that in the first two examples here the particle was not preceded by such a negation, whilst in the third instance the distance between what they were supposed to be doing wrong, and the particle, was too great (ML 1:188-89). Moreover, it is interesting to note I-H's concluding argument that *kallā* occurs at what he calls 'the beginning of speech', i.e., in verse 6 of Sūra XCVI (The Blood-Clot), which was the first sūra to be revealed. This Sūra begins: 'Recite: In the name of thy Lord, who created, created man of a blood clot. Recite: And thy Lord is the Most Generous, who taught by the Pen, taught Man that he knew not'; this is then followed immediately by: *kallā inna l-insāna la yaṭghā* 'No indeed; surely Man waxes insolent'.

What I-H's own position is on this is not entirely clear, but it appears that the meaning most favoured by him for the particle *kallā*, in addition to the main one cited above, is that of 'inception', with the same sense as the particle *alā* This is almost certainly his interpretation of the particle in those verses above.

kull

Of all the particles and quasi-particles not to be found in the principal works on this subject other than ML, the word *kull* is perhaps one of the most surprising omissions. To judge by I-H's treatment of this word in ML it is clearly important on both a formal and a semantic level.

As we saw earlier (see the section on *al* above), *kull* is a noun which was posited 'to encapsulate the totality of individual (entities) of an indefinite noun' (*li istighrāq afrād al-munakkar*), as in, for instance, Sūra III vs.182: *wa kullu nafsin dhā'iqatu l-mawti* 'Every soul shall taste of death'; 'the individual (entities) of a plural definite noun' (*al-muʻarraf al-majmūʻ*), as in, for example, Sūra XIX vs.95: *wa kulluhum ātīhi yawma l-qiyāma fardan* 'Every one of them shall come to Him upon the Day of Ressurection, all alone'; or 'parts of a definite singular noun' (*ajzā' al-mufrad al-muʻarraf*), as in, for example, *kullu zaydin ḥasanun* 'all of Zayd is good' (ML 1:193).

In addition, there is an important distinction to be made in the following examples. If you say *akaltu kulla raghīfin li zaydin* 'I ate all of Zayd's loaves of bread', then the function of *kull* is for 'the generality of individual (entities)' (*li ʻumūm al-afrād*). But if you annexe the word *raghīf* 'loaf' to Zayd, i.e., *akaltu kulla raghīfi zaydin*, the function now becomes 'the generality of parts of one individual' (*li ʻumūm ajzā' fard wāḥid*), whilst the meaning becomes 'I ate the whole of Zayd's loaf'.

I-H cites several verses from the Qur'ān to indicate that the form (*lafẓ*) of *kull* is always masculine singular. However, its meaning runs according to what it is annexed to; thus if it is annexed to an indefinite noun the meaning must be preserved. In other words, the following syntactic elements will agree in gender, number and so on with the noun annexed to *kull*. An interesting exception to this occurs in a verse of poetry by ʻAntara which provoked a disagreement between Ibn Mālik and Abū Ḥayyān (ML 1:198):

jādat ʻalayhi kullu ʻaynin thārratin
fa tarakna kulla ḥadīqatin ka l-dirhami
(Every spring abounding in water bestowed upon it
And left every garden like a dirham)

The argument here concerns the use of the verb *tarak* in the feminine plural rather than singular form. I-H offers the following explanation for this:

'What makes their dispute clear to me is that the *kull* annexed to the singular, if it is intended to be related to each one then the singular (of the noun) is essential, as in *kullu rajulin yushbi'uhu raghīfun* 'Every man is filled up by a loaf of bread'. If (it is intended to be related) to the plural, then the plural is necessary (as in the above piece of poetry). In this piece, what is intended is that each single one of the springs has been bounteous, but the group of springs has done the 'leaving'. By the same token you can say *jāda 'alayya kullu muḥsinin fa aghnānī*...or *fa aghnūnī* 'Every charitable person was generous to me and he / they made me rich', according to the meaning you want (ML 1:198).

Further evidence of the importance of a semantic orientated interpretation of *kull* may be adduced from an issue (*mas'ala*) discussed by I-H based on what the *bayāniyyūn* said about its relationship to the negative (*nafy*) (ML 1:200-201). The essence of their interpretation is that if *kull* falls within the domain (*ḥayyiz*) of the negative, it reduces the force of the negative from one of completeness (*shumūl*) to one of affirming the verb in at least some of its individual aspects (*afrād*) of a given sentence, as in, for example, *mā jā'a kullu l-qawmi* 'Not all the people came (but some did)', or *lam ākhudh kulla l-darāhimi* 'I did not take all the dirhams'.

However, if the opposite situation obtains, and the negative falls within the domain of *kull* then each individual must be negated (*iqtaḍā l-salb 'an kull fard*). This could be exemplified by the reply of the Prophet Muḥammad to a question about whether he had forgotten to pray, or if the number of prayers had been reduced. He said *kullu dhālika lam yakun* 'Nothing of the sort'. Another example of this type is the following verse by Abū l-Najm:

qad aṣbaḥat ummu l-khiyāri tadda'ī
'alayya dhanban kullu(a)hu lam aṣna'
'Umm al-Khiyār has begun to blame me
For something I had nothing to do with'.

Yet in spite of these two distinct categories, I-H raises the problem of the interpretation of the *bayāniyyūn* of the first category above in the light of Sūra LVII vs.23: *wa allāhu lā yuḥibbu kulla mukhtālin fakhūrin* 'God loves not any man proud and boastful' (ML 1:201). He alludes to the fact that if one applied the rule of the first category above it would necessitate a meaning that God loves at least some proud and boastful men; but this could hardly be the case. What is clear from the signification of this verse is that pride and boastfulness are strictly forbidden; thus in such instances one must look beyond the situation outlined above to determine exactly what is meant. Although I-H does not specify the exact means by which to do this it is likely that associative indications would be relevant here.

al-lām al-mufrada

This particle has twenty-two meanings according to I-H (ML 1:208), of which the main ones have been recorded adequately elsewhere in Western grammars of Arabic and need not detain us here (e.g., Wright 1933 2:147-57). I-H devotes more space to his analysis of this particle than any other in ML, although our attention to it here will be restricted to a few selected elements.

In the first instance I-H notes three separate senses of this particle which some scholars subsumed under one heading. Its original (*aṣl*) meaning was *ikhtiṣāṣ* 'denoting that something is ascribed to one as his own', as in, for example, *al-jannatu li l-mu'minīna* 'paradise is for the believers'. According to I-H (ML 1:208) there are two other closely related meanings worth noting in this connection; *istiḥqāq* 'showing that he has a right to it', as in *al-ḥamdu li allāhi* 'Thanks be to God', in which the particle always occurs between an abstract noun (*ism ma'nan*) and a concrete noun (*ism dhāt*), and *milk* 'indicating the right of property', as in, for instance, Sūra IV vs.169: *lahu mā fī l-samawāti wa mā fī l-arḍi* 'To Him belongs all that is in the heavens and in the earth'.[31]

In a section on *li* as an 'emphatic of a negative' (*tawkīd li l-nafy*) (ML 1:211-12), I-H disputes the view held by a number of grammarians that the particle in Sūra XIV vs.47: *wa in kāna makruhum li tazūla minhu l-jibālu* 'though their devising were such as to move mountains', is the *lām* of 'denial' (*juḥūd*) on the assumption that the particle *in* has the meaning of the negative here. However, not only is this form of the negative uncommon, but the agents of the two verbs are clearly very different. I-H argues that the *lām* here must be the one meaning 'in order to' like the particle *kay*, and that the *in* occurs here in its conditional sense. This means that the sense of the verse is that God's recompense for their devising will be greater than their devising, no matter how great that may be, just as you say *anā ashjaʿu min fulānin* 'I am braver than so-and-so', even if he is prepared for all possible calamities.

It has been indicated on several occasions so far that I-H's own contribution to semantic and syntactic related issues was frequently not original. But one of the techniques which he employs so successfully throughout ML is to clarify recondite arguments that had endured for many centuries. One such technique is in operation in his section on the *lām al-tabyīn* '*lām* of clarification' where I-H claims to resolve matters left unclear by Ibn Mālik and others (ML 1:220-21). One of the principal functions of this particle is to distinguish the object from the agent (*tubayyinu l-mafʿūl min al-fāʿil*). I-H notes that in this context the *lām* occurs after a verb of surprise/admiration (*taʿajjub*) or an elative (*ism tafḍīl*) conveying the meaning of love or hate. Therefore, if you say *mā aḥabbanī (mā abghaḍanī) li fulānin* you are the agent of the love (or hate) and the other person is the object. In other words it means 'How much I love (or hate) him!'. On the other hand, if you replace the *lām* with *ilā* the meaning is reversed; thus *mā aḥabbanī ilayhi* means 'How much he loves me!'.

What should also have emerged during the course of this study to date is that a single verse of the Qur'ān, for example, whose interpretation may rest on a correct assessment of the function of one particle within that verse, can result in the application of a grammatical or semantic law which should be adhered to in such matters. A useful example of this type of argument occurs in the second section of this particle on its capacity to function as an operator on the jussive mood (*ʿāmila li l-jazm*) (ML 1:226). In Sūra XIV vs.36: *qul li ʿibādī alladhīna āmanū yuqīmū l-ṣalāta* 'Say to My servants who believe, that they perform the prayer', there were three different interpretations of the elided *lām*, i.e., *li yuqīmū*. In the first place I-H advances a very important precept to discount the views of Sībawayhi and al-Khalīl who maintained that the jussive in this verse conveys the essence of request (*nafs al-ṭalab*) because it implies the meaning of the conditional particle *in* (*li mā taḍammanahu min ma'nā 'in al-sharṭiyya'*), which is also the reason why the conditional nouns put the verb in the jussive mood. Of this argument I-H says the following:

'Elision (*ḥadhf*) and implication (of sense) (*taḍmīn)* share the fact that they are both a violation of the original structure (*khilāf al-aṣl*). However, implication changes the meaning of the original structure, whereas elision does not. Similarly, to give the verb the implied meaning of the particle either happens rarely or not at all' (ML 1:226).

The second interpretation of the above verse rested on the belief that the jussive was for request on account of its taking the place of the jussivizer (*jāzim*), which is the reconstructed condition (*al-sharṭ al-muqaddar*). Once again I-H applies a semantic law by stating the following:

'The substitute of something must convey its meaning; but request does not convey the meaning of condition (*nā'ib al-shay' yu'addī ma'nāhu wa l-ṭalab lā yu'addī ma'nā l-sharṭ*).

The third interpretation, which is the one favoured by I-H, maintains that the jussive is based on a reconstructed conditional after the request.

In earlier chapters we have attempted to show that principles of agreement (*ittifāq*) and disputation (*ikhtilāf*) were such an important corollary of grammatical debate in the medieval period. Nowhere is the contrast between the two so visible as in the section on the inoperant (*ghayr al- 'āmila*) *lām* (ML 1:228) where, for instance, it is agreed upon that the particle can occur after the noun of *inna*, with the imperfect indicative which resembles the noun, and with the adverb, but where dispute prevailed on the acceptability of its occurring with the stationary (*al-jāmida*) verbs, such as *'asā*, the simple past tense with *qad*, and the conjugated (*mutaṣarrif*) simple past tense verb without *qad* This helps to substantiate the view that it was often very difficult or even infelicitous for a grammarian to attempt to put forward a definitive opinion on the function of a given particle; in such cases the most appropriate service he could provide was to present as many sides of a particular issue as possible in order that the reader decide for himself on the most satisfactory explanation.

lā

There is one particular verse in the Qur'ān in which the status of the particle *lā* is not only indeterminate, but it is not discussed in any of the other major works on the particles.[32] This occurs in Sūra X vs.63: *wa mā ya'zubu 'an rabbika min mithqāli dharratin fī l-arḍi wa lā fī l-samā'i wa lā aṣghara min dhālika wa lā akbara (illā fī kitābin mubīnin)* 'and not so much the weight of an ant in earth or heaven escapes from thy Lord, neither is aught smaller than that, or greater, (but in a Manifest Book)' (ML 1:241). The value of bringing this issue to light becomes clear when I-H tells us that even if the coordination of the *lā* and its ensuing sentence, viz., *lā aṣghara min dhālika wa lā akbara* with *mithqāl* is acceptable on a formal level, it is unacceptable on a semantic level. In other words, an assertion of the Book (*al-kitāb*) constitutes an affirmation of the escaping (*'uzūb*), just as when you say *mā marartu bi rajulin illā fī l-dāri* 'I only passed by a man when he was at home' you confirm your passing by a man at home. Although I-H does not elaborate on such an interpretation of the verse in specific terms, we may construe that this interpretation demands that the Book is the only thing in which the weight of an ant escapes from the Lord, which is preposterous since everything is known to the Lord in the Book. According to I-H there must be a pause on the word *samā'*, and what follows it must be inceptive (*musta'nif*). He does elaborate a little when he adds that some scholars allowed coordination in the verse on the basis that the verb *ya'zubu* did not have the sense of *yakhfā* 'to be hidden', but rather *yakhruju ilā l-wujūd* 'to become existent', which would then bring about a meaning that all these things are only revealed in the Book.

law

I-H presents a very detailed and pertinent analysis of this particle which possesses several categories and meanings. We would argue that for the most part his interest in the function of this particle is essentially a semantic one. Versteegh (1991) now provides a penetrating analysis of what I-H had to say on this particle, and the reader is referred to that work for more information. In the meantime, to conform with the objectives of this study the following represents the main substance of I-H's discussion.

As a starting point it is important to note that *law* was not immediately accepted as a conditional particle, in spite of the treatment it has received in traditional Western grammars of Arabic. Versteegh (ibid.:78) notes that as far as the Arab grammarians were concerned, 'since the construction with the jussive is regarded as the primary construction for conditional sentences, only those words which are construed with the jussive are regarded as true *ḥurūf al-sharṭ*'. It is the fact that the particle *law* does not operate upon a jussive which was of more interest to the majority of Arab grammarians than the type of conditionality which it conveyed (cf. ibid.:79). The following discussion will attempt to show that *law* was a conditional particle of a different kind, particularly in the relationship between the two parts of the conditional sentence which had to be taken into account.

According to I-H (ML 1:255) the first category of *law* may be found in the situational example *law jā'anī la akramtuhu* 'If he had come to me I would have honoured him'. He says that the particle in this example conveys three things:

(i) conditionality (*sharṭiyya*), by which he means 'binding the cause and the (thing) caused' (*ʻaqd al-sababiyya wa l-musabbabiyya*) between the two sentences following it.

(ii) restricting the condition to the past time (*taqyīd al-sharṭiyya bi l-zaman al-māḍī*): this is in contrast to the conditional particle *in* which has a future meaning. According to some it also had precedence over *law* because the future has precedence over the past. I-H adds in this connection that when you say *in ji'tanī ghadan akramtuka* 'If you come to me tomorrow I will honour you', and tomorrow ends and he has not come, you say *law ji'tanī amsi akramtuka* 'If you had come to me yesterday I would have honoured you'.[33]

(iii) 'impossibility' (*imtināʻ*) of the 'cause' (*sabab*).

On this third point in particular I-H has much to say. Some scholars denied that it conveyed the idea of impossibility, but this view provokes a retort from I-H in which he refers to the need for an instinctive (*badīhī*) understanding of the concept of impossibility. He adds that when you hear *law faʻala*... 'If he had done...' then the fact that the verb has not taken place should be understood immediately (ML 1:256). Others, principally the grammarians and those concerned with *i'rāb*, held that it conveyed the impossibility of both the conditional and the result components of the conditional sentence. I-H cites several verses from the Qur'ān to refute this idea (cf. Versteegh 1991:83) on the basis that everything that is made impossible means that its opposite is affirmed (*kull shay' imtana'a thubita naqīḍuhu*). By way of a useful situational example in this regard I-H adds that if *mā qāma* 'He did not get up' is made impossible, then *qāma* 'He got up' is affirmed.[34]

More semantic considerations emerge from I-H's refutation of the view that the element of impossibility is restricted to the conditional clause, and that it in no way signifies the impossibility or affirmation of the result clause. I-H presents some interesting corroborative evidence to demonstrate that this is not always the case, particularly if the result clause is equal to the conditional in terms of generality (*'umūm*). For instance, when you say *law kānat al-shamsu ṭāli'atan kāna l-nahāru mawjūdan* 'If the sun had come up the day would have come into existence', the result clause is impossible, since the day never exists without the sun coming up. In this instance we see how the result clause is wholly dependent on the conditional, if the whole statement is not to be falsified. However, if the result is more general than the condition, as in, for example, *law kānat al-shamsu ṭāli'atan kāna l-ḍaw'u mawjūdan* 'If the sun had come up then it would have become daylight', the result clause is not dependent on the conditional because it is possible to have daylight without sun.

I-H maintains that the sentences in which the second statement is wholly dependent on the first one for either its fulfillability or falseness are a matter for Revelation and the intellect (*al-shar' wa l-'aql*), exemplified by the examples from the Qur'ān and the examples above concerning the sun. However, there is also a type of sentence in which the intellect alone can play a role in determining exactly what is meant, as in, for instance, *law jā'anī akramtuhu* 'If he had come to me I would have honoured him'. Versteegh (1991:83) refers to this neatly as a case where 'there is no exclusive causal relationship between the two sentences as such, but common sense makes it probable that the only cause for the second is contained in the first'. In other words, the intellect could argue that you could have honoured him without his coming to you, but custom and usage (*al-'urf wa l-isti'māl*) demand that negation of the condition brings about automatic negation of the result (ML 1:258).

Now to the definition of the particle *law* with which I-H appears to have been particularly preoccupied. I-H sets out a firm refutation of the view propounded in some quarters that *law* is a particle of impossibility (of something) because of the impossibility (of something else). In fact, he favours the definition put forward by Sībawayhi some six centuries earlier: a particle indicating what might have happened at the time of something else happening (*ḥarf li mā kāna sa yaqa'u li wuqū' ghayrihi*). However, this can only be correct if the *li* in this definition is interpreted as the *lām al-tawqīt* 'of timing', (or 'simultaneity', Versteegh 1991:84) and not as the causal (*ta'līl*) *lām*. I-H cites several verses from the Qur'ān to substantiate this, such as Sūra XVII vs.102: *law antum tamlakūna khazā'ina raḥmati rabbī idhan la amsaktum khāshiyata l-infāqi* 'If you possessed the treasures of my Lord's mercy, yet would you hold back for fear of expending'. In this verse the 'holding back' and so on would not be caused by their possessing the treasures, but by their being niggardly; in other words they would hold back whatever the case.

The definition which runs closest to I-H's own interpretation of *law* is the one proposed by Ibn Mālik: *ḥarf yadullu 'alā intifā' tālin wa yalzamu li thubūtihi thubūt tālīhi* 'a particle indicating the impossibility of what follows it (i.e., the condition), whilst the truthfulness of this first clause necessitates the truthfulness of the second'. Nonetheless, I-H offers a more accurate definition (ML 1:260) which he refers to as the most excellent of expressions: *law ḥarf yaqtaḍī fī l-māḍī mā yalīhi wa istilzāmuhu li tālīhi* 'a particle which necessitates the impossibility of what follows it and where what follows it is implied by it'.

To conclude the discussion on what is a fascinating particle, it is clear that I-H had many things to say on the issue of condition regarding *law*. In fact, his approach seems to underline the very essence of this study; that I-H was rarely in a position to offer wholesale innovation on a given subject, although he was never reluctant to offer novel interpretations or to develop existing arguments in a unique fashion, as we have just seen. On the other hand, he was always prepared to accept the views of his predecessors if they were founded on firm and enduring principles, as he did with Sībawayhi's definition of *law*. Although our opinion of I-H's technique applies to the whole of his work, Versteegh also identifies this varied approach with regard to this present subject of condition. On the one hand Versteegh (1991:84) identifies what he calls 'some hints at a pragmatic analysis of language use, as for instance when he (I-H) discusses the relevance of the fact that it is possible to use *lākinna* + negation after a sentence with *law*, proving that the condition has not been fulfilled';[35] this reflects to some degree at least the sophisticated nature of I-H's approach to language. On the other hand, we would also agree with Versteegh's conclusion (1991:89) that 'even grammarians such as Ibn Hishām, who were interested in semantic aspects of language as well, could not escape in the end the pressure of this syntacticism'. More will be said on this later.

lākinna

The main function of this particle, *istidrāk* 'amendment', was never really disputed. Once again we see I-H demonstrating a particular interest in the semantic aspects of sentences involving this particle.

In the first of the interpretations of its meanings I-H notes (ML 1:290) how amendment is based on what follows the particle being a logical contradiction to what precedes it, either as a direct contradiction, as in *mā hādhā sākinan lākinnahu mutaḥarrikun* 'this is not stationary, but mobile', or as an opposite of it (in meaning), as in *mā hādhā abyaḍa lākinnahu aswadu* 'this is not white, but black'. Some allowed a complete (semantically unrelated) contrast, as in *mā zaydun qā'iman lākinnahu shāribun* 'Zayd is not standing, but drinking'.

What is essentially understood by amendment, then, is a correction of the previous statement. This is more or less what I-H means (ML 1:290-91) in his second category for *lākinna*, which was put forward by some scholars, that regards the sense of this particle as amendment, and sometimes emphasis (*tawkīd*). Their interpretation of *istidrāk* is that it revokes what was wrongly affirmed (*raf' mā yatawahhamu thubūtuhu*), as in, for instance, *mā zaydun shujā'an lākinnahu karīman* 'Zayd is not brave but honourable'. I-H makes the observation that the two adjectives here are closely related in meaning, but according to their definition of *istidrāk*, the negation of the first adjective also gives the wrong impression that the other one should be negated. Another example of where there should be a semantic correspondence is in *mā qāma zaydun lākinna 'amran* 'Zayd did not get up, but 'Amr did'. In this case there should be a correspondence and similarity in the *ṭarīqa* 'behaviour' of the two men.

As for emphasis, this may be seen in the example which occurred in the previous section on *law*: *law jā'anī akramtuhu lākinnahu lam yaji'* 'If he had come to me I would have honoured him, but he did not come'. In this context *lākinna* emphasizes the impossibility conveyed by *law*. Moreover, there is no place here for *istidrāk* because it is known that he did not come before the particle *lākinna* came into speech.[36]

min

This particle is among those that have received most attention from the Arab grammarians themselves in the medieval period. Moreover, it has also been dealt with in a reasonably comprehensive fashion by Western grammars of Arabic (e.g., Wright 1933 2:129-39). One plausible explanation for the treatment it has received from the former group in particular is that it constitutes what we might call a neatly self-contained particle which, in spite of its many meanings, has a fundamental sense to which most of its meanings appear to relate back. Even the earlier grammarians acknowledged that the principal meaning of *min* was *ibtidā' al-ghāya* 'beginning point of a (specific) aim'. I-H notes (ML 1:318) how some scholars claimed that all its meanings relate back to this particular sense.[37]

As we mentioned earlier, it was also viewed as the antithesis to the particle *ilā*, which was also often quoted by the medieval linguists when they wished to give an illustration of what constituted a particle. Ibn Ya'īsh (*Sharḥ*, 8:10), for instance, compares the two particles on the basis that every action must have a beginning and an end, with the particle *ilā* conveying the latter meaning, of course. It is significant that Ibn Ya'īsh adds that al-Zamakhsharī began his section on the particles in the *Mufaṣṣal* with the particle *min* 'because of its frequent occurrence in speech, and the extent of its behaviour and meanings. Yet in spite of its many meanings, they are closely related' (*li kuthrat dawrihā fī l-kalām wa sa'at taṣarrufihā wa ma'ānīhā wa in ta'addadat fa mutalāḥima*). There is also evidence in ML that I-H believed that many of the senses of this particle which some other scholars interpreted as being other than *ibtidā' al-ghāya* did, in fact, have this as their meaning.

There are several occasions when I-H offers an alternative interpretation of a particular sense of *min* in a given context in which the sense of *ibtidā'* is apparent. One such occasion concerns a view put forward by Ibn Mālik that one of the meanings of *min* is *faṣl* 'separation', in which the particle precedes the second of two opposites, as in, for instance, Sūra II vs.219: *wa allāhu ya'lamu l-mufsida min al-muṣliḥa* 'God knows well him who works corruption from him who sets aright', or Sūra III vs.173: *ḥattā yamīzu l-khabītha min al-ṭayyibi* 'till He shall distinguish the corrupt from the good'. I-H suggests (ML 1:322) that the (idea of) separation can be determined from the operator (*mustafād min al-'āmil*), i.e., the verb in each case. In the first example here, knowledge (*'ilm*) is, naturally, one of God's attributes which by its very essence requires specification (*tamyīz*); in the second example, the meaning of separation is contained in the nature of the verb itself. I-H's conclusion, therefore, is that the *min* in question can only be for *ibtidā'*, or with the sense of *mujāwaza* 'going beyond'. In either case the starting point would be the good person, although if the latter sense applied here it would entail going beyond the good person to distinguish him from the bad one.

Another instance where I-H refutes the opinion of Ibn Mālik is in the situational example *wa kadhā akhadhtahu min zaydin* 'You took such and such from Zayd'. Ibn Mālik claimed that the sense of the particle here is for going beyond, but I-H suggests that it is for *ibtidā'*, since 'the taking began from him and ended up with you' (*al-akhdh ubtudi'a min 'indahu wa intahā ilayka*) (ML 1:322).

There are two further categories of the meaning of *min* which merit comment here. In the situational examples *mā jā'anī min rajulin* 'Not one man came to me' and *mā jā'anī min aḥadin* 'Not one person came to me', it was generally agreed that the particle in both cases is superfluous (*zā'ida*), since it fulfils the three conditions of superfluity set out by I-H (ML 1:323), i.e., that it is preceded by a negative (or prohibition or interrogative with *hal*), its noun is indefinite, and it is either an agent, direct object or topic (of a nominal sentence). However, according to I-H the function of the *min* in the two examples is very different. In the first instance, the particle is for *al-tanṣīṣ 'alā l-'umūm* 'signifying the generality', because it could have been considered a negation of the oneness before the inclusion of the *min*. In other words, one could have added '...but two men (came to me)' (*bal rajulāni*), with the sense of retraction (*iḍrāb*). In the second example, however, retraction is not possible, because of the generality of the word *aḥad*; therefore, I-H calls this category *tawkīd al-'umūm* 'emphasizing the generality'.[38]

One final point for consideration here concerns Sūra XXV vs.18: *mā kāna yanbaghī lanā an nuttakhadha min dūnika min awliyā'a* 'It did not behove us to take unto ourselves protectors apart from Thee'. I-H refutes the reading of the verb *nuttakhadha* in this form (ML 1:324), and refers to it as anomalous. Moreover, he objects to Ibn Mālik's interpretation of the particle as superfluous and to his view that the word *awliyā'* is a circumstantial accusative/dependent case (*ḥāl*) as a result of his accepting the anomalous reading. This is partly because Ibn Mālik considered that the verb *ittakhadha* can take only one object, whereas most other scholars agreed that it could take two; therefore, *awliyā'* would become a second object. I-H notes, however, that the anomalous reading and Ibn Mālik's interpretation lead to a corruption of the meaning. In other words, we would assume that the resulting meaning in that case would be that they (the angels) were taken as protectors instead of God. I-H alludes to this interpretation when he adds that it is just like when you say *mā kāna laka an tattakhidha zaydan fī ḥālat kawnihi khādhilan laka* 'You did not have to take Zayd unto yourself at the time when he was being a disappointment to you'. In this case you are confirming his disappointing behaviour whilst prohibiting the taking of him. Likewise, in the verse above such an interpretation would imply that the angels confirmed the position of protector for themselves.

na'am (and balā)

The particle *na'am* may occur after negative or affirmative sentences, as we shall presently. It is also worth including the particle *lā* within this discussion, which only occurs after non-negative sentences, whether they are affirmative (*khabarī*), or interrogative (*istifhāmī*). I-H notes (ML 1:345) that Sībawayhi recorded the meanings of *na'am* as promise (*'ida*) and verification (*taṣdīq*), as in, for example, when one asks *hal qāma zaydun* 'Did Zayd get up ?', so you reply *na'am* 'Yes' to verify that he did. However, I-H adds that he did not record the meaning of informing (*i'lām*) which is also an important one. For instance, you do not say to someone who has asked the preceding question *ṣadaqta* 'You have spoken the truth', because that would be non-affirmative (*inshā'ī*), not affirmative (*khabarī*) (cf. Larcher 1990). Therefore, the particle performs the function of informing in this regard (ML 1:346).[39]

In general terms the particle *balā* occurs as a contradiction to a negative statement, and is therefore to be found in response to sentences containg negative particles, or sentences which may be interpreted as negative, as in, for example, Sūra XXXIX vs.57: *law anna allāha hadānī* 'If only God had guided me', to which the reply is to be found in vs.60: *balā qad jā'atka āyātī* 'Yes indeed! My signs did come to thee' (ML 1:346).[40]

For the purposes of comparison between the functions and meanings of *na'am* and *balā* (and. to a lesser extent, *lā*), the following table may help as an illustration:

	jumla 'sentence'	***taṣdīq*** 'verification'	***takdhīb*** 'denial'
(i)	*qāma zaydun*	*na'am*	*lā*
	Zayd got up"	Yes, he did'	'No, he did not'
(ii)	*mā qāma zaydun*	*na'am*	*balā*
	'Zayd did not get up'	'No, he did not'	'Yes, he did'
(iii)	*a qāma zaydun*	*na'am*	*lā*
	'Did Zayd get up ?'	'Yes, he did'	'No, he did not'
(iv)	*a lam yaqum zaydun*	*na'am*	*balā*
	'Did Zayd not get up ?'	'No, he did not'	'Yes, he did'
(v)	*a lam u'ṭika dirhaman?*	*na'am*	*balā*
	'Did I not give you a dirham?'	'No, you did not' (according to the form (*lafẓ*) and the *lugha*)	'Yes, you did'
		na'am	
		'Yes, you did' (according to the meaning (*ma'nā*) and customary usage (*'urf*)	
(vi)	*a lastu bi rabbikum?*	*na'am*	*balā*
	'Am I not your Lord?' (Sūra VII vs.172)	'No, you are not'	'Yes, you are'
		na'am	
		'Yes, you are' (according to customary usage)	

There are a number of observations to be made here. In examples (i) and (ii), the response is for confirmation (*taqrīr*) in reply to affirmative speech (*kalām khabarī*), i.e., in the form of either a statement or question here (al-Irbilī, *Jaw,* 446). In examples (iii) and (iv), the response is neither for confirmation nor verification, but for pure affirmation (*maḥḍ khabar*), which is in response to a question in these two instances (al-Irbilī, *Jaw*, 446). According to Ibn ʻUṣfūr, in example (v) some claimed that the response with *naʻam* is for confirmation because it can assume the status of the pure negative (*ajrat al-ʻarab al-taqrīr fī l-jawāb mujrā l-nafy al-maḥḍ*), even if the reply itself is positive in meaning (ML 1:347). Therefore, there were two possible interpretations of the response to this type of sentence, as the table above shows. First, if it were to be interpreted according to the (grammatical) form (*lafẓ*), one would expect *naʻam* to confirm the negative aspect of the question, viz., 'Yes, you did not give me a dirham'. On the other hand, an affirmative reply would suggest that a dirham was actually handed over according to the meaning (*maʻnan*). Finaly, in example (vi) from the Qur'ān, most scholars argued that to say *naʻam* implied heresy (*kufr*). However, it was also claimed that *naʻam* would be possible for confirmation on the grounds that the idea is to convey the meaning of the interrogative sentence, which is, of course, positive, i.e., 'I am your Lord...', to which the reply would be 'Yes (*naʻam*), You are my Lord' (al-Irbilī, *Jaw*, 447). This reply would be according to customary usage in the same way as the second interpretation of example (v).

hal

The distribution of the particle *hal* is much more restricted than that of the interrogative *hamza* which was discussed earlier in this section. I-H notes (ML 1:350) that there are ten differences between them, the most significant of which is probably that *hal* is for requesting positive verification (*ṭalab al-taṣdīq al-ījābī*), but not for establishing the individual (concerned with the verb) (*al-taṣawwur*), unlike the *hamza* which is possible for both. The restricted nature of the former means, for instance, that the speaker does not have so many options for displacement in the sentence. Therefore, pre-posing (*taqdīm*) of a noun is not permitted, as in *hal zaydan ḍarabta*

'Did you beat Zayd ?', because as we saw earlier, *taṣdīq* requires an establishment of the relationship (*idrāk al-nisba*) between the components of a given sentence, i.e., did / does something happen or not. However, the pre-posing of Zayd in the above sentence implies that there is no doubt that the beating did take place; rather you are trying to establish who was beaten. The same situation obtains in sentences containing *hal* and the conjunctive *am* (*al-am al-muttaṣila*), as in *hal zaydun qā'imun am 'amrun* 'Is Zayd or 'Amr standing ?', where you already know that one of them is standing (ML 1:349).

The particle *hal* is only to be found in affirmative (*ījābī*) questions. Therefore, it is perfectly acceptable to say *hal zaydun qā'imun* 'Is Zayd standing ?', but not *hal lam yaqum zaydun* 'Did he not stand up?'. Yet when I-H notes (ML 1:351) how the real intention of an interrogative involving *hal* is negation, what he appears to mean is that when its predicate is preceded by either the particle *illā* of exception, as in Sūra LV vs.60: *hal jazā'u l-iḥsāni illā l-iḥsānu* 'Shall the recompense of goodness be other than goodness ?', or the particle *bā*, for example, it denotes negation. In other words, the meaning of the verse here must be that only goodness can be the recompense of goodness. Another such example is that you can say *hal qāma illā zaydun* 'Only Zayd got up', but you cannot say *a qāma illā zaydun.*

A similarly potential outcome may be seen in I-H's review of an instance where one could argue that the *hamza* in Sūra XVII vs.42: *a fa aṣfākum rabbukum bi l-banīna* 'What, has your Lord favoured you with sons?', fulfils the same function, since there is little doubt here that God did not actually bestow this upon them. I-H proceeds to explain, however, that the function of the particle here is denial (*inkār*), as he noted in the section on the *hamza* (see above). In this case the denial is used against anyone who claims that something actually took place (*al-inkār 'alā man idda'ā wuqū'a l-shay'*), where it assumes the status of negation, but is not essentially a negative. I-H adds another category of denial to this, which is also exclusively for the *hamza*, that of denying what someone has actually done (*al-inkār 'alā man awqa'a l-shay'*), where the verb has actually been carried out. An example of this is *a taḍribu zaydan wa huwa akhūka* 'Would you beat (i.e., how could you beat...) Zayd even though he is your brother ?', where the beating has already taken place, but you are expressing your dismay at the fact. The third category of denial noted by I-H is exclusive to the particle *hal*, as exemplified by Sūra XV vs.60 above. I-H calls this denial of the occurrence of the thing (*al-inkār li wuqū' al-shay'*), where the event did not happen at all; the meaning is therefore negative.

wāw

There is one section in particular in I-H's discussion of the particle *wāw* which merits some attention here. He notes two types of *wāw* which must be followed by either a noun in the nominative/independent case, or a verb in the nominative/ independent mood (*yartafi'u mā ba'dahumā*). The first of these types is the one of recommencement (*isti'nāf*), which may be exemplified by Sūra XXII vs.6: *li nubayyina lakum wa nuqirru fī l-arḥāmi mā nashā'u* 'that We may make clear to you. And we establish in the wombs what We will'. In this verse there is no justification in arguing for the second verb, viz., *nuqirru,* to be in the same mood as the first verb because the first verb is connected to what precedes it, whereas the second verb begins a new clause. I-H corroborates this point with an interesting situational example (ML 2:359) in which the second verb can only be for recommencement, and can only be in the nominative/independent mood:

'(When they say)...*da'nī wa lā a'ūdu* 'Leave me alone (i.e., stop punishing me) and I will not repeat it', if the verb were in the accusative/dependent mood, i.e., for coordination (*'aṭf*) the meaning would bring together the idea of your refraining from hitting me, and my refraining from doing what I am being instructed not to do. Yet this is absurd, because the request is that the punishment should stop now (*fī l-ḥāl*); but if refraining from the thing being forbidden is tied to the present too, then the intention of the educator does not get home (*fa idhā taqayyada tark al-munhā 'anhu bi l-ḥāl lam yaḥṣul gharaḍ al-mu'addib*)'. The reason for the non-permissibility of coordination here is that an affirmative (*khabar*) cannot be coordinated to an imperative (*amr*).

The second type of *wāw* in this section is the circumstantial (*wāw al-ḥāl*) which was called the *wāw* of commencement (*ibtidā'*). In fact, I-H concludes (ML 2:360) that this is essentially the same as the function of recommencement. The characteristic of the second type here is that it precedes nominal sentences, as in, for example, *jā'a zaydun wa l-shamsu ṭāli'atun* 'Zayd came when the sun was rising'. I-H notes that Sībawayhi and the earlier grammarians implied that it had the meaning of the word *idh* 'at the time that'. However, according to I-H they could not possess the same sense since the particle cannot be synonymous with the noun. (*lā yurādifu l-ḥarf al-ism*). What they should have said is that the particle and what follows it are tied to the preceding verb (*qayd li l-fi'l al-sābiq*) (ML 1:359-60).

yā

In the section on the particle *bā'* (ML 1:105-106) I-H observes how it possesses certain syntactic and semantic privileges over other particles of oath in its capacity as the original (*aṣl*) particle of that group.

A similar type of hierarchical situation obtains for the vocative (*al-nidā'*) particle *yā*, which is the most widely used of the vocative particles in speech. For this reason, it is the only one of its type which can be reconstructed in a case of elision, as in, for example, Sūra XII vs.29: *yūsufu a'riḍ 'an hādhā* 'Joseph, turn away from this'. What is implied here is *yā yūsufu*..(ML 2:373).

The foregoing discussion on some of the more interesting and perhaps unusual aspects of the particles has attempted to show that I-H's concern with their meanings often extended beyond that of their more formal syntactic function. There is undoubtedly much more to be said not only on the particles discussed above, but on those which were omitted from this study. The reader may understandably question, for instance, the omission of such important particles as *fa* or *fī*. This decision was based on the principal consideration that there was little in I-H's treatment of these particles, and others, which suited our objectives, and which have not been adequately dealt with elsewhere. It is true that the need for more extensive research into the particles and their meanings remains, but the reader is referred in the meantime to such works as Carter (1981) for a more detailed account than most, or Wright (1933), or Reckendorf (1967) for a brief summary of the most important functions of some of the particles at least.

Let us now turn to the question of the possible substitution of certain particles for others which has already been mentioned in passing during this study.

The particles and synonymy according to I-H in ML[41]

Although I-H does not attempt to provide a theory on the notion of synonymy in ML, there is some evidence to suggest that he was one of several scholars who held that certain particles could be replaced by another in certain contexts without any effect on the meaning. The aim of the ensuing discussion is to determine what were the restrictions, if any, on this process. It is interesting to note that discussion on the subject of synonymy was essentially the business of the legal theorists, to whom we owe much gratitude for their efforts on discussion of linguistic issues, as we have already seen. It seems that opinion was deeply divided about the existence of synonymy in Arabic. The opponents held that synonymy in any language placed unneccessary demands on the language learner who was obliged to learn the additional expressions for a given extra-linguistic object. Those who supported its existence acknowledged that it enriched the language, and allowed the speaker many more options of expression for the same idea. In fact, the possible existence of synonymy represented just one of the many linguistic features, such as that of opposites (*aḍdād*), which gave credence to the argument of those like Ibn Fāris who championed Arabic over other languages.

In a work like ML, then, which specialises in part in a study of the particles, the issue of synonymy is obviously restricted to the potential interchangeability of these words. Synonymy between the lexical items which make up the language is naturally a much wider subject, but equally fascinating. In fact, I-H even makes a cursory reference to this aspect of synonymy when he notes (ML 2:607) that 'the right of two synonyms is that they should be able to take the place of each other' (*ḥaqq al-mutarādifayni ṣiḥḥat ḥulūl kull minhumā maḥall al-ākhar*). It is the potential synonymy of the particles which interests us here, however, although the term *murādif* 'synonym, synonymous' is to be found at various points in ML in the context of the particles, the issue seems to depend on the phenomenon of *niyāba* 'substitution', and its verbal derivatives, *nā'ib, yanūbu*. I-H notes in the section on *al-lām al-mufrada* (ML 1:226) that the function of the substitute of a thing (*nā'ib al-shay'*) is to 'convey its meaning' (*yu'addī ma'nāhu*). I-H affirms (ML 1:111), however, that the Basrans did not accept the concept of substitution for the particles at least. But there is evidence of at least a restricted form of exchange of one particle for another in ML, and this will constitute the basis of our discussion here.

The prevelant view amongst linguists of Western languages is that total synonymy rarely occurs, if at all. Jackson (1980:65) notes that 'two words are synonyms if they can be used interchangeably in all sentence contexts'.[42] Since this definition of strict synonymy rarely holds in language, the most realistic point of departure for our discussion here is to follow the view that what one can hope for at best is a form of loose synonymy (ibid.:66) where words can be substituted for each other in certain contexts, but not in all cases.

The incidence of loose or partial synonymy in ML rests predominantly with the category of prepositions / particles of obliqueness (*ḥurūf jarr*). Only rarely does I-H acknowledge the possible substitution of non-prepositional particles. Of particular interest in the context of the exchange of prepositions is the terminology used by I-H which is, with little exception, very consistent. He employs a range of terms to convey the idea of substitution, such as *murādif li* 'synonymous with', *muwāfiq li* 'corresponding to', *makāna* 'in place of' and, to a lesser degree, *ka* 'like', e.g., preposition 'a' is like preposition 'b'. Occasionally he uses the term *bi manzila* 'in the category of'. It is worth noting that the use of the term *bi ma'nā* 'with the meaning of' tends to be restricted more to non-prepositions, as in, for example, the particle *aw* may occur with the meaning of *ilā* as end point of a (specific) aim (*intihā' al-ghāya*) (ML 1:67), although it does occur occasionally in the context of prepositions.

To what extent, then, can some particles, principally prepositions, take the place of others? The particle which appears to be the most flexible in terms of the number of other particles whose meanings it can convey, or for which it may be substituted, is *al-lām al-mufrada*. It corresponds to (*muwāfiqa ilā*) seven other prepositions: *ilā, 'alā, fī, ba'da, ma'a, min,* and

ʿan (ML 1:212-13), in addition to the noun particle *ʿinda*. This correspondence in meaning could be exemplified by *samiʿtu lahu ṣurākhan* 'I heard cries from him' in which the original *min* has been substituted for the *lām*. Another illustration of this is Sūra XXXV vs.14: *wa kullun yajrī li ajlin musammā* 'each of them running to a stated term', in which the *lām* has replaced *ilā*.[43] Yet the customary vagueness with which I-H presents these correspondences, with just a few citations from the Qur'ān or poetry, for instance, means that one is not quite certain as to which of the several meanings of *ilā* the particle *li* is supposed to correspond. Could it possibly be all of them ? The answer to this, of course, is negative. After all, what emerges from a closer study of this whole issue is that a particle, normally a preposition, will only correspond to another in the latter's literal (*ḥaqīqī*) meaning, as is the case with *li* and *ilā*, although I-H does note the occasions when a figurative sense may also apply (e.g., ML 1:212). Further evidence of this may be found in the section on the preposition *fī* (ML 1:169) where I-H acknowledges that it can occur as a synonym (*murādifa*) of the *bā'* in very limited contexts, and also the preposition *min*. In the case of the former it can only be synonymous with it in terms of its original meaning of adhesion (*ilṣāq*) (al-Shamunnī, *Munṣif*, 2:5), since there are several meanings they do not share. The same situation obtains with *min* because the partial synonymy here involves only its original meaning of *ibtidā' al-ghāya*.

To continue this line of argument we see how the particle *ḥattā* may occur with the same semantic and operating status as *ilā* but that there are three fundamental differences between them even on that basis (ML 1:125). An important point emerges too in the section on *ilā* in its capacity to function with the meaning of with-ness (*maʿiyya*). One may initially conclude that on this basis it could occur without restriction in place of the preposition *maʿa*, but this is clearly not the case. In fact, I-H qualifies this by adding that this can only take place in the context of joining something to something else (*idhā ḍamamta shay'an ilā ākhar*). You cannot say, therefore, *ilā zaydin mālun* 'Zayd has money', even though you can say *maʿa zaydin mālun*. Another interesting example concerns the substitution of *bā'* for the preposition *ʿan* in the latter's capacity of *mujāwaza* 'going beyond', which is its literal meaning. An example of this substitution is the occurrence of the *bā'* in Sūra XXV vs.61: *fa is'al bihi khabīran* 'ask any informed of Him!'. Once more I-H is not specific about any restrictions in this regard, but one of the commentators on ML (al-Damāmīnī, *Sharḥ*, 295) observes that if you say *ramaytu bi l-qawsi* 'I fired from the bow', the particle here occurs with the senses of *isti'āna* 'the instrument used for assistance', and not for *mujāwaza* which is the normal sense of *'an* in *ramaytu 'an al-qawsi*.

In addition to the range of terminology noted earlier which I-H employs to denote the substitution of particles one for another, there are other ways in which he acknowledges this phenomenon. Sometimes he will state the meaning first and then state the particle to which that meaning corresponds, as in, for example, the particle *'alā* which can assume the meaning of *muṣāḥaba* 'accompaniment', like *'an* (ML 1:143). On other occasions he will cite the meaning, such as *'an* occurring for *ta'līl* 'cause' (ML 1:148), or *isti'lā'* 'elevation' (ML 1:147), and leave the reader to conclude from the textual evidence cited what the corresponding particle is, and whether the two particles are interchangeable with that meaning in all contexts.

There are also grammatical considerations which appear to come into play in determining the interchangeability of particles. A useful example of this occurs in the section on *min* in which I-H discusses briefly (ML 1:321) an example in which Ibn Mālik described the meaning of *min* as *mujāwaza* in *zaydun afḍalu min 'amrin* 'Zayd is preferable to 'Amr'. I-H appears to doubt this interpretation on the grounds that if it were for *mujāwaza* it could appropriately be replaced by *'an*. However, we are then informed that *min* is the only preposition which can occur with elative nouns (al-Shamunnī, *Munṣif*, 2:89).[44]

Overall, there is no doubt that I-H subscribed to the view that certain particles, particularly prepositions, could replace others in specific contexts. This is reinforced by a section in the final chapter of ML in which I-H assesses a selection of what he calls the beauties (*mulaḥ*) of speech in which two different expressions may have the same grammatical rules (*taqāruḍ al-lafẓayni fī l-aḥkām*), such as *ghayr* functioning like *illā* for *istithnā'*, or the conditional *idhā* performing the same grammatical function as *matā* with the jussive mood (ML 2:697ff.). He notes at the end of this section that if he had discussed prepositions here he would have given many examples (ML 2:700). However, that I-H was fully cognizant that any form of synonymy here was only partial is borne out by his view that the belief of some scholars that 'some prepositions may be substituted for others' (*yanūbu baʿḍ ḥurūf al-jarr ʿan baʿḍ*) should be modified by the insertion of the word *qad* 'may'.

It is now time to turn once more to the second section of ML in which I-H continues to present a neatly classified analysis of both the structural and semantic elements of the Arabic language. Although he concentrates in the second part on the sentence rather than individual particles, it should already be clear that the two aspects are inextricably linked. Indeed, the influence of the particle within this wider context will continue to be seen, although the particles cease to be I-H's point of departure in this section.

NOTES

1 al-Murādī, *al-Janā*, 85.

2 In addition to the insightful nature of Fischer's article it is also a good source of reference for many of the articles and books which have broached the question of the meaning of the term *ḥarf*.
Given that the tripartite division of speech acknowledged by Sībawayhi has been one of the bastions of language studies since Greek times, it is not surprising that some scholars have looked for a possible Greek influence on the ideas of the Arab grammarians in this connection. See, for instance, Versteegh (1977:43-45 esp.).

3 I-H's neat categorization of these extra 'bits' underlines what some modern scholars consider to be one of the major drawbacks of the traditioal presentation of Arabic grammar. According to El Sayed Omran (1991:306-7) the creation of a new category of speech, in addition to the tripatite one of nouns, verbs and particles, was one of the reforms called for by Fu'ād Ṭarzī in his work *Fī Sabīl Taysīr al-ʿArabiyya wa Taḥdithīha* 'Towards the Simplication and Modernization of Arabic'.

4 On the subject of terminology it would be useful to mention the valuable section on the prepositions by Ibn Qutayba in his *Adab al-Kuttāb*. Although a study of his ideas is not proposed here, such an undertaking would no doubt produce some fascinating results, particularly if it were carried out in conjunction with the commentary by al-Baṭalyawsī. For the moment, it suffices to mention that the prepositions were called *ḥurūf al-ṣifāt* by Ibn Qutayba, which we are told was a Kufan term (al-Baṭalyawsī, *Sharḥ*, 2:295; Ibn Yaʿīsh, *Sharḥ*, 8:7). al-Baṭalyawsī's explanation for this choice of term is worth recounting in full here. He notes that the term *ṣifāt* was employed because the prepositions (can) take the place of, i.e., assume the status of, the adjectives (also *ṣifāt*). Therefore, if you say *marartu bi rajulin min ahli l-Kūfa* 'I passed by a man from the people of Kufa', the sense (*maʿnā*) is really *marartu bi rajulin kā'inin min ahli l-Kūfa* 'I passed by a man (an existing one) from the people of Kufa', in which

the preposition *min* has taken the (syntactic) place of the adjective *kā'inin* here. Another such example provided by al-Baṭalyawsī is *ra'aytu rajulan fī l-dār* 'I saw a man in the house' of which the sense is *ra'aytu rajulan mustaqirran fī l-dār* 'I saw a man (situated) in the house. In this second example the reconstructed 'descriptive word' (*ṣifa*) is taken care of by the preposition *fī*. The significant point here is that this description may only apply to the prepositions, since it was not uncommon for grammarians to reconstruct an adjective as in the examples here; therefore the scope of Ibn Qutayba's particles is rather limited because it does not go beyond the prepositions. A possible explanation for this is that the earlier grammarians in particular were bound more by the form of a sentence and sought to explain away case-endings, predicates and so on by arguing for the existence of either explicit or implicit operants. It was this technique, of course, which led to one of the criticisms of the grammarians by Ibn Maḍā' in his *al-Radd ʿalā l-Nuḥāt.* For this point see El Sayed Omran (1991:300).
On the term *adawāt* Carter (1981:393,21.02 n.1) notes that although it was thought to be a Kufan term it is to be found on one occasion in Sībawayhi's *Kitāb.*
For an analysis of the status of prepositions as a member of the family of particles, see Levin (1987).

5 To put this issue into perspective the limited number of particles which may undergo elision works to the advantage of the argument here that the particles in medieval Arabic bear considerable significance. It is only a few of the arguably less important ones such as *qad* in its capacity as a simple past tense marker (ML 2:636), or the vocative particle (*ḥarf al-nidā'*) (ML 2:641-42) which may be elided without causing considerable disturbance to the syntax in many cases.

6 It is regrettable that I was unable to obtain the work carried out on the particle by D.E. Kouloughli entitled 'Les Particules ont-elles un sens ? (Autour d'une controverse dans la tradition grammaticale arabe', in the *Bulletin de Linguistique Appliquée et Générale,* 13, Université de Besançon.)

7 For the employment of these terms in the literature on Western languages see, for instance, Eco (1976:67) or

Weinreich (1980:277). Ullmann (1962:44) suggests 'autosemantic' for the so-called full words, and 'synsemantic' for the form words. Frank (1981:287ff.) is an excellent reference for the use of such terms as 'syncategorematic' with regard to the medieval Arabic situation. An appreciation of the unique role of the particles can be found in Ḥassān (1979: 123ff. esp.). He acknowledges that not only are the *adawat* the essential pivot of a sentence but they are also one of the most important elements of *ta'līq* 'syntactico-semantic connection' (ibid.: 127). One could suggest here that Ḥassān's treatment of this category of a speech is a more refined version of what I-H was actually trying to show, which only serves to underscore once again the relatively sophisticated approach of I-H.

8 Compare, for example, I-H's discussion of the particle *innamā* (ML 1:307ff.) with that of al-Jurjānī (*Dalā'il*, 228ff.) where the latter goes into considerably more detail on the concept of word order.

9 For all this see Ibn Ya'īsh, *Sharḥ*, 8:2. Compare this idea with the view put forward in the introduction to al-Murādī's *al-Janā*, 90. Here the editor notes that the same applies to the definite article *al*, for instance, i.e., if you say *al-ghulām* 'the slave boy', the combination of the definite article plus the noun conveys the idea of definiteness, whereas *al* by itself does not actually convey a meaning.

10 See Wehr (1976:10). It is clear that the term *adawāt* was used for nouns (and probably nouns and adverbs) resembling the particle by at least the time of al-Murādī. He notes, for instance, that *in* is the main conditional tool (*umm adawāt al-sharṭ*) (*al-Janā*, 228). Yet we have already seen that some conditional words were nouns and not particles. On a more contemporary note we find the terms *ḥurūf* and *adawāt* employed for 'particles' in a fairly comprehensive Western grammar of Arabic (Wright 1933 1:267). Wright affirms that there are 'four sorts (of particle)...prepositions, adverbs, conjunctions and interjections'. This categorisation is much closer to the mark, but still falls short of describing which nouns and verbs resemble these particles and fall within this class of words.

11 See, for instance, al-Irbilī (*Jaw*, 558) who creates a separate category for this type of word which he calls *mushtarak* 'shared (meaning)'.

12 The question of lack of syntactic status will be tackled in more depth in Chapter Six. For the moment it suffices to mention that what is meant here is essentially that they do not bear any syntactic status themselves within the sentence or context in which they are being discussed. What should be made clear, however, is that this acknowledgement by I-H does not undermine the importance held by the particles as 'cultural units' (cf. above Chapter Two). In other words he would not necessarily have been consciously aware of their semantic value, but would almost certainly have recognised their 'cultural' value within the extra-linguistic context, which prompted him to promote the particle to the forefront of his linguistic study.

13 For a useful explanation of *taṣawwur* and *taṣdīq* see Isbir/Junaydī (1981:14). In their view the former is for *idrāk al-mufrād* 'establishing the individual' and the latter is for *idrāk al-nisba* 'establishing the relationship'.

14 On a point of terminology, note how al-Mālaqī (*Raṣf*, 46), for example, calls the former category *ījāb* 'affirmation' for the verification of speech (*taḥaqquq al-kalām*), with the meaning of *istikhbār* 'enquiry'.

15 Once again we cannot overemphasize the fascinating question of the variant terminology employed by the specialists on the particle. In this instance it is worth noting the views of al-Irbilī (*Jaw*, 30) who draws a distinction between the category of *taqrīr* and that of *ilzām*, which I-H does not list. According to al-Irbilī the former is only used in negative sentences whereas the latter is employed in affirmative ones. Moreover, *taqrīr* merely affirms the sentence whilst *ilzām* not only affirms it, but also seeks acknowledgement of it.

16 To set this discussion in context, I-H has preceded it with a long section on the function of the particle *an* as a 'verbal noun' particle (ML 1:27-28), in which he explores the relationship between the verbal noun and the subjunctive (dependent) mood of the verb. Thus the verbal construction in Sūra II vs.185, for example: *an taṣūmū khayrun lakum* 'and

that you should fast is better for you', can be replaced by *al-ṣiyāmu khayrun lakum* lit.'Fasting is better for you', with no change in meaning.

17 The editor of this edition of ML, in one of his rare notes, indicates that I-H means *qaṣr iḍāfī* 'additional restriction' here when he says *ḥaṣr muqayyad.* In other words it is only God who has oneness, although there may be other things revealed to him.

The term *qaṣr* denotes a very important rhetorical device which is part of the inimitability of the Qur'ān. For a detailed discussion of this see, for example, Isbir/ Junaydī (1981:675-78).

18 The word Shechina is Arberry's representation of the Arabic *sakīna* which is a singularly difficult word to translate. Its general meaning, however, is the tranquility brought about by the presence of God in one's heart.

19 A further example of the variant terminology used by writers on the particles can be found in al-Irbilī (*Jaw*, 381). In the case of I-H's second category here al-Irbilī uses the term *iḥāṭiyya* 'all-encompassing', and he adds that previous writers on the subject had been far too general to include it.

20 It was suggested by al-Shamunnī (*Munṣif*, 120) that *ammā* is one of the most unique (*aghrab*) particles because of its capacity to perform the function of a conditional particle and a conditional sentence. It is also worth pointing out here that this particle, like so many of the particles, is discussed at length by other scholars, especially al-Irbilī who relies quite heavily on al-Astarābādhī; this fact in itself lends a more complex and almost philosophical flavour to the former's work. We would even go so far as to suggest that it is unlikely that I-H would have seen this work because it contains a richness that he would probably have found difficult to ignore.

21 A particularly penetrating analysis of the posited function of *aw* and *immā* is given by al-Irbilī (citing al-Astarābādhī) (*Jaw*, 259-60). He notes the following: 'Let it be known that permitting connection (*jam'*) between two things in, for instance, *ta'allam al-naḥwa aw al-fiqha* (which is an example of *ibāḥa*) is not known from the particles themselves, since

they were only posited for one of two things in every situation; rather it is known from what comes before *aw* and after it (together). (In the case of the example above), acquiring knowledge is a blessing, and increasing that knowledge is also a blessing...(since all these meanings) are only acquired through other accidental (*'āriḍa*) things. Thus division (*tafṣīl*) is known through the speaker's intention to divide (things); doubt (*shakk*) is known from ignorance; obscurity (*ibhām*) is known from hiding something from the one being addressed; unlimited choice (*ibāḥa*) is known from connecting two things from which merit (*faḍīla*) is derived, and limited choice (*takhyīr*) (from those connected items) from which merit is not derived'. What this illustrates above all, of course, is not only the importance of external factors in these, and other cases, but also the ultimate function of the meaning of a particle being in something else.

22 For a more detailed discussion of *niyāba* , see Gully (1994 (a)). It is also discussed briefly at the end of this chapter.

23 It is important to note that the identifying context for the particle *ilā* is often the particle *min* 'from'(al-Irbilī, *Jaw*, 422), presumably because in some ways the meanings of these two particles are both opposites and mutual complements, i.e., one normally does something *from* a place or time *to* a place or time. On a note of terminology - and this is a fascinating subject which would merit further study as we have already mentioned - al-Irbilī qualifies the meaning of *ilā* as *intihā' al-ghāya* by saying that it is of two types: *ḥissiyya* 'perceptible', as in, for example, *sirtu ilā Baghdād* 'I travelled to Baghdad', or *ḥukmiyya* 'rational' (?), as in, for instance, *maylu qalbī ilayka* 'My heart is inclined towards you'. The associative indication here is that you can put the particle *min* in both examples in order to say *min al-Baṣra* (*ilā Baghdād)* and *minnī (ilayka)*.

24 For a convincing case for translating *inshā'* as non-affirmative (or non-referential) see Larcher (1990:200 esp.). According to Larcher (p.208, n.14) *inshā'* is anything which is not *khabar* 'affirmative (referential)'; in other words, 'every utterance which can neither be true nor false, nor verified nor falsified' (transl. of al-Astarābādhī as cited by Larcher).

25 cf. Sībawayhī (*Kitāb,* 4:217) who says that this is its original meaning, even if other meanings diversify from it. This was also duly noted by al-Irbilī (*Jaw*, 36)who described this situation in a manner more akin to the language of the later scholars. He said that 'the *bā'* was used (to convey) other meanings, but adhesion can be seen in (all of) them' (*wa qad ustu'milat li ma'ānin ukhrā lākinna l-ilṣāqa mulāḥaẓa fīhā*). It should be pointed out that al-Rummānī (*Ma'ānī*, 36) preferred to use the term *iḍāfa* 'annexation' in preference to *ilṣāq.*

26 See also Isbir/Junaydī (1981:272) where *tajrīd* is acknowledged as a vehicle of *badī'*, one of the three main prongs of *balāgha.*

27 For an informative account of the particle *bal* in its rhetorical capacity see Isbir/Junaydī (1981:252-53).

28 On a light-hearted, but not insignificant note, references to the Doctor of *ḥattā*, based on an alleged PhD thesis devoted exclusively to that subject, are to be found in Arabic literature and in Arabic films, although the exact references elude me for the moment.

29 See also Wright (1933 2:165-66,178) where the function of *'inda* is reasonably well-documented, together with its counterparts *ladun* and *ladā*. In ML, I-H discusses their similarities and differences under *'inda* to avoid creating three separate categories.

30 For the translation of *ishtighāl* as 'preoccupation' see Carter (1981:477). For 'occupation' see Owens (1990:287). For more information, see below, Chapter Six, p. 218.

31 The translations for these meanings here are taken from Wright (1933 2:149).

32 It is, however, to be found in al-Zamakhsharī (*Kashshāf,* 3:279). Given the nature of that work one may observe how the type of issues discussed by I-H underline his interest in exegetical issues like the one in hand.

33 This example provides us with firm evidence that the conditional element of *law* is essentially tied to the past, which is clearly a restriction not recognised by modern grammars. It is also important to realize that this idea can be found at least as early as al-Rummānī (*Ma'ānī,* 102).

34 This technique of argument is almost certainly derived from logic (cf. Versteegh 1991:83), as is the one used on at least one other occasion by I-H that negation of a negative equals a positive (*nafy al-nafy ithbāt* (e.g., ML 1:17). Also, notice here how it is once again the grammarians and the *mu'ribūn* who are implicitly accused by I-H of not fully understanding the significance of *law.*

35 He is referring here to the example cited above, viz., *law jā'anī akramtuhu* to which you may add *lākinnahu lam yaji'* 'but he did not come' to emphasize that the verb of the conditional did not take place.

36 For an analysis of the pragmatic elements of the particle *lākinna* in selected later medieval Arabic grammatical literature, see now Larcher (1992).

37 See, for instance, al-Irbilī (*Jaw*, 335) who notes that this was the view of one as early as al-Mubarrad.

38 It is worth noting that al-Irbilī (*Jaw*, 340-41) subsumes these two senses of *min* within one category, that of *istighrāqiyya* 'totality', whether that entails totality of one of a type of species, or all of its individuals.

39 It is important to note at this juncture that I-H was fully cognizant of the distinction between the terms *khabar* and *inshā'*. On one occasion (ML 2:406) he acknowledges explicitly that he is talking about the *khabar* whose condition is the probability of falsehood or truth, i.e., the counterpart of *inshā'*, not the *khabar* 'predicate' of the topic (*mubtada'*). See also n.24 above.

40 For I-H's discussion of *balā* within its own section, see ML 1:113-14.

41 For a much more detailed version of the following discussion, which includes more reference to other sources, see Gully (1994 (a).

42 For other definitions see Gully (ibid.) .

43 A pertinent example of how circumspect one must be in assuming that one preposition can substitute for another in certain contexts is provided by Wright (1933 2:147-48). He says that *li* is etymologically related to *ilā* , but differs in that the latter 'mostly expresses concrete relations, local or temporal, whilst (the former) generally indicates abstract or

ideal relations. Hence *li* is rarely employed *li l-intihā'*. Although Wright acknowledges that this is its function in Sūra XXXV vs.14 (as above), he notes that 'its principal use is to show the passing on of the action to a *more distant* object'. This type of additional information is often lacking in ML.

44 It should not be overlooked that I-H was often criticized by his commentators for inconsistencies of argument. An illustration of this is his remark that *'an* is synonymous with *ba'da* (ML 1:148). We have already seen that I-H himself said that a particle cannot be synonymous with a noun (ML 2:360), yet he notes that *ba'da* is a noun; therefore , how can it be synonymous with a particle ? (al-Damāmīnī, *Sharḥ*, 295).

Chapter Six

FURTHER SEMANTIC AND STRUCTURAL ASPECTS IN PART TWO OF *ML*

> '...rather I wrote ML for the benefit of those who are concerned with exegesis as well as the Arabic language' (ML 1:650).

It is worth reminding ourselves that I-H's concern throughout ML is with *iʿrāb*. This chapter will continue to investigate to what degree the scope of this term may be extended beyond the notion of 'terminational syntax/inflection', 'mood and case markers', or 'parsing', to assume wider syntactic implications. When one talks about syntax, it cannot be assumed ipso facto that a study of that aspect of the language will necessarily reveal salient semantic features. We have already seen that when the earlier grammarians in particular discussed meaning within the context of *iʿrāb*, it did not entail anything more than grammatical meaning in many cases. Furthermore, when the grammarians concerned themselves with such phenomena as *taqdīr* it was not incumbent on them to produce new information about the semantics of a sentence. In other words, when they acknowledged that the underlying structure of the sentence *zaydan ḍarabtuhu* was *ḍarabtu zaydan ḍarabtuhu*, viz., where the accusative/dependent case of zayd is explained away by the reconstructed verb, they were not presenting any new information about the meaning of the sentence which is clear from the surface structure (cf. Versteegh *to appear*). In our study so far, then, we have attempted to show that I-H was concerned to demonstrate that there was much more substance to the relationship between structure and meaning than many of his predecessors had identified. On the evidence so far, a rather appropriate term to describe the content of some of ML might be 'grammatical semantics' (Bohas et al. 1990:118ff.).

At this stage it could be said that what I-H attempted to do was to bring together various related aspects of syntax and semantics which were either left unclear in the studies of his predecessors, or were apparently overlooked by many because those aspects, in particular what pertained to the *iʿjāz* 'inimitability' of the Qur'ān, constituted what was generally held to be the business of the exegetes and rhetoricians. Two general points which will be elaborated on shortly may help to corroborate the issues raised here. First, I-H distinguishes between two categories of sentence in the second part of ML, each of which has several types (ML 2:382ff.). The first category he calls *al-jumal allatī lā maḥalla laha min al-iʿrāb* 'sentences which do not have a syntactic function (within the sentence under discussion)' (cf. 'sentence filling a functional position', Bohas et al. 1990:125). Clearly the ideas of parsing and syntactic function are closely related because the manner in which one parses a given sentence is the way to determining its status and function. Second, the overlap between syntactic and semantic considerations may be seen particularly in one of the sentences with no syntactic function, that of the parenthetical sentences which were mentioned earlier. We may recall that according to I-H, the function of this type of sentence was to reinforce and embellish speech, although he implies that the grammarians did not see it in this way. This same convergence of syntactic and semantic elements is also to be found in the detailed discussion of elision. At once it becomes clear that certain elements of elision are to be interpreted on a structural level, while others offer firm evidence of the importance of semantic considerations (cf. Owens 1988:186). It is with I-H's analysis of the categories of elision that we shall begin here.[1]

Although the concepts of elision and reconstruction (*taqdīr*) can be seen at work throughout ML, I-H's long and detailed analysis (ML 2:603-50) brings together many of the various types of each, which in the process underlines how the two go very much hand in hand. As we have seen, *taqdīr* is, in essence, the restoration of those elided items, providing a reconstruction of the underlying structure. As for elision, Ibn Jinnī, who is considered by many to have influenced I-H's writings, made a significant contribution to the subject when he said that 'nothing can be deleted, unless there is something which refers to it in the context, and unless there is an awareness of it in its absence' (Owens 1988:186). One should not overlook here the concept of *iḍmār* 'suppression' which was an equally prominent feature of the studies of the earlier grammarians in particular. Carter notes (1991:123, n.7) that 'we might contrast *iḍmār* and *ḥadhf* as follows: (the former) is the mental act of suppressing the agent, while (the latter) denotes the physical cutting out of the agent morphemes from the verb'. Obviously this quotation is made within a specific context, since the scope of elision is much wider than this, but it does give a plausible illustration of the difference between the two.[2] Of particular interest and significance in ML, however, is that in the section on elision the role of *iḍmār* is less prominent. In fact, Carter (ibid.:122-23) notes an especially relevant point made by I-H (ML 2:604, 610) in this connection - to which context the above quotation belongs - that in the sentence *ḍarabanī wa ḍarabtu zaydan* 'He (Zayd)hit me, and I hit Zayd', the agent of *ḍarabanī* is elided, not suppressed, 'where *ḍarabanī* is clearly analysed not as 'struck (he)' with a hidden agent pronoun according to the normal rules for the agent of a verbal sentence but as *ḍarabanī <zaydun>* with the agent *zaydun* elided'. We would certainly agree with Carter that a full analysis of the relationship between these terms is required.

There are a total of eight conditions (*shuruṭ*) on which elision depends.[3] The first of these is that which depends on contextual considerations, or the existence of a *dalīl* 'indication / signification'. These indications may be related to either the grammatical form (*ṣinā'ī*), or the meaning (*ghayr ṣinā'ī*). In other words, the context is either structural or semantic, although it should be borne in mind that even in the case of the latter an ellipted word can always be restored to take its rightful grammatical place in the sentence.

To begin with the *ghayr ṣinā'ī* type, it can depend on one of two contexts: context of situation (*dalīl ḥālī*) which may be exemplified by your saying to someone who has raised a whip in order to strike someone: *zaydan*! 'Zayd', with the suppression (*iḍmār*) of the command *iḍrib* 'Beat!'; or verbal context (*dalīl maqālī*) which can be illustrated by your saying to someone who asks *man aḍrib ?* 'Who should I beat ?': *zaydan*! 'Zayd!'. Not only can complete sentences be elided, however, but also one of the two fundamental parts (*rukn*) of the sentence, viz., either the topic or predicate, as in Sūra LI vs.25: *qāla salāmun qawmun munkarūna* 'he said 'Peace! You are a people unknown to me', in which the predicate *'alaykum* is elided from the first sentence, and the topic *antum* is elided from the second one. There is also a type of elision where the elided part is an expression (*lafẓ*), which communicates a meaning on which the sentence is based, as in, for example, Sūra XII vs.85: *ta allāhi tafta'u* 'By God, thou wilt never cease', in which the prohibitive particle *lā* is elided (ML 2:603). I-H also raises a significant issue when he notes (ML 2:603-604) that the elision of an *'imād* 'structurally indispensible element' (c.f. Carter 1991:127) requires a context of situation, but the elision of a structural element which is redundant (*faḍla*) (c.f. Owens 1988:75: 'the optional sentential items like object, circumstance, etc.) does not require one.[4] However, this situation only obtains if the process of elision leads neither to a flaw in the meaning (*ḍarar ma'nawī*), as in, for example, *mā ḍarabtu illā zaydan* 'It was only Zayd I hit', in which the elision of Zayd would mean that the recipient of your hitting became unknown, or a flaw in the grammatical form (*ḍarar ṣinā'ī*), as in, for instance, *zaydun ḍarabtuhu* 'I hit Zayd' (ML 2:604). In this instance, I-H tells us (ML 2:610) that the elision of the object (*maf'ūl*), i.e.,*-hu,* would mean that you would be left with the construction *zaydun ḍarabtu* which is incomplete and incorrect. In this case, the construction would only be acceptable if *zaydun* became *zaydan*, viz., were put into the accusative/dependent case.

According to I-H the more structural (*ṣinā'ī*) type of context is the one in which the grammarians specialized (ML 2:605) because 'it was known only from the point of view of grammatical form' (*innamā 'urifa min jihat al-ṣinā'a*). This could be exemplified by the verse from poetry *innahā la iblun am shā'un* 'Are they camels or sheep ?', in which the underlying structure is *am hiya shā'un* because the disjunctive *am* particle can only be coordinated to sentences. In a sense, of course, I-H is indicating that his understanding of elision goes much deeper than that of the grammarians, especially as elision is very much one of the trademarks of the inimitability of the Qur'ān, and one of its more obscure qualities (*mubhamāt*).[5]

Another type of context discussed by I-H is what he calls *dalīl lafẓī*. In fact, we would also propose to translate this as verbal context because it seems to be subject to the same requirements as the *dalīl maqālī* (ML 2:606). The important factor here is that the *dalīl lafẓī* is dependent on its corresponding to the elided item in meaning. Therefore, you cannot say *zaydun ḍāribun wa ʿamrun*, i.e., *ʿamrun ḍāribun*, if you mean by the second *ḍāribun* the lesser-known meaning of 'journeying'. Similarly there was a consensus that allowed *zaydun qāʾimun wa ʿamrun* and *inna zaydan qāʾimun wa ʿamrun* 'Zayd is standing and (so is) ʿAmr', but not *layta zaydan qāʾimun wa ʿamrun* 'If only Zayd and ʿAmr were standing', since the mentioned predicate, i.e., *qāʾimun* is 'wished or hoped for' (*mutamannan aw mutarajjan*), whereas the elided predicate cannot be like that because it is the predicate of the topic. In other words, there would be a contradiction inasmuch as the first one would not have happened, but the second predicate must have already happened.

The *dalīl lafẓī* could be further exemplified by Sūra LXXV vs.3: *a yaḥsabu l-insānu an lan najmaʿa ʿiẓāmahu balā qādirīna* 'Does man reckon We shall not gather his bones ? Yes indeed; We are able'. According to al-Farrāʾ the underlying structure here is *bal yaḥsabūna qādirīna* in which the mentioned verb in the verse has the meaning of 'thought', and the elided one 'knowledge'. However, I-H favours the view put forward by Sībawayhi that *qādirīna* in the verse is an accusative of circumstance (*ḥāl*) with an underlying meaning of *balā najmaʿuhā qādirīna* 'Indeed, we gather them up ably', since the verb of 'gathering' is closer in meaning to the verb of 'reckoning'. Moreover, *balā* is a particle which makes positive a negative, and the verb of 'gathering' in the verse is negated. If one is to accept the opinion of al-Farrāʾ, it must be on the understanding that the 'reckoning' in the verse does not have the meaning of 'thought', but 'conviction' and 'certainty' (*iʿtiqād wa jazm*), since this would underline the extent of their infidelity.

If we pursue the more semantic elements of these contextual considerations we find examples of when elision may or may not occur, depending on whether it results in an impairment of the meaning. Thus you cannot elide the qualified noun (*mawṣūf*) in *raʾaytu rajulan abyaḍa* 'I saw a white man', because if you removed the word 'man' you would not know what the adjective 'white' was describing. On the other hand, you can say *raʾaytu rajulan kātiban* 'I saw a man, (who is) a writer', and elide the qualified noun 'man' here. In the same way you cannot delete the first term of the *iḍāfa*, i.e., *ghulāmu* in *jā'a ghulāmu zaydin* 'Zayd's slave boy came', even though it may be elided in Sūra LXXXIX vs.22: *jā'a rabbuka* '(and) thy Lord comes', because the first term of the *iḍāfa*, ie., God's command (*amr*) is immediately understood, and it could not be the Lord himself who comes.

A further interesting issue emerges in this connection with the interpretation of the verb *raghiba* 'to desire / detest', depending on whether it takes the preposition *fī* in the first case, or *'an* in the second. I-H notes how the preposition may not be elided in, for example, *raghibtu fī an taf'ala* 'I wanted you to do...', nor in *raghibtu 'an an taf'ala* 'I detested your doing', but he finds a way to explain the absence of the preposition in Sūra IV vs. 127: *wa targhabūna an tankiḥūhunna* 'and yet desire to marry them'. He says that the preposition here has been elided due to the presence of a *qarīna* 'associative indication'; but scholars disagreed on the original preposition because of the dispute on the reason for the sending down (*nuzūl*) of the verse. I-H adds that the source of the dispute lies, in fact, in the associative indication for the appropriate verb (ML 2:604).

We now move on to more examples of elision involving *ikhtiṣar* 'brevity' and *iqtiṣār* 'restriction'. In the first instance, I-H is in no doubt that one of the main objectives of elision is brevity. This may be seen explicitly on at least one occasion (ML 2:608) when I-H discounts the possibility of the elided item's being emphasized (*mu'akkad*), as in, for example, *alladhī ra'aytu zaydun* 'The one whom I saw was Zayd', where you cannot emphasize the elided relator (*al-'ā'id al-maḥdhūf*), i.e., *-hu*, on the verb *ra'aytu*, with, say, *nafsuhu* 'himself', i.e., Zayd himself. The reason for this, according to I-H, is that the emphasizer is employed to lengthen speech, but the elider (*ḥādhif*) brings about the opposite result. In fact, length of speech is the prerequisite for the occurrence of elision, so long as the elided item has not already undergone some form of abbreviation, as in, for instance, the noun that functions as a verb (*ism al-fi'l*) (cf. Owens 1988:190).

Of equal significance to the above is the section in which I-H looks at the elision of the object (of a verb) which he claims the grammarians called brevity (*ikhtiṣār*) and restriction (*iqtiṣār*) (ML 2:611ff.). He goes on to explain that brevity was intended when a contextual indication was present to denote the elided item, while restriction was employed in the absence of such an indication. What is particularly important here is that such examples are not necessarily part of elision at all. According to I-H there are three specific occasions when the object is absent, and each case requires a different explanation:

(i) when the intention is merely to convey that the action took place, without specifying who carried it out or who acted upon it. In an example like *ḥaṣala ḥarīqun / nahbun* 'A fire / plundering took place', the verbal noun is attributed to a verb of a general event (*fi'l kawn 'āmm*). This is not to be considered an instance of elision.

(ii) when the aim is to inform about the verb and its agent, as in Sūra II vs.261: *rabbī alladhī yuḥyī wa yumītu* 'My Lord is He who gives life and makes to die', of which the meaning is *rabbī alladhī yaf'alu l-iḥyā'a wa l-imāta* 'My Lord who performs the action of making life and death', or Sūra XXXIX vs.13: *hal yastawī alladhīna ya'lamūna wa alladhīna lā ya'lamūna* 'Are they equal - those who know and those who know not', of which the meaning is *hal yastawī man yattaṣifu bi l-'ilm wa man yantafī 'anhu al-'ilm* 'Are they equal who are described as having knowledge and those who are denied it'.

In these and similar examples, the object is neither mentioned, nor even intended. Moreover, they cannot be considered part of elision because the verb is intended to convey the idea of what does not require an object. This is what I-H calls *iqtiṣār*, where no contextual indication is required.

(iii) when the intention is to attribute the verb to its agent and (semantically) connect it to its object. In this case, both the agent and the object are mentioned, as in, for example, Sūra III vs. 125: *lā ta'kulū l-ribā* 'devour not usury'. However, if the object is not mentioned it must have undergone elision, as in, for instance, Sūra XCIII vs.3: *mā wadda'aka rabbuka wa mā qalā* 'Thy Lord has neither forsaken thee nor hates thee'. There are also occasions whan the grammatical form (*lafẓ*) requires the object, and if it is absent it has to be reconstructed, as in, for example, Sūra XXV vs.43: *a hādhā alladhī ba'atha allāhu rasūlan* 'is this he whom God sent forth as a Messenger', where the pronoun *-hu* which should be attached to the verb *ba'atha* must be restored to the sentence.

These examples serve to illustrate further I-H's objectives to clarify complex issues which in many cases were not properly understood by the grammarians in his estimation.

As part of I-H's policy of providing rules for as many grammatical and semantic categories as possible - and it is quite clear from the way he sets out his material and often supports it with sections for practice that he always has in mind either the *mu'rib* or the *mubtadi'* 'beginner', or both - he considers the various aspects of the sentence in which elision or related concepts appear in order to decide which parts take precedence, and which should be the last to undergo elision. Once more he seems to employ a system of hierarchy in this regard (ML 2:618ff.). For instance, if one has to select either the topic or the predicate of a nominal sentence for elision, it should always be the topic because the predicate is the 'essential conveyor of full meaning' (*maḥaṭṭ al-fā'ida*) (ML 2:618). Indeed, earlier in ML, I-H discounts the view of al-Akhfash that the elision of the predicate is widespread by saying that its elision is only essential if there is something to take its place (*lā yuḥdhafu wujūban illā in sadda shay' masaddahu*) (ML 2:602). One must apply a similar equation to the question of which item should be deleted in the case of when the verb is elided to leave the agent, or the topic is elided to leave the predicate (ML 2:619). I-H notes that in the case of the latter, the topic is the essence (*'ayn*) of the predicate, which would mean that the elided item would be the essence of the established (*thābit*), i.e., the predicate here, and it would be tantamount to there being no elision at all (*fa yakūnu al-ḥadhf ka lā ḥadhf*). However, this relationship does not obtain for the verb and its agent because the verb is not the same as the agent (in essence) (*ammā al-fi'l fa innahu ghayr al-fā'il*). Therefore, the result of this calculation is that the elision of the topic to leave the predicate is more appropriate than the elision of the verb to leave the agent.[6]

I-H presents a long and detailed exposition of all the various types of grammatical properties which can be deleted (ML

2:623-49), such as the first and second terms of the *iḍāfa*, the qualified noun (*al-mawṣūf*), the adjective, either part of the coordinated sentence (*al-ma'ṭūf / al-ma'ṭūf 'alayhi*), the circumstantial (*ḥāl*), specification (*tamyīz*), and so on, including certain particles. What is of particular interest to the argument maintained throughout this study that I-H set out with the intention of penetrating the field of *i'rāb* much more deeply than the grammarians, is where he concludes the section on elision by making more reference to the shortcomings of grammarians because they were only concerned with grammatical form (ML 2:649-50). He notes one or two occasions when they managed to go beyond this into the realms of exegesis, but acknowledges their efforts as an 'unwelcome intervention into the art of clear-exposition' (*fa innahu taṭafful minhum 'alā ṣinā'at al-bayān*). This surely constitutes more evidence that I-H was interested in more than just structural issues.

The inextricable link between elision and reconstruction (*taqdīr*) was indicated at the beginning of this chapter, and it is to the latter phenomenon which we turn now. I-H presents clearly defined categories for *taqdīr*, although the presence of elision is never far away, as Owens notes (1988:187) when he says that 'ellipsis can only occur when the ellipted item is (immediately) recoverable from the context'. In other words, the function of *taqdīr* is to restore the missing surface elements brought about by elision as directly as possible. Although some parallels may be drawn between the Arabic situation and modern transformational theory, there are also many differences, as Owens indicates. In fact, it is worth adding here Owens' remarks in this connection that unlike in modern transformational theory, 'the postulation of an intermediate structure would imply that it is not immediately recoverable'. This view may be corroborated by I-H's remark (ML 2:449) that 'good elision is when the deleted item is known immediately at the point of its reconstruction' (*wa innamā ḥusn al-ḥadhf an yu'lama 'inda mawḍi' taqdīrihi*).

On a structural level, then, the objective of restoring the underlying structure should be implemented as economically as possible. For this reason, the reconstruction of only two grammatical items in *ḍarbī zaydan qā'iman* 'my beating Zayd took place (when he was) standing', where what is understood is *ḍarbuhu qā'iman* 'the beating of him (happened while he was) standing', is preferable to the five restored items suggested by some, such as *ḥāṣilun idhā kāna* 'happened when he was (standing)', in which the word *ḥāṣilun* and its hidden pronoun, *idhā*, and *kāna* and its hidden pronoun, constitute five reconstructed elements. I-H refers to the former as 'less in terms of reconstruction' (*aqallu taqdīran*) which is preferable because it reduces the violation of the (underlying) original structure (*taqillu mukhālafat al-aṣl*). The above example comprising only two implied items is also preferred because it is taken from the existing grammatical structure in the form of the topic (ML 2:615,617; cf. al-Shamunnī, *Munṣif,* 2:251).

The last point of the immediately foregoing discussion is also testimony to the requirement of *taqdīr* that the restored item be inserted, if possible, on the basis of what has been mentioned, i.e., in the surface form. An illustration of when this is possible may be found in the phenomenon of *ishtighāl* 'occupation / preoccupation'. As we saw earlier, this occurs when a noun which would normally be the direct object of the verb in the accusative/dependent case, or the object of a preposition that goes with the verb, appears before the verb, as in *zaydan ḍarabtuhu* 'I hit Zayd'. In this case one must reconstruct a verb, i.e., *ḍarabtu* before the accusative *zaydan* since the verb in the example is preoccupied with the pronoun and cannot be the operant on the word *zaydan* (cf. Owens 1990:253). In this example, then, the restored item is inserted from what has already been expressed, so you say *ḍarabtu (muqaddar) zaydan ḍarabtuhu.* However, structural or semantic considerations may contrive to render this process of direct reconstruction impossible, as the following examples will attempt to show.

A structural obstacle (*māniʿ ṣināʿī*) to the restored elements being inserted from the existing expression can be exemplified by *zaydan marartu bihi* 'I passed by Zayd'. One may not reconstruct the verb *marartu* before *zaydan* because this would mean that the intransitive verb had made itself transitive. Therefore, the only solution according to I-H (ML 2:448) is to restore the transitive verb *jāwaztu* 'I passed by', i.e., *jāwaztu zaydan marartu bihi*. An example of a semantic obstacle (*māniʿ maʿnawī*) could be illustrated by *zaydan ḍarabtu akhāhu* 'I hit Zayd's brother', in which you cannot reconstruct the verb *ḍarabtu*, viz., *ḍarabtu zaydan* 'I hit Zayd', because that it is not what you wanted to say; rather the meaning in that case would be impaired. Therefore, one must restore the verb *ahantu* 'I humiliated', i.e., *ahantu zaydan ḍarabtu akhāhu* since hitting Zayd's brother is considered a humiliation of Zayd. However, I-H acknowledges that there are exceptions to both of these obstacles (ML 2:617). In the first instance, certain verbs that require a particle, such as *shakara li* 'to thank someone', or *naṣaḥa li* 'to give someone advice', can also be transitive verbs by themselves, without their prepositions; so in the example *zaydan naṣaḥtu lahu* 'I gave advice to Zayd', you can restore the verb *naṣaḥtu* and say *naṣaḥtu zaydan naṣaḥtuhu*. This is preferable to restoring an item which has already been expressed. Similarly, there is no semantic obstacle to reconstructing the verb *ahantu* 'I humiliated' before the example *zaydan ahantu akhāhu* 'I humiliated Zayd's brother', i.e., 'I humiliated Zayd and his brother', since you can say that humiliating his brother is tantamount to humiliating him.[7]

The discussion in this chapter so far has centred on the vitally important concepts of elision and reconstruction in Arabic grammatical theory. What I-H did was not only to piece together much of what had been said previously, but he also clarified and elaborated on these views in accordance with his own objectives. These last few examples have shown once again that for the most part he seemed to have a dual purpose to any argument; to illustrate both structural and semantic aspects of linguistic issues. Many of these examples from the immediately preceding discussion were, in fact, taken from a section entitled 'How to restore the semantically connected item in accordance with the meaning' (*kayfiyyat taqdīr al-muta'allaq bi i'tibār al-ma'nā*). Let us now turn to another key area of analysis by I-H in the second part of ML which highlights further the pursuit of semantic trends.

In Chapter Four of ML, in which I-H instructs the student or scholar of *i'rāb* on types of very common grammatical categories and their differences, he compiles an extremely useful section on the various aspects of coordination (*'aṭf*). There are three categories in particular which merit elaboration here, not least because the distinction which may be drawn between them demands an acute understanding on the part of the grammarian if he is not to misinterpret the subtleties of each. We shall concentrate princpally on the third of these aspects after brief discussion of the other two because that is the one most relevant to the question of meaning.

The first type of coordination noted by I-H (ML 2:473) is what may be called coordination according to the grammatical form (*al-ʿaṭf ʿalā l-lafẓ*). An example of this is *laysa zaydun bi qāʾimin wa lā qāʿidin* 'Zayd is neither standing nor sitting'. The condition required for the occurrence of this category is that the operator be applied to the coordinated item (*al-maʿṭūf*). In the example, the *bāʾ* operates on the word *qāʿidin* even though the particle is not repeated. However, one must be discerning in this connection because in the example *mā jāʾanī min imraʾatin wa lā zaydun* 'neither a woman nor Zayd came to me', *zaydan* can only be in the nominative/independent case because the superfluous particle *min* does not operate upon definite nouns. Yet the point here is that in spite of the different case endings, Zayd is still negated by the verb in the same way as the woman. Therefore, Zayd is coordinated in the nominative case according to the grammatical status (*ʿalā l-mawḍiʿ*).

The second aspect of coordination discussed by I-H in this section is coordination according to the (grammatical) status (*al-ʿaṭf ʿalā l-maḥall*). This could be exemplified by *laysa zaydun bi qāʾimin wa lā qāʿidan* 'Zayd is neither standing nor sitting', in which *qāʿidan* is in the accusative/dependent case as the predicate of *laysa,* and the function of the *bāʾ* which was effective with *qāʾimin* does not apply because of the intervention of the *lā.* [8]

Our main concern in this section on coordination, however, is with the category which I-H calls *al-ʿaṭf ʿalā l-tawahhum.* Earlier in this study (see above, Chapter Three), it was noted that the word *tawahhum* 'misconception' was one of the armoury of terms applied by I-H to the various erroneous views held by certain grammarians on linguistic matters. Nonetheless, it was also acknowledged that this term was also employed by I-H in a special, positive sense; it is this sense which is intended here. In a perceptive article Baalbaki (1982) discusses the ambiguity of this term, and examines the way in which Sībawayhī's use of the term was misinterpreted not just by many later scholars of the medieval period, but also by some modern scholars.[9] Baalbaki notes that I-H was one of the few later grammarians who appears to have understood what Sībawayhi meant by the term (ibid.:243; cf. ML 2:478). That being the case, I-H would seem to have developed the idea of *tawahhum* a little further. As a starting point we shall borrow Baalbaki's translation of the term as 'comprehension', with the additional idea of its conveying 'the speaker's restoration of elided parts in the utterance...in this sense... a synonym for *iḍmār* or *taqdīr*' (ibid.:235).[10]

In a similar way to *taqdīr*, the concept of *tawahhum* is significant in both a structural and a semantic context. The first example of *al-ʿaṭf ʿalā l-tawahhum* noted by I-H is essentially a structural one, as exemplified by *laysa zaydun qā'iman wa lā qāʿidin* 'Zayd is neither standing nor sitting', in which *qāʿidin* is in the genitive/oblique case (*khafḍ*) 'because of the restoration/understanding of the *bā'* preceding the predicate' (*ʿalā tawahhum dukhūl al-bā' fī l-khabar*) (ML 2:476). I-H adds that the condition of its being permitted is the soundness of the insertion of the understood operator (*ṣiḥḥat dukhūl dhālika l-ʿāmil al-mutawahham*). Even more important, perhaps, is that the 'condition of its excellent usage lies in the frequency of its occurring in that position'. In addition to this type of coordination occurring with the oblique items, it also occurs with the jussive verb, the nominative/independent noun, the accusative/dependent noun, and the subjunctive/dependent verb, as well as with compound structures (*murakkabāt*) (ML 2:476-77).

What is of particular interest to the discussion here is that there appears to be an establishable link between I-H's use of the terms *al-ʿaṭf ʿalā l-tawahhum* and *al-ʿaṭf ʿalā l-maʿnā*. When assessing the syntactic status of the sentence after the *fā'* in a particular conditional sentence of the Qur'ān, I-H concludes that the verse under analysis is an example of what is called *al-ʿaṭf ʿalā l-maʿnā* 'coordination according to the meaning'. He then makes the significant remark (ML 2:423) that in contexts other than the Qur'ān it is known as *al-ʿaṭf ʿalā l-tawahhum*. It appears that the latter term was never applied overtly, in fact, to such examples in the Qur'ān, although the terms *tawahhum* and *mutawahham* may be used when discussing a particular aspect of a verse such as Sūra XII vs.91 in which the verb *yaṣbir* 'he is patient' is in the jussive mood according to I-H (ML 2:477) because of the implication of the meaning of *man*' (*'alā tawahhum ma'nā man*), or in Sūra LXIII vs.11 where the suppressed (*muḍmara*) particle *an* and the verb after the *fā'* (ML 2:478) are to be interpreted as a verbal noun coordinated with a verbal noun which is understood from what precedes it (*maṣdar mutawahham mimmā taqaddama*). This is to discount the widely held view that the verb after the *fā'* in Sūra LXIII: *law lā akhkhartanī ilā ajlin qarībin fa aṣaddaqa wa akun* 'if only Thou wouldst defer me unto a near term, so that I may make freewill offering, and so I may become...', is in the jussive mood. We might suggest, therefore, that the reason for the non-application of the rubric *al-'aṭf 'alā l-tawahhum* to semantic related issues in the Qur'ān was probably due to the potential and seemingly widespread misunderstanding of the term *tawahhum*. After all, if grammarians had chosen to describe a particular interpretation of a verse as *tawahhum*, it might have led some to believe that the interpretation was erroneous, i.e., a misconception, even though the opposite was intended.

More evidence of the importance of the term on both a structural and semantic level may be seen in I-H's support of Sībawayhi's interpretation (ML 2:478) of the situational example *qāma al-qawmu ghayru zaydin wa 'amran* 'the people stood up except for Zayd and '*Amr*'. Sībawayhi argued that this is an example of *tawahhum* 'comprehension'. On a structural level *ghayr* must be interpreted as possessing the same grammatical status (*mawḍi'*) as the *illā* of exception, i.e., to account for the accusative/dependent case of *'amran*; on a semantic level, however, *ghayr* must have the meaning of 'except' here, otherwise it could imply that Zayd got up as well as the people (cf. Carter 1981:405).

I-H gives an indication, however, that coordination according to comprehension is a rather esoteric business, and should be avoided wherever possible. For example, there appears to be a connection between Sūra II vs.260: *a lam tara ilā alladhī ḥājja* 'Hast thou not regarded him who disputed...', and vs.261: *aw ka alladhī marra 'alā qaryatin* 'or such as he who passed by a city'. However, I-H notes (ML 2:479-80) that it is easier to interpret this on the basis of a suppressed (*muḍmar*) verb before the second verse, such as *aw ra'ayta mithla alladhī...* 'or have you seen such as he who...', because its meaning is already signified by the first verse, than it is to coordinate according to implication, which would result in a meaning like *a ra'ayta ka alladhī ḥājja aw ka alladhī marra* 'have you regarded such as he who disputed or such as he who passed by'. The first suppressed element here, viz., *aw ra'ayta mithla alladhī* was elided because it is already signified, and because both of the verses render the idea of surprise (*ta'ajjub*).

In this section on coordination according to comprehension/ implication, I-H includes an important note (*tanbīh*) (ML 2:480-81) in which he further underlines the importance of this phenomenon. According to the Basrans, the example *la alzamannaka aw taqḍiyanī ḥaqqī* 'I shall indeed stick close to you until you give me my right'[11] is of the coordination according to the meaning (*al-ma'nā*) type. In this instance the dependent/subjunctive form of the verb, i.e., *taqdiya*, is with the suppression of the subjunctivizing particle *an*, and the *an* particle with the verb are interpreted as a verbal noun coordinated with an understood (*mutawahham*) verbal noun, so you get *la yakūnanna luzūmun minnī aw qaḍā'un minka la ḥaqqī* 'Indeed my sticking (to you) or a giving from you is my right'. Of this type also is Sūra XLVIII vs.16: *tuqātilūnahum aw yuslimū* 'to fight them, or they surrender', provided that one follows the reading of the Qur'ān which deleted the *nūn* in the second verb. Otherwise, according to the majority (*jumhūr*) it would be an example of coordination according to the grammatical form (*al-'aṭf 'alā l-lafẓ*), whereby it concurred with the preceding verb, or even an example of suspending the connection (*qaṭ'*) by reconstructing *aw hum yuslimūna*.[12]

After presenting these optional interpretations, I-H extends the note by considering some controversial and ambiguous examples in which *al-'aṭf 'alā l-ma'nā* appears more likely than either of the two previous options. In the example *mā ta'tīnā fa tuḥaddithanā* 'You are not coming to talk to us', if the verb 'talk' is in the subjunctive/dependent mood then the meaning is clearly that your not coming precludes your talking to us, i.e., if you do not come, how can you talk to us ? There is also a possibility that it could merely be a denial of the 'talking' in the sense that you could come to us and do something other than talk. However, if this is compared to Sūra XXXV vs.33: *a yuqḍā 'alayhim fa yamūtū* 'they shall neither be done with nor die', only the first of the above meanings may apply, i.e., if they are not done away with, how can they die ? On the other hand, it is not possible for them to be done away with but not die. Once more the coordination in the verse is more likely to be according to the meaning, although the *lafẓ* and *qaṭ'* options would be acceptable. Of course, in the 'coming to talk' example, coordination according to the form, in which the verb was in the imperfect/dependent mood, would entail a negation of both verbs. With suspension of the connection, the 'talking' would be essential.

However, in the following examples, there is little doubt that coordination according to the meaning takes precedence over the form: *mā ta'tīnā fa tajhala amranā* 'You are not coming to us so you will be ignorant of our affair', and *lam taqra' fa tansā* 'You did not read so you will forget'. If these two examples were instances of coordination according to the form the verb 'to be ignorant' would be negated; therefore you would not be ignorant. Yet how could that be the case if you did not come ? In the second example, the verb *tansā* would have to be in the jussive mood.

As a final note on this subject it is worth pointing out that on one occasion, I-H notes how his interpretation of part of a line of poetry on the basis of something understood (*mutawahham*) impressed his former teacher Abū Ḥayyān a great deal (ML 2:528). This is one further illustration of the subtle nature of this concept which was clearly not identified by the majority of grammarians. We have seen how it bears similarities with the more widely known *al-'aṭf 'alā l-ma'nā,* and was itself used within the context of meaning. Indeed, it would be useful to determine whether any fundamental differences exist between these two terms. Let us now move on, however, to what I-H calls the quasi-sentence (*mā yushbihu l-jumla*) which constitutes another very important subject in the second part of ML.

The quasi-sentence consists of either the operator of the genitive/oblique case (*jārr*), i.e., the prepositions, and the genitive/oblique element, or the adverb (of time and space) (*ẓarf*). These elements have no structural value in themselves, but they must be (syntactico)-semantically connected (*muta'alliq*) to either the verb or its equivalent, or even to what is interpreted as its equivalent or to what indicates its meaning. If none of these four items exists it must be reconstructed (ML 2:433). It is worth adding here that the translation of *ta'alluq* as (syntactico)-semantic connection is more or less a literal translation of I-H's definition of the term in this section (ML 2:440) where he refers to it as *al-irtibāṭ al-ma'nawī* 'semantic connection'. The decision to add the term 'syntactico-' has been made to illustrate the inextricable relationship between any semantic link and the syntax of the sentence.

The issue of *ta'alluq* arose earlier in this study in Chapter Four, where we witnessed its importance for a correct understanding of speech, particularly in specific verses of the Qur'ān. Likewise, much of the discussion earlier in this chapter on elision and reconstruction hinged on the role of semantic connection. It is perhaps somewhat ironic, then, that these ostensibly structurally redundant parts of speech assume such importance when they occur in their rightful place with one of the above four categories. Yet this is no less than a reinforcement of the pivotal role played by all particles in the Arabic language system. For instance, in a section on the exceptions to when the preposition requires a semantic connection, I-H tells us that one of these exceptions is the superfluous *bā'*. Apparently, the superfluous particle only became part of speech to fortify and emphasize it, not to connect parts to it. However, 'the original rule was that verbs were all transitive, and unable to reach out to nouns, but the prepositions helped them to do this' (*wa l-aṣl anna af'ālan quṣirat 'an al-wuṣūl ilā l-asmā' fa u'īnat 'alā dhālika bi ḥurūf al-jarr*) (ML 2:440).

The rather intricate way in which the phenomenon of the quasi-sentence and its essential property of semantic connection works could be demonstrated by an example of where it is connected to something that is interpreted as resembling the verb (*mā uwwila bi mushbih al-fi'l*) (ML 2:434). In Sūra XLIII vs.84: *wa huwa alladhī fī l-samā'i ilāhun wa fī l-arḍi ilāhun* 'and it is He who in heaven is God and in earth is God', the original structure is *wa huwa alladhī huwa ilāhun fī l-samā'i*, so the preposition *fī* is semantically connected to *ilāhun.* I-H notes that *ilāhun* is, of course, a noun, not an adjective, since it can be described but cannot describe. Moreover, it is appropriate to semantically connect something to it because of its being interpreted as something worshipped (*ma'būd*); this is what gives it its verbal force.

One of the issues concerning the operator of the genitive/oblique case and the genitive/oblique element, and the adverb (of time and space), which produced considerable difference of opinion, was whether they could be semantically connected to the particles. The majority did not permit this, but I-H, following the views of Ibn al-Ḥājib as he does on many occasions, puts forward a cogent argument against this majority view (ML 2:438). In each of the following instances, taken from the Qur'ān and situational examples, the secret of the interpretation is that the preposition or the adverb is always semantically connected to the negative particle, and not to the verb as one may be tempted to suggest:

(i) Sūra XLIV vs.38: *lan yanfa'akum al-yawma idh ẓalamtum* 'It shall not profit you today, since you did evil'. In this example, the adverb *al-yawma* can be, according to Ibn al-Ḥājib, either an adverb (of time) of the 'negated' profit, or of the negative sense contained in the particle *lan*, i.e., all profit will cease as from today, in which case the negation is of an unrestricted profit (*naf' muṭlaq*). The latter is more likely, therefore, because otherwise 'the profit would be restricted to today' (*naf' muqayyad bi l-yawm*).

(ii) Sūra LXVIII vs.2: *mā anta bi ni'mati rabbika bi majnūnin* 'thou art not, by the blessing of thy Lord, a man possessed'. Once again, the second *bā'* here must be semantically connected to the negative, viz., *mā*, because if it were connected to *majnūn* it would convey the negation of a specific madness (*junūn khāṣṣ*) emanating from God's blessing. However, there is no such thing as a madness that is a blessing, and neither is a specific madness intended here.

(iii)(a) *mā ḍarabtuhu li l-ta'dīb* 'In order to teach him some manners I did not beat him'.

(b) *mā akramtu l-musī'a li ta'dībihi* 'In order to teach him some manners I did not honour the unpleasant person'.

(c) *mā ahantu l-muḥsina li mukāfa'atihi* 'In order to reward him I did not despise the good person'.

On example (iii) here I-H has much to say. In example (iii) (a), if the preposition *li* is semantically connected to the verb, i.e., to beat, it means that you did actually beat him, but not with the intention of teaching him some manners. However, if the preposition is connected to the negative particle *mā* it negates the beating altogether and conveys the idea that the reason for not beating him was to teach him some manners, since some people can be educated without being beaten. The same situation obtains for examples (iii) (b) and (c), since semantically connecting the preposition *li* to the verb would impair the meaning. In other words, according to I-H's interpretation, in example (b) the unpleasant person would learn some manners by not being honoured, as opposed to a meaning which implies that he was not honoured to teach him manners, but for another reason, and in (c) the good person would be rewarded without being despised, whereas a semantic connection with the verb would suggest that you despised the good person for a reason other than to reward him.

What is significant about this section in particular is that I-H is unequivocal on the fact that the majority of the grammarians did not permit semantic connection with the particle (*jumhūr al-naḥwiyyīna lā yuwāfiqūna ʿalā ṣiḥḥat al-taʿalluq bi l-ḥarf*) (ML 2:438). I-H refers to this preceding section as *kalām badīʿ* 'innovative speech', which is a term he uses in ML whenever he senses that his interpretation of meaning demonstrates a much more profound knowledge than that of the grammarians. The results of this section show unquestionably that the different interpretations of semantic connection lead to very diverse meanings.

If we return briefly to the concepts of *taqdīr* and *ḥadhf* there are two important elements of which one must always be restored to sentences involving any of the essential components of the quasi-sentence when they bear the grammatical status of one of the following: adjective, circumstantial clause, relative clause, predicate, or when they put the overt noun in to the nominative/independent case. This is because those components of the quasi-sentence must be semantically connected to something in the sentence. These two elements in hand are what the grammarians called an unrestricted being (*kawn muṭlaq*), and a particular being (*kawn khāṣṣ*) (ML 2:448-49). The following examples illustrate how these elements functioned.

In the example *zaydun fī l-dāri* 'Zayd is in the house', the preposition *fī* is semantically connected to a semantic connector which has been elided. In this particular example, and in those categories listed above, the reconstructed element normally takes the form of the unrestricted entity; the restored word is either *kā'inun* 'exists', or *mustaqirrun* 'is settled' (or their respective imperfect or past tenses if either the present, future or past is intended). Thus the situational example here would become *zaydun kā'inun / mustaqirrun fī l-dāri.*[13]

The 'particular being' involves the reconstruction of a word like *qā'im* 'standing', or *jālis* 'sitting', for instance. This type of semantic connector can only be implied, however, when there is a contextual indication (*dalīl*). Therefore, it is far less specific than the *kawn muṭlaq*, and will normally be construed on the basis of the semantic content of the sentence. Thus its elision was considered permissible, but not essential. The following example will illustrate the nature of the 'particular being', and its semantic relationship with the rest of the sentence.

According to I-H, a group of grammarians including Abū Ḥayyān believed that the elision of the particular entity was not permitted, even though I-H and many other grammarians agreed that the predicate may be deleted so long as there remained a contextual indication. Therefore, in Sūra LXV vs.1: *fa ṭalliqūhunna li ʿiddatihinna* 'divorce them when they have reached their period', in which the reconstructed element is *mustaqbilātin ʿiddatihinna*, i.e., a particular entity, Abū Ḥayyān interpreted the *lām* as a particle of timing (*tawqīt*); hence the verse would have had the underlying structure of *li istiqbāli ʿiddatihinna*, after which the first term of the *iḍāfa*, i.e., *istiqbāl*, would have been elided. According to Abū Ḥayyān's interpretation, then, this verse would not have contained a particular entity even in the original structure.

There are other instances cited by I-H which exemplify semantic connection in which the particular being is preferable to the unrestricted one. Once again, the criteria for reaching this decision are based on the economy of restored elements; in other words, the fewer the better, and the fact that the excellence of elision is when the elided item is known immediately at the point of reconstruction, as we saw earlier. An example of this is the famous *is'al al-qarya* 'Ask the village' example in which the word *ahl* 'people' is understood to come before the village. As an illustration of the preference for the *kawn khāṣṣ* over the *kawn muṭlaq* I-H cites Sūra II vs.173: *al-ḥurru bi l-ḥurri wa l-ʿabdu bi lʿabdi wa l-unthā bi l-unthā* 'freeman for freeman, slave for slave, female for female'. In I-H's view the restored element must be a particular entity, i.e., *al-ḥurru maqtūlun* or *yuqtalu bi l-ḥurri* and so on, whereas if it were of the other kind, the underlying structure would be *qatl al-ḥurri kā'in bi qatli l-ḥurri* which not only necessitates an elaborate and complex application of reconstruction, but which also delays one's knowing the meaning of the first term of the *iḍāfa,* i.e., *qatl* which is restored with the topic here, until after speech has been completed.

To conclude this discussion on semantic connection and the function of the *jārr/majrūr* and the *ẓarf*, I-H discussed them in another of his very short, but important, works (*Iʿrāb,* 113-14). Their inclusion in that work serves to underline their significance for our understanding of the syntactico-semantic elements of Arabic at that time. In addition, I-H discusses them in their own section as one of the eleven categories which make up the final chapter of ML (ML 2:693-94). He notes that the Arabs allowed more flexibilty in sentences comprising either the adverb or the word operated upon by the preposition than they did with other similar features(*yattasiʿūna fī l-ẓarf wa l-majrūr mā lā yattasiʿūna fī ghayrihimā*).[14] In all the examples cited by I-H in this connection, what seems to be taking place is indeed a form of syntactic disruption caused by the inclusion of elements of the quasi-sentence between two components of a sentence which are mutually dependent, such as the incomplete (*nāqiṣa*) verb *kāna* and the word it operates upon, as in, for example, *kāna fī l-dāri - aw ʿindaka - zaydun jālisan* 'Zayd was sitting in the house - or with you', or between the first and second terms of an *iḍāfa*, as in, for instance, *hādhā ghulāmu wa allāhi zaydin* 'this is, By God, Zayd's slave boy', or even between the preposition and the noun it operates upon, as in *ishtaraytuhu bi wa allāhi dirhamin* 'I bought it, By God, for a dirham'.

The story so far in this final chapter has been a pursual of the technique adopted by I-H in ML which he explicitly acknowledges in the chapter entitled 'On the nature of *i'rāb*'. That is to say that we have attempted thus far to elucidate some of the more significant structural and semantic issues of the second part of ML after having examined some of the smaller elements (*mufradāt*) in the previous chapter. As we saw earlier, I-H described the most important role of the *mu'rib* to be an assessment of the *mufradāt* and their properties followed by a thorough analysis of the sentence. I-H has shown on more than one occasion that many of the grammatical rules set out by the grammarians were subject to a system of hierarchy, in which certain parts of the sentence were considered to be more important than others; an example of this was the debate on whether the topic or the predicate could be elided from the sentence. We have also seen how certain particles took precedence over others. Of course, these issues were not determined by personal choice, but in many cases by considerations which gave due deference to the meaning of a sentence. I-H has undoubtedly demonstrated that structural considerations were only part of the picture. The basis of the argument here - and in a fashion which perhaps encapsulates I-H's objectives in ML - has been appropriately described by Weiss (1987:344) who notes that 'the constituent elements of language...form a hierarchy...with the syntactic structures representing the highest degree of complexity (in absorbing all other elements within them)'. That ML has received such widespread acclaim over the centuries is due in no small way to its comprehensive eclecticism on grammatical and semantic related issues. For the remainder of this chapter the focus will continue to be on selected points of interest to both the structuralist and the semanticist.

One of the elements of ML which has caught the eye of scholars is I-H's analysis of the sentence, its various types, and the rules for their formation. Among its many interesting features are the requirements for a sentence to constitute a verbal (*fi'liyya*) one. It is well-known that the main prerequisite of the verbal sentence should be that it begin with a verb, as in *qāma zaydun* 'Zayd stood up', or *ḍuriba l-liṣṣu* 'the thief was struck', and so on. I-H adds to this section (ML 2:376), however, that the occurrence of a particle before the verb does not affect the status of the sentence - the same applies to the nominal (*ismiyya*) type of sentence too. Thus the sentence *a qāma zaydun* 'Did Zayd stand up?', or *in qāma zaydun* 'If Zayd stands up...' retain their status as verbal sentences. In the same way, a sentence such as *a zaydun akhūka* 'Is Zayd your brother?' is still a nominal sentence. In other words, the occurrence of the *musnad* 'topic/agent' or the *musnad ilayhi* 'comment/verb' (Owens 1988:181) at the head of the sentence (*ṣadr al-jumla*) would take precedence, and their status would not be affected by a preceding particle.[15] With regard to the verbal sentence, the same situation obtains for sentences in which the verb is the first item in the original structure (*aṣl*). For instance, in the sentence *kayfa jā'a zaydun?* 'How did Zayd come?', or Sūra XL vs.81: *fa ayya āyāti allāhi tunkirūna* 'then which of God's signs do you reject?', these sentences also have verbal status because the nouns which precede them are, in fact, intended to be post-posed (*fī niyyat al-ta'khīr*). Also of interest here is that the grammarians considered the sentence *yā 'abda allāhi* 'O, 'Abd Allāh' to be a verbal one because of the restored verb *ad'ū* 'I call', or Sūra IX vs.7: *aḥadun min al-mushrikīna istajāraka* '(and if) any of the idolaters seeks of thee protection', on the basis that the underlying structure is *in istajāraka aḥadun*.

As with many grammatical categories, though, the issue was not as straightforward as it may seem, and there were several instances where a sentence could be interpreted as either a verbal or nominal one. This might ultimately be determined by the perceived difference of reconstructed elements, or merely by agreeing to accept that the grammarians had differed on a given point, and that both interpretations were acceptable. The following example serves as an illustration of this.

In the sentence *idhā qāma zaydun fa anā ukrimuhu* 'When Zayd gets up I shall honour him', the argument rested on determining the element which operates upon the particle *idhā* (ML 2:377). If one supports the view that it is the result verb, then the nominal sentence, i.e. *anā ukrimuhu* is the first part of speech because the particle *idhā* has been pre-posed from a post-posed position, and what follows it completes the speech with it because it is annexed to it. This example is just like *yawma yusāfiru zaydun anā musāfirun* 'I shall travel the day Zayd travels'. However, if one proposes that the operator upon the particle *idhā* is the conditional verb, i.e., *qāma*, and that the particle is not, in fact, the first term of an *iḍāfa*, then the first part of speech must be the verbal sentence, in which the adverb *idhā* has been pre-posed, as in *matā taqum fa anā aqūmu* 'Whenever you get up I shall get up'.

In another of his works (*I'rāb...*) I-H lists very briefly seven types of sentence which do not have a functional status, and seven types that do, as we mentioned at the beginning of this chapter. Given the apparent popularity of that work, according to I-H, it is no surprise that he chose to develop its brief, but pertinent, ideas in ML. What is of further interest is that I-H adds two categories to those sentences that do have a functional status which he claims were neglected by the grammarians. These are *al-jumla al-mustathnā* 'the excepted sentence', and *al-jumla al-musnada ilayhā* 'the predicated sentence' (ML 2:427). The latter, for instance, could be exemplified by Sūra II vs.5: *sawā'un 'alayhim a andhartahum...*'whether thou hast warned them', in which the predicated sentence can assume functional status if the particle *sawā'un* is parsed here as the predicate, and the verb *andhartahum* as the topic with the underlying structure of the verbal noun, i.e., *indhār*.

But perhaps one of the most significant aspects of the sentences with no syntactic status (*al-jumal allatī lā maḥalla lahā min al-i'rāb*) which is particularly relevant to this study is that the first three types; *isti'nāfiyya* 'inceptive', *mu'tariḍa* 'parenthetical', and *tafsīriyya* 'explanatory', all merit consideration on a semantic level to a certain degree.

The inceptive sentence was also known as the *jumla ibtidā'iyya*, but since that could lead to confusion between what is intended here, and the type of sentence beginning with a topic (*mubtada'*), the choice of *isti'nāfiyya* clarifies the matter, as I-H notes (ML 2:382). The inceptive sentence is of two kinds: one with which a particular pronouncement is made, the beginning of speech, as in, for instance, *zaydun qā'imun* 'Zayd is standing', where Zayd is the first thing you say, or, for example, the first verses of each sūra in the Qur'ān. The other type of inceptive sentence is the one which is cut off from what precedes it (*al-jumla al-munqaṭi'a 'ammā qablaha*). This could be exemplified by *māta fulānun raḥimahu allāhu* 'so-and-so died, God Bless him', or Sūra XVIII vs.83: *qul sa atlū 'alaykum minhu dhikran, innā makkannā lahu fī l-arḍi* 'Say: 'I will recite to you a mention of him'. We establish him in the land...'. Another interesting example is where the operator is nullified because of its being post-positioned, as in *zaydun qā'imun aẓunnu* 'Zayd is standing, I think', in which the verb *ẓanna*, which would normally put the second object, i.e., 'standing', into the accusative/dependent case, has lost its operating power because of its position. It is interesting to compare this example with *zaydun aẓunnu qā'imun* which I-H records as another example of a sentence with no functional status, but on this occasion it is of the parenthetical type because the verb comes between the topic and comment here, but has still lost its operating power.

Worthy of note in this connection are two further sub-categories of the inceptive sentence (ML 2:383-84). One of these was called *bayāniyya* 'elucidatory', and was acknowledged specifically by those rhetoricians called *bayāniyyūn*. The context of this usage is when the inceptive sentence functions as a reply to a reconstructed question, as in Sūra LI vs.25: *hal atāka ḥadīthu ḍayfi ibrāhīma l-mukramīna idh dakhalū 'alayhi fa qālū salāman qāla salāman* 'Hast thou received the story of the honoured guests of Abraham ? When they entered unto him, saying 'Peace!' he said 'Peace!'. According to I-H, the second occurrence of speech in this verse, i.e., when he said 'Peace!', is a reply to a reconstructed question *mādhā qāla lahum* 'What did he say to them ?'. Therefore it is separated from the first one, and is thus not coordinated to it. The other type of inceptive sentence was called *naḥwiyya* 'syntactic'. There would be seem to be a slight irony attached to the use of the term here, since I-H lists some examples of syntactic inception which might be difficult to perceive without a deeper analysis, and in which the meaning would be distorted if the relevant sentences were not interpreted as such. In most cases it was the rhetorician's art which determined the more esoteric aspects of meaning. In spite of this, however, there is no clear indication that the use of one type is considered to be more meritorious than the other, but further study would no doubt clarify this matter. It would be particularly interesting to determine whether the rhetoricians themselves made this distinction.

At any rate, the syntactic inception may be represented by Sūra XXXVII vs.7: *wa ḥifẓan min kulli shayṭānin māridin lā yassamma'ūna ilā l-malā'i l-a'lā* 'and to preserve against every rebel Satan; they listen not to the High Council'. I-H notes (ML 2:383) that one might initially interpret *lā yassamma'ūna* as a descriptive sentence (*ṣifa*) of *kulli shayṭānin*, or as its circumstantial qualifier (*ḥāl*). However, I-H believes this to be nonsense, because preserving from a devil that does not listen (nor try to create discord) has no meaning (*lā ma'nā li l-ḥifẓ min shayṭān lā yassamma'u*). I-H concludes that this is an example of syntactic inception in which the inceptive element is *lā yassamma'ūna*. If it were of the *bayānī* type, the meaning would be impaired because it would imply that *lā yassamma'ūna* was a reply to a reconstructed question about the condition of the devils after they had been protected from.[16]

Syntactic inception may be further exemplified by Sūra XXXVI vs.75: *fa lā yaḥzunka qawluhum innā na'lamu mā yasurrūna wa mā yu'linūna* 'so do not let their saying grieve thee: assuredly we know what they keep secret and what they publish'. In this instance, one might be misled into thinking that the sentence beginning *innā...* was actually what they said, but recounted in reported speech here.

A final example, again representing a semantic concern, is from Sūra XXIX vs.18: *a wa lam yaraw kayfa yabda'u allāhu l-khalqa thummā yu'īduhu* 'Have they not seen how God originates creation, then brings it back again'. I-H notes (ML 2:384) that the re-creation of creation has not yet happened for them in order to be able to establish having seen it. Therefore, the inception in the verse from *thumma yu'īduhu* conveys the idea that it is yet to happen. This is further supported by the verse immediately following it, i.e., 'then God causes the second growth to grow'.

Once again we have seen the importance of I-H's discussion on theological issues which can only be resolved by a sound understanding of the meaning of a particular verse. What these preceding examples have shown is that the parts of the relevant verses which I-H has focused on are to be seen as a separate part of the context to which they belong; this is what puts them into the category of sentences with no functional, or syntactic status, in the sense that they bear no immediate function in relation to the other parts of the sentence. It hardly needs to be added that within themselves they are structurally significant.

The second type of sentence with no functional status which we mentioned above is the parenthetical sentence. This was discussed in Chapter Three of this study and will not detain us here.

The third category of sentence from this type is the explanatory sentence (*al-jumla al-tafsīriyya*). This comprises the structurally redundant element which reveals the reality of what it follows (*al-faḍla al-kāshifa li ḥaqīqat mā talīhi*),[17] or as I-H later qualifies it (ML 2:402), that which reveals the reality of the intended meaning (*al-kāshifa li ḥaqīqat al-ma'nā l-murād bihi*).

An example of this is Sūra III vs.52: *inna mathala 'Īsā 'inda allāhi ka mathali ādama khalaqahu min turābin thumma qāla lahu kun fa yakūnu* 'Truly, the likeness of Jesus, in God's sight, is in Adam's likeness; he created him of dust, then said He unto him, 'Be', and he was'. The sentence beginning *khalaqahu...* is an explanation (*tafsīr*) of how Jesus' creation was like Adam's creation. However, the crucial point here is that it is not describing the likeness from the point of view of the outward form of the sentence (*ẓāhir lafẓ al-jumla*), i.e., that he was created after being foreordained as dust; rather it is describing it from the point of view of the meaning, which is to show that Jesus was like Adam in their uniqueness of not being born out of two parents (ML 2:399). Let us turn now to some of the sentences which do have a functional status (*al-jumal allatī lahā maḥall min al-i'rāb*).

A further significant example in this section is Sūra XXI vs.3: *wa asarrū l-najwā alladhīna ẓalamū ; hal hādhā illā basharun mithlukum* 'The evildoers whisper one to another; Is this aught but a mortal like to yourselves?' (ML 2:399). I-H notes that in this example the interrogative is explanatory for the 'whispering' (*al-najwā*), i.e., it explains exactly what they were whispering to each other, and the particle *hal* is for the negative (*al-nafy*). He returns to this point (ML 2:401) to add that what is meant here is that the interrogative is for negation to explain the meaning, and to fulfil the requirements of the grammatical form (*al-ṣinā'a*). In other words, the exceptive particle *illā* in this context must be preceded by a negation of some sort. He also notes that the category of explanation by itself does not require all this; obviously the context is the most important factor.

Among the sentences of this category is the one that follows a single entity (*al-tābiʿa li mufrad*). One of these types is the sentence which is coordinated with a particle, of which the *fā'* can be one, as in Sūra XXII vs.63: *a lam tara anna allāha anzala min al-samā'i mā'an fa tuṣbiḥu l-arḍu mukhḍārratan?* 'Hast thou not seen how that God has sent down out of heaven water, and in the morning the earth becomes green ?'. The *mufrad* in this verse is, according to I-H (ML 2:424), the word *mā'an*. Now, according to Abū l-Baqā, the verb *anzala* is coordinated with a pronoun after the *fā'*, i.e. *fa hiya tuṣbiḥu*. I-H discounts this view, however, by saying that there is no need to restore this pronoun, although he notes that its insertion could be for inception, i.e., to begin a new part of speech. Abū l-Baqā' also claimed that the verb *tuṣbiḥu* could have the meaning of *aṣbaḥat* 'became', and could thus be coordinated to the verb *anzala* without any syntactic status. I-H looks closely at this issue, and advances what he calls an innovative view (*badīʿ*) in response to this claim that the verb coordinating with the verb *anzala*, which functions as the predicate here, is without functional status. He argues that the *fā'* occupies the grammatical status of one sentence with the two sentences. Therefore, the one pronoun in the verb *tuṣbiḥu* is sufficient for both sentences. Moreover, the predicate is the combination of the two sentences, i.e., beginning with *anzala*, just like the conditional and result sentences which occur as a predicate. The grammatical status, therefore, is derived from this combination, and each of them is only a part of the predicate; in other words, in isolation they do not have grammatical status, but together they do. This is the *badīʿ*, according to I-H.

He develops this argument further (ML 2: 425) by noting that on the above basis, the *fā'* in sentences such as *zaydun yaṭīru l-dhubābu fa yaghḍabu* 'the flies are flying all around Zayd so he is getting angry', must be exclusively for introducing a clause denoting the result of the previous clause (*li maʿnā l-sababiyya*), not for coordination, just as it does in the conditional clause. There is another type of sentence which also lends itself well to this type of argument, which can be represented by *qāla zaydun ʿabd ullāhi munṭaliqun wa ʿamrun muqīmun* 'Zayd said that 'Abd Allāh is leaving and 'Amr is staying'. According to I-H the first sentence, *'abd ullāhi munṭaliqun*, is not in the status of the accusative/dependent case with the following sentence behaving in the same manner; rather the two sentences together are in the status of that 'case', whilst neither of them has individual grammatical status. This is because the speech (*qawl*), i.e. what Zayd said, is a combination of the two, and each sentence is a part of what was said, just as both parts of each sentence, i.e., *'abd ullāhi munṭaliqun* or *'amrun muqīmun* do not have any status with regard to what was said. It is in this capacity that we see I-H at his most inspirational.

To complete the picture the other types of sentence without syntactic status are the following:

> the one which follows an oath (*al-mujāb bihā l-qasam*) as in, for instance, Sura XXI vs.57: *wa ta allāhi la akīdanna aṣnāmakum* 'And, by God, I shall assuredly outwit your idols' (ML 2:403).
>
> the one which occurs as the result of a non-jussive conditional sentence which begins with the particles *law, law lā, lammā,* and *kayfa,* because the jussive element appears in the verbal expression itself (*li ẓuhūr al-jazm fī lafẓ al-fi'l*); or a jussive conditional sentence which is not connected (to its result clause) by either a *fā'* or the particle *idhā* of surprise, as in, for example, *in taqum aqum* 'If you get up I shall get up', because the second verb here derives its logical predicament from the jussive of the first verb (*li'anna l-maḥkūma li mawḍi'ihi bi l-jazm al-fi'l*) (ML 2:409)
>
> the one which occurs as a relative clause (*ṣila*) to a (relative) noun or a particle, as in, for example, *jā'a alladhī qāma abūhu* 'the one whose father got up came', in which the relative pronoun is in the nominative/independent case, and the relative clause does not fulfil a functional role because it has the status of a particular (*juz'*) of a noun (al-Shamunnī, *Munṣif,* 2:132), which itself has no status (ML 2:409).

the one which follows a sentence which itself does not have syntactic status, as in *qāma zaydun wa lam yaqum abūhu* 'Zayd got up and his father did not get up', so long as the particle *wāw* here is of the coordinating (*'āṭifa*) type (ML 2:410).

What this section seems to show is that the sentences without syntactic status are only interpreted as such in accordance with the context in which they occur, and in relation to the other parts of the sentence. Whilst there appears to be no single rule which one can apply to every example, the general picture presented by I-H is that the sentences of this type are subordinate to what is seen as the main vehicle of the meaning in a sentence. Such instances are to be found in the examples above of oath and condition. The criteria for determining this type of sentence appear to be both structural and semantic. As we have shown, certain elements of the inceptive and the explanatory sentence require semantic considerations. On the other hand, the role of the relative sentence above appears to be strictly formal. In this connection it is worth citing the view of Bohas et al. (1990:125) who compares the treatment of the relative sentence by the grammarians with that of the 'secondary sentence' by the rhetoricians. He notes the following:

> 'the rhetorical notion of secondary sentence does not correspond with the grammatical notion of sentence filling a functional position (*jumla lahā maḥall min al-i'rāb*). For example, relative sentences are not considered as sentences filling a functional position in grammar, while, quite obviously, they would be considered as secondary sentences in rhetoric, since they necessarily play a qualifying role of some sort in an utterance. This fact, if correctly considered, would in itself suffice to show how deep the difference of approach is between grammar and rhetoric'.

This observation is once more very pertinent, but we would suggest that I-H's analysis of the sentence reflects more than just a formal interest, as do so many of his discussions. This is borne out not only by some of the examples cited above, but also in the section on the parenthetical sentence which, as was demonstrated in Chapter Three, seems to contain a combination of elements which would appeal, and be relevant to, both the grammarian and the rhetorician.

To conclude this (regrettably) brief look at the contents of Chapter Two of ML it is worth noting the various types of sentence which do have syntactic status, or which fulfil a functional role according to I-H. In addition to the two extra ones mentioned earlier, these are the following:

> the one which occurs as a predicate with nominative/ independent status with the topic (*mubtada'*), or with accusative/dependent status with *kāna* and *kāda* (ML 2:410).
>
> the one which occurs as the circumstantial qualifier (*ḥāl*) with accusative/dependent status, as in Sūra IV vs.46: *lā taqrabū l-ṣalāta wa antum sukārā* 'draw not near to prayer when you are drunken' (ML 2:410-11).
>
> the one which occurs as an object with accusative/ dependent status (ML 2:412).
>
> the one which occurs as the element which is annexed to (*al-muḍāf ilayhā*) in the status of the genitive/oblique case, as with the nouns of time (*asmā' al-zamān*) in, for example, Sūra XIV vs.44: *wa andhir al-nāsa yawma ya'tīhim al-'adhābū* 'And warn mankind of the day when the chastisement comes on them' (ML 2:419).
>
> the one which occurs after the *fā'* or *idhā* as a result clause of a jussive conditional, as in, for instance, Sūra VII vs.185: *man yuḍlil allāhu fa lā hādiya lahu* 'Whomsoever God leads astray, no guide he has'.
>
> the one which follows a single entity (*mufrad*), such as the one which functions as an adjectival qualifier (*al-man'ut bihā*), as it occurs, for instance, in the accusative/dependent case after the word *yawman* in Sūra II vs.281: *wa ittaqū yawman turja'ūna fīhi* 'And fear a day wherein you shall be returned' (ML 2:424)

the one which functions appositively to a sentence which has functional status of its own (*al-tābi'a li jumla lahā maḥall*).[18] This applies to only two of the appositival categories, *nasaq* 'sequential coordination', and *badal* 'substitution', since the other appositives do not occur with sentences (al-Shamunnī, *Munṣif*, 2:142). The second category here is of particular semantic significance, as can be seen in Sūra XXVI vs.13: *wa ittaqū alladhī amaddakum bi mā ta'lamūna amaddakum bi an'āmin wa banīna wa jannātin wa 'uyūnin* '(so fear you God, and obey you me;) and fear Him who has succoured you with what you know, succoured you with flocks and sons, gardens and fountains'. According to I-H the prerequisite of this category is that the second element, i.e., the substituting part, must carry out the meaning more specifically than the first element (*sharṭuhu kawn al-thāniya awfā min al-ūlā bi ta'diyat al-ma'nā l-murād*). In the example here, God's blessings are actually specified in the second part after the repetition of *amaddakum* (ML 2:426).

In the case of sentences with syntactic status, it appears that those sentences carry either functional status in the sense that they are an essential part of the structural context in which they appear, or that they convey additional meaning to that context. Again there would seem to be a convergence of interests in I-H's categories above. Let us turn now to some of the other important aspects of I-H's syntactic analysis in the second part of ML.[19]

In Chapter Four of ML, I-H begins by analysing some important issues such as how to distinguish the topic from the predicate, the noun from the predicate, and the agent from the object (ML 452-53). We shall concentrate on the second and third categories here. In order to distinguish the noun from the predicate, one has to identify three occasions when the two occur together: when they are both either definite or indefinite entities, or one of each. The first two types are of particular interest because unlike many of the grammatical rules defined by the early grammarians, the speaker and the recipient of speech actually have a role to play in certain cases.

When both the noun and the predicate are definite entities, and the listener knows one but not the other, the known entity is always the noun, and the unknown entity the predicate. Therefore, one would say *kāna zaydun akhā ʿamrin* 'Zayd was ʿAmr's brother' to one who knew Zayd but did not that he was a brother of ʿAmr. Similarly one would say *kāna akhū ʿAmrin zaydan* "ʿAmr's brother was Zayd' to one who knew that ʿAmr had a brother but did not know that it was Zayd. However, if both the noun and the predicate are known, but the relationship between the two is unknown (*wa yajhalu intisāb aḥadihima ilā l-ākhar*), and one of them is more defined, then that would be chosen as the noun. In other words, you would say *kāna zaydun al-qāʾima* 'Zayd was the one standing' to someone who had heard about Zayd, and about a man standing, so that he knew about each of them in essence, but not that one was the other, i.e., that Zayd was the man standing or that the man standing was Zayd. If neither of them is more defined than the other then the speaker may choose whether he wishes to say, for example, *kāna zaydun akhū ʿAmrin* or *kāna akhū ʿAmrin zaydan.*

If the noun and the predicate are both indefinite entities and there is a justification (*musawwigh*) for either of these entities to be predicated, the speaker may choose which is the noun and which is the predicate, as in, for example, *kāna khayrun min zaydin sharran min ʿAmrin* 'A better one than Zayd was a worse one than ʿAmr', and vice-versa. However, if there is a justification for only one of them to be predicated, it must be the noun, as in *kāna khayrun min zaydin imraʾatan* 'A better one than Zayd was a woman'.

When the noun and predicate differ in that one is definite and the other is indefinite, the noun will always be the definite entity, as in *kāna zaydun qāʾiman* 'Zayd was standing'. The only exception to this occurs sometimes in poetic licence (*ḍarūra*).

We now come to an ingenious testing device which I-H employs to distinguish the agent from the object (ML 2:454-55). This serves to illustrate not only the dexterity of his own mind, but also the extent to which he was prepared to go in order to assist his students in their efforts to comprehend the complexities of *iʿrāb*. The most obscure instances of the agent and the object appear to involve a combination of a relative noun (*ism nāqiṣ*), so called because it requires a supplementary element to make its signification clear, and a complete (ordinary) noun (*ism tāmm*). The process for the application of this testing device, which clearly made an impression on later writers (cf. al-Suyūṭī, *Ashbāh*, 2:68-69), is as follows:

Step (i)

(a) replace the complete noun, if it is in the nominative/independent (*rafʿ*) case, with the first person singular (attached) pronoun of the *rafʿ* case.

(b) if the noun is in the accusative/dependent (*naṣb*) case, replace it with the first person singular (attached) pronoun of the same case.

Step (ii)

substitute for the relative noun a noun that has a rational or a non-rational sense (*maʿnāhu fī l-ʿaql aw ʿadamihi*)

Step (iii)

if the problem turns out to be correct after the application of these principles, it was correct beforehand. If not, it was incorrect at the outset.

Example

Can you say, for instance, *aʿjaba zaydun mā kariha ʿAmrun* 'Zayd liked what ʿAmr disliked', if you assume that *mā* is for something rational here ? To test this one would first put the first person singular nominative pronoun on the verb, in place of Zayd which was also in the nominative; this would give you *aʿjabtu*, and you would then replace *mā* with a non-rational noun like *thawb* 'garment'. Then you ask yourself if it is possible to say *aʿjabtu al-thawba* 'I liked the garment'; the answer, in fact, is no.

However, if Zayd were in the *naṣb* case it would be possible to say *aʿjabanī l-thawbu* where the first person pronoun in the *naṣb* case has replaced Zayd.

A further possibility here is that if the *mā* were taken as something rational, the *rafʿ* case would be possible too, since you can say *aʿjabtu l-nisāʾa* 'the women liked me' (lit. I pleased the women). Both the *rafʿ* and *naṣb* cases would be possible if the relative noun in the initial example were *man* or *alladhī*.

I-H then divides this category into further examples. You can say, for instance, *amkana l-musāfira al-safaru* 'the traveller was able to travel', with *musāfir* in the accusative case, because you can say *amkananī l-safaru* 'I was able to travel', but you can not say *amkantu l-safara* in order to achieve the same meaning. Furthermore, you can say the following:

(a) *mā da'ā zaydan ilā l-khurūji* 'What prompted Zayd to go out ?', because you can say *mā da'ānī ilā l-khurūji* 'What prompted me to go out'.

In the first example, Zayd is the object, and the hidden pronoun of *mā* is the agent.

(b) *mā kariha zaydun min al-khurūji* 'what Zayd detested about going out', because you can say *mā karihtu minhu* 'what I detested about him'.

In the first example, Zayd is the agent, and the elided pronoun of *mā* is the object.

However, you cannot put Zayd in example (a) into the nominative case because if you applied the testing device of (i) (a) and (ii) above, you would get *da'awtu l-thawba ilā l-khurūji* 'I invited the garment out'. Neither can you put Zayd into the accusative case because if you applied the testing device of (i) (b) and (ii) above, you would get *karihanī l-thawbu min al-khurūji* 'the garment detested my going out'.[20] Both of these instances are, of course, absurd.

What is particularly interesting about this device employed by I-H is that not only does it establish a number of syntactic possibilities, but more important, it is directed by semantic considerations. It is only the resulting sense of a sentence after the application of this device which distinguishes the agent from the object. On the subject of testing devices in general, Carter (1983(b)) assesses a device employed by Sībawayhi on the morphological range of Arabic nouns, using proper names as his yardstick. According to Carter (ibid.:116) 'Sībawayhi's successors, being for the most part prescriptive in approach, lost interest in such experimental techniques'. It is interesting, then, that I-H should reintroduce the technique of testing, but not surprising that he based it on semantic principles, as well as structural, in contrast to the morphological interests of Sībawayhi.

Among the many semantic related terms in I-H's repertoire we find frequent occurrences of the word *fā'ida* 'communicative meaning'. As was pointed out at the beginning of this chapter, and at various points during this study so far, structural and semantic issues are, more often than not, inextricably linked. To get to the bottom of a problem of meaning often requires a systematic breaking-down of numerous grammatical elements in order to determine whence the real meaning actually emanates. Often a given piece of speech may be understood on a superficial level, although the process by which that meaning is conveyed may be obscured, as the following example indicates.

In a short section on the parsing of the conditional and interrogative nouns and such like (ML 2:467), I-H includes a note on the question of whether the predicate of the noun of condition (*ism al-sharṭ*) is the conditional verb or the result verb in a conditional sentence, when the noun of condition is a topic of that sentence. In *man yaqum...* 'whoever stands up', *man* is considered a complete noun, and the conditional verb, viz., *yaqum*, contains a pronoun relating back to it. I-H adds here a supplementary item of information which should be borne in mind for the outcome of his discussion here, when he notes that if the above sentence did not have the conditional meaning it would assume the status of *kullun min al-nāsi yaqūmu...* 'each of the people stands up'. Is the conditional verb alone, therefore, the predicate of the noun of condition, or is it the result verb, or both?

After all, the result verb is the element through which the full meaning is communicated (*al-fā'ida tammat bihi*), and it contains a pronoun that refers back to the noun of condition. Besides, in similar examples like *alladhī ya'tinī fa lahu dirhamun* 'He who comes to me will get a dirham', the result clause is the predicate, or the predicate could be a combination of the two, as in *man yaqum aqum ma'ahu* 'whoever stands up I shall stand up with him', when it is in the status of *kullun min al-nāsi in yaqum aqum ma'ahu* 'if each of the people stands up I shall stand up with him'.

The conclusion to all this, however, is that the predicate of the noun of condition has to be the conditional verb, because 'the communicated meaning only depends on the result verb in terms of semantic connection, not in terms of predication' (*innamā tawaqqafat al-fā'ida 'alā l-jawāb min ḥaythu l-ta'alluq lā min ḥaythu l-khabariyya*).

The question of *fā'ida* arises again in a section on when the sentence may legitimately begin with an indefinite noun (*musawwighāt al-ibtidā' bi l-nakira*) (ML 2:467ff.). On this occasion, I-H criticises those early grammarians who only looked at this concept in terms of the communicated meaning; it was up to the later ones to acknowledge that they did not all lead to the essence of the communicated meaning (*mawāṭin al-fā'ida*). It is worth noting here that I-H's views in this connection were well received once more by later writers (cf. al-Suyūṭī, *Ashbāh,* 2:46-48), even though Ibn 'Aqīl (*Sharḥ,* 1:198) would have provided a sound source of reference for his comprehensive analysis of this subject. One of the more attractive elements of I-H's approach, perhaps, is its conciseness: he restricts the number of categories within this section to ten, in comparison with Ibn 'Aqīl who subsumed them into more than twenty categories.

According to the grammarians, the topic of a sentence could be an indefinite noun if it were qualified by an adjective (*mawṣūf*), or if it were an adjective taking the place of an implied noun (*khalf min mawṣūf*). However, I-H clarifies this view by noting that it can be qualified by an adjective according to either form, reconstruction, or sense. Furthermore, - and this is where he disputes their opinions on the nature of *fā'ida,* - not every adjective communicates a full meaning (*laysat kull ṣifa tuḥaṣṣilu l-fā'ida*). For example, it is not acceptable on this basis to say *rajulun min al-nāsi jā'anī* 'a man from the people came to me' because *min al-nās* is in the status of an adjective which does not communicate a full meaning.

At any rate, the three types noted by I-H are illustrated by some rather interesting examples (ML 2:467-68). The first type, that of form, may be exemplified by Sūra II vs.221: *wa lā 'abdun mu'minun khayrun min mushrikin* 'a believing slave is better than an idolater', or *rajulun ṣāliḥun jā'anī* 'a virtuous man came to me', where the adjective agrees with the noun in the normal way. In the case of reconstruction, the adjective may even be a preposition or a pronoun, as in *al-samnu manwāni bi dirhamin* 'two manas of ghee are for a dirham', in which the restored element is (*manwānī*) *minhu* '(two manas) of it'. With regard to the indefinite noun which is qualified by an adjective according to meaning, and which occurs as a topic, I-H cites two interesting examples which can only be of this type, even though one may be tempted to subsume them within the category of reconstruction. These examples are *rujaylun jā'anī* 'a small man came to me', in which the meaning of 'a small man' is contained within the word *rujaylun* because of its being a diminutive form. The other example is *mā aḥsana zaydan* 'how wonderful Zayd is!', which contains the meaning of *shay'un 'aẓīmun ḥassana zaydan* 'a great thing made Zayd wonderful'.

If we stay with this question of sentences beginning with indefinite nouns we find more material which serves as evidence that I-H's interpretation of this category was quite different to that of many other grammarians. It was mentioned above how Ibn 'Aqīl wrote at length on this subject, but, if we understand I-H correctly, the former would seem to have fallen into the same trap as the earlier grammarians by adopting a rather traditional approach to the subject. One such example is where Ibn 'Aqīl includes *mu'minun khayrun min kāfirin* 'a believer is better than an infidel', which he considers to be an example of the indefinite noun being an adjective in place of the implied noun (*khalf min mawṣūf*), i.e., *rajulun mu'minun*. However, I-H includes the examples *rajulun khayrun min imra'atin* 'a man is better than a woman', and *tamratun khayrun min jarādatin* 'a date is better than a locust'. In his view, the words *rajulun* and *tamratun* are nouns in their own right (*an takūna murādan bihā ṣāḥib al-ḥaqīqa min ḥaythu hiya*), as indeed would be the example *mu'minun.*

Two further possibilities for the indefinite noun to be the topic of the sentence are worth noting here; and it is perhaps significant that neither is to be found in Ibn 'Aqīl's work. We might suggest, in fact, that both examples lend themselves more to the rhetorical aspects of Arabic. The first one is where 'the establishment of the predicate for the indefinite noun is an extraordinary occurrence' (*an yakūna thubūt dhālika l-khabar li l-nakira min khawāriq al-'āda*) (ML 2:470), as in *shajaratun sajadat* 'a tree bowed down', or *baqaratun takallamat* 'a cow spoke'. These occurrences are, to say the least, unusual; therefore, to predicate such nouns with these occurrences communicates a (real) meaning. This may be contrasted with an example like *rajulun māta* 'a man died', which does not communicate a real meaning because communication should be based on conveying new information about something already known. With regard to (common) indefinite nouns, of course, one can never be talking about something already known because indefinite nouns, by their very nature, have not been previously referred to. The exceptions to this are when the information brought forth in conjunction with the indefinite noun is out of the ordinary.

The other example in this section which is akin to the category described above inasmuch as it would have an effect on the listener, is when the indefinite noun occurs after the particle *idhā* of 'surprise' (ML 2:471), as in, for instance, *kharajtu fa idhā asadun* 'I went out and there was a lion'. The significance of this is that under normal circumstances one would not expect to find a lion (or a man, and so on) outside the door as soon as one goes out. The impact made by the indefinite noun, therefore, is that one has no previous knowledge of the lion or whoever maybe waiting outside the door.

Another important context in which the concept of *fā'ida* features is in a section on the pronoun of separation (*ḍamīr al-faṣl / 'imād*), in which I-H alludes to the deficient analyses of many of the grammarians. This pronoun communicates three types of meaning, one formal (*lafẓī*), and two semantic (*ma'nawī*) (ML 2:496). In the formal case, the role of the pronoun is to inform that what follows it is actually a predicate, and not an appositive (*tābi'*). It is called the pronoun of separation because it separates the predicate from the appositive, or pronoun of support because the meaning of speech actually depends on it. I-H notes two faults here on the part of the grammarians. First, most of them only discussed this particular *fā'ida* of the pronoun. Second, many of them did not distinguish between the adjective and the appositive, although the application of the latter term in this context is much more accurate, as we can see from the occurrence of the pronoun in, for example, Sūra V vs.117: *kunta anta l-raqība 'alayhim* 'Thou wast Thyself the watcher over them'. I-H notes that pronouns are never described, nor qualified by adjectives; therefore, *al-raqība* can only be an appositive, and not an adjective.

The second *fā'ida* of the pronoun of separation is emphasis (*tawkīd*), which is a semantic consideration. For this reason it would not occur beside another emphatic device like *nafs* in, for instance, *zaydun nafsuhu huwa l-fāḍilu* 'Zayd himself, he is the eminent one'.

The third type was also based on semantic considerations. This was the one favoured by the *bayāniyyūn* such as al-Zamakhsharī. In fact, some of them restricted the function of this pronoun to the category of *ikhtiṣāṣ* 'particularization'. With regard to Sūra II vs.4: *wa ūlā'ika hum al-mufliḥūna* 'those are the ones who prosper', al-Zamakhsharī incorporated the three types of *fā'ida* when he made the important observation that the meaning communicated by the pronoun is to signify that what follows it is a predicate, not an adjective, and is used for emphasis, and to affirm that the meaning communicated by the predicate (*al-musnad*) is established solely for its topic (*musnad ilayhi*) (ML 2:496).

We might add here that there would seem to be little difference between the first and second categories, especially as the Kufans also called this pronoun the pronoun of support (*ḍamīr al-di'āma*) because it strengthened amd emphasized speech. The question remains, therefore, why should the first category constitute a formal one and the second category a semantic one ? The answer appears to be in the fact that in the formal category, the function of the pronoun appears to be one of simply informing that what follows it is a predicate, even if the meaning of the speech actually depends on that informing. However, in the semantic context the pronoun would seem to emphasize the relationship between the *musnad* and the *musnad ilayhi*.

To continue with meaning related issues it is worth focusing momentarily on a discussion of al-Zamakhshari's interpretation of a couple of verses from the Qur'ān to which we find I-H agreeing in part, but to which he also proposes a counter-argument (ML 482-83). This example is taken from a section called 'coordinating affirmative speech to non-affirmative speech and vice versa' (*'aṭf al-khabar 'alā l-inshā' wa bi l-'aks*) (cf. Larcher 1990). The verse in hand is Sūra II vs.23: *wa bashshir alladhīna āmanū wa 'amilū l-ṣāliḥāti* 'Give thou good tidings to those who believe and do deeds of righteousness'. To complete the picture, however, some supplementary information must be provided. Immediately preceding this verse are the words *ittaqū l-nāra* 'then fear the Fire (whose fuel is men and stones, prepared for unbelievers)'. In turn, this is a response to those who refuse to bring a sūra like one that has already been sent down, i.e., a response to the unbelievers, which begins 'And if you do not - and you will not - then fear the Fire...'.

Now, I-H agrees with al-Zamakhsharī that the coordination of the *wāw* here in *wa bashshir...* is not with the command *bashshir*, but rather links the reward of the believers, viz., 'gardens underneath which rivers flow...' and so on, to the punishment of the infidels (mentioned above). This is just like when you say, for example, *zaydun yu'āqabu bi l-qaydi wa bashshir fulānan bi iṭlāqihi* 'Zayd is being punished with the shackles, and go and give so-and-so the news for his release'. I-H adds that al-Zamakhsharī should have noted that the meaning is not entirely clear, and that what is actually meant is *wa alladhīna āmanū wa 'amalū l-ṣāliḥāti lahum jannātun fa bashshirhum bi dhālika* 'those who believe and do deeds of righteousness will have gardens, so give them the good tidings about that'.

What I-H objects to in al-Zamakhsharī's interpretation, however, is his view that the 'command' *bashshir* is coordinated with *ittaqū* in the above verse. Such an interpretation would entail that *bashshir* be a result of the conditional clause 'and if you do not (bring a Sūra like it)' from the previous verse, which would be incorrect because the command to bring good tidings is not conditional upon the infidel's failure to bring a Qur'ān like it.

It is probably fair to say that there are very few areas of the language dealing with syntactic or semantic concerns that escaped I-H's attention. At the end of Chapter Four of ML, for instance, he has two sections, one on the types and forms of the verb which can only be intransitive, and the other that looks at the elements which make some of the intransitive verbs transitive (ML 2:524). These sections constitute what is better known in the West as the derived forms of the verb. I-H's interest is in both their formal and semantic elements. For example, one of the verbs from the first section here is formed on the pattern *infa'ala*, such as *inṭalaqa* 'to depart'. I-H notes that while this is the formal analysis, the semantic element present here is that it is a 'reflexive form of a verb that can take one object' (*muṭāwiʿ li mutaʿaddin ilā wāḥid*).

Now the point of all this is that in the second section here (*al-umūr allatī yataʿaddā bihā l-fiʿl al-qāṣir*), I-H takes issue with a claim by al-Zamakhsharī that a difference exists between the occurrence in the Qur'ān of the verb *nazzala* with the doubling of the medial consonant (*taḍʿīf al-ʿayn*), and *anzala* with the *hamza* of transitivity (*hamzat al-taʿdiya*). It is true that these forms of the verb both incorporate transitivizing mechanisms, but al-Zamakhsharī perceived a distinction in the following from Sūra III vs 2-3: *nazzala ʿalayka l-kitāba bi l-ḥaqqi...wa anzala l-tawrāta wa l-injīla min qablu* 'He has sent down upon thee the Book with the truth...and He sent down the Torah and the Gospel aforetime'. According to al-Zamakhsharī the verb *nazzala* was used about the Qur'ān because it was revealed in instalments (*munajjaman*), whereas the other two books, i.e., the Torah and the Bible, were sent down all at one time (*jumla wāḥida*), so the verb *anzala* was used in the latter case. I-H notes that al-Zamakhsharī uses the verb *anzala* himself with regard to the Qur'ān in his own introduction to the *Kashshāf*, his major work on exegesis, as an antithesis to *nazzala* which, as we have already seen, conveys the idea of instalments, and was used in the context of the sending down of the Qur'ān from the heavens of this world (*al-samā' al-dunyā*) to the Prophet Muḥammad over a period of twenty-three years. In his introduction to the *Kashshāf*, al-Zamakhsharī says *al-ḥamdu li allāh alladhī anzala l-Qur'ān kalāman mu'allafan munaẓẓaman wa nazzalahu bi ḥasab al-maṣāliḥ munajjaman* 'Praise be to God who sent down the Qur'ān as an organised book, and revealed it in instalments according to need'. I-H suggests that he employed the verb *anzala* with the intention of conveying the sending down from the 'preserved tablet' (*al-lawḥ al-maḥfūẓ*) to the heavens of this world. On the whole, then, I-H agrees with al-Zamakhsharī on this point, but he cites examples from the Qur'ān itself in which the verb *nazzala* occurs even when the idea of its being revealed all at one time is being conveyed, which runs contrary to his argument. An instance of this is Sūra XXV vs.33: *wa qāla alladhīna kafarū law lā nuzzila ʿalayhi l-*Qur'ān*u jumlatan wāḥidatan* 'the unbelievers say, 'Why has the Koran not been sent down upon him all at once ?'.

In a work such as ML it is not surprising that a concept like *taḍmīn* 'implication (of meaning)' recurs at various points. In fact, I-H notes on one occasion (ML 2:686) that examples of *taḍmīn* in Arabic are so common that it was once said that if a book were compiled on the subject it would be several hundred pages long. One of the aspects of *taḍmīn* not mentioned so far is that in addition to its capacity to permit one word to convey the meaning of two, it can also extend the function of that word by making, say, an intransitive word transitive (ML 2:525). This could be exemplified by the verb *raḥuba* 'to be wide' which can extend to an object (*'addā ilā maf'ūl*) when it has the implied meaning of *wasi'a*. More than this, *taḍmīn*, which is unique among transitivizing elements according to I-H, is able to make a verb transitive by more than one degree. In other words, a verb such as *alā* with the meaning of *qaṣura* 'to hold back', can be transformed from an intransitive verb to a verb extending to two objects, provided it assumes the meaning of *mana'a* 'to hold back something from someone', as in *lā ālūka juhdan* 'I would spare you no efforts', i.e., I would do all I can for you. Some verbs can even extend to three objects on this basis.

We now come to a section in Chapter Six of ML in what are ostensibly grammatical considerations, i.e., whether a part of speech is the *maf'ūl bihi* 'direct object' or the *maf'ūl muṭlaq* 'absolute object', reveal a deeper semantic concern or, even more important in this case, a logical or even theological one. As a crucial starting point to this issue we may cite Sūra XXIX vs.43: *khalaqa allāhu l-samawāti* 'God created the heavens and the earth'. In this instance most of the grammarians interpreted the word *al-samawāti* as a direct object of the verb *khalaqa*. However, I-H advances the idea that it is, in fact, an absolute object (ML 2:660-61), although he acknowledges later that this was also the opinion of al-Jurjānī and Ibn al-Ḥājib, but that they were of a minority view. I-H defines what he perceives as the role of these two categories:

> 'The absolute (unrestricted) object is what the noun (object) can occur for without restriction (*bilā qayd*), as in when you say *ḍarabtu ḍarban* 'I beat a beating'. The direct object is what the noun (object) can only occur for with restriction through your asserting it', as in *ḍarabtu ẓaydan* 'I beat Zayd'. If you say

that the word *al-samawāt* is an object, just as you say *al-ḍarb* is an object, then that is correct. However, if you say that *al-samawāt* is a direct object just as Zayd is a direct object, then that is incorrect' (ML 2:661).

The key to this distinction in the verse in question, and other similar examples, is that the direct object is used for 'what exists before the verb which operates upon it' (*mā kāna mawjūdan qabla l-fi'l alladhī 'amila fīhi*). In this case the agent bestows upon it a verb. As for the absolute object, 'the verb that brings it into existence is the one which operates upon it' (*mā kāna al-fi'l al-'āmil fīhi huwa fi'l ījādihi*). I-H notes that the grammarians always assumed that the absolute object was used for instituting mankind's actions (*inshā' af'āl al-'ibād*), not for substances (*dhawāt*), and that it was only connected with events (*ḥawādith*). However, God (who is in the context of the verse above) is, of course, the creator of both substances and events. Therefore, the word *samawāt*, one of God's creations, must be an absolute object. I-H adds that the same principle applies to *ansha'tu kitāban* 'I composed a book', or *'amila fulānun khayran* 'so-and-so did a good deed', or Sūra II vs.23: *wa āmanū wa 'amilū l-ṣāliḥāti* 'and those who believe and do deeds of righteousness'. What needs to be comprehended in these two situational examples is that there appears to be an intrinsic semantic relationship between the verb and its object, which in these examples is an absolute object as opposed to a direct object. In other words, to bring a book into creation requires compilation; in the second example, a good deed actually needs to be carried out. What seems to be at issue here, particularly in a theological context as demonstrated by the verses from the Qur'ān, is a phenomenon in which the result of the act did not actually exist before the act started, but was brought into existence by the act itself.

There is also a case for considering the relevance of semantic connection in this regard. I-H cites one or two examples put forward by Ibn al-Ḥājib with which he disagrees, such as *anba'tu zaydan 'Amran fāḍilan* 'I informed Zayd that 'Amr is an excellent chap'. Ibn al-Ḥājib claimed that Zayd is a direct object, but that 'Amr and *fāḍil* are absolute objects because they are the essence of the informing (*nafs al-naba'*). In

I-H's opinion, what Ibn al-Ḥājib claimed are absolute objects are merely semantically connected to Zayd.

Another unequivocal indication of where I-H's real interest in the language appears to lie emerges in a section devoted to the semantic nature of the verb *kāda* 'to almost...', and its negative *mā kāda / lam yakad* 'to scarcely...(do something)'. This verb belongs to a semantic class of verbs denoting 'being near' (*muqāraba*). Worthy of note above all in this connection is that I-H gives no supplementary information about the other verbs of its type, nor of the grammatical rules pertaining to its usage. His sole concern is to provide a corrective interpretation of what the grammarians said about its meaning (ML 2:661-63).

The grammarians said that when *kāda* occurs in the affirmative, it means the negative, and vice-versa. If you say *kāda yaf'alu* it means he did not do it, and if you say *lam yakad yaf'alu* it means he did do it. They then cited two instances from the Qur'ān as proof of their argument. However, I-H has other views. He notes that this verb is no different from any other verb in that 'their negation is a negation, and their affirmation is an affirmation' (*nafyuhā nafy wa ithbātuhā ithbāt*). Given that its meaning is 'being near, on the point of', it is obvious that *kāda yaf'alu* means 'he was on the point of the action' (*qāraba l-fi'la*), and that *mā kāda yaf'alu* means that 'he was not on the point of the action'. However - and this is the inevitable fact of I-H's argument - its predicate will always be negated. If the verb *kāda* is negated, the meaning of negation is clear anyway, since a negation of the 'being near' aspect of the verb will denote in the mind of someone (*'aqlan*) that the action has not actually taken place. This could be exemplified by Sūra XXIV vs.41: *idhā akhraja yadahu lam yakad yarāhu* 'when he puts forth his hand, wellnigh he cannot see it'. According to I-H it is more meaningful (*ablagh*) to use the verb *kāda* here in preference to saying *lam yarahu* 'he did not see it', since he who did not see it might have been on the point of seeing it.

Yet what is the situation if the verb is in the affirmative? The answer to this rests on an acceptance, according to customary usage (*'urfan*), that conveying the idea of the nearness of something (*qurb al-shay'*) necessitates its non-occurrence. This is exemplified by the fact that it is not considered good speech, according to customary usage, to say to someone who has prayed, or who has not prayed, that the time for prayer has drawn near, until it has actually drawn near. There is a verse in the Qur'ān, however, which the grammarians cited to corroborate their view that if the verb *kāda* occurs in the negative, the action has been done. This verse is Sūra II vs.67: (*fa dhabaḥūhā*) *wa mā kādū yafʿalūna* '(and therefore they sacrificed her), a thing they had scarcely done'. The grammarians argued, therefore, that the sacrificing had obviously been carried out. However, I-H's counter-argument to this is based once more on the importance of context, as we have seen many times before. He notes that the verbs in this verse, i.e., *mā kādū yafʿalūna*, are relaying the situation of those in question in the beginning when they were far from being in a position to sacrifice her. This is signified elsewhere in the Sūra by their obstinacy. It is these contextual indicators that are of vital importance to an understanding of the meaning of the verb here. We turn now to the shortest, yet no less significant, chapter in ML, which is the one entitled 'On the nature of *iʿrāb*'.

One of the issues raised earlier was that all the significative or formal elements have a name. For instance, the *wāw* is a particle of 'coordination', and one always refers to it as a *wāw*, not a /w/ phoneme. The subject marker 't' of *ḍarabtu* 'I struck, hit' is an agent (*fāʿil*), and one always says that the *tā'* is an agent, not the phoneme /t/. As has been put elsewhere (Carter 1981:15, n.3) 'the name of a thing is a noun'.[21] I-H develops this idea in this chapter which is aimed, for the most part, at the beginner of *iʿrāb*. When you say that *ḍaraba* 'he hit, struck' is a simple past tense verb, *ḍaraba* in this context is a noun to which you have given a predicate by saying it is a past tense verb. This is obviously a different method of describing it to when one says of the verb that it signifies an event and time. Here, *ḍaraba* does not indicate that at all. In other words, it is not being described in a parsing context. Further proof of this is that a verb will never occur without an agent in composite speech, but of course *ḍaraba* here does not have an agent. In effect, it is being used here in a similar way to the English infinitive, i.e., to beat. If it were being used in a parsing context, as in, for instance, *ḍaraba zaydun* 'Zayd struck...', one would say that Zayd here is in the nominative/independent case because of *ḍaraba* (*marfūʿ bi ḍaraba*), or the agent of *ḍaraba* (*fāʿil bi ḍaraba*). In this case, the particle of obliqueness (*al-jārr*) is associated with it. Therefore, its occurring as a noun operated upon by the particle here is further proof of its 'noun-ness'.

I-H takes this argument even further when he notes (ML 2:665-66) that although there may seem to be a contradiction in saying that *ḍaraba* - which is a noun here as we have seen - is a verb of the past tense, i.e., how can a noun be a verb, the same is meant here as when you say *zaydun qā'imun* 'Zayd is standing'; in other words, in this example you are informing about Zayd in terms of his nominatum, the thing signified by Zayd, not just with regard to the expression 'Zayd'. Likewise, in the example of *ḍaraba* above you are informing about its nominatum, which is the fact that *ḍaraba* signifies event and time. The corollary to all this, then, is that *ḍaraba* is 'an expression whose nominatum is also an expression' (*lafẓ musammāhu lafẓ*), as is the case with the names of the Sūras of the Qur'ān, or the names of the letters of the alphabet. This view clearly assumes philosophical dimensions which are elaborated on by one of the commentators on ML (al-Shamunnī, *Munṣif,* 2:273) who adds that in the title of the Sūra of the House of Imran, for instance, the expression *āl 'imrān* is 'a name whose nominatum (signified) is the particular Sūra composed of the words (that make up the Sūra)' (*ism musammāhu l-sūra al-makhṣūṣa al-mu'allafa min al-kalimāt*).

It is in this chapter, in fact, that I-H is at his most instructive and prescriptive. One could be forgiven for anticipating that such a short section, whose subject matter represents the principal reason for which ML was written, would be more poignant, and would tackle matters of a more esoteric nature. It seems that most of this has been done elsewhere in ML, as this study has been attempting to show. In what could easily be described as a section written in an almost conversational style I-H outlines the meticulous qualities required of the beginner in his technique of parsing so that he leaves no analysis ambiguous nor open to debate.

In this section one finds some brief, but rare, instances of issues pertaining to changes brought about by certain morphophonemic combinations, such as those involving defective verbs. Acknowledgement of these phenomena is, of course, all part of the parsing process if one is to avoid assuming, for instance, that the nunation on *qāḍin* 'judge' in *marartu bi qāḍin* 'I passed by a judge', is not a marker of the genitive/oblique case brought about by the preposition *bi* (ML 2:670). On the whole, though, the aim is to alert the beginner to the type of errors which may result from either an insufficient knowledge of *i'rāb*, or an incorrect application of that knowledge. The latter could be represented by Sūra CII vs.1: *alhākum al-takāthuru* 'Gross rivalry diverts you' (ML 2:668). According to I-H he heard someone parse this sentence with *alhākum* as a topic, and *al-takāthur* as a predicate, on the basis that the former was a noun with a definite article. Similar errors have occurred, he notes, where the scholar of *i'rāb* has learned that the *wāw* and the *fā'* are both particles of coordination, and has then proceeded to parse the past tense verbs *wa'aẓa* and *fasakha* as the coordinating particle and the verbs *'aẓa* and *sakha* respectively.

I-H's disdain for those whose knowledge of the Arabic language is anything less than approaching perfection may be seen in a very amusing example of a solecism (*laḥn*) cited from the *Kitāb al-Taṣḥīf* 'The Book of Grammatical Mistakes' by Abū Hilāl al-'Askarī. Unfortunately the humorous elements do not really appear in the translation, but in the absurdity of the erroneous case-endings applied by the unfortunate perpetrator. Someone said to another: *mādhā fa'ala abūka bi ḥimārihi* 'What did your father do with his donkey', to which the other replied *bā'ihi* 'He sold it' (is what he intended to say). So he was asked: 'Why did you say *bā'ihi* and not *bā'ahu* ?' To this the man replied: 'Why did you say *bi ḥimārihi* ?' He said: 'I put it in the genitive/oblique case with the preposition *bā'*. So the other man said: 'Why should your *bā'* put things in the genitive case and not mine?' (ML 2:669).

I-H's technique here is to recount several examples of such errors which he has either read about or witnessed during his teachings. As we attempted to show in Chapter Three, he is at once alerting his own students to the inelegance of such ignorance and carelessness, while reasserting his own position within the 'club' of language experts. One more interesting example to note here is the possible influence of what may well be a colloquial pronunciation infiltrating the classical Arabic. I-H tells of how he was once relating that some of the legal theorists make an error in speech (*yalḥanūna*) by saying *al-bāyi'* 'the seller', instead of *al-bā'i'*, to which someone replied: 'But God said (in the Qur'ān) in Sūra LX vs.10: *fa bāyi'hunna* 'test them'. Once more this is a clear illustration of the type of grammatical errors made by those with an inadequate knowledge of Arabic and *i'rāb*. In this example, the word *bāyi'* for *bā'i'* is an incorrect active participle, whilst the Qur'ānic example is an imperative command from a third form verb (ML 2:669).

If one believes that the style, conciseness, and general content of this chapter on *i'rāb* is rather unique, the same could easily be said of the final chapter in ML which is concerned, for the most part, with both structural and semantic issues, either in cases where they are interrelated, or where they are separate concerns. It is to the content of this chapter that we turn now.

The translation of this final chapter is somewhat problematic. However, given the eleven precepts (*qawā'id*) presented by I-H in this chapter, a suggestion for translation might be 'On universal rules by which unlimited particular concepts can be interpreted' (*fī dhikr umūr kulliyya yatakharraju 'alayhā mā lā yanḥaṣiru min al-ṣuwar al-juz'iyya*). An indication of what is meant here may be found in Weiss (1966:106) who says that 'the identity of particulars...is known, not from the expression itself, but from an identifying context (*qarīna mu'ayyana*)'.

That there was a prevailing debate in the medieval period amongst scholars about the role of universals and particulars is well-known. The linguistic significance of this issue appears to have reached its zenith during the period of those who specialized in studies of *waḍ' al-lugha*. This is not to suggest that I-H had formulated such a scholastic view of the relevant merits and importance of an understanding of universals and particulars. In fact, it became a multi-faceted issue that ultimately appears to have attempted to reconcile the two by means of a delicate systematic analysis of the role of all the significative elements of language both in isolation and in context (Weiss ibid.:95). Nonetheless, the concepts of universals were centuries old by the time of I-H, and it is not unlikely that the issue of an identifying context, which was taken to extremes by the scholars of *waḍ'*, and which is frequently to be found in ML, lies at the root of the content of the final chapter. In other words, I-H has identified several principles which could be referred to as universals, but which are based on particulars in the form of those semantic or structural properties responding to the context, as the following examples will attempt to illustrate. In essence, the role of signification is pivotal to this section.[22]

This final chapter of ML is arguably one of the most fascinating. The first of the eleven precepts selected by I-H to illustrate this category of universal rules has been tackled briefly by Owens (1988:235). He maintains that I-H showed a more profound understanding than most linguists of the 'notion of grammatical form vs. meaning'; this was an issue discussed earlier in this study (see above, Chapter Four esp.). According to Owens 'form and meaning are not always in one to one correspondence'. While there is much to be commended in Owens' observations, to which he adds that I-H 'uses this lack of correspondence to explain what would otherwise be anomalous patterns', it would seem that there is a more positive side to these apparent anomalies. What is not clear from Owens' description is that there are other precepts within this section of ML which indicate that contrary to containing anomalies which need to be accounted for, this lack of correspondence would appear to be yet another illustration of the 'beauties' of Arabic which serve to illustrate its uniqueness. We would argue that the precepts on implication of meaning (*taḍmīn*), or metathesis (*qalb*), or the correspondence of two expressions in grammatical status (*taqāruḍ al-lafẓayni fī l-aḥkām*), for example, constitute further illustration of this point which I-H has been attempting to underline at various junctures throughout ML.[23] It is worth making the point here that al-Suyūṭī includes a chapter called *wuqūʿ al-badāʾiʿ al-balīgha fīhā* 'occurrences of eloquent innovation' in one of his works (*Muʿtarak*, 1:373ff.) which contains material very similar to that of the final chapter of ML. More on this later.

The first precept discussed by I-H is 'something which can be given the status of what it resembles' (*qad yuʿṭā l-shayʾ ḥukm mā ashbahahu*), and is divided into three parts; what it resembles:

(i) in its meaning (*fī maʿnāhu*)

(ii) in its form (*fī lafẓihi*)

(iii) in its meaning and form (*fīhimā*).

Type (i) may be exemplified by the following (ML 2:674-75):

(a) the *bā'* occurring with the predicate of the particle *anna* in Sūra XLVI vs.33: *a wa lam yaraw anna allāha alladhī khalaqa l-samawāti wa l-arḍi wa lam ya'ya bi khalqihinna bi qādirin* 'Have they not seen that God, who created the heavens and earth, not being wearied by creating them, is able...'. The *bā'* occurs here because the predicate has the meaning of *a wa laysa allāhu bi qādirin* 'or is God not able...', and the *bā'* is often attached to the predicate of *laysa*. I-H adds that the reconstruction (*taqdīr*) here was facilitated by the distance in the verse between the restored *laysa* and the *bā'*. He notes that it is not restored, however, in Sūra XVII vs.101: *a wa lam yaraw anna allāha alladhī khalaqa l-samawāti wa l-arḍi qādirun 'alā an yakhluqa mithlahum* 'Have they not seen that God, who created the heavens and earth, is powerful to create the like of them', because of the proximity of the *bā'* and *laysa*. Once more it would seem that contextual indications determine what is permissible in such cases.

(b) the admissibility of eliding the predicate of the topic, as in, for example, *inna zaydan qā'imun wa 'Amrun* 'Zayd is standing (and so is) 'Amr' (ML 2:675), where the one predicate of *inna*, i.e., *qā'imun*, is sufficient, because the meaning is simply *zaydun qā'imun* 'Zayd is standing'. However, this would not be acceptable with a particle like *layta* 'if only', for instance, because 'it does not convey the idea of either truth (*ṣidq*) or falsehood (*kidhb*)' (al-Shamunnī, *Munṣif,* 2:275). In other words, the unit 'Amr ('is standing') resembles 'Zayd is standing' in meaning here because they are both standing, even though the predicate *qā'imun* is not repeated.

(c) the acceptability of saying *anā zaydan ghayru ḍāribin* lit. 'I am other than beating Zayd' (ML 2:675-76) because it possesses the meaning of *anā zaydan lā aḍribu* 'I am not beating Zayd'. If it does not have that meaning, i.e., if it conveys the meaning of 'I am beating (someone) other than Zayd, you cannot say it in this way, because the second term of the *iḍāfa*, Zayd, cannot then pre-pose the first term, *ghayru ḍāribin*, and therefore neither can the element operated upon by it. You cannot say, for instance, *anā zaydan awwalu ḍāribin* 'I am the first to beat Zayd', nor *anā zaydan mithlu ḍāribin* 'I am like someone who beats Zayd'.

(d) the occurrence of the 'exhaustive exception' (*al-istithnā' al-mufarragh*) (Carter 1981:402) in the affirmative (ML 2:676).[24] This could be represented by Sūra II vs.41: *wa innahā la kabīratun illā 'alā l-khāshi'īna* 'for grievous it is, save to the humble', because the meaning of the verse is that it is only easy for the humble ones; or Sūra IX vs.33: *wa ya'bā allāhu illā an yutimma nūrahu* 'and God refuses but to perfect His light', in which the meaning is that God only wants to perfect it.

I-H adds two important notes to this section. The first concerns something that he calls even more meaningful (*ablagh*) than 'their giving an existing expression the status of another expression because of its possessing its meaning' (*tanzīluhum lafẓan mawjūdan manzilat lafẓ ākhar li kawnihi bi ma'nāhu*). The device he is referring to here is when they give a non-existent expression whose existence is perfectly valid the status of the existing (expression) (*tanzīluhum al-lafẓ al-ma'dūm al-ṣāliḥ li l-wujūd bi manzilat al-mawjūd*), as in the following line of poetry:

badā liya annī lastu mudrika mā maḍā wa lā sābiqin shay'an idhā kāna jā'iya

In this verse the word *sābiqin* is in the genitive/oblique case on the assumption of an understood preposition *bā'*. What is significant here is that the understood element is not *muqaddar*, but *mutawahham*, and is considered a fine example of *tawahhum* which was discussed earlier in this chapter (cf. Baalbaki 1982:236). The understood preposition would then be added to what is already the predicate of *laysa* in the verse, even though the other predicate of *laysa* which appears in the first line, i.e., *mudrika*, takes the accusative/dependent case ending which is also normal for predicates of *laysa*. It is worth pointing out here the difference between this example and (a) above. In the latter, the preposition *bi* was already present in Sūra XLVI vs.33, and it was only *laysa* that was restored. However, in the piece of poetry, it is already there with a predicate; but to assume a preposition with the other predicate alternative is, as I-H notes, even more commendable.

The other note worth recording here concerns things which have the meaning of something else, but which may not be given its status (ML 2:679). This is exemplified by the verbal noun which may not be given the status of the particles *anna* or *an* and their conjunctive sentences (*ṣilatuhumā*), and vice-versa. For instance, the latter two may permit an elided preposition, but not the verbal noun. Thus you may say *'ajibtu annaka qā'imun* 'I was astonished at your standing', but you cannot say *'ajibtu qiyāmaka.* In a similar way the verbal noun may not be given their status 'in their taking the place of the two parts of predication' (*fī saddihimā masadd juz'ay al-isnād*). Therefore, you can say *ḥasibtu annahu qā'imun / an qāma* 'I assumed he was standing / had stood up', but you cannot say *ḥasibtu qiyāmaka* until you supply the predicate. On the other hand, *an* and *anna* with their respective clauses cannot have the status of the verbal noun in its being substituted for the adverb of time in *ji'tuka ṣalāt al-'aṣr* 'I came to you at mid-afternoon prayer time'. In other words, you cannot say *ji'tuka an tuṣallī l-'aṣr.*

Let us turn now to type (ii) of the first precept mentioned above - that of when something is given the status of what it resembles in form, not meaning. This could be exemplified by the following:

(a) the attachment of the *lām* of inception to the negative *mā* because of the latter's similarity in form to the relative *mā* (*mawṣūla*) which also occurs as the topic of the sentence. Therefore, the *la* in the poetic verse *la mā aghfaltu shukran* 'I did not forget to thank you', is interpreted according to the similarity in form between the *mā* here and in *la mā taṣna'ahu ḥasanun* 'Indeed whatever you do is good'. Both *mā*'s have positional and formal similarity, and for this reason the *la* of the former example is permitted. That the two *mā*'s have a different meaning is incidental (ML 2:680; cf. Owens 1988:235-36).

(b) emphasizing the imperfect indicative mood with a *nūn* after the negative *lā* in accordance with the form which may occur with the prohibitive *lā* (*al-nāhiyya*) (ML 2:680). An example of this is in Sūra VIII vs.25: *wa ittaqū fitnatan lā tuṣībanna alladhīna ẓalamū minkum khāṣṣatan* 'and fear a trial which shall surely not smite in particular the evildoers'. This agrees in form, for instance, with Sūra XIV vs.44: *wa lā taḥsabanna allāha ghāfilan* 'deem not that God is heedless'. The significant point here, as I-H notes, is that if the *lā* of Sūra VIII vs.25 (and similar verses) was interpreted initially as the prohibitive *lā* there was subsequently no need for the agreement in form.

Type (iii) above is rare (ML 2:682), and was only attested for two instances of when the form and meaning of the elative noun and the verb of surprise concurred. This need not detain us here, except to note that in spite of its rarity the grammarians appear to have formulated and accepted a rule for it.

The fourth precept recorded by I-H is worth dwelling on. This is where he has selected instances of when two things are of a similar kind, or share similar characteristics, and one word or term is chosen to represent both (ML 2:686-88). In effect it takes precedence over the other represented type (*annahum yughallibūna 'alā l-shay' mā li ghayrihi li tanāsub baynahumā aw ikhtilāṭ*).

With regard to similarity in kind (*tanāsub*), this is represented by such nouns as *al-abawayni* 'parents' coined for both the word *ab* 'father' and *umm* 'mother'. Similarly they used the word *al-khāfiqāni* for *al-mashriq* and *al-maghrib* 'East and West', because *al-maghrib* was known figuratively as *al-khāfiq*. Another well-known example is the employment of the word *al-qamarāni* 'the two-moons' for *al-qamar* 'moon' and *al-shams* 'sun'.

The category of *ikhtilāṭ* 'mixture' is more interesting. This occurs principally where two different types of thing, although not unrelated, occur in close proximity in a text. To judge by the examples adduced by I-H it appears that this device pertained almost exclusively to the Qur'ān. Thus we find the word *man* 'he who, whoever', normally used only for rational things, being employed for irrational things, as in Sūra XXIV vs.44: *fa minhum man yamshī 'alā baṭnihi wa minhum man yamshī 'alā rijlayni wa minhum man yamshī 'alā arba'a* 'and some of them go upon their bellies, and some of them go upon two feet, and some of them go upon four'. According to I-H the idea of *ikhtilāṭ* here had already been initiated previously in the Sūra (vs.43) in the words *kullu dābbatin min mā'in* 'every beast of water'. Thus in the above verse we see the word *man* being applied to animals. Within this verse, there is also another example of *ikhtilāṭ* in the words *man yamshī 'alā rijlayni*, because both man and birds are being referred to here.

Another example of this device is to be found in Sūra II vs.19: *u'budū rabbakum alladhī khalaqakum wa alladhīna min qablikum la'allakum tattaqūna* 'serve your Lord Who created you, and those that were before you; haply so you will be goodfearing'. Here, the noun of those being addressed (*ism al-mukhāṭabīna*) takes precedence over those absent (*al-ghā'ibīna*) - or in other terms, the second person plural is used in preference to the third person plural. This can be determined because the particle *la'alla* is semantically connected to *khalaqakum*, not to *u'budū*. Therefore, the pronoun of *la'alla* and the following verb must be referring to those who have been created after those being addressed in the first part of the verse. One would normally anticipate third person grammatical parts in this case.

One of the most important qualities required of the exegete was the ability to interpret a given verse from the Qur'ān beyond the surface level. In other words there was not always an immediate demand for the reconstruction of a part of the text in order to return the syntax to an acceptable form, say, if it was *prima facie* grammatically unsound. Nonetheless, if a given verse was syntactically correct the exegete might be required to offer an interpretation which transcended the outward meaning of the text, basing his interpretation on a sound consideration of the (semantic) nature of the accompanying text. It is this technique which appears to be in operation in the fifth precept discussed by I-H. This particular section concerns the verb.

Naturally the underlying rule for the verb is that its action and purport actually take place (*al-aṣl wuqū'uhu*) (ML 2:688-

90). However, in this section I-H notes three additional potential meanings of the verb whose application must be judged from the context. The first of these is *mushārafa* 'being on the point of' which may be represented by Sura II vs.231: *wa idhā ṭallaqtum al-nisā'a fa balaghna ajalahunna fa amsikūhunna* 'when you divorce women, and they have reached their term then retain them honourably'. The implication in this verse is that because the term (*al-ajal*) is reached at the end of the *'idda* 'period of time during which a woman may not remarry after being divorced or widowed', the retaining (*al-imsāk*) must take place before that time. Therefore, one could imply *fa shārafna inqiḍā'a l-'idda* 'and they are on the point of, on the way towards the completion of the period' in place of *fa balaghna ajalahunna*.

The next potential meaning of the verb is its intention (*irādatuhu*) in the sense that when a past tense verb occurs after the conditional particles *idhā* or *in*, it often assumes the idea of 'wanting' or 'intending'. This would appear to be because the verb in the result clause is normally in the command mood, and the time sequence, although possible, makes less sense. This could be illustrated by Sūra V vs.8: *idhā qumtum ilā l-ṣalāti fa ighsil* '(and) when you stand up to pray wash your faces', in which the idea is that if you intend to get up for the prayer you must wash. Another useful example of this is Sūra VII vs.10: *laqad khalaqnākum thumma ṣawwarnākum thumma qulnā li l-malā'ikati usjudū li ādama* 'We created you, then We shaped you, then We said to the angels: Bow yourselves to Adam'. I-H notes that if one accepts that one of the functions of the particle *thumma* is for ordering (*tartīb*), it is clear that the two verbs *khalaqa* and *ṣawwara* cannot be interpreted according to their outward form. Therefore, the idea of intention must be applied to each in order that the sequence of time and events makes sense, i.e., the angels bowed to Adam before those being addressed in the verse were created.

The final mode pertaining to the verb in this section is the ability to carry it out (*al-qudra 'alayhi*). This could be represented by Sūra XXI vs.104: *wa'dan 'alaynā innā kunnā fā'ilīn* 'a promise binding on us; so We shall do', where it is implied that they are capable of making it return (*qādirīna 'alā l-i'āda*). I-H notes that this is because the 'verb is originally brought about by intention and ability' (*al-fi'l yatasabbabu 'an al-irāda wa l-qudra*). He adds that one of the phenomena of the verb is when the cause (*sabab*) takes the place of the caused (*musabbab*), and vice-versa. The former may be illustrated by Sūra XLVII vs.33: *wa nabluwa akhbārakum* 'and try your tidings'. In this instance the underlying meaning is that 'we know your tidings' (*wa na'lamu akhbārakum*). However, the knowing is presumably the thing caused, and is arrived at by trial (*ibtilā'*), the cause which is tantamount to testing (*ikhtibār*) from which knowledge is derived. The opposite process takes place in Sūra II vs.22: *fa ittaqū l-nāra* 'then fear the Fire'. In this case the caused, which is hell, i.e., the fire, replaces the cause, which is the obstinacy (*al-'inād*) that inevitably leads to hell.

The seventh precept described by I-H is once again important from a semantic viewpoint. This is where the intended meaning of something is not in immediate correspondence with its form, although this lack of correspondence may be explained away by what we might suggest is an intention of dramatic effect. This precept is based on the past and the future being expressed as though they were something in the present. The aim behind this, of course, is to bring the event of the verb into the mind of the recipient as though he is experiencing or seeing it at the time of its being conveyed. I-H cites several examples of this phenomenon, although it is worth noting that the majority of those are taken from the Qur'ān, such as Sūra IV vs.141: *wa inna rabbaka lā yaḥkumu baynahum yawma l-qiyāmati* 'and God will judge between you on the Resurrection Day'. The *lām* of inception here with the verb would normally represent the present (*al-ḥāl*). However, there is a contradiction in that case between the present and the Day of Judgement; therefore, it appears that the present tense is being employed here for the effect of bringing the idea of (final) judgement more immediately into the minds of those being addressed. This type of device is further represented in Sūra XXXV vs.10: *wa allāhu alladhī arsala l-riyāḥa fa tuthīru saḥāban* 'God is He that looses the winds, that stir up cloud'. The intention here with the words *fa tuthīru* is 'to bring forth this unique picture that signifies the wonderful power as a result of stirring up the clouds' (*iḥḍār tilka l-ṣūra al-badī'a al-dālla 'alā l-qudra al-bāhira min ithārat al-siḥāb*), from the moment they appear as isolated parts until they become a conglomeration (ML 2:690).

Also included as part of this device are instances of what would probably be known today as the historical present (*ḥikāyat al-ḥāl al-māḍiya*), in which the past is represented in the text by a present tense marker which dramatises the effect of the situation. The same can also obtain for a future tense situation in which the present marks an event that has occurred at the time of the reported speech, but which was yet to take place at the moment it was revealed. An example of this is Sūra II vs.68: *wa allāhu mukhrijun mā kuntum taktumūna* 'and God disclosed what you were hiding', where the idea at the point of dispute about the exact nature of the cow for sacrifice was that it was always part of God's plan that he would reveal what they were hiding at that time (ML 2:691). It is only from the context that the use of this device can be determined.

The eighth precept in this chapter deals with examples of syntax involving mainly particles (ML 2:692-93). The rule at issue here is that the repetition of the particle is not permitted because of grammatical constraints, as in, for example, *rubba rajulin wa akhīhi* 'many a man and his brother'. What is meant here is 'many a man and many a brother of his', but the rule pertaining to *rubba* is that it may only put indefinite nouns into the genitive/oblique case. Therefore, the force of *rubba* is carried over to *akhīhi*, but the particle is not repeated. Of particular interest in this connection is I-H's explanation of the operation which is in process here. He says that 'what can rarely be excused from the first (part of speech) may often be excused from the second' (*kathīran mā yughtafaru fī l-thawānī mā lā yughtafaru fī l-awwal*). It is as if these rules are viewed as a positive and economical aspect of syntax which may be ascertained from the meaning and the context at any rate.

Considerations of both form and meaning are essential in the tenth precept which is metathesis (*qalb*). I-H admits that most examples of this are to be found in poetry. However, this does not undermine the importance of this phenomenon for the purposes of this study, because it stands as a further illustration that the two concepts of form and meaning went hand in hand in all forms of Classical Arabic, although it often happened that one took precedence over the other, as we shall see now.

There are occasions when a structural metathesis occurs which does not ultimately affect the meaning. This could be illustrated by the half line of poetry *yakūnu mizājahā 'asalun wa mā'un* 'her temperament is always (like) honey and water' (ML 2:695). In this example, what is in the status of the predicate, i.e., *mizājahā* has become the definite entity (*ma'rifa*), and the two topics, viz., *'asalun* and *mā'un* have become the indefinite item (*nakira*). This is contrary to what is expected, and indeed accepted, according to customary formal considerations. It is true that in the translation of this piece of poetry one perceives that *mizājahā* would normally be the topic, and *'asalun* and *mā'un* the predicate. This would also be the case in the Arabic if *mizāj* were in the nominative/independent case, and *mā'* and *'asal* were in the accusative/dependent case. In other words, the meaning here is subordinate to the form.

On the other hand, we find the opposite process taking place elsewhere. I-H cites several examples of metathesis (ML 2:696; cf.al-Shamunnī, *Munṣif*, 2:283) in which the meaning is the principal consideration, while the form is subordinate to it, even though the meaning has been inverted. Thus an example such as *'araḍtu l-nāqata 'alā l-ḥawḍ* 'I showed the she-camel to the trough' is actually an inversion of what the Arabic really means, i.e., *'araḍtu l-ḥawḍa 'alā l-nāqa* 'I showed the trough to the she-camel'.

The eleventh and final precept discussed by I-H is one which was mentioned briefly earlier. This is a category comprising some of the so-called beauties (*mulaḥ*) of speech in which two different forms compete for grammatical status (*taqāruḍ al-lafẓayni fī l-aḥkām*). This may be exemplified by the particles *lam* and *lan* for instance, which are both negative in meaning, but the former always operates upon the verb in the jussive mood, and the latter in the subjunctive mood. At this level they share the meaning of negation. However, there is textual evidence to suggest (ML 2:697-98) that they may 'borrow' each other's grammatical form in some contexts, as in, for example, Sūra XCIV vs.1: *a lam nashraḥa* 'Did we not expand...'. In this instance, we find the *lam* operating upon the subjunctive mood. Likewise, in the line of poetry *lan yakhib al-āna min rajā'ika* 'He will not disappoint you now', the particle *lan* assumes the status of *lam* in the jussive mood (ML 2:698; cf. Owens 1988:237). Another example of this phenomenon may be seen in cases where the agent is given the syntactic status of the object, and vice-versa, so long as this does not affect the meaning nor cause confusion. For example, in *kharaqa l-thawbu al-mismāra* 'the gown pierced the nail', there is no doubt about what is meant, i.e., that the nail pierced the gown, even though the case-endings (*i'rāb*) of the two nouns suggest otherwise. A similar example to this cited by I-H is *kasara l-zajjāju al-ḥajara* 'the glass broke the stone'.

Perhaps the most significant aspect of this final section of ML is that I-H's analysis reflects an unequivocal link with a long-standing tradition of recognition of some of the more unusual phenomena mentioned above. As early as the third century A.H. Abū 'Ubayda had noted many examples of this type, such as the use of the masculine form for the feminine, or the plural for the singular (Versteegh 1990:285). Even al-Kisā'i (d.189/905) noted that the Arabs were not averse to interpreting something according to its opposite (*al-'arab qad taḥmilu l-shay' 'alā ḍiddihi*) (al-Baṭalyawsī, *Sharḥ*, 2:266); this was also a phenomenon which persisted throughout the Arabic linguistic tradition. Scholars such as Ibn Jinnī and Ibn Fāris were consistent in their views that phenomena like synonymy and opposites were nothing less than a reflection of the superiority of Arabic over other languages.

Yet it is interesting to note that a previous reference to the phenomenon referred to above of *taqāruḍ al-lafẓayni fī l-aḥkām* by I-H (ML 1:91) was accompanied by a remark that Sībawayhi and his followers paid no attention to this type of incongruity. This is particularly important because it suggests that many grammarians were not concerned with such aspects of the language which appear to have been of more interest to those scholars whose views seem to have been more in line with I-H's. After all, we have made frequent reference to Ibn Fāris in this study because of his pertinent opinions on issues of relevance to ML, and it has often been said that I-H was influenced in no small way by the writings of Ibn Jinnī. Moreover, it was mentioned in Chapter Two that many of the earlier attitudes to the concept of meaning were inspired by exegetical studies, but that this tradition changed quite rapidly to the more 'formal-syntactic' (Versteegh *to appear*) approach with Sībawayhi. What we would suggest, therefore, is that I-H could well be linked to this earlier tradition of exegesis, and that a future study to attempt to assert this could prove very fruitful.

To conclude this analysis of some of the semantic and structural aspects of the second part of ML, then, it is hoped that further illustration has been given of the kind of issues that interested I-H. As much as possible we have attempted to demonstrate that much of the grammatical analysis displays a richness from the point of view of meaning and form. At times it was possible for the grammatical rules to be violated so long as the meaning remained unimpaired. On other occasions certain things could not be said if they infringed grammatical rules. In other cases it was contextual considerations that determined the meaning of a particular piece of text. On occasions when the grammatical form and meaning appeared to be unsychronised, as seemed to be the case in the examples of the final section of ML, I-H reconciled these apparent incongruities by presenting a more positive side to them. In other words one is left with the impression that many of these devices worked to the benefit of the Arabic language by helping to illustrate its uniqueness as perceived by many scholars at that time.

NOTES

1 For an excellent analysis of elision in general, but with several specific references to I-H and ML, see now Carter (1991).

2 Other insightful analyses of *iḍmār* have been provided by Cuvalay (see Carter 1991:123, n.7 who says that she suggests that it takes place at a much deeper level than elision on the basis that the latter 'can only really occur once the phonological form of the utterance has been determined, (whereas the former) would seem to belong to a stage before any syntactic categories at all are selected'). Also, Ayoub (1990) sees the essential difference between *iḍmār* and *taqdīr* to be that the former involves suppression by the speaker, while the latter is merely the business of the grammarian whose task it is to reconstruct the original structure.

3 It seems that I-H's classification of the conditions of elision made a significant impact on important later scholars like al-Suyūṭī who chose to cite his conclusions in considerable detail (*Mu'tarak*, 1:309ff.).

4 According to Carter (ibid.:127) 'this suggests that the context can itself be an *'imād* or supporting element of an utterance, an idea which is latent in Sībawayhi's treatment of the speaker as an operator and which surely has important semantic as well as structural implications'. I-H is almost teasing in his rather cursory reference to what is almost certainly a much larger subject.

5 For a brief, but adequate, description of some of the more important structural conditions of elision discussed by I-H (and Ibn Jinnī), see Owens (1988:187-90).

6 A clearer illustration of what I-H means here is provided by al-Shamunnī (*Munṣif*, 2:253). An example of the topic/predicate relationship could be your saying *zaydun* in reply to the question *man qāma* 'Who stood up ?', in which the *i'rāb* is that *zaydun* is the predicate of an elided topic, of which the underlying structure is *al-qā'imu zaydun* 'the one standing is Zayd'. This is more appropriate than parsing it as an agent of an elided verb of which the underlying structure is *qāma zaydun* 'Zayd stood up'.

7 For all this see ML 2:448,617. An interesting point to note here is where I-H uses the term *sababī* on one occasion in place of *ma'nawī* to describe this last example of preoccupation. This term is normally used in conjunction with adjectives, and has been translated as 'semantically linked' (Carter 1981:245, n.11.5), which would render the idea perfectly here. See also Carter's analysis of the term *sabab* in the earlier literature in particular (1985), where we find examples very similar to those given by I-H.

8 I-H's analysis of the categories of coordination clearly made an impression on al-Suyūṭī (*Ashbāh*, 2:95ff.) who, not for the first time, borrows from him word for word, especially in the first part here.
The employment of such terms as *mawḍi'* and *maḥall* is a fascinating subject in relation to syntax; the reader is referred to Versteegh (1981) for a penetrating analysis of these and other related terms.

9 For a correct modern interpretation, however, see now Isbir/Junaydi (1981:600-601).

10 In the light of new evidence discussed earlier in this chapter (e.g., Ayoub 1990), to talk of the terms *taqdīr* and *iḍmār* as synonyms is now questionable.

11 The particle *aw* here occurs with the sense of *ilā* (ML 1: 67), or *ḥattā* (al-Rummānī, *Ma'ānī*, 79), i.e., with the meaning of 'until'. This is what is meant by coordination according to the meaning, since *aw* is a coordinating particle like *wāw* and *fa*, for instance.

12 The term *qaṭ'* is 'typically Kufan' (Versteegh 1993: 133), and is used for what Sībawayhī would refer to as a *ḥāl*. Owens (1990: 123) is of a similar view since he notes that al-Farrā' uses the term *qaṭ'* when it 'refers to some sort of structural/semantic break between predicative element and modifiers'. Thus not for the first time do we find I-H drawing on terminology which is generally held to represent the Kufan tradition.

13 See also above, p. 199, n. 4.

14 The term *ittisā'* which is the technical term associated with this verb here, is a fascinating one. Although it appears to render the idea of 'flexibility' in this context (cf. Carter

1981:353 who translates it as 'latitude'), the meaning of the term clearly developed from its earlier technical usage by Sībawayhi. Versteegh (1990: 293) provides an excellent account of the development of the term where he notes that *ittisāʿ* was originally 'used for certain specific syntactic phenomena, all concerning cases where the normal relationship between form and meaning is disrupted', but which later became a synonym for *majāz*. I-H's usage of the concept here seems to tie in neatly with the earlier meaning of the term.

15 The terms *musnad/musnad ilayhi* represent a complex problem which has been tackled in an insightful way by Owens (1988;1990). He notes that the situation regarding these terms had changed to a degree by the time of al-Sarrāj (d.316/928). Perhaps the best way to illustrate this change is to cite Owens' useful comparison of the way in which the earlier grammarians, principally Sībawayhi and al-Mubarrad, and the later ones, viewed the sentence *qāma zaydun*. According to Owens (1990:104), the earlier grammarians viewed the verb as the *musnad*, and the noun as the *musnad ilayhi*; on the other hand, the later group considered the opposite to be the case. Both groups agreed on the status of the terms of the nominal sentence, however, i.e., that the *musnad* is the topic, and the *musnad ilayhi* the comment. Judging by I-H's analysis, it appears that he adhered to the later view on the status of each term within the verbal sentence.

16 For an opposite view see al-Zamakhsharī (*Kashshāf*, 3:335), and also al-Shamunnī (*Munṣif*, 2:121) who seems perplexed by I-H's conclusion here. He notes that the sentence could conceivably be of the elucidatory type if the question were about the reason for their having to be protected from the devils, i.e., that they do not listen. Yusuf Ali's translation and notes (1934: 1191) are particularly useful here. He inserts the word 'So' before the sentence 'they should not strain their ears' (c.f. Arberry's 'they listen not'). The context is determined by the depiction of what Yusuf Ali calls the 'Court of the Most High' (representing Good) which the Devil

(or Evil) tries to approach in order to overhear its proceedings.

17 al-Shamunnī (*Munṣif*, 2:127) makes the valuable observation that what I-H means here by *faḍla* is 'sentences which do not fulfil a functional role'!

18 If our understanding of this category is correct, I-H must mean *tābi'* in the technical sense here, as in *tawābi'* 'appositives, satellites', such as the adjective, emphasis, substitution, and so on. The sentences referred to in ML 2:410,424, for example, must be functioning in their entirety in this capacity, either with or without syntactic status as the case may be.

19 A fine example of what it means for a sentence to fulfil or not to fulfil a functional role is provided by al-Baṭalyawsī (*Sharḥ*, 2:287-88). He says that the two sentences *irkab 'alā ismi allāhi* 'carry out your life in God's name' and *irkab 'alā l-farasi* 'Get up onto the horse' do not have the same status (*manzila*). The reason for this is that in the latter example, *'alā* is semantically connected to the essence of the outward verb, so it does not have syntactic status. On the other hand, in the former example *'alā* is semantically connected to an elided item, so it does have syntactic status because it is semantically connected to a circumstantial (*ḥāl*) whose place it has taken; in other words there is a reconstructed element, which is *mu'tamidan* 'depending on', viz., *irkab mu'tamidan 'alā ismi allāhi*.

20 For this last example, either I-H or the original editor appears to have made an error in the text, since what is actually written is *kariha min al-khurūji* which does not fit in with the rules of the testing device. This is duly noted by the editor of our version (ML 2:454)

21 This idea is not new. Carter notes that even in Sībawayhi's *Kitāb* we learn how 'al-Khalīl catches out students who cannot tell the difference between the phoneme /k/ and the name *kāf*.

22 It is worth noting at this juncture the views of Nīl (1985:503-504) who suggests that the material for the final chapter of ML is based on that of the precepts of legal theory (*'ilm al-uṣūl wa l-fiqh*). This ties in neatly with the argument being

put forward here concerning signification, which was very much the domain of the legal theorists.

23 It is only fair to note here what seems to be an exception to this argument. In the section in this chapter on when 'something is given the status of what it resembles in form not meaning' (ML 2:681-82), I-H records an example of *ikfā'* 'the substitution of some cognate letter for the *rāwī*' in poetry (Wright 1933:356-57). According to Wright this device was considered a violation of the rules of poetry. There is a case, of course, for arguing that even violations of this nature could be perceived as yet another example of the uniqueness, and even superiority, of Arabic.

24 This occurrence of 'exhaustive exception' is clearly an anomaly because as Carter notes (1981:403), 'exhaustive exception is confined to negative sentences'.

CONCLUSION

The preceding study has attempted to show that ML is a work which more than deserves a detailed analysis of this nature. It is clear that not only was I-H a highly esteemed grammarian during the era in which he lived, and immediately beyond that, but that his reputation has remained intact until the present day. Even more important is that we have seen on many occasions how scholars who lived in the wake of I-H made frequent recourse to ML, particularly on issues which had been dealt with in a unique manner, or at least in much more detail than by I-H's predecessors. Native students of Arabic in Arabic-speaking countries study ML even now as part of the advanced syllabus in schools and universities; it is not surprising, therefore, that its reputation as a unique work persists. But it is not only in Arab circles that ML has enjoyed such recognition, and in which the implicit demands for a thorough assessment of this work have persisted. More than a decade ago Carter (1981:305) made the observation that 'the whole work (ML) awaits a proper evaluation'. That is not to say that this present study has unveiled all of the unique characteristics of ML; nor has it remotely attempted to tackle all the important issues raised by I-H in it. Indeed, in many respects this is a modest representation in comparison to the riches it contains. One area which undoubtedly requires further investigation, for example, is the significance of the citations of poetry in relation to I-H's objectives, as we mentioned in the introduction.

At any rate, let us remind ourselves that I-H wrote ML as a response to previous works which he considered did not constitute an adequate representation of the complex question of *i'rāb*. Perhaps two of the more important issues to be raised at this final stage, therefore, are: i) on the basis of the subject matter of ML, is there scope to argue that the concept of *i'rāb* assumes a significance that brings it closer to what is understood by the term 'syntax' in Western languages ?, and ii) does I-H approach anything like what could be considered a (separate) theory of semantics in ML ?

The answer to the first question is that the hypothesis set forth at the outset that I-H's presentation of *iʿrāb* shows a certain conformity with Silvestre de Sacy's translation of it as 'terminational syntax' still holds. There is no doubt that the case endings of nouns, or mood markers of verbs, are essential components of an inflectional system in which meanings can change according to those endings or markers. These components play an unequivocal role in denoting the syntactic function of a given noun or verb, and so on. One corroborating factor in this issue of syntactic relevance is that whole sentences can assume the grammatical status of single entities, as I-H acknowledges explicitly in ML (2:412). Of course, all the grammarians had more than just a passing interest in the concept of *iʿrāb*; in fact, it was central to an understanding of the theory of Arabic grammar. However, what I-H showed in ML is that case-endings and the like were not always just a formal issue, and that it was not always simply a matter of whether a noun, for example, should be in the nominative/independent case. Indeed, he demonstrated on many occasions that a profound interpretation of the syntax of a sentence could lead to a rewarding understanding of a deeper meaning of the texts. On balance, however, it would be fair to conclude that the issue of meaning was very important in the context of syntax for I-H, but that in many cases it could not be disassociated from formal considerations. We are reminded of Versteegh's observation noted earlier (1991:89) that scholars such as I-H could not free themselves entirely from syntactic constraints, no matter how much they busied themselves with semantic issues.

In a way, the syntactico-semantic function of *iʿrāb* as we see it in ML leads into an answer to the second question here. There is little justification to argue that I-H develops what could be called a semantic theory in ML, not least because of the formal constraints just mentioned. In essence one could say that his presentation of the semantic nature of Arabic is function linked, rather than a set of rules, to help solve problems of exegesis which had persisted for centuries. It is in this capacity in particular that I-H's technique would seem to display the qualities more characteristic of an exegete than a grammarian. There is certainly substantial evidence to suggest that this is how I-H would have preferred to be regarded in any case. We have also seen how he appears to champion the views of the rhetoricians over the grammarians on many points, specifically because the former group were justifiably regarded on the whole to be the ones who possessed the insight into the more profound aspects of meaning in the Arabic language, especially with regard to the sacred texts. It would be inaccurate to suggest that he even attempts to develop theories as expounded by later rhetoricians such as al-Taftazānī and al-Sakkākī. Moreover, he often falls short of developing ideas on rhetoric related issues as found in the works of al-Jurjānī. Yet there are many occasions when I-H appears to be heading in that direction, to the extent that his knowledge of such matters extends way beyond that of the scholar of *iʿrāb*. There are also elements of what would be called pragmatic interests, to use a modern linguistic term, to be found in ML, as we have seen. In addition, his theories on elision, and the insightful views on implication of meaning (*taḍmīn*) and syntactico-semantic connection (*taʿalluq*) which are to be found in various sections in ML, are all representative of a mind which was not only extremely dexterous, but one that recognised these three phenomena in particular as a fundamental key to unlocking the issues of *iʿrāb*, as I-H puts it in his introduction. Moreover, these three phenomena are especially relevant to any discussion of meaning within the medieval Arabic context, as is the role of contextual considerations which were clearly also important to I-H. If these factors are taken together it is not unreasonable to suggest that I-H was certainly one of the most sophisticated Arab grammarians.

One fact which cannot be overlooked is that I-H appears to have understood in some depth the composite nature of Arabic, and the idea that meaning is to be regarded as a whole. This is borne out, of course, by his revealing quote at the end of Chapter Six in ML when he notes that in order to analyse the language properly, one must begin with the single entities, and progress to the sentences. What emerged from the study of these single entities, in fact, was that the particles, whose meaning is essentially their function, are not to be viewed in isolation, but rather as an integral part of the whole language system. Even in the second part of ML on the sentences it was clear that the particles played a major role: in fact, it is worth reiterating that they appear to be the pivot of meaning in the Classical Arabic situation as it is represented in ML.

The foregoing study has also attempted to show the value of ML not just as the subject of grammatical analysis, but also in a much wider sense as a work that provided an inestimable service to Islam. Whether I-H succeeds consistently in his objective to offer the uninitiated or inexperienced scholar of *iʿrāb* a work in which the rudiments of parsing and syntax unfold, is open to question. There are many occasions when the abstruse nature of certain arguments would surely be beyond the learner. In addition, we have also seen how the attempts by the author to demonstrate the notion of wisdom, and the extremes of scholastic debate, can actually work to the detriment of the less experienced scholar as the author seeks to impose his own authority on an issue by casting doubt on much of what went before, yet by not always arriving at a firm conclusion himself.

That ML was a relatively late work has, on balance, been a mixed blessing. It has certainly been beneficial to set I-H's views against those of so many of his predecessors from the fields of lexicography, rhetoric, legal theory, and, of course, grammar; such is the eclectic nature of ML. On the other hand, I-H's frequent failure to record his source for a particular argument, or to present a full discussion of a certain point has sometimes been frustrating, if understandable. As was previously indicated, the very act of recording information of this type provided a valuable service to Islam and the community, and the source of information was not always relevant provided it was presented by an authoritative scholar in a cogent manner. It is also likely that much of I-H's reading public would have been aware of a certain amount of existing debate on a given subject, since it is almost certain that he would have been addressing an educated elite at that time.

Whatever one's subjective views on whether I-H deserved the accolade of being referred to as the 'second Sībawayhi', it is highly appropriate that ML was written at the other end of the spectrum in a chronological sense. Its encyclopaedic nature is a characteristic which the *Kitāb* could never have possessed, but the impact which ML has made on subsequent studies of the language is no less significant than the work of the great master of Arabic grammar. If this present study has in some way helped to illuminate some of the qualities of ML it will have achieved its aim.

BIBLIOGRAPHY

Primary Arabic sources

Abū Ḥayyān, *Manhaj* = Abū Ḥayyān al-Gharnāṭī. *Manhaj al-Sālik 'alā Alfiyyat Ibn Mālik.* ed. by S.Glazer. Connecticut: American Oriental Society, 1947.

al-Āmidī, *Iḥkām* = 'Alī ibn Abī 'Alī l-Āmidī. *al-Iḥkām fī Uṣūl al-Aḥkām*. Cairo: Maṭba'at al-Ma'ārif, 1914.

al-'Askarī, *Furūq* = Abū Hilāl al-'Askarī. *al-Furūq fī Fiqh al-Lugha.* 2nd ed. Beirut: Dār al-Āfāq al-Jadīda, 1977.

al-Astarābādhī, *Sharḥ* = Raḍī l-Dīn al-Astarābādhī. *Sharḥ al-Raḍī 'alā l-Kāfiya.* 2 vols. Benghazi: Manshūrāt al-Jāmi'a, 1973.

al-Baṣrī, *Mu'tamad* = Abū l-Ḥusayn Muḥammad ibn 'Alī l-Baṣrī. *Kitāb al-Mu'tamad fī Uṣūl al-Fiqh.* 2 vols. ed. by M. Ḥamīd Allāh. Damascus: al-Ma'had al-'Ilmī l-Faransī li l-Dirāsāt al-'Arabiyya, 1964.

al-Baṭalyawsī, Ibn al-Sīd. *al-Iqtiḍāb fī Sharḥ Adab al-Kuttāb.* 4 vols. ed.by M. al-Siqā and H. 'Abd al-Majīd. Cairo: al-Hay'a al-Miṣriyya al-'Āmma li l-Kitāb. 1982.

al-Baṭalyawsī, *Inṣāf* = Ibn al-Sīd al-Baṭalyawsī. *al-Inṣāf fī l-Tanbīh 'alā l-Asbāb allatī awjabat al-Ikhtilāf bayna l-Muslimīna fī Ārā'ihim*. Damascus: Dār al-Fikr, 1974.

al-Damāmīnī, *Sharḥ* = Muḥammad ibn Abī Bakr al-Damāmīnī. *Sharḥ Mughnī l-Labīb.* Cairo, 1888.

al-Dasūqī, *Ḥāshiya* = Muḥammad ibn Aḥmad al-Dasūqī. *Ḥāshiyat al-Dasūqī 'alā Matn Mughnī l-Labīb*. Cairo: Bulaq, 1869.

al-Ghazālī, *Mustaṣfā* = Muḥammad Abū Ḥāmid al-Ghazālī. *al-Mustaṣfā min 'Ilm al-Uṣūl.* 2 vols. Baghdad: Maktabat al-Muthannā, 1970.

al-Harawī, *Uzhiyya* = 'Alī ibn Muḥammad al-Harawī. *Kitāb al-Uzhiyya fī 'Ilm al-Ḥurūf.* ed. by A.M. al-Mallūḥī. Damascus: Majma' al-Lugha al-'Arabiyya, 1975.

Ibn al-Anbārī, *Nuzha* = 'Abd al-Raḥmān ibn al-Anbārī. *Nuzhat al-Alibbā' fī Ṭabaqāt al-Udabā'*. 2nd ed. Baghdad: Maktabat al-Andalus, 1970.

Ibn al-Anbārī, *Luma'* = 'Abd al-Raḥmān ibn al-Anbārī. *Luma' al-Adilla fī Uṣūl al-Naḥw.* 2nd ed. Damascus: Dār al-Fikr, 1971.

Ibn al-Anbārī, *al-Inṣāf* = 'Abd al-Raḥmān ibn al-Anbārī. *Kitāb al-Inṣāf fī Masā'il al-Ikhtilāf bayna l-Baṣriyyīna wa l-Kūfiyyīna.* ed. by M.al-Dīn 'Abd al-Ḥamīd, Cairo, 1955.

Ibn 'Aqīl, *Sharḥ* = 'Abd Allāh ibn 'Abd al-Raḥmān ibn 'Aqīl. *Sharḥ Ibn 'Aqīl 'alā Alfiyyat Ibn Mālik.* ed. by M.D.'Abd al-Ḥamīd. 2 vols. Cairo: Maṭba'at al-Sa'āda, 1947.

Ibn Fāris, *Ṣāḥibī* = Abū l-Ḥusayn Aḥmad ibn Fāris. *al-Ṣāḥibī fī Fiqh al-Lugha.* ed. by Aḥmad Ṣaqr. Cairo: 'Īsā l-Bābī l-Ḥalabī, n.d.

Ibn al-Ḥājib, *Amālī* = Abū 'Amr 'Uthmān ibn 'Umar ibn al-Ḥājib, *Amālī Ibn al-Ḥājib.* 2 vols. ed. by F. Qadāra. 'Ammān: Dār 'Ammār. 1989.

Ibn Ḥazm, 'Alī ibn Aḥmad. *al-Iḥkām fī Uṣūl al-Aḥkām.* ed. by A.Shākir. 8 vols. Cairo: Maṭba'at al-'Āṣima, n.d.

Ibn Hishām, *Qaṭr* = Jamāl al-Dīn 'Abd Allāh ibn Yūsuf ibn Hishām. *Qaṭr al-Nadā wa Ball al-Ṣadā.* 12th ed. by M. 'Abd al-Ḥamīd. Cairo: Maṭba'at al-Sa'āda, 1966.

Ibn Hishām, *Shudhūr* = Jamāl al-Dīn 'Abd Allāh ibn Yūsuf ibn Hishām. *Sharḥ Shudhūr al-Dhahab.* ed. by M. 'Abd al-Ḥamīd. Cairo, n.d.

Ibn Hishām, *I'rāb* = Jamāl al-Dīn 'Abd Allāh ibn Yūsuf ibn Hishām. 'al-I'rāb 'an Qawā'id al-I'rāb' in al-Maydānī, 1981. 108-127.

Ibn Hishām, Jamāl al-Dīn 'Abd Allāh ibn Yūsuf. *Mughnī l-Labīb 'an Kutub al-A'ārīb.* ed. by M.'Abd al-Ḥamīd, n.d.

Ibn Hishām, Jamāl al-Dīn 'Abd Allāh ibn Yūsuf. 'Mūqid al-Adhhān wa Mūqiẓ al-Wasnān' in *Min Rasā'il Ibn Hishām al-Naḥwiyya.* ed. by Ḥ.Ī.Marwā. Damascus: Maktabat Sa'd al-Dīn. 1988. 99-129.

Ibn Jinnī, *Khaṣ* = Abū l-Fatḥ 'Uthmān ibn Jinnī. *al-Khaṣā'iṣ.* 3 vols. ed. by M.'Abd al-Najjār. Beirut: Dār al-Hudā, 1974.

Ibn Kamāl Bāshā *Asrār al-Naḥw.* 'Ammān: Dār al-Fikr, 1982.

Ibn Maḍā', *Radd* = Ibn Maḍā' al-Qurṭubī. *al-Radd 'alā l-Nuḥāt.* ed. by M. Ibrāhīm al-Bannā'. Cairo: Dār al-I'tiṣām, 1979.

Ibn Sīda, *al-Mukhaṣṣaṣ.* 14 parts. Beirut: al-Maktab al-Tijārī, n.d.

Ibn Taymiyya, *Īmān* = Abū l-'Abbās Taqī l-Dīn ibn Taymiyya. *Kitāb al-Īmān.* Cairo: Dār al-Ṭibā'a, n.d.

Ibn Ya'īsh, *Sharḥ* = Aḥmad ibn 'Abd al-Ḥalīm ibn Ya'īsh. *Sharḥ al-Mufaṣṣal.* 10 parts. ed. by M.K.Ḥarrās. Beirut: 'Ālam al-Kutub, 1978.

al-Irbilī, *Jaw* = 'Alā' al-Dīn ibn 'Alī l-Irbilī. *Jawāhir al-Adab fī Ma'rifat Kalām al-'Arab.* ed. by H.A.Nīl. Cairo: Maktabat al-Nahḍa al-Miṣriyya, 1984.

Ibn Qayyim al-Jawziyya, *Badā'i'* = Muḥammad ibn Abī Bakr Ibn Qayyim al-Jawziyya. *Badā'i' al-Fawā'id.* 4 vols. Beirut: Dār al-Kitāb al-'Arabī, n.d.

Ibn Qayyim al-Jawziyya, *Mukhtaṣar* = Muḥammad ibn Abī Bakr Ibn Qayyim al-Jawziyya. *Mukhtaṣar al-Sawā'iq al-Mursala.* 2 vols. Saudi Arabia: Maktabat al-Riyāḍ al-Ḥadītha, n.d.

al-Jurjānī, *Dalā'il* = Abū Bakr 'Abd al-Qāhir ibn 'Abd al-Raḥmān al-Jurjānī. *Dalā'il al-I'jāz.* Cairo: al-Maktaba al-Jumhūriyya al-Tijāriyya, n.d.

al-Jurjānī, *Ta'rīfāt* = 'Alī ibn Muḥammad. al-Jurjānī *Kitāb al-Ta'rīfāt.* ed. by G.Flügel. Beirut: Librairie du Liban, 1969. Reprint of 1845 Leipzig ed.

al-Mālaqī, *Raṣf* = Aḥmad ibn 'Abd al-Nūr al-Mālaqī. *Raṣf al-Mabānī fī Sharḥ Ḥurūf al-Ma'ānī.* ed. by A.M. al-Kharrāṭ. Damascus: Majma' al-Lugha al-'Arabiyya, 1975.

al-Maydānī, Aḥmad ibn Muḥammad. *Nuzhat al-Ṭarf fī 'Ilm al-Ṣarf.* ed. by Lajnat Iḥyā' al-Turāth al-'Arabī. Beirut: Dār al-Āfāq al-Jadīda, 1981.

al-Murādī, *al-Janā* = al-Ḥasan ibn al-Qāsim al-Murādī. *al-Janā l-Dānī fī Ḥurūf al-Ma'ānī.* ed. by Ṭ. Muḥsin. Baghdad: Jāmi'at al-Mawṣil, 1976.

al-Rāzī, *Maḥṣūl* = Fakhr al-Dīn Muḥammad ibn 'Umar al-Rāzī. *al-Maḥṣūl fī 'Ilm Uṣūl al-Fiqh.* 2 vols. Dār al-Kutub al-'Ilmiyya: Beirut, 1988.

al-Rummānī, *Ma'ānī* = 'Alī ibn 'Īsā l-Rummānī. *Kitāb Ma'ānī al-Ḥurūf.* 2nd ed. ed by A.F. Shalabī. Jeddah: Dār al-Shurūq, 1981.

al-Sarrāj, *Mūjaz* = Abū Bakr ibn al-Sarrāj. *al-Mūjaz fī l-Naḥw.* ed. by M. al-Shuwaymī and B.S. Dāmirjī. Beirut: Mu'assasat A. Badrūn li l-Ṭibā'a wa l-Nashr, 1965.

al-Shamunnī, *Munṣif* = Aḥmad ibn Muḥammad al-Shamunnī. *al-Munṣif min al-Kalām 'alā Mughnī Ibn Hishām.* Cairo, 1888.

al-Shawkānī, *Badr* = Muḥammad ibn 'Alī al-Shawkānī. *al-Badr al-Ṭāli'.* 2 vols. Beirut: Dār al-Ma'rifa, 1978.

Sībawayhi, *Kitāb* = 'Amr ibn 'Uthmān Sībawayhi. *al-Kitāb.* ed. by 'Abd al-Salām Hārūn. 5 vols. Beirut: 'Ālam al-Kutub li l-Ṭibā'a wa l-Nashr, 1982. Reprint of 1966-75 Cairo ed.

al-Suyūṭī, *Bughya* = Jalāl al-Dīn Abū l-Faḍl 'Abd al-Raḥmān ibn Abī Bakr al-Suyūṭī. *Bughyat al-Wu'āt.* Beirut: Dār al-Ma'rifa, n.d. Reprint of 1908 Cairo ed.

al-Suyūṭī, *Muz* = Jalāl al-Dīn Abū l-Faḍl 'Abd al-Raḥmān ibn Abī Bakr al-Suyūṭī. *al-Muzhir fī 'Ulūm al-Lugha.* 3rd ed. 2 vols. Cairo: Dār al-Turāth, 1945.

al-Suyūṭī, *Ashbāh* = Jalāl al-Dīn Abū l-Faḍl 'Abd al-Raḥmān ibn Abī Bakr al-Suyūṭī. *al-Ashbāh wa l-Naẓā'ir.* 2nd ed. 4 vols. Hyderabad: Dā'irat al-Ma'ārif al-'Uthmāniyya, 1940-42.

al-Suyūṭī, *Itqān* = Jalāl al-Dīn Abū l-Faḍl 'Abd al-Raḥmān ibn Abī Bakr al-Suyūṭī. *al-Itqān fī 'Ulūm al-Qur'ān.* 2 vols. Cairo: Muṣṭafā l-Bābī l-Ḥalabī, 1978.

al-Suyūṭī, *Mu'tarak* = Jalāl al-Dīn al-Suyūṭī. *Mu'tarak al-Aqrān fī I'jāz al-Qur'ān.* ed. by A.M. al-Bajāwī. 3 vols. Beirut: Dār al-Fikr al-'Arabī, 1969-73.

al-Yamanī, *Ṭirāz* = Yaḥyā ibn Hamza al-Mu'ayyad Billāh al-Yamanī. *al-Ṭirāz al-Mutaḍammin li Asrār al-Balāgha wa 'Ulūm Ḥaqā'iq al-I'jāz.* 3 vols. Tehran: Mu'assasat al-Naṣr, 1968. Reprint of 1914 Cairo ed.

al-Zajjājī, *Īḍāḥ* = 'Abd al-Raḥmān ibn Isḥāq. *al-Īḍāḥ fī 'Ilal al-Naḥw.* 4th ed. ed. by M. al-Mubārak. Beirut: Dār al-Nafā'is, 1982.

al-Zamakhsharī, *Mufaṣṣal* = Maḥmūd ibn 'Umar al-Zamakhsharī. *al-Mufaṣṣal.* 2nd ed. ed. by M. Badr al-Dīn al-Ḥalabī. Beirut: Dār al-Jīl, 1979. Reprint of 1906 Cairo ed.

al-Zamakhsharī, *Kashshāf* = Maḥmūd ibn 'Umar al-Zamakhsharī. *al-Kashshāf 'an Ḥaqā'iq al-Tanzīl.* 4 vols. Cairo: Muṣṭafā l-Bābī l-Ḥalabī, 1966.

al-Zamlukānī, *Burhān* = 'Abd al-Wāḥid ibn 'Abd al-Karīm al-Zamlukānī. *al-Burhān al-Kāshif 'an I'jāz al-Qur'ān.* Baghdad: Maṭba'at al-'Ānī, 1974.

al-Zarkashī, *Burhān* = Muḥammad ibn 'Abd Allāh al-Zarkashī. *al-Burhān fī 'Ulūm al-Qur'ān.* 2nd ed. 4 vols. Cairo: 'Īsā l-Bābī l-Ḥalabī, 1972.

al-Zubaydī, Muḥammad ibn al-Ḥasan. *Ṭabaqāt al-Naḥwiyyīn wa l-Lughawiyyīn.* ed. by M.A.F. Ibrāhīm. Cairo: al-Khānjī, 1954.

Ṭāshkubrīzādah, *Miftāḥ* = Aḥmad ibn Muṣṭafā Ṭāshkubrīzādah. *Miftāḥ al-Sa'āda wa Miṣbāḥ al-Siyāda fī Mawḍū'āt al-'Ulūm.* 3 vols. Cairo: Dār al-Kutub al-Ḥadītha, 1968.

Secondary Arabic sources

'Abd al-Bāqī, M.F. n.d. *al-Mu'jam al-Mufahras li Alfāẓ al-Qur'ān al-Karīm.* Beirut: Dār Iḥyā' al-Turāth al-'Arabī.

al-Afghānī, Sa'īd. 1968. *Min Tārīkh al-Naḥw wa l-Nuṣūṣ*. Beirut: Dār al-Fikr.

al-Aḥmadnagarī, 'Abd al-Nabī. 1975. *Jāmi' al-'Ulūm fī Iṣṭilāḥāt al-Funūn*. 2nd ed. 4 vols. Beirut: al-Mu'assasa al-A'lā li l-Maṭbū'āt.

al-Ashtar, Ṣāliḥ. 1965. 'Ibn-Hishām anḥā min Sībawayhi', *Revue de l'academie arabe de Damas*, 40.

al-Faḍlī, 'Abd al-Hādī. *Fihrist al-Kutub al-Naḥwiyya al-Maṭbū'a.* Jordan: Maktabat al-Manār. 1986.

Ḥammūda, T.S. *Dirāsat al-Ma'nā 'inda l-Uṣūliyyīn.* Alexandria: al-Dār al-Jāmi'iyya li l-Ṭibā'a wa l-Nashr, 1973.

Ḥassān, Tammām. 1979. *al-Lugha al-'Arabiyya: Ma'nāha wa Mabnāha*. Cairo: al-Hay'a al-Miṣriyya li l-Kitāb.

Isbir,M.S. and Junaydī,B. *al-Shāmil: Mu'jam fī 'Ulūm al-Lugha al-'Arabiyya wa Muṣṭalaḥātihā.* Beirut: Dār al-'Awda, 1981.

Majma' = Majma' al-Lugha al-'Arabiyya. Proceedings of meetings 1934-35. 181-99.

Makram, 'Abd al-'Āl Sālim. *al-Madrasa al-Naḥwiyya fī Miṣr wa l-Shām fī l-Qarnayn al-Sābi' wa l-Thāmin min al-Hijra.* Beirut: Dār al-Shurūq, 1980.

Nīl, 'Alī Fawda. 1985. *Ibn Hishām al-Anṣārī : Āthāruhu wa Madhhabuhu l-Naḥwī.* al-Riyāḍ: 'Imādat Shu'ūn al-Maktabāt.

Secondary Western sources

al-Azmeh, Aziz. 1986. *Arabic Thought and Islamic Societies.* London: Croom Helm.

Almagor, Ella. 1979. 'The Early Meaning of *Majāz* and the Nature of Abū 'Ubayda's Exegesis'. *Studia Orientalia Memoriae D.H.Baneth Dedicata*, 307-26. Jerusalem: Magnes.

Ali, Abdullah Yusuf. 1934. *The Holy Qur'an* (translation and commentary). Birmingham: Islamic Propagation Centre.

Arberry, A.J. 1964. *The Koran Interpreted.* Oxford: University Press.

Arkoun, M. 1972. 'Logocentrisme et Verité Religieuse dans la Pensée Islamique d'après al-I'lām bi Manāqib al-Islām d'al-'Āmirī'. *Studia Islamica* 35. 5-51.

Ayoub, Georgine. 1990. 'De ce qui 'ne se dit pas' dans le livre de Sībawayhi: la notion de tamthīl', in Carter and Versteegh (eds). 1-15.

Ayoub, M. 1984. *The Qur'an and its Interpreters*. Albany: State University of New York Press.

Baalbaki, R. 1978. *A Study of the Analytical Methods of the Arab Grammarians of the 2nd and 3rd centuries*. Phd. School of Oriental and African Studies, London.

Baalbaki, R. 1979. 'Some aspects of harmony and hierarchy in Sībawayhi's grammatical analysis'. *Zeitschrift für Arabische Linguistik* 2. 7-22.

Baalbaki, R. 1982. '*Tawahhum*: an ambiguous concept in early Arabic grammar'. *Bulletin of the School of Oriental and African Studies* 45. 233-44.

Baalbaki, R. 1983. 'The relation between *naḥw* and *balāgha*: a comparative study of the methods of Sībawayhi and Jurjānī'. *Zeitschrift für Arabische Linguistik* 11. 7-23.

Baalbaki, R. 1991. 'A *balāghī* approach to some grammatical *shawāhid*', in Devenyi and Ivanyi (eds.). 89-101.

Bakalla, Muḥammad Ḥasan. 1983. *Bibliography of Arabic Linguistics*. 2nd ed. London: Mansell.

Berger, P. 1969. *The Social Reality of Religion*. London: Faber and Faber.

Bloomfield, Leonard. 1970. *Language*. 11th ed. London: Allen and Unwin.

Bohas, Georges and Guillaume, Jean-Patrick. 1984. *Études des théories des grammairiens arabes. 1. Morphologie et Phonologie*. Damas: Institut Francais de Damas.

Bohas, Georges, Guillaume Jean-Patrick and Kouloughli, Djamel Eddin. 1990. *The Arabic Linguistic Tradition*. London and New York: Routledge.

Brockelmann, C. 1943. *Geschichte der Arabischen Litteratur*. 2 vols. and 3 Suppl. Leiden: E.J.Brill.

Cachia, P. 1973. *The Monitor: a Dictionary of Arabic Grammatical Terms*. Beirut: Librairie du Liban.

Carter, Michael G. 1968. A Study of Sībawayhi's Principles of Grammatical Analysis. PhD. University of Oxford.

Carter, Michael G. 1972. 'Les Origines de la Grammaire Arabe'. *Revue des Études Islamiques* 40. 69-97.

Carter, Michael G. 1973. 'An Arab Grammarian of the Eighth Century'. *Journal of the American Oriental Society* 93. 146-57.

Carter, Michael G. 1980. 'Sībawayhi and Modern Linguistics'. *Histoire Épistémologie Langage* 2 (1). 21-26.

Carter, Michael G. 1981. *Arab Linguistics: An Introductory Classical Text with Translation and Notes*. Studies in the History of Linguistics (Amsterdam Series) 24. Amsterdam: John Benjamins.

Carter, Michael G. 1983 (a). 'Language Control as People Control in Mediaeval Islam'. *al-Abḥāth* 31. 65-84.

Carter, Michael G. 1983 (b). 'The Use of Proper Names as a Testing Device in Sībawayhi's *Kitāb* ' in Versteegh, Koerner and Niederehe (eds).

Carter, Michael G. 1985 (a). 'The term *sabab* in Arabic grammar'. *Zeitschrift für Arabische Linguistik*. 15. 53-66.

Carter, Michael G. 1985 (b). 'When did the Arabic word *naḥw* first come to denote Grammar ?'. Language and Communication 5. 265-72.

Carter, Michael G. 1990 (a). 'Arabic Grammar'. *The Cambridge History of Arabic Literature, Religion, Learning and Science in the 'Abbasid Period* ed. by Michael J. L.Young, J.Derek Latham and Robert B.Serjeant, 118-38. Cambridge: University Press.

Carter, Michael G. and Versteegh, Kees (eds.). 1990 (b). *Studies in the History of Arabic Grammar II*. Amsterdam: John Benjamins.

Carter, Michael G. 1991. 'Elision', in Devenyi and Ivanyi (eds.). 121-33.

Carter, Michael G. 1993. 'Language and Law in the *Ṣāḥibī* of Ibn Fāris'. *Zeitschrift für Arabische Linguistik* 25. 139-47.

Cawthra, G. 1985. 'Philology vs Traditional Grammar'. *Proceedings of the Spring Meeting of the Linguistics Association of Great Britain*. Salford.

Concise Dictionary of English. 1982. 5th ed. England: Omega.

Cooke, M. 1984. 'Ibn Khaldūn and Language: From Linguistic Habit to Philological Craft', in *Ibn Khaldūn and Islamic Ideology*. ed. by B.B.Lawrence. Leiden: E.J.Brill.

Coward, R and Ellis, J. 1977. *Language and Materialism: Developments in Semiology and the Theory of the Subject*. London: Routledge and Kegan Paul, 1977.

Crystal, D. 1965. *Language, Linguistics and Religion*. London: Burns and Oates.

Crystal, D. 1980. *A First Dictionary of Linguistics and Phonetics.* London: Andre Deutsch.

Culler, J. 1975. *Structuralist Poetics: Structuralism, Linguistics and the Study of Literature*. London: Routledge and Kegan Paul.

Culler, J. 1976. *Saussure*. Glasgow: Fontana.

Culler, J. 1981. *The Pursuit of Signs*. London: Routledge and Kegan Paul.

Derrida, J. 1967. *De la Grammatologie*. Paris: Éditions de Minuit.

Devenyi, Kinga and Ivanyi, T. (eds.). 1991. *Proceedings of the Colloquium on Arabic Grammar (Budapest Studies in Arabic 3-4)* Budapest.

Eco, U. 1976. *A Theory of Semiotics*. Indiana: University Press.

Eco, U. 1984. *The Name of the Rose*. London: Picador.

Fischer, Wolfdietrich. 1989. 'Zur Herkunft des grammatischen Terminus *ḥarf*'. *Jerusalem Studies in Arabic and Islam* 12. 35-145.

Fleisch, H. 1961. *Traité de Philologie Arabe*. 2 vols. Beirut: Imprimerie Catholique.

Fleisch, H. 1954-. art. 'Ibn Hishām'. *Encyclopaedia of Islam*. III. 2nd ed. Leiden: E.J. Brill. 801-802.

Fleisch, H. 1954-. art. 'I'rāb'. *Encyclopaedia of Islam*. IV. 2nd ed. Leiden: E.J.Brill. 1248-50.

Frank, R.M. 1981. 'Meanings are spoken of in many ways: The earlier Arab grammarians'. *Le Muséon* 94. 259-319.

Fück, J. 1955. *al-'Arabiyya*: *Recherches sur l'histoire de la langue et du style arabe*. trans. C. Denizeau. Paris: Didier.

Gardet, L. 1981. *La Cité Musulmane: Vie Sociale et Politique*. 4th ed. Paris: Vrin.

Goldziher, I. 1871. 'Beiträge zur Geschichte der Sprachgelehrsamkeit bei den Arabern'. *Sitzungsberichte der Akademie der Wissenschaft in Wien* 67. 207-51.

Gully, Adrian John. 1991. *Aspects of Semantics, Grammatical Categories and Other Linguistic Considerations in* Ibn-Hishām's *Mughnī al-Labīb*. Ph.D. University of Exeter, U.K.

Gully, Adrian. 1994 (a) 'Synonymy or not synonymy: That is the question. The case of the particle in mediaeval Arabic'. *Zeitschrift für Arabische Linguistik*, vol. 27, pp. 36-46.

Gully, Adrian. 1994 (b) 'Medieval Arabic as a form of social contract, with special reference to Ibn Hishām's *Mughnī l-Labīb*', in *Arabic Sociolinguistics: Issues and Perspectives*. ed. by Yasir Suleiman. London: Curzon Press. 251-273.

Haarmann, U. 1974. 'Religiöses Recht und Grammatik im Klassischen Islam'. *Zeitschrift für Deutschen Morgenländischen Gesellschaft* 12, suppl. II. 149-69.

Harris, R. 1980. *The Language Makers*. London: Duckworth.

Heinrichs, Wolfhart. 1984. 'On the Genesis of the *ḥaqīqa-majāz* dichotomy'. *Studia Islamica* 59. 111-140.

Hourani, Albert. 1991. *A History of the Arab Peoples.* London: Faber and Faber.

Ibn Khaldūn. 1986. *The Muqaddimah*. trans. F.Rosenthal. 3rd ed. 3 vols. London: Routledge and Kegan Paul.

Jackson, H. 1980. *Words and their Meanings*. England: Longman.

Larcher, Pierre. 1990. "Éléments pragmatiques dans la théorie grammaticale arabe post-classique', in Carter and Versteegh (eds.). 195-214.

Larcher, Pierre. 1992. 'La particule *lakinna* vue par un grammairien arabe'. *Historiographia Linguistica* 19. 1-24.

Lass, R. 1980. *On Explaining Language Change*. Cambridge: University Press.

Leech, G. 1969. *Towards a Semantic Description of English*. England: Longman.

Leech, G. 1981. *Semantics: The Study of Meaning*. 2nd ed. England: Penguin.

Levin, Aryeh. 1987. 'The views of the Arab grammarians on the classification and syntactic function of prepositions'. *Jerusalem Studies in Arabic and Islam* 10. 342-367.

Lewis, C.S. 1964. *The Discarded Image: An Introduction to Mediaeval Renaissance and Literature*. Cambridge: University Press.

Lloyd, G.E.R. 1987. *Revolutions of Wisdom: Studies in the Claims and Practice of Ancient Greek Science.* Berkeley: University Press of California.

Long, A.A. 1971. *Problems in Stoicism*. London: Athlone Press.

Lyons, J. 1968. *Introduction to Theoretical Linguistics*. Cambridge: University Press.

Lyons, J. 1977. *Semantics.* 2 vols. Cambridge: University Press.

Lyons, J. 1981. *Language, Meaning and Context*. London: Fontana.

Mahdi, M. 1970. 'Language and Logic in Classical Islam', in *Logic in Islamic Culture*. ed. by G. Von Grunebaum. Wiesbaden: Otto Harrassowitz. 51-83.

Makdisi, George. 1981. *The Rise of Colleges: Institutions of Learning in Islam and the West.* Edinburgh: University Press.

Makdisi, George. 1990. *The Rise of Humanism in Classical Islam and the West: with special reference to Scholasticism*. Edinburgh: University Press.

Mey, J. 1977. 'Linguistics as a Practical Science', in *Studies in Descriptive and Historical Linguistics* 4. ed. by P.Hopper. Amsterdam: John Benjamins. 235-263.

Norris, C. 1982. *Deconstruction: Theory and Practice*. London: Methuen.

Omran, El Sayed M.H. 1991. 'Arabic Grammar: Problems and Reforms', in Devenyi and Ivanyi: (eds.). 297-311.

Owens, Jonathan. 1984. 'Structure, Class and Dependency: Modern Linguistics and the Arabic Grammatical Tradition'. *Lingua* 64. 25-62.

Owens, Jonathan 1988. *The Foundations of Grammar: An Introduction to Medieval Arabic Grammatical Theory*. Amsterdam: John Benjamins.

Owens, Jonathan. 1990. *Early Arabic Grammatical Theory: Heterogeneity and Standardization*. Studies in the History of the Language Sciences 53. Amsterdam and Philadelphia: John Benjamins.

Peters, J.R.T.M. 1980. 'La Théologie Musulmane et l'Étude du Langage'. *Histoire Épistémologie Langage* 2, fasc.1. 9-19.

Peterson, D. 1972. 'Some Explanatory Methods of Arabic Grammarians'. *8th Regional Meeting of Chicago Linguistic Society, Chicago*. 504-15.

Reckendorf, H. 1967. *Die syntaktischen Verhältnisse des Arabischen*. Leiden: E.J.Brill. Reprint of 1898 ed.

Rescher, O. 1908. 'Studien über Ibn-Ginni und sein Verhältnis zu den Theorien der Basri und Baghdadi'. *Zeitschrift für Assyriologie* 23. 1-54.

Robins, R.H. 1979. *A Short History of Linguistics*. 2nd ed. London: Longman.

Robins, R.H. 1980. *General Linguistics: An Introductory Survey*. 3rd. ed. England: Longman.

Rosenthal, F. 1970. *Knowledge Triumphant: The Concept of Knowledge in Medieval Islam*. Leiden: E.J.Brill.

Saussure F. de 1966. *Course in General Linguistics*. 2nd ed. New York: Mcgraw Hill.

Sezgin, Fuat. 1982. *Geschichte des arabischen Schriftums*. Band IX: *Grammatik bis ca.430 H.* Leiden: E.J.Brill.

Sharabi, Hisham. 1988. 'The Neopatriarchal Discourse: Language and Discourse in Contemporary Arab Society', *Arab Civilization: Challenges and Responses. Studies in Honor of Constantine K. Zurayk*. Ed. by G. Atiyeh and I.M. Oweiss. New York: State University Press. 149-165.

Todorov, Tzvetan. 1983. *Symbolism and Interpretation*. trans. C. Porter. London: Routledge and Kegan Paul.

Troupeau, G. 1962. 'La Grammaire à Baghdad du IXe au XIIIe siècle'. *Arabica* 9. 397-405.

Ullmann, S. 1962. *Semantics: An Introduction to the Science of Meaning*. Oxford: Blackwell.

Versteegh, Cornelis H.M. 1977. *Greek Elements in Arabic Linguistic Thinking*. Leiden: E.J.Brill.

Versteegh, Cornelis H.M. 1978. 'The Arabic terminology of syntactic position'. *Arabica* 25. 261-80.

Versteegh, Kees. 1980. 'Logique et grammaire au dixième siècle'. *Histoire Épistémologie Langage* 2, fasc.1. 39-52.

Versteegh, Koerner and Niederehe (eds.) 1983. *The History of Linguistics in the Near East*: Studies in the History of Linguistics. vol. 28. Amsterdam: John Benjamins.

Versteegh, Kees. 1983 (a) 'A dissenting grammarian: Qutrub on declension', in Versteegh, Koerner and Niederehe (eds.). 167-193.

Versteegh, Kees. 1983 (b). 'Arabic grammar and the corruption of speech'. *al-Abḥāth* 31. 139-60.

Versteegh, Kees. 1989. 'A sociological view of the Arab grammatical tradition: Grammarians and their professions'. *Studia Linguistica et Orientalia Memoriae Haim Blanc Dedicata*. ed. by Paul Wexler, Alexander Borg, Sasson Somekh. Wiesbaden: Otto Harrassowitz. 289-302.

Versteegh, Kees. 1990. 'Freedom of the Speaker: The term *ittisāʿ* and related notions', in *Studies in the History of Arabic Grammar II*. ed. by Kees Versteegh and Michael G.Carter. Amsterdam: John Benjamins. 281-93.

Versteegh, Kees. 1991(a). art. 'Maʿnā'. *Encyclopaedia of Islam* VI. 2nd ed. Leiden: E.J.Brill. 346.

Versteegh, Kees. 1991(b). 'Two conceptions of irreality in Arabic Grammar: Ibn Hishām and Ibn al-Ḥājib on the particle *law*'. *Bulletin d'Études Orientales* XLIII, Damas. 77-92.

Versteegj, C.H.M. 1993. *Arabic Grammar and Qur'anic Exegesis in Early Islam*. Leiden: E.J. Brill.

Versteegh, Kees. *to appear*. 'The Role of Meaning in Arabic Linguistics'.

Wansbrough, J. 1977. *Qur'anic Studies*. Oxford: University Press.

Wansbrough, J. 1978. *The Sectarian Milieu*. Oxford: University Press.

Wehr, H. 1976. *Dictionary of Modern Written Arabic*. 3rd ed. ed. by J.M. Cowan. Wiesbaden: Otto Harrassowitz.

Weil, G. 1915. 'Zum Verständnis der Methode der Moslemischen Grammatiker'. *Festschrift Eduard Sachau*. Berlin: Reimer. 380-92.

Weinreich, Uriel. 1980. *On Semantics*. Philadelphia: University of Pennsylvania Press.

Weiss, B. 1966. *Language in Orthodox Muslim Thought: A study of waḍ' al-lugha and its development*. PhD. University of Princeton.

Weiss, B. 1976. 'A Theory of the parts of speech in Arabic: A study in *'ilm al-waḍ'* '. *Arabica* 23. 23-36.

Weiss, B. 1984 'Language and Law: the Linguistic Premises of Islamic Legal Science', in *In Quest of an Islamic Humanism*. ed. by A.H. Green. Cairo: AUC Press. 15-21.

Weiss, B. 1985. 'Knowledge of the Past: the theory of *tawātur* according to al-Ghazālī'. *Studia Islamica* LXI. 81-105.

Weiss, B. 1987. ''ilm al-waḍ': an Introductory Account of a later Muslim Philological Science'. *Arabica* 34, fasc.3. 339-56.

Wright, W. 1933. *A Grammar of the Arabic Language*. 3rd ed. 2 vols. Cambridge: University Press.

INDEX

'Abd al-Wārith ibn Sa'īd al-Anbārī 166
Abū 'Alī l-Fārisī, al-Ḥasan ibn Aḥmad 76-7, 82
Abū l-Baqā', Ayyūb ibn Mūsā 100, 234
Abū l-Dardā', 'Umaymir ibn Zayd 89
Abū Ḥayyān al-Gharnāṭī, Muḥammad ibn Yūsuf
    ḥadhf 226
    Ibn 'Aqīl 8
    I-H 1, 65, 76-8, 83, 222
    Ibn Mālik 75, 174
    imperative 141
    innovation 57
    particles 126, 143-4
    waḍ' 29, 34
Abū Hilāl al-'Askarī al-Ḥasan ibn 'Abd Allāh 254
Abū l-Najm al-Ijlī, al-Faḍl ibn Qudāma 97, 175
Abū 'Ubayda, Ma'mar ibn al-Muthannā 40, 78, 266
accusative case *see ḥāl, tamyīz*
adab (literature) 21n.35, 79
adawāt (particles/tools) 119, 122, 126, 127, 131-2
    see also particles
aḍdād (opposites) 32, 193, 266
adjectives 215, 237, 243-6
adverbs 56, 118-9, 128, 134-5, 223-4, 227
agent *see fā'il*
al-Akhfash, Sa'īd ibn Mas'ada 110, 157, 214
al 39, 121, 146-8
alā 19, 173
āla (tool) 126
'alā 106, 134, 194, 196
alif 38, 54, 110, 137-41
    see also hamza
alladhī 89, 104, 109, 235, 240
alphabetical arrangement 16, 132
am 145-6, 190, 210
al-Āmidī, 'Alī ibn Abī 'Alī 57, 63n.38, 124
'āmil (operator) 17, 20, 118, 131
ammā 148-9
amr see imperative
an 101, 104, 141-4, 221, 259
'an 131, 195-6, 212
al-Anbārī, Abū Bakr Muḥammad ibn al-Qāsim 119
anna 46, 109, 144, 257, 259
annamā 144
'Antara ibn Shaddād 174
appositives 124, 238, 245
Aquinas, Thomas 81
Arkoun, M. 35, 44
'asā 134, 136, 178
aṣl (primary form/original structure) 44, 112
al-Astarabādhī, Raḍī al-Dīn Muḥammad ibn al-Ḥasan x, 90, 127-8

'aṭf (coordination) 33, 125, 130-1, 137, 150, 165, 215, 217-22, 234, 246-7, 252, 254
authenticity x, xiii, 62-3
aw 34, 101, 149-52, 221n.11
ayna 127
Ayoub, M. 20
al-Azmeh, A. 28, 32, 36

bā' 38, 42, 47, 56-8, 125, 127, 137, 141, 160-5, 190, 192, 195-6, 218, 223, 224, 254, 257, 258-9
Baalbaki, R. xiii, 4, 11, 88, 218-19
ba'da 194, 196n.44
badal (substitution) 103, 238
badī' see innovation
Baghdad 7
Baghdadi school 21, 74-5
ba'īd 105
bal 145, 165-6
balā 128, 187-8, 211
balāgha see rhetoric
basīṭa (simple/made of one part) 137
Basran school xi, 21, 74-5, 155, 173, 194
al-Baṣrī, Muḥammad ibn 'Alī 124
al-Baṭalyawsī, Ibn al-Sīd 'Abd Allāh ibn Muḥammad 51, 55, 97, 119n.4
bayān ('ilm al-) (science of clear speech) 4-5, 77-8, 88, 215, 231, 246
    see also rhetoric
bayāniyyūn (rhetoricians) *see* bayān *and* rhetoric
bayda 129
bi 56-8, 160-5
    see also bā'
Bible 248
bid'ah see innovation
biographical dictionaries 1, 73, 75, 76, 77n.9
Bloomfield, L. 40
Bohas, G. ix, 5, 18, 87-8, 236
borrowing 80-3, 130-3, 138
al-Bukhārī, Muḥammad ibn Ismā'īl 89-90
bureaucracy 12

Cairo 1
Carter, M.G. 8-9, 11-12, 35, 48, 75, 80, 83, 116, 209, 241, 273
case (grammatical) 237, 240-1, 265
    see also ḥāl, iḍāfa, marfū', tamyīz
Cawthra, G. 13
Christianity 10-11, 36, 64
class 13-14
classical fallacy 57, 84, 85
colloquial language 7, 254
commentators (Qur'ānic) *see mufassirūn,* Qur'ān
communicative meaning 29, 43-4, 87-8, 112, 126-7, 242-7
conditional *see sharṭ and* sentences - conditional
Confucian texts 7
consensus 10, 50-2, 54-5, 61, 91

contractualism 49-66, 84
coordination *see 'aṭf*
correspondence *see muṭāqaba, taqārud*

ḍa'īf (weak) 79, 105-6
dalā'il (signs) 9
dalāla see signification
dalīl (contextual indication) 32, 48-9, 90, 108, 209, 226
dalīl lafẓī (verbal context) 210-11
al-Damāmīnī, Muḥammad ibn Abī Bakr 38, 79, 142
ḍamīr al-di'āma (pronoun of support) 246
ḍamīr al-faṣl (pronoun of separation) 88, 245-6
Dante Alighieri 81
ḍa'ufa (to be weak) 98
deep structure 44
definite article *see al*
Derrida, J. 31n.9
descriptivism 11-17
dictionaries 56-8, 87, 121, 123
see also lexicographers
disagreements *see khilāf*
displacement 88-9
disputes *see khilāf*

Eco, U. 35-6
education 74
Egypt 7-8, 75, 76
elative 177, 196, 260
elision *see ḥadhf, taqdīr*
empty forms 119-20
epistemology *see* knowledge
errors, 12, 14-16, 40, 52-3, 61, 64-5, 77, 85, 98, 101-2, 104-5, 108-11, 113, 254-5
see also speech errors

fā' 103, 148-9, 192, 219-20, 234, 235, 237, 254
faḍla (redundant) 210, 233n.17
fā'ida see communicative meaning
fā'il (agent) 29, 39, 62-3, 88, 214, 239, 252, 266
faqīh see legal theorists
al-Farrā', Yaḥyā ibn Ziyād 4, 77, 119, 211
fasada (to be unsound) 98
faṣl (separation) 185
fī 192, 194, 212, 226
figurative meaning *see majāz*
fi'l see verbs
Fischer, W. 116-117
Fleisch, H. 11
form *see lafẓ, ṣinā'a*
Frank, R.M. 122
full forms 119
fuṣaḥā' (eloquent speakers) 45
future tense 158, 168-9

gender 174-5, 266
ghalaṭ see errors, speech errors
ghayr 129, 153-5, 196, 220
ghayr ṣinā'ī (related to meaning) 164, 209-10
al-Ghazālī, Abū Ḥāmid Muḥammad ibn Muḥammad 59-60, 124

grammarians
  biographical dictionaries 73, 75, 76, 77n.9
  borrowing 80-3, 130-3, 138
  communicative meaning 243-5
  consensus 50-2
  education 74
  errors 12, 15-16, 51-4, 64-5, 98, 101-2, 108-11, 113
  ḥadhf 3, 9, 60, 112, 214, 226
  I-H 52-3, 64-5, 75-80, 83, 100-1, 103-5, 108-11, 113, 228, 266, 276-7
  i'rāb 15-17, 19, 207, 215, 274
  kāda 251-2
  khilāf 52-3, 54-6, 178
  law 34, 51
  lexicographers 85-6
  ma'ānī 80
  maf'ūl muṭlaq 249-51
  ma'nā 3, 30, 96-7
  mufassirūn 83-4
  nouns 243-4
  particles 58-60, 116-19, 123, 126-34, 152, 158
  Qur'ān 3-4, 8-9, 12, 16, 19, 46-8, 80, 83-4
  rhetoric 84-9, 275
  schools of grammar xi, 7, 21, 44, 74-5, 119, 142, 155, 173, 194, 246
  semantic principles 3-4
  status 12, 73, 80, 84-5
  ta'alluq 224-5
  Traditions 89-90
  'ulamā' 74
  waḍ' 38-41
Greek epics 7
Greek language 49, 117n.2
Greek society 81-2, 84-5

ḥadhf (elision) 48, 88, 96, 98, 100, 112, 226, 275
  Abū Ḥayyān 226
  aṣl 44
  dalīl lafẓī 210-11
  ghayr ṣinā'ī 209-10
  grammarians 3, 9, 60, 112, 214, 226
  Ibn Jinnī 208
  iḍāfa 212
  ikhtiṣār 212
  illā 155
  iqtiṣār 212-13
  lafẓ 210
  lām 177
  ma'ānī 5
  majāz 41
  ma'nā 30
  nouns 211-13
  object 213
  particles 120, 215
  predicate 214, 228, 257
  pronouns 241
  Qur'ān 30, 41, 210
  sentences 209-10
  Sībawayhi 9, 211
  ṣinā'ī 209-10
  ta'alluq 226
  taḍmīn 178
  taqdīr 207-8, 215-17, 225-6
  topic 214, 228, 257

verbs 128, 158, 214
yā 192
ḥadīth see Traditions
hal 37-8, 39, 79, 119, 189-91, 233
ḥāl (accusative of condition/circumstantial qualifier) 107-8, 135, 191, 215, 237
ḥāmil (non-operator) 118, 131
ḥaml ʻalā l-maʻnā (correlation of meaning) 41, 47
hamza 38, 42, 87, 132, 137-41, 162-3, 189-90
see also alif
Ḥanbalī school 33
ḥaqīqa (literal meaning) 27, 39-40, 88n.23, 161
al-Harawī, ʻAlī ibn Muḥammad 80, 130, 132, 145-6
ḥarf (defintion of) 116-18
see also mufradāt, particles
al-Ḥarīrī, al-Qāsim ibn ʻAlī 85
Harris, R. 10-11, 49-52, 54, 56-9, 61
ḥasan (good) 106
ḥāshā 132
ḥaṣr (restriction) 144
ḥattā 18-19, 37, 59, 131, 166-8, 195
ḥaythu 101, 119
Heinrichs, W. 40, 88n.23
Hermogenes 49
hierarchy of responsibility 61
historical enquiry 61-2
Hourani, A.H. 50
ḥuḍūr (presence) 170
ḥurūf al-maʻānī see ḥarf, mufradāt, particles
hurūf zā'ida (superfluous particles) 30, 110, 137, 148, 163-4, 186, 218, 223

ibāḥa (unlimited choice) 83n.17, 151-2
ibhām (obscurity) 150
Ibn al-Anbārī, ʻAbd al-Raḥmān ibn Muḥammad 45, 51-2
Ibn ʻAqīl, ʻAbd Allāh ibn ʻAbd al-Raḥmān 5, 8, 60n.35, 243-4
Ibn Durustawayhi, ʻAbd Allāh ibn Jaʻfar 54
Ibn Fāris al-Qazwīnī, Abū l-Ḥusayn Aḥmad 17, 37, 48, 111n.11, 124, 193, 266
Ibn al-Ḥājib, ʻUthmān ibn ʻUmar 29, 76-7, 83, 99, 224, 249-51
Ibn Jinnī, Abū l-Fatḥ ʻUthmān 21
aḍdād 266
ḥadhf 208
I-H xii, 2
khilāf 77
sharīʻa 12, 53
ṣināʻa 96
al-Suyūṭī 63
synonymy 266
Ibn Kamāl Bāshā, Aḥmad ibn Sulaymān 85n.19

Ibn al-Khabbāz, Muḥammad ibn Abī Bakr 54
Ibn Khālawayhi, al-Ḥusayn ibn Aḥmad 79
Ibn Khaldūn, 'Abd al-Raḥmān ibn Muḥammad 1-3, 7, 9
Ibn Maḍā', Aḥmad ibn 'Abd al-Raḥmān 6
Ibn Mālik, Muḥammad ibn 'Abd Allāh
  Abū Ḥayyān 75, 174
  I-H 75, 77, 83
  ibṭāl 165
  'inda 170
  isti'āna 161
  kharq 54
  lām 177
  law 182
  min 185-6, 196
  poetry 46
  prescriptivism 12
  qad 171
  tafrīq 151
  Traditions 89-90
  al-Zamakhsharī 76
Ibn Mas'ūd, 'Abd Allāh ibn Ghāfil 91, 104, 111
Ibn al-Naḥḥās, Aḥmad ibn Muḥammad 126
Ibn Qayyim al-Jawziyya, Muḥammad ibn Abī Bakr 33n.12, 37n.16, 124
Ibn Qutayba, 'Abd Allāh ibn Muslim 78, 119n.4
Ibn al-Shajarī, Hibat Allāh ibn 'Alī 78, 150
Ibn Sīda, 'Alī ibn Ismā'īl 126
Ibn al-Ṭabbā' (teacher of Abū Ḥayyān) 75
Ibn Taymiyya, Aḥmad ibn 'Abd al-Ḥalīm 33, 40
Ibn 'Uṣfūr, 'Alī ibn Mu'min 55, 146, 189
Ibn Ya'īsh, Aḥmad ibn 'Abd al-Ḥalīm 59, 127-8, 131-2, 184-5
ibṭāl (retraction/invalidation) 165
ibtidā (inception/recommencement) 99, 168, 171, 191, 259, 263
ibtidā' al-ghāya (beginning of a specific aim) 37, 167, 184-5, 191-2
Icelandic sagas 7
'ida (promise) 187
iḍāfa (annexation) 87, 108, 130-1, 212, 215, 237
idh 192
idhā 103, 136, 156-60, 172, 196, 216, 229-30, 235, 237, 245, 262
iḍmār (suppression) 5, 48, 120, 208-9, 219, 220-1
iḍrāb (retraction) 145-6, 165
ighrā' (inducement) 106
ījāb (necessity) 106
i'jāz (inimitability) 5, 29, 42, 84, 85, 208, 210
al-Ījī, 'Abd al-Raḥmān ibn Aḥmad 38
ijmā' see consensus
ikfā' (substitution) 256n.23
ikhtilāṭ (association/mixture) 160, 260-1
ikhtiṣār (brevity) 212, 252

ikhtiṣāṣ (particularization) 176, 212, 246
ilā 37, 100, 155-6, 166-7, 172, 184-5, 194-5
i'lām (informing) 187
illā 100, 144, 153-5, 190, 220, 233
'ilm see knowlege
ilṣāq (adhesion) 42, 56-7, 127, 160, 161, 195
ilzām (acknowledgement) 140n.15
'imād (structurally indispensible element) 210
immā 55, 149-52
imperative 141, 191
imtinā' (impossibility) 180-2
in 42-3, 119, 127, 176-7, 180, 262
'inda 134, 170, 195
indefiniteness 60, 238-9, 244-5
infinitive 252
inflections *see i'rāb, mabnī, mu'rab*
inkār (denial) 132, 190-1
inkār ibṭālī (invalidatory denial) 42, 139
inkār tawbīkhī(reproachful denial) 140
inna 119, 125, 178, 257
innamā 125, 144
innovation xi, 57, 82, 225, 234, 256
interrogative *see* istifhām
intihā' al-ghāya (end of specific aim) 37, 100, 155, 166, 194
iqtiṣār (restriction) 212-3
i'rāb (inflection/parsing) 6-7, 81, 252-3
  'āmil 17, 20
  errors 14, 15, 53, 254-5
  grammarians 15-17, 19, 207, 215, 274
  i'tirāḍ 86
  ma'nā 17-19, 167, 207, 274-5
  mufradāt 20
  particles 20
  prescriptivism 15-17
  sentences 208
  al-Yamanī 125
irāda (intention) 262-3
al-Irbilī, 'Alā' al-Dīn ibn 'Alī 21, 44, 80, 130-1, 133, 137, 140n.15, 161-2
irtibāṭ ma'nawī (semantic connection) 99, 124, 223
ishtighāl (occupation/pre-occupation) 171, 216
ism see nouns
ism tafḍīl see elative
isti'āna (assistance) 161, 196
istidrāk (amendment) 183-4
istifhām (interrogative) 37-9, 42, 103, 127-8, 132, 134-5, 138-40, 145-6, 171, 189-91
istiftāḥ (introduction) 19
istiḥqāq (ascription of right) 176
isti'lā' (elevation) 161, 196
istimrār (continuity) 168
isti'nāf (recommencement) 191
istiqbāl (future) 168

istirshād (seeking guidance) 137
istithnā' (exception) 100, 110, 124, 153, 196, 220, 258
iṭbāq (agreement) 50
i'timāl (functionality) 161
i'tirāḍ (parenthesis) 78, 86-7
ittifāq (agreement) 50, 55
ittisā' (flexibility) 227n.14

Jackson, H. 194
jam' (connection) 32-3, 151
jamā'a (group) 50, 54, 55
jarr see prepositions
al-Jawharī, Ismā'īl ibn Ḥammād 85
jazm (certainty) 152
  see also jussive
jihāt (grammatical categories) 96
juḥūd (denial) 176
jumhūr (group) 50, 54-6, 61, 98, 158, 221
jumla see sentences
al-Jurjānī, 'Abd al-Qāhir ibn 'Abd al-Raḥmān
  I-H 4-5, 8-9
  maf'ūl muṭlaq 249
  particles 123
  rhetoric 4, 42, 87-9, 125, 275
  waḍ' 29-30, 42
jussive 177-8, 180, 235, 237, 265

kāda (to be on the point of) 237, 251-2
kāf 78, 104
kalam khabarī see sentences - affirmative
kallā 172-3
kāna (to be) 106, 227, 237
kawn khāṣṣ (particular being) 226-7
kawn muṭlaq (unrestricted being) 226-7
kay 177
kayfa 127, 129, 134-5, 235
khabar see predicate
al-Khaḍrāwī, al-Ḥasan ibn 'Abd al-Raḥmān 79
khalā 132
al-Khalīl ibn Aḥmad al-Farāhīdī 39, 177-8
kharq (breach) 54
khaṭā' see errors, speech errors
khilāf (disagreement) 52-3, 54-6, 63-5, 75-80, 178
al-Kisā'ī, 'Alī ibn Ḥamza 160, 266
knowledge 9, 31-2, 48, 60, 63-4, 79-82
Kufan school 21, 44, 74-5, 119, 142, 246
kull 97, 132, 134, 147-8, 174-6

lā 110, 125, 171, 179, 187-8, 210, 218, 260
la'alla 261
ladā 170n.29
ladun 170n.29
lafẓ physical expression/form) 18, 27-8, 30, 32, 36, 88, 96-7, 99, 207, 210

laḥn see colloquial language, errors
lākinna 59, 183-4
lam 125, 265
lām 138, 162, 171, 176-8, 194-5, 217, 225, 226, 259
lammā 143, 235
lan 125, 224, 265
laqad 143, 171
Larcher, P. x
Lass, R. 61-3, 64
Latin language 10-11, 73
law (jurisprudence) 12, 33-4, 45, 51, 60, 124
  see also legal theorists, *sharī'a*
law (particle) 46, 119, 179-83, 184, 235
law lā 235
law schools 6, 33
laysa 218, 257, 258-9
layta 119, 257
legal theorists 27, 37, 51, 62, 86, 88n.23, 89, 123-4, 193, 254-5, 256n.22
  see also law, *sharī'a*
Lewis, C.S. 81
lexicographers 85-6
lexicography *see* dictionaries
lexis 120
li see lām
librarians 74
Lloyd, G.E.R. 81-2
logocentrism 28, 31-5, 38, 44, 90
logos 120
Lyons, J. 119-20
mā 15, 47, 89, 101, 125, 127, 144, 224, 225, 240-1, 259-60
ma'a 129, 134, 194, 195
ma'ānī ('ilm al-) (science of meanings) v, 5, 28-9, 80, 85-6
  see also ma'nā
mabnī (uninflected) 16, 119
maf'ūl see object
maf'ūl muṭlaq (absolute object) 135, 249-51
al-Mahdawī (commentator on *al-Duraydiyya*) 61
mahmā 129, 134, 137
ma'īb (defective) 52
majāz (figurative language) 27, 33-4, 39-43, 63, 88n.23, 161
Makdisi, G. 9-10, 54-5, 74
Makkī ibn Abī Ṭālib 78
al-Mālaqī, Aḥmad ibn 'Abd al-Nūr 59, 80, 130-2, 137, 155, 162
Mamluks 7-8
man 97, 127, 240, 242, 261
ma'nā (meaning) 62
  communicative meaning 43-5
  grammarians 3, 30, 96-7
  ḥadhf 30
  ḥaqīqa 39-40
  innovation 57
  i'rāb 17-19, 167, 207, 274-5
  lafẓ 88, 99, 207
  majāz 39-43
  muṭāqaba 32, 36

particles 36-9, 56-7, 59, 119-22, 126-8
qalb 264-5
Qur'ān 42-3, 46-8
ṣinā'a 53, 96-7
taḍmīn 43
taqāruḍ 256-67
verbs 88
waḍ' 27-9
marfū' (nominative case) 63, 237
see also case
masā'il (isolated issues) 106-7
maṣdar (verbal noun) 139, 259
matā 196
Mattā ibn Yūnus 57
metathesis *see qalb*
Mey, J. 13
milk (right of property) 176
min 36-7, 99, 107, 156n.23, 167, 170, 184-7, 194-6, 218
Mongols 7
mood *see* jussive, subjunctive
morphology *see ṣarf*
al-Mubarrad, Muḥammad ibn Yazīd 155, 157, 162, 165
mubhamāt (obscurities) 210
mubtada' see topic
mudh 172
mufāja'a (surprise) 103, 147, 156-7, 172, 260
mufassirūn (exegetes) 3-4, 46-8, 79, 83-5, 274
mufradat (single entities) 7, 16, 20, 29, 41-2, 118, 134, 274
see also ḥarf, particles
muḥaddithūn see Traditions
mujāwaza (going beyond) 185, 196
mulaḥ (beauties of speech) 196, 265
muqābala (recompense) 163
mu'rab (inflected) 16
see also i'rāb
al-Murādī, al-Ḥasan ibn al-Qāsim 80, 129-34, 170, 172
murādif see synonymy
murakkab (compound/made of more than one part) 29, 41, 137, 219
mu'rib see grammarians
muṣāḥaba (accompaniment) 196
mushārafa (being on the point of) 262
Muslim ibn al-Ḥajjāj 89-90
musnad (topic/agent) 229, 246
see also predicate, topic
muta'alliq see ta'alluq
al-Mutanabbī, Aḥmad ibn al-Ḥusayn 79
muṭāqaba (correspondence) 32, 36
mutashābihāt (obscurities) 19, 107, 111
Mu'tazilites 40n.21, 41, 76, 102, 163

na'am 128, 187-9
nafy (negation) 125, 130, 166, 175-6, 190, 224, 233, 265
naḥw (syntax) 1, 16-17

see also grammarians, *i'rāb*
nahy (prohibition) 166, 260
names 252-3
see also proper names
name-relation 38-40
naql (transmission) 50, 55, 61-3, 80-1, 86, 89-90
nasaq (sequential coordination) 238
naṣb see subjunctive
naẓm (composition) 4n.7
negatives *see nafy*
neologisms 57
niyāba (substitution) 155, 194-7
nouns 55-6, 60, 118, 126-9, 131-5, 174, 211-13, 215, 237-45
see also maṣdar and sentences - nominal
number 174-5, 266
nunation *see tanwīn*
nuzūl (sending down) 212, 248

oaths 78, 87, 104, 158, 235
object 88, 137, 213-14, 249, 266
opposites *see aḍdād*
origin of language 31-3, 50
originality *see* innovation
orthography 45, 109-10
Owens, J. 20, 44-5, 96, 215, 256

parenthesis *see i'tirāḍ*
parsing *see i'rāb*
particles 7, 35, 60
al 39, 121, 146-8
alā 19, 173
'alā 106, 134, 194, 196
alif 38, 54, 110, 137-41
alladhī 89, 104, 109, 235, 260
am 145-6, 190, 210
ammā 148-9
an 101, 104, 141-4, 221, 259
'an 131, 195-6, 212
anna 46, 109, 144, 257, 259
annamā 144
'aṣā 134, 136, 178
aw 34, 101, 149-52, 221 n.11
ayna 27
bā' 38, 42, 47, 56-7, 125, 127, 137, 141, 160-5, 190, 192, 195-6, 218, 223, 224, 254, 257, 258-9
ba'da 194, 196
bal 145, 165-6
balā 128, 187-8, 211
bayda 129
bi 56-7, 160-5
fā' 103, 148-9, 192, 219-20, 234, 235, 237, 254
fī 192, 194, 212, 226
ghayr 119, 153-5, 196, 220
hal 37-8, 39, 79, 119, 189-91, 233
hamza 38, 42, 87, 132, 137-41, 162-3, 189-90
ḥāshā 132

ḥattā 18-19, 37, 59, 131, 166-8, 195
ḥaythu 101, 119
idh 192
idhā 103, 136, 156-60, 172, 196, 216, 229-30, 235, 237, 245, 262
ilā 37, 100, 155-6, 166-7, 172, 184-5, 194-5
illā 100, 144, 153-5, 190, 220, 233
immā 55, 149-52
in 42-3, 119, 127, 176-7, 180, 262
'inda 134, 170, 195
inna 119, 125, 178, 257
innamā 125, 144
kāf 78, 104
kallā 172-3
kay 177
kayfa 127, 129, 134-5, 235
khalā 132
kull 97, 132, 134, 147-8, 174-6
lā 110, 125, 171, 179, 187-8, 210, 218, 260
la'alla 261
ladā 170n.29
ladun 170n.29
lākinna 59, 183-4
lam 125, 265
lām 138, 162, 171, 176-8, 194-5, 217, 225, 226, 259
lammā 143, 235
lan 125, 224, 265
laqad 113, 171
law 46, 119, 179-83, 184, 235
law lā 235
laysa 134, 218, 257, 258-9
layta 119, 257
mā 15, 47, 89, 101, 125, 127, 144, 224, 225, 240-1, 259-60
ma'a 129, 134, 194, 195
mahmā 129, 134, 137
man 97, 127, 240, 242, 261
matā 196
min 36-7, 99, 107, 156n.23, 167, 170, 184-7, 194-6, 218
mudh 172
na'am 128, 187-9
qad 39, 170-2, 178, 197
qaṭṭu 172
rubba 54, 264
sīn 137, 168-9
thumma 105, 129, 262
wāw 32-3, 39, 78-9, 83n.17, 104, 110, 137, 150-1, 191-2, 236, 247, 252, 254
yā 54, 192
and Abū Ḥayyān 126, 143-4
    'aṭf 137
    borrowing 80-1
    dictionaries 58
    empty forms 119
    full forms 119

grammarians 58-60, 116-19, 123, 126-34, 152, 158
ḥadhf 120, 215
ḥurūf zā'ida 30, 110, 137, 148, 163-4, 186, 218, 223
Ibn Fāris 37
i'rāb 20
al-Irbilī 21
istifhām 38, 103
al-Jurjānī 123
legal theorists 123-4
majāz 41-2
ma'nā 36-9, 56-7, 59, 119-22, 126-8
nafy 125, 224, 265
niyāba 194-7
poetry 48
prescriptivism 16
referents 26, 58
rhetoric 125
sentences 121-3, 229
Sībawayhi 4, 39, 59, 116-17, 123
al-Suyūṭī 126, 128
synonymy 193-7
ta'alluq 99-103, 137
tawkīd 212
al-Zajjājī 126-7
past tense 158, 169-72, 178, 264
phonology 5, 137
plagiarism 83
see also borrowing
poetry xii-xiii, 6, 14-15, 46-8, 52, 55, 65, 90, 138, 174-5, 264
power 80
pre- and post-positioning *see taqdīm wa-ta'khīr*
predicate 44, 214, 228, 238-9, 242, 244-6, 257, 265
prepositions 119n.4, 194-7, 212, 223-4, 227, 243
prescriptivism 11-17, 52-3, 241
prohibitive *see nahy*
pronoun suffixes 39
pronouns 146, 147, 160, 241, 243, 245-6
see also alladhī, ḍamīr al-di'āma, ḍamīr al-faṣl
proper names 241
see also names

qad 39, 170-2, 178, 197
qalb (metathesis) 256, 264-5
qarīb (near) 105
qarīna/qarā'in (associative indication) 40, 63, 88n.23, 151-2, 155-6, 212
qasam see oaths
qaṣr qalb (restriction of reversal) 144
qaṭ' (suspension) 221-2
qaṭṭu 172
qawī (strong) 105
qirā'āt (readings) 91
qiyās (analogy) 11, 21, 45-6
quasi-sentences 222-7
qudra 'alayhi (ability to fulfil) 262-3
Qur'ān xii
'aṭf 219-20
consensus 55
dalā'il 9

grammarians 3-4, 8-9, 12, 16, 19, 46-8, 80, 83-4
ḥadhf 30, 41, 210
I-H 6-7, 9, 46, 64, 87-91, 97-106, 108-12, 135-6, 139-91, 195-6, 210-13, 219-27, 229-38, 243, 245-55, 257-64
i'jāz 5, 29, 42, 84, 85, 208, 210
i'tirāḍ 86
khilāf 63-4
majāz 41-3
ma'nā 42-3, 46-8
mubhamāt 210
mufassirūn 3-4, 46-8, 79, 83-5, 274
mutashābihāt 19, 107, 111
nuzūl 212, 248
orthography 45, 109-10
qirā'āt 91
revelation 60, 63
Sībawayhi 8-9
tawahhum 219-20
al-Zamakhsharī 46-7, 105-6, 108-10, 142-3, 248
see also sacred texts

rad' (averting) 173
rasm see orthography
rationality 63-4
al-Rāzī, Fakhr al-Dīn Muḥammad ibn 'Umar 62-3, 85
referents 35-7, 58
revelation 60, 63
rhetoric xiii, 9, 21, 91, 178
grammarians 84-9, 275
al-Jurjānī 4, 42, 87-9, 125, 275
ma'ānī 5
particles 125
poetry 175
Sībawayhi 4
see also bayān
ri'āsa (leadership) 80
Robins, R.H. 10, 121
rubba 54, 264
ruling class 13-14
al-Rummānī, 'Alī ibn 'Īsā 130-1

sababiyya (causation) 161-3, 234
sacred texts xiii, 7, 10-11, 30-1, 48, 50, 64-5, 73, 90-1, 275
see also Qur'ān, Traditions
ṣadāra (initial position) 103
sahw (carelessness) 12, 52, 77
al-Sakkākī, Yūsuf ibn Abī Bakr 6, 275
sama' (reporting) 46
ṣarf (morphology) 2, 5
Saussure, F.de 31-2, 36
scholars 81-2
see also 'ulamā'
scholasticism 9-10, 64, 81, 255
schools of grammar xi, 7, 21, 44, 74-5, 119, 142, 155, 173, 194, 246

see also Basran, Baghdadi, Kufan schools
semantic connection *see ta'alluq*
semantic principles 3-4, 60, 241, 273-4
semiotics 32, 35, 37
sentences 7, 60
  affirmative (*khabariyya*) 187-9
  conditional (*sharṭiyya*) 152, 172, 180-3
  conjunctive/ coordinated (*ma'ṭūf*) 215, 259
  descriptive 232
  elucidatory (*bayāniyya*) 231-2
  equational 157
  excepted (*mustathnā*) 230
  explanatory (*tafsīriyya*) 230, 233, 236
  inceptive (*musta'nifa*) 161, 230-2, 236
  nominal (*ismiyya*) 5, 44, 60, 110, 156, 172, 192, 229
  parenthetical (*musta'riḍa*) 78, 230, 231, 233, 236-7
  predicated (*musnada ilayhi*) 230
  prohibitive 111
  quasi-sentences 222-7
  relative 87, 104, 235, 236
  secondary 236
  syntactic (*naḥwiyya*) 231-8
  verbal 5, 228-9
  and *ḥadhf* 209-10
    i'rāb 208
    particles 121-3, 229
shādhdh (anomalous material) 46, 91
Shāfi'ī school 33
shakk (doubt)
al-Shamunnī, Aḥmad ibn Muḥammad 79
Sharabi, H.B. 31
sharī'a (revealed law) 12, 53
  see also law, legal theorists
sharṭ (condition) 103, 127-8, 134-5, 148, 158-60, 177-8, 180-3, 242-3
  see also sentences - conditional
shawāhid (textual evidence) 6, 14-15
al-Shawkānī, Muḥammad ibn 'Alī 77n.9
shechina 146
Sībawayhi, 'Amr ibn 'Uthmān
  ḥadhf 9, 211
  I-H xii, 2-3, 5-6, 7-9, 85, 276
  imperative 141
  jussive 177-8
  kallā 173
  khilāf 77
  al-Kisā'ī 160
  law 182-3
  na'am 187
  niyāba 155

nouns 241-2
particles 4, 39, 59, 116-17, 123
pronouns 160
Qur'ān 8-9
rhetoric 4
taqārud 266
tawahhum 218-20
Traditions 89
wāw 192
ṣifa see adjectives
signification 9, 32, 35, 48, 82, 255-6
Silvestre de Sacy, A.I. 17, 274
simile *see tashbīh*
sīn 137, 168-9
ṣinā'a (form) 53, 96-8, 106, 209-10, 215, 233, 264-5
see also ḥadhf
ṣinā'ī/ghayr ṣinā'ī
single entities *see mufradāt*
al-Sīrāfī, al-Ḥasan ibn 'Abd Allāh 55, 57
Spain 7, 75
speech errors 6, 13-14, 78, 255
see also errors
status (of grammarians) 12, 73, 80, 84-5
subject markers 39, 252
subjunctive 265
substitution *see badal, ikfā', niyāba*
al-Suhaylī, 'Abd al-Raḥmān ibn 'Abd Allāh 162
superfluous particles *see ḥurūf zā'ida*
al-Suyūṭī, 'Abd al-Raḥmān ibn Abī Bakr 81
adawāt 119
I-H xii, 33, 60, 66
Ibn Jinnī 63
innovation 256
majāz 41
naql 81
particles 126, 128
qirā'āt 91
al-Rāzī 62
synonymy 193-7, 266
syntactico-semantic connection *see ta'alluq*
syntax *see naḥw, i'rāb and* sentences - syntactic

ta'adhdhur (non-feasibility) 77
ta'ajjub (astonishment) 135, 177, 221
ta'alluq (syntactico-semantic connection) 12, 53, 60, 99-103, 122, 137, 222-7, 274-5
ta'assuf (incorrect usage) 77
ta'ayyun (determination) 46
al-Ṭabarī, Muḥammad ibn Jarīr 85
tābi' see appositives
tabyīn (clarification) 177
taḍmīn (implication) 10, 43, 60, 99, 164, 178, 249, 256, 275
tafrīq (differentiation) 151
tafṣīl (elaboration) 148-9, 151
tafsīr see mufassirūn, Qur'ān

al-Taftazānī, Mas'ūd ibn 'Umar 275
taḥqīq (certainty) 191
tajrīd (absolution) 162
takdhīb (denial) 188
takhrīj (interpretation) 47
takhyīr (limited choice) 150
ṭalab (request) 78n.13, 150-1
ta'līl (expressing cause) 161-2, 182, 196
tamyīz (accusative of specification) 107, 185, 215
tanāsub (similarity in kind) 260
tanbīh (drawing attention) 19
tanfīs (amplification) 168
tanwīn (nunation) 129, 254
taqāruḍ (correspondence) 196-7, 256-67
taqdīm wa-ta'khīr (pre- and post-positioning) 3, 5, 41, 189-90, 229-31
taqdīr (reconstruction) 18, 31, 40, 44, 120, 145, 207-8, 215-17, 219, 225-6, 257
ta'qīb (immediate consequence) 143
taqlīd (repetition) 35
taqrīb (nearness) 152
taqrīr (confirmation) 140, 189
taqsīm (division) 151
tartīb (arranging) 262
taṣdīq (verification) 37, 138, 187-8, 190
tashbīh (simile) 162
Ṭāshkubrīzāda, Aḥmad ibn Muṣṭafā 118, 119
tawahhum (misconception) 77, 218-20, 222, 258
tawaqqu' (expectation) 170
tawātur (transmission) 62-4
tawbīkh (reprimand) 132
ta'wīl see mufassirūn, Qur'ān
tawkīd (emphasis) 41, 143, 149, 164, 176, 183, 186, 212, 246
tawqīt (timing) 182, 226
tawsī' (extension) 168
ta'yīn (determination) 46
tense *see* future tense, past tense
terminology 9
testing 239-42
thabata (to assert/establish) 45-6
al-Tha'labī, Aḥmad ibn Muḥammad 79
theology 10
thumma 105, 129, 262
time 157-9, 172, 180, 237
    see also future tense, past tense, *tawqīt*
topic 214, 228, 237, 243-4, 257, 265
Torah 248
Traditions 6, 7, 86, 89-90
    see also sacred texts
transformation theory 44, 215
transitivity 162-4, 216-17, 223, 247-9
transmission *see naql*, *tawātur*

'ulamā' (religious scholars) 7-8, 13, 50, 54, 63-5, 74, 82-4
Ullmann, S. 122
universals 255-6
uṣūl al-dīn (foundations of religion) 51
uṣūliyyūn see legal theorists

Vedas (Indian epic poetry) 7
verbs 37, 133-4, 262-3
  'aṣā 134, 136, 178
  ḍa'ufa 98
  fasada 98
  ḥāshā 132
  kāda 237, 251-2
  kāna 106, 227, 237
  khalā 132
  laysa 134, 218, 257, 258-9
  thabata 45-6
  and future tense 158, 168-9
    ḥadhf 128, 158, 214
    imperative 141, 191
    infinitive 252
    jussive 177-8, 180, 235, 237, 265
    ma'nā 88
    past tense 158, 169-72, 178, 264
    sentences 5, 228-9
    ṭalab 78n.13, 150-1
    transitivity 162-4, 216-17, 223, 247-9
Versteegh, C.H.M. 3-4, 7, 8, 17-18, 73-4, 179-83, 274
vocative 54, 73, 192

waḍ' (establishment of speech) 27-34, 38-45, 133, 255
wāḍiḥāt (grammatical categories) 19
wahm (misconception) 108
Wansborough, J. 8, 14, 34, 50
waṣf (descriptive element) 154
wāw 32-3, 39, 78-9, 83n.17, 104, 110, 137, 150-1, 191-2, 236, 247, 252, 254
Weiss, B.G. 28, 30, 33, 38, 52-8, 59-61, 62, 65, 124, 228, 255
Western Europe 10-11, 56-8
wisdom *see* knowledge
word order *see* displacement *and taqdīm wa-ta'khīr*
works (of I-H) 1n.3
  al-I'rāb 'an qawā'id al-i'rāb 19, 59, 84, 122, 227, 230
  Mūqid al-adhhān wa mūqiẓ al-wasnān 14
  Mukhtaṣar al-Intiṣāf 101n.5
  Qurāḍat al-dhahab fī'ilmay al-naḥw wa l-adab 21
  Shudhūr al-dhahab 46
Wright, W. 131n.10, 146

yā 54, 192
al-Yamanī, Yaḥyā ibn Ḥamza al-Mu'ayyad Billāh 85-8, 125

… (outward form) 112
…irī school 6, 33
…-Zajjāj, Ibrāhīm ibn al-Sarī 80, 157
al-Zajjājī, 'Abd al-Raḥmān ibn Isḥāq 16-17, 117, 126-7, 129-30, 134
zajr (rebuking) 173
al-Zamakhsharī, Maḥmūd ibn 'Umar
    ammā 149
    ḍamīr al-faṣl 246
    ibāḥa 83n. 17
    I-H 97, 102
    Ibn Mālik 76
    mīn 185
    poetry 46
    Qur'ān 46-7, 105-6, 108-10, 142-3, 248
    ṣarf 5
    sīn 168-9
    wāw 247
ẓarf see adverbs
al-Zarkashī, Muḥammad ibn 'Abd Allāh 119, 133
al-Zubaydī, Muḥammad ibn al-Ḥasan 75
Zuhayr ibn Abī Sulmā 65

For Product Safety Concerns and Information please contact our EU
representative GPSR@taylorandfrancis.com
Taylor & Francis Verlag GmbH, Kaufingerstraße 24, 80331 München, Germany

www.ingramcontent.com/pod-product-compliance
Lightning Source LLC
Chambersburg PA
CBHW071154300426
44113CB00009B/1208
* 9 7 8 1 1 3 8 8 6 9 8 3 7 *